Beginning Joomla!

From Novice to Professional

Dan Rahmel

Apress®

Beginning Joomla!: From Novice to Professional

Copyright © 2007 by Dan Rahmel

ISBN-13 (pbk): 978-1-59059-848-1

ISBN-10 (pbk): 1-59059-848-2

Printed and bound in the United States of America 9 8 7 6 5 4 3 2 1

Lead Editor: Jason Gilmore
Technical Reviewer: Stephen Burge
Editorial Board: Steve Anglin, Ewan Buckingham, Gary Cornell, Jonathan Gennick, Jason Gilmore,
    Jonathan Hassell, Chris Mills, Matthew Moodie, Jeffrey Pepper, Ben Renow-Clarke,
    Dominic Shakeshaft, Matt Wade, Tom Welsh
Project Manager: Tracy Brown Collins
Copy Edit Manager: Nicole Flores
Copy Editors: Nicole Flores, Damon Larson, and Marilyn Smith
Assistant Production Director: Kari Brooks-Copony
Production Editor: Katie Stence
Compositor: Linda Weidemann, Wolf Creek Press
Proofreaders: Linda Seifert and Elizabeth Berry
Indexer: Toma Mulligan
Artist: April Milne
Cover Designer: Kurt Krames
Manufacturing Director: Tom Debolski

Distributed to the book trade worldwide by Springer-Verlag New York, Inc., 233 Spring Street, 6th Floor, New York, NY 10013. Phone 1-800-SPRINGER, fax 201-348-4505, e-mail orders-ny@springer-sbm.com, or visit http://www.springeronline.com.

For information on translations, please contact Apress directly at 2855 Telegraph Avenue, Suite 600, Berkeley, CA 94705. Phone 510-549-5930, fax 510-549-5939, e-mail info@apress.com, or visit http://www.apress.com.

The source code for this book is available to readers at http://www.apress.com in the Source Code/ Download section.

Contents at a Glance

Contents

About the Author

■**DAN RAHMEL** is an author best known for his work relating to database servers, PHP, and Visual Basic. He has more than 14 years of experience designing and implementing information systems and deploying midsize client/server solutions using MySQL, Microsoft SQL Server, Microsoft Access, and Visual FoxPro. Dan began work as a writer for various magazines including *DBMS*, *American Programmer*, and *Internet Advisor*.

Author of over a dozen books, his writing has been translated into Chinese, Japanese, Spanish, French, and Portuguese. In 2006, Focal Press issued a special edition of *Nuts and Bolts Filmmaking* for release in India.

About the Technical Reviewer

■**STEVE BURGE** is the CEO of Alledia (www.alledia.com), one of the leading Joomla development companies in the world. He is the author of the Joomla SEO eBook and writes a daily blog about Joomla and search engine optimization at a www.alledia.com/blog. Originally from the United Kingdom, he now lives and works close to Atlanta, Georgia.

Acknowledgments

It was a pleasure to work with the people at Apress on this book. The superior Apress staff often made the difficult seem easy. I'd like to thank Jason Gilmore for believing in the book from the start and shepherding it down the long, hard road to publication. Tracy Brown Collins, who lives in a distant land, thanks for all your help and the small e-mails of encouragement. I'd also like to thank Damon Larson, Marilyn Smith, Katie Stence, and all the others who had to work tirelessly in production and editing to produce this book.

I must thank the twin stars of my life—my wife, Elizabeth, and my daughter, Alexandra—for their untiring patience as I crafted this book. Elizabeth put up with all the late nights and lost weekends with seldom a complaint. Meeting her was the best thing that ever happened to me and I am eternally grateful that serendipity introduced me to my better half.

I'd like to thank my siblings (David and Darlene) and friends (David Rahmel, Greg Mickey, John Taylor, Juan Leonffu, Ed Gildred, and Weld O'Connor) for their unconditional support. I'm very grateful to Sandra Villagran who kept the munchkin at bay and happy while I focused on the writing.

The Joomla! development team deserves all of our highest praise. They work tirelessly with small thanks and smaller remuneration to create the most fantastic open source application in the world. We all benefit from their generosity.

Most of all, I'd like to thank you, the reader. By buying this book, you make it possible for all of us in the publishing industry to labor to produce good work. I hope the information in this book will play a part in helping you achieve your dreams. Thanks.

## CHAPTER 1

Introduction to Joomla!

I'm more excited about Joomla than any other web product I've seen in years. Joomla exploded onto the web scene in 2005 and drastically simplified web design, development, deployment, and maintenance. It's also done its fair share to beautify the web world. By using Joomla, you can instantly banish ugly, poorly structured interfaces from your web sites—even the default installation shown in Figure 1-1 shows how pleasing a Joomla web site can look. Adding content or updating the design of your entire web site is a snap . . . and that's just for openers!

This book will guide you through nearly every aspect of the Joomla system, from basic deployment to writing your own extensions. By the time you've reached the last page, you'll be able to make Joomla do almost anything that a manually designed web site can do—and in a fraction of the time. Before we get started, let's take a quick glance at what makes Joomla such as revolutionary technology. The sections that follow describe the advantages of using a content management system (CMS) like Joomla, in addition to the features and benefits that make Joomla a compelling choice.

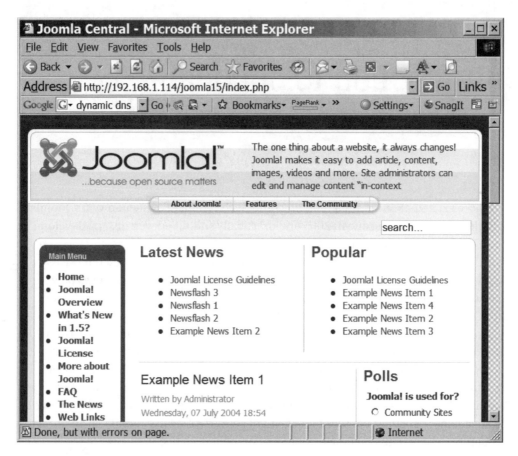

Figure 1-1. *The home page of a default Joomla installation*

THE HISTORY OF MAMBO AND THE BIRTH OF JOOMLA!

Although Joomla debuted in 2005 as version 1.0, its roots stretch back to 2001 when the open source content management system (CMS) named Mambo was first released. Mambo began life as an internal CMS product created by engineers at the Miro Corporation of Australia. In April 2001, Mambo was initially released to the open source community. For its time, Mambo was an amazingly advanced CMS application to be freely available with full source code.

Mambo gained worldwide popularity and spawned a cottage industry of vendors selling plug-ins and templates. The developer community flourished in an environment where people could freely share ideas and source code. Mambo was well on its way to becoming the most popular open source CMS application.

Yet in 2005 there was a substantial disagreement between the open source developers of Mambo and the nonprofit foundation that had been created to guide Mambo development. Finally in August 2005, the Mambo development staff abandoned the Mambo project and began toiling to create a new CMS from the ashes of the old.

A short time later, Joomla 1.0 was released. While this new CMS was fundamentally compatible with most aspects of Mambo, the user interface and site management had been streamlined. The problems with the Mambo foundation caused the open source community to shun that product and throw all their weight behind Joomla development.

In the short time since Joomla was born, use and development of the CMS has exploded. Within its first year of release, Joomla was downloaded more than 2.5 million times. At the time of this writing, there are over 65,000 registered Joomla developers, and there are countless web sites deployed with Joomla. Even more amazing is the international embrace of Joomla. The Joomla CMS has been adopted by webmasters from Brazil to the Netherlands, from the United States to Italy, and from Australia to China.

Content Management System Overview

When the World Wide Web was born, creating even the simplest web page required learning the language of the Web: HTML. Since then, great strides in the power of web authoring software have been made with the availability of professional web editors such as Adobe Dreamweaver and Microsoft FrontPage. These types of editors have made the creation and maintenance of a web site much easier by providing a graphical user interface for web construction and minimizing the amount of HTML coding required by the webmaster.

Despite these advances, when a web site grows beyond a few simple pages, even these advanced editors begin to crack under the pressure. Maintaining a web feature as simple as a site map can quickly become a tedious affair, swallowing webmasters' time and energy with every update. Other routine tasks, such as monitoring broken links, implementing a menu system, and adding a user forum, can make web site deployment a full-time job. Then there are broader challenges, such as ensuring that new content has a look and feel consistent with the rest of the site and providing web visitors a site search option.

To solve these problems, large media publishers (e.g., TIME and Newsweek) turned to a special type of software called a *content management system* (CMS). The CMS application not only automated site content management, but also allowed nontechnical writers and journalists to contribute articles directly into the system via a custom user interface. This type of interface required no knowledge of HTML or other technical skills, minimizing the potential for problems or inconsistencies to be introduced into the publishing process.

With the implementation of a CMS, most of the headaches of site management disappear. Features such as a site map and a site search will automatically update without the need for custom programming. Additional features such as forums, shopping carts, and picture galleries are either built in to the software or widely available as plug-ins. All of this serves to minimize the amount of custom development (and the substantial number of bugs and security concerns that go with it) required for more traditional web site deployment.

For web designers, the core of CMS site presentation rests on visual templates that can be set for the entire site or even associated with individual pages. These templates determine the visual representation of content to the user. When a remote author adds a new article to a web site, for example, the item is instantly published with a standardized site template, ensuring that the entire site retains the same look and feel or theme.

For large corporations, CMS use grew dramatically in the 1990s. But with deployment costs running into the hundreds of thousands of dollars, this technology remained out of reach of smaller organizations and individual users. Even if the cost wasn't prohibitive, the professional systems generally had complicated "everything and the kitchen sink" management interfaces that would allow a large organization to maintain control over thousands of articles and hundreds of users. Simple maintenance required an expert's knowledge of the CMS application.

Enter Joomla. Not only is Joomla free, but it also has one of the most easy-to-use interfaces of any CMS. Almost anyone can download, install, and have Joomla up and running on a web server in 20 minutes or less. When people in the technology community discuss the second generation of Internet-based services commonly referred to as Web 2.0, Joomla is one application that makes this new web world not only possible, but appealing as well.

Content Management System Adoption

So why hasn't everyone switched to a Joomla already? There are several answers to that question, with the first and most likely response being inertia. When people become accustomed to a way of doing things—no matter how antiquated—they are often loathe to switch. Climbing the mountain of web development from HTML to advanced web application design takes years and a great deal of work. It can be almost painful to minimize those hard-won skills with an automated solution.

Another factor slowing the move to a CMS solution is the existing hundreds of web pages that will need to be converted from their raw HTML format. For a substantial web site, content migration can pose a daunting challenge. Needless to say, the initial time investment porting to a CMS will pay for itself many times over in maintenance time-savings in the future.

The only real technical barrier to moving to a CMS is the requirement that the web host provide support for dynamic content in the form of PHP and MySQL hosting. Five years ago, there weren't many service providers who offered this option, but times have changed dramatically for the better. Now web hosting from companies such as Go Daddy (www.godaddy.com) and SiteGround (www.siteground.com) provide inexpensive access to servers that can run CMS technology without breaking a sweat.

Joomla! Benefits

With numerous CMS programs available, it's interesting to note that Joomla alone has been embraced by a wide spectrum of individuals, corporations, nonprofit organizations, boutique businesses, and public organizations.

One reason for Joomla's wide adoption is its ease of use. If you have any experience with web site construction or CMS design, you can use Joomla once and understand why people and businesses have adopted it in such large numbers.

Joomla's ease of use is matched only by its built-in professional features. In addition to Joomla's robust native feature set, over 200 free and commercial plug-ins are available to use with it. This vast array of extensions makes it possible to deploy a Joomla system that can do almost anything you need, from chat rooms, to online auctions, to classified ads, to inventory management.

Despite the gold-medal capabilities of the system, however, I think the primary reason Joomla is so popular is the award-winning user interface aesthetics the application offers to even the most novice users. The professionally designed user interface templates, both those included with the default installation and those available from the large third-party market, can instantly make almost any web site a "sight to behold." Gone are the days when a web site required a dedicated professional web designer to look immaculate. Joomla allows the most humble blog site to stand toe to toe with a multimillion-dollar web site without blinking. That means a professional web presence is available to site creators with no graphic arts experience. The aesthetics of a Joomla site are unparalleled by any other system.

Further, many CMS systems nearly require an advanced degree to set up and maintain. Joomla, in contrast, enables you to perform all maintenance tasks through a simple and elegant administration screen (see Figure 1-2). Since Joomla administration is web based, a Joomla site can be managed from wherever you happen to be—even if you're resting comfortably on a beach in Maui with a piña colada in one hand and laptop with a Wi-Fi connection in the other.

In the sections that follow, you'll be introduced to various Joomla features and learn, in a nutshell, how the application works.

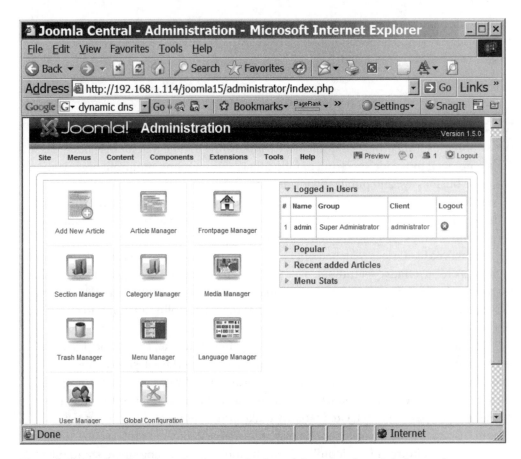

Figure 1-2. *Joomla administration is completely web based and straightforward.*

Joomla! Features

The power and simplicity of the Joomla application may be difficult to understand if you don't have previous experience with a CMS. However, any webmaster can see that the included administrative features are compelling:

- Complete management possible via a robust web interface

- Web-based management of site assets such as graphics, files, and other media

- Content approval features allow moderating of remote author postings

- Hierarchical user group management

- Automated menu management

- Content publication scheduling for automatic publishing and deletion of articles

- User security and contact management

Even more impressive is Joomla's ability to handle content and provide interaction with site visitors. Joomla's content capabilities include the following:

- Multiple built-in "What You See Is What You Get" (WYSIWYG) editors

- Automatic full text search of site content

- Full support for newsfeeds in RSS or Atom format

- Built-in user polling

- Banner advertising management

- Plug-ins for e-commerce solutions, including shopping cart, picture gallery, inventory management, and point of sale

- Multilingual internationalization features

- Accessibility options for the disabled

Finally, Joomla offers a good number of system advantages, including the following:

- Full open source license with free download of the application and source code

- Availability on all major operating systems (Windows, Mac OS, Linux)

- Page caching for improved performance

The robust plug-in architecture has made adding missing features affordable in terms of both time and money. Joomla is completely open source, so you can make desired changes to the system, and you can also contribute your work to the Joomla community if you want. This sort of community contribution often pays dividends later as other users build on your improvement and post back their own enhancements.

Now that you understand the reasons to adopt Joomla for your web site needs, let's take a look at how Joomla works.

How Joomla! Works

A CMS is a fair bit more complicated than a simple web server, but you will need to know only the basics to use Joomla effectively. If you understand the general process that Joomla uses to retrieve content, format it, and return it to the requesting web browser, you will be able to see how you can configure the Joomla system to present content in a manner that best suits your needs.

Figure 1-3 presents a block diagram of a simple web server. Interaction begins when a web browser requests a page of the web server. The web server retrieves the HTML code from the requested static HTML file (e.g., `http://www.example.com/index.html`) and returns it to the browser. The HTML file is called a *static* web page because the page returned to the browser is exactly the content contained in the file stored on the server—nothing more, nothing less. That's about as simple as it gets.

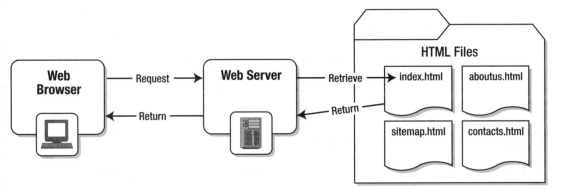

Figure 1-3. *Serving process of a basic web server*

Now let's take a look at the process executed by a request to the Joomla CMS, as shown in Figure 1-4. The web browser requests a page (e.g., `http://www.example.com/index.php`) of the web server. Although the address of the page requested in the browser's address bar may appear similar to the request for a simple HTML page, it actually activates a whole processing system. The request causes a part of Joomla to load into the web server and begin executing on the server's PHP engine. Joomla analyzes the request to determine what content is requested, and then the Joomla system opens a connection to a database server and requests the specified article from the database.

Once the article contents are retrieved, Joomla formats the article using the style selected as the user template. Joomla creates the HTML display content and sends it back to the browser, where it appears to the user in the same form as if a static HTML file was retrieved.

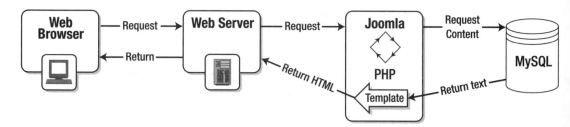

Figure 1-4. *Serving process of the Joomla CMS*

A CMS will dynamically feed content that has been retrieved from a database and formatted through one of the site templates to the web browser. Because the article content is stored as data, the presentation can be changed by simply altering the Joomla template. If you want an entirely new look for your web site, you can select a different template, and instantly a visitor to your site would see the original content in a completely new presentation style.

Differences Between Joomla! 1.0 and 1.5

As explained earlier in the sidebar titled "The History of Mambo and the Birth of Joomla," Joomla has roots in the Mambo open source CMS. Joomla's first version (1.0) departed from Mambo primarily in the user interface. Joomla and Mambo's shared lineage was apparent from their structural similarities to their complete mutual compatibility of modules, components, and plug-ins.

It really wasn't until the significant upgrade to version 1.5 that Joomla came into its own. If you've used Joomla version 1.0, the update will be like a breath of fresh air. There is a new administrative interface, and complex project deployment has been simplified. If you plan to program Joomla, the 1.5 update is a revolution. The new Joomla source code implementation loads painlessly into a standard HTML editor such as Dreamweaver or FrontPage (something that was never simple with the original PHP coding).

Some of the changes in the upgraded version include the following:

- Completely revamped Administration interface

- Improved template preview

- New plug-in manager

- Multi-CSS file editing

- Full support for Atom 1.0 and RSS 2.0 feeds

- Improved accessibility options

- Increased focus on internationalization, including full UTF-8 support, RTL support, and translation using INI files

- Native LDAP support

- XML-RPC support

- A streamlined component call interface that allows easy implementation of Ajax applications

- Completely overhauled Joomla programming framework

Because many readers have likely used previous versions of Joomla, I've included notes throughout the book where important differences exist. If you've never used Joomla before, you can ignore the notes specifying the version differences. Given Joomla 1.0's widespread adoption, utilities that aid in the transition to the new version have already begun to appear, and it's unlikely that you'll have to manage a previous installation.

Life As One of the 50 Most Important Open Source Projects

Joomla has won a vast number of awards and continues to rack them up. At the time of this writing, Joomla just won the Best Linux Open Source Project award at UK Linux and Open Source Awards for the second year in a row. In 2006, Joomla was selected as one of the 50 most important open source projects in the world at the Desktop Linux Summit. Since receiving that honorable designation, Joomla has continued to expand in breadth of deployment and depth of features. Joomla's features make it likely to remain the dominant open source CMS in the future.

And all this for free! Joomla can do most anything you want to do with it. If you want to do a quick and easy setup, no problem. If you want to do advanced development of a custom extension, the resources available to you are astounding. Whether you need to deploy an e-commerce store or write a daily blog, Joomla should be able to fit your needs.

Conclusion

If you didn't understand the utility and power of using a CMS application before you began reading this chapter, I hope you now agree with me that manually constructing a web site is a distant second-place finisher when it comes to site capabilities and maintainability. Joomla has the power and flexibility to serve the needs of almost any individual or organization. Deployment has never been easier, and you can't beat Joomla's price tag: free!

The best way to experience Joomla is to dive in feet first. With that in mind, the next chapter will take you on a "Quickstart" tour. The Quickstart will guide you through installation, configuration, and deployment of a basic Joomla site. So fire up your computer and begin taking advantage of the software that will make your web site as powerful as it is attractive.

■■■

## CHAPTER 2

Quickstart: Setting Up a Joomla! Site in 20 Minutes

Joomla installation can be a tricky process, because it leverages the operating system's security functions as well as three independently developed server systems: web server, code execution engine (PHP), and MySQL. Running into at least one problem during installation is more likely than not.

For this reason, I've tried to include as many screen shots as possible in this Quickstart chapter, so you can see what's going on at each step of the process. If you encounter a problem, please take a deep breath and don't worry—you won't be left to your own devices. If you can't find the solution to your problem in the "Troubleshooting" section of the next chapter, you can turn to the thousands of people on the Joomla forums (http:// forum.joomla.org) for help. It's been my experience that if you do so, you'll receive a quick and clear answer.

The figures included here are mostly from an installation performed on the Windows platform. Joomla is cross-platform, however, so regardless of whether your final deployment server runs Windows, you can execute design and development experiments on a different operating system.

Let's jump right in!

■**Note** You have several ways to install Joomla. I chose to outline the manual approach in this chapter because it applies to the greatest number of users. However, your web hosting provider may have a custom installer available through a control panel or cPanel utility that executes the installation via a script like those available from Fantastico (http://netenberg.com/fantastico.php). If you choose that route of installation, make sure the Joomla version available matches the most current version on the Joomla site. Also, you can use Joomla Stand Alone Server (JSAS; http://jsas.joomlasolutions.com) if you want a turnkey installation for all the required servers.

Installing Joomla!

Before you begin, make certain that your web host can handle the Joomla system. The minimum system requirements are as follows:

- Apache 1.13 or above

- PHP 4.2 or above

- MySQL 3.23 or above

Almost all web hosts that support these technologies will have more advanced versions than the minimums just listed. Nonetheless, if your host provides at least the bare minimum requirements, most likely you will be able to install Joomla.

Don't spend too much time trying to track down the version numbers, as web hosting providers are notorious for not documenting these sorts of things. If you run into problems with the installation, checking version numbers may put you on the right track toward resolving your problem.

■Caution The PHP installation must also include support for MySQL, XML, and zlib (these are additional modules outside the vanilla PHP installation). In most cases, you won't be able to find whether these modules have been installed on the support section of your web host. If the host complies with the other requirements, you're probably best just trying a Joomla installation. The installer performs a preinstallation check and will let you know if these capabilities are missing.

Modern web browsers will have no trouble viewing either the user front-end or the Administrator interface of Joomla. Any version of Internet Explorer after 5.5 will work fine. All versions of Mozilla Firefox and Apple Safari will display a Joomla site properly. For viewing the default front page of Joomla, a web visitor will not need JavaScript enabled, although many of the Joomla plug-ins use JavaScript to improve user interaction. The Administrator interface requires JavaScript, however, so be sure to have it enabled before you begin the installation.

The examples in this chapter are demonstrated using a web server running on Linux and a Windows XP desktop machine for browser and FTP access. If your configuration is different from this one, you should still be able to follow the instructions, even if the graphical user interfaces don't match exactly. Once Joomla is installed and running, nearly all interaction will take place through the Joomla web interface, which should look identical on most platforms.

Downloading the Joomla! CMS

To begin, you'll need to download the Joomla archive with the *most current stable release.*
When I tried to download Joomla for the first time, I was confused by all the files that
appeared in the download list. The Joomla development team frequently releases patches
to eliminate bugs or mend possible security holes. Therefore, the files that head the list
on the Joomla web site tend to be the newest patches. Since you're doing a new installation, you need a complete installation of a stable release.

To start, go to the Joomla web site at `www.joomla.org` and click the Download link as
shown in Figure 2-1. This will take you to the list of available download files.

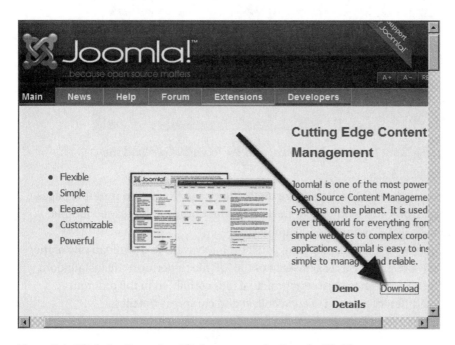

Figure 2-1. *Click the Download link to access the Joomla file library.*

Look through the list until you locate a file titled something like the following, where
VVV is the current version:

```
Joomla_VVV-Stable-Full_Package.zip
```

Figure 2-2 shows the Joomla download page and the list of files available. Since
Joomla releases new versions frequently, it's a certainty that the version numbers on the
files listed in the figure will not match the ones you see on your screen. You need to
select the newest complete package (labeled "stable" or "full") equal to or greater than
version 1.5.

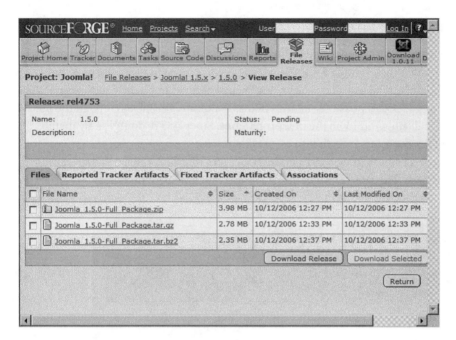

Figure 2-2. *Find the latest full or stable package on the Joomla download site.*

If you don't see the stable full package on the first page, you'll find multiple pages and navigation arrows at the bottom of the list. The first time I downloaded Joomla, I had to go to page 8 of 8 to find the full archive!

If you're running on a Linux platform, you'll probably want to download one of the tarball archives (.tar.gz or .tar.bz2) instead of the ZIP file to perform the installation. There should be no difference between the actual files contained in the different archives—only a different method used to collect and compress the files.

Click the desired Joomla link and save the file to your local drive.

Extracting the Joomla! Files

Once the package file has been saved to your local drive, you will need to extract the installation files from the archive before you can upload them to the web server. If you're running Windows XP or later, you can simply double-click the ZIP archive to open it. If you're running an older version of Windows, you'll have to download one of the numerous popular ZIP applications, such as WinZip or 7-Zip, from the Web in order to open the archive.

In Figure 2-3, you'll see that I've opened the file. While the files in your archive probably won't exactly match those shown in the figure, the folders and number of files should be similar. To extract them to your local drive, simply drag and drop them to the folder where they will be stored.

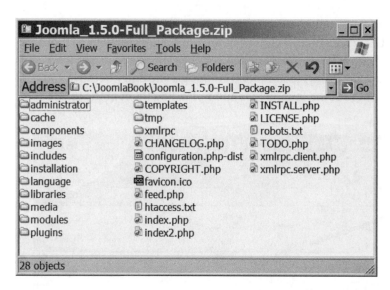

Figure 2-3. *The opened archive shows all of the Joomla files and folders.*

I created a folder called \Joomla1_5install and extracted all of the Joomla files and folders into it. What you name this folder isn't important as long as you remember its location on your hard drive. In the next step, you'll use FTP to copy the files to your web server.

Uploading Files to Your Web Host FTP

Most FTP programs are very similar because FTP applications are specialty transfer utilities that serve one function and do it very well. If you have FTP software that you are already accustomed to using, please continue using that software here, as you should be able to easily adapt these instructions to your situation. If you don't have a preferred FTP program, I recommend downloading FileZilla from http:// filezilla.sourceforge.net.

FileZilla is a full-featured, free, open source, multiplatform (Windows, Linux, Mac OS X, and Mac OS 9) FTP client. I use FileZilla here to demonstrate the Joomla upload. These general steps should parallel the process you'll use for most FTP applications.

■**Note** There is also a free FileZilla FTP server available at the FileZilla web site if you would like to run an FTP server. If you will be running the web server that's hosting Joomla, you can install the FTP server to allow yourself or others to access files through an FTP program.

When you have FileZilla installed, execute it (or open your current FTP application). To access your FTP server, you can either put the parameters for your FTP site into the Quickconnect fields at the top of the screen or click the Site Manager icon (see Figure 2-4) to create a new site. I recommend creating a site entry because you will probably be editing some of the Joomla files and uploading them in the future.

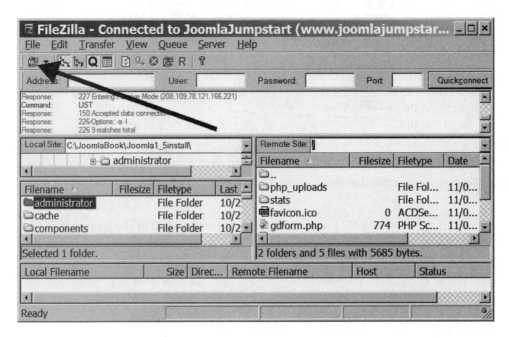

Figure 2-4. *Click the Site Manager icon to create a new site.*

For the host, enter the address of your FTP server (likely it will be something like ftp.example.com). The standard FTP port is 21; that will work for most users. If you have problems connecting, check your firewall settings to make sure port 21 isn't blocked.

For logontype select Normal so FileZilla will send the username and password. Enter the username and password for the FTP server. Note that some web providers supply a different username/password for their FTP sites than their main web logins. Be sure to check the support area of your web provider's site for information on FTP configuration.

■**Note** If your web host is Go Daddy, the FTP address that goes in the Host field in FileZilla will be the core of the URL from your web site (e.g., www.example.com) instead of an address that starts with ftp. Also, your FTP login will be the same username and password that you selected when you initially created the Go Daddy site.

When you have entered the FTP information, click the Connect button. FileZilla will return you to the main screen and display the login progress. When you have connected, the window labeled Remote Site should populate with the files on the web server. Most FTP sites on web servers navigate directly to the root directory of the web site. If your FTP host does not take you to the root automatically, navigate to it now.

For the Local Site directory in your FTP program, change the directory until it matches the folder where you earlier extracted the Joomla files and folders. Once you've reached the proper directory, select all of the files and folders in the Joomla installation folder. You're now ready to upload Joomla.

In FileZilla, you can right-click any of the highlighted files or folders and select the Upload option. The selected items will begin uploading, and the bottom-right corner of the FileZilla window (see Figure 2-5) will display the total kilobytes in the queue to be transferred to the server. As the files upload, this queue total will decline until it reaches zero.

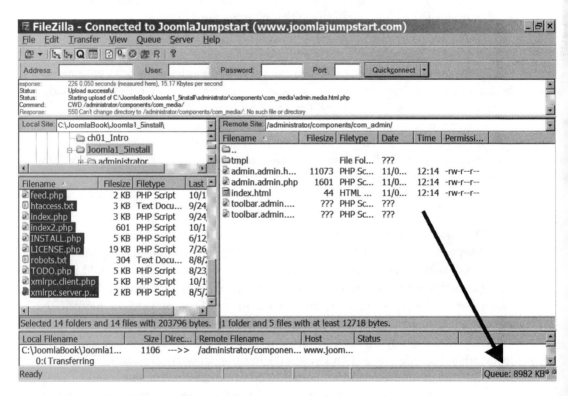

Figure 2-5. *FileZilla shows the file upload progress in the bottom-right corner.*

Once the files are uploaded, you're ready to configure MySQL for Joomla to store content data. When MySQL is ready, you can move to the "Using the Joomla Installation Wizard" section of this chapter to complete the Joomla setup.

■**Note** Don't delete the files for the Joomla installation on your local drive. You'll need them for a modification or two later.

Preparing Go Daddy for Joomla!

Go Daddy (www.godaddy.com) is a very popular and inexpensive web hosting provider that makes a good host for a Joomla web site. Go Daddy was chosen for this Quickstart because of its general popularity and accessibility.

If you are using another web hosting provider, the following process may closely mirror the setup you will perform. The procedure described here is generally similar to the process used for many PHP/MySQL applications.

If you want to set up your own web server and run Joomla, I suggest turning to the next chapter and looking over the installation instructions there.

■**Tip** Some providers that specialize in hosting Joomla web sites are said to have better performance because they are specifically tuned to the needs of Joomla. That gives them advantages over Go Daddy, especially for sites with high visitor volume. Therefore, if you haven't already selected a web hosting provider, be sure to do a web search for recommendations on the best Joomla host. You can find a list of some Joomla hosts at http://forum.joomla.org/index.php/topic,6856.0.html. Doing a little research will help you make an informed choice when considering the various factors (support, performance, price, etc.) of Joomla hosting.

The process described in this section is for manually installing Joomla on a Go Daddy web site account. You might have noticed that Go Daddy already includes Joomla as a Value-Added Application (VAA). You may be thinking that it would be much easier to simply use the version of Joomla that is available for free through your account. VAA installation is easier, but there are two reasons that I recommend you perform the installation by hand: directory location and version control.

With the Go Daddy VAA installation, you can't control the directory location of the installation. The Value-Added option sets the location automatically, and it's not at the root directory of your web site path, but instead within a folder named \joomla. Given that location, the URL to the Joomla site must include the folder name, so it would appear like this:

http://www.example.com/joomla/index.php

For most people, this directory allocation is not ideal, even if they don't want Joomla at the root directory. By installing Joomla yourself, the URL can appear as you would expect it:

```
http://www.example.com/index.php
```

The other disadvantage of using the VAA installation is the lack of control over choosing which version of Joomla will be used. The version of Joomla on the Go Daddy site may not be (and often isn't) the most current. New versions have added features, important bug fixes, and strengthened security. When you install a version of Joomla available on www.joomla.org manually, you can choose exactly the revision you want.

Determining the Go Daddy Operating System

Before you begin the installation process, you'll need to make sure you can execute Joomla on the Go Daddy server, which means your account must be set to handle Linux/PHP. If your account is set to Windows/ASP, you won't be able to execute the PHP code to run Joomla. Don't worry if you currently have the account set to Windows, though—you can change it easily enough. Just be aware that once you change this setting, you will no longer be able to run your ASP applications on that site.

Log in to the Go Daddy site and display your Managed Host list. In Figure 2-6, you can see my joomlajumpstart.com account in the list. Click the Open link in the Control Panel column of the site row.

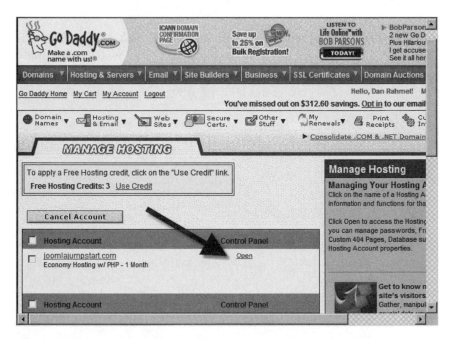

Figure 2-6. *Click the Open link to display the account Control Panel.*

The Control Panel displays the configuration information for your account. In the Account Summary area, you will see the operating system that is currently selected for this account. To host Joomla, the account operating system should be Linux, as it is in Figure 2-7.

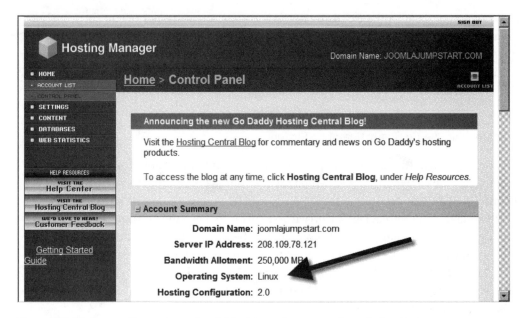

Figure 2-7. *The operating system should be Linux for proper Joomla hosting.*

If the wrong operating system is active, return to the Manage Host window. Select the check box to the left of the account you want to change. Click the Switch Operating System link (see Figure 2-8) to change the operating system to Linux.

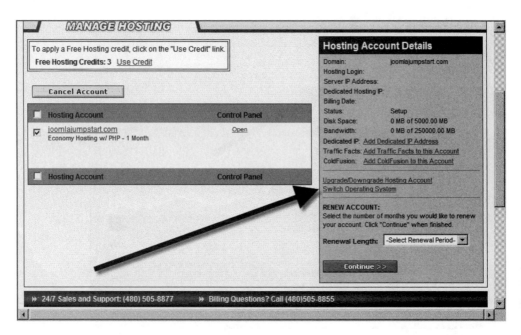

Figure 2-8. *The Switch Operating System link will take you to the reconfiguration page.*

Creating a MySQL Database

Before you run the Joomla installer, you will create a MySQL database where Joomla can write content and settings. Database creation generally requires special permissions that many web providers restrict from automated access. If you create the database by hand, you can still let Joomla do the heavy lifting of creating the tables and inserting the data into the database.

Note If you have administrator privileges on your MySQL server, you can let Joomla create the database for you. Since the procedure detailed here presumes that you're installing on a web hosting service, it instructs you on creating the database manually. See Chapter 3 if you want more information on Joomla automatic database creation.

Return to the Control Panel window if you left it to change the operating system. Scroll down until you reach the Databases area, which contains the MySQL button as shown in Figure 2-9. Click the MySQL button to open the page that provides management for the MySQL databases.

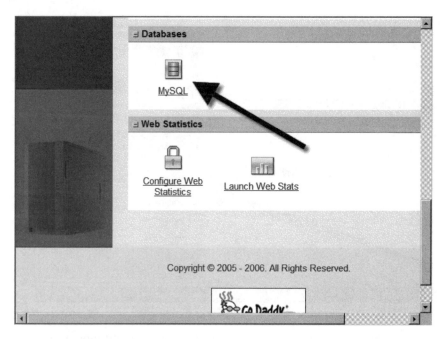

Figure 2-9. *Click the MySQL button to open the database administration page.*

The MySQL administration page will display the currently available databases. On my site shown in the figure, there are currently no databases. Below the database list is a Create New Database button. If you haven't already created the Joomla database, click the button (see Figure 2-10).

Joomla will take you to the template screen to enter the information to create a database. Enter **JoomlaDB_Main** in the Description field. Enter the same text in the User Name field (see Figure 2-11).

This may be slightly confusing, but the User Name field will actually be the name of the database that is created. Setting this field to the same text as the description makes things easier to manage. Note that the User Name is limited to 16 characters and must be unique on the shared MySQL server. On Go Daddy, many users share the same database server, and the database name must not match one already created by another user. Enter a password and a confirmation of that password, and then click the Continue button.

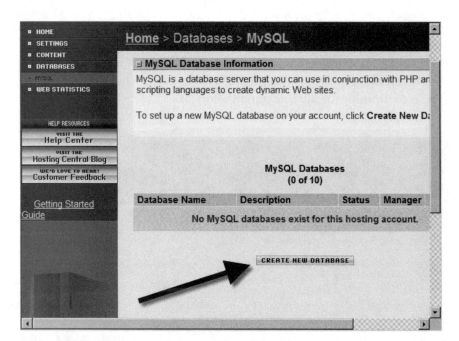

Figure 2-10. *To add a new database, click the Create New Database button.*

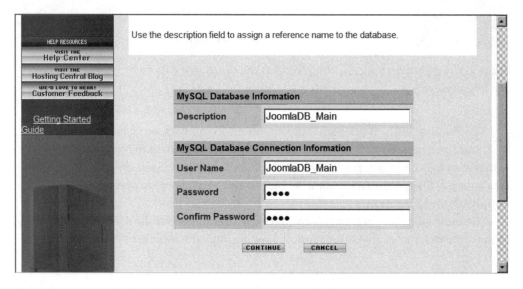

Figure 2-11. *Enter the database name in the User Name field.*

You will be asked to verify the entered information. Click the Create Database button to continue. Once Go Daddy creates the database, you'll be returned to the MySQL administration screen. Your database should be visible, as shown in Figure 2-12, and the entry in the Status column will most likely read Pending Setup. That means that the Go Daddy server is performing the administration setup tasks.

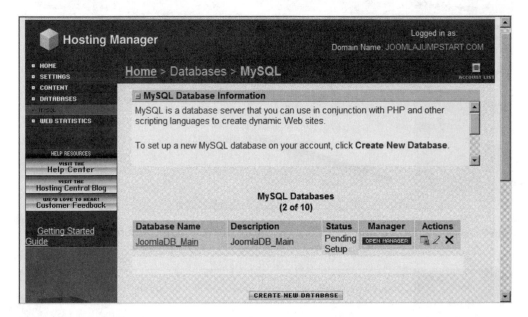

Figure 2-12. *Go Daddy shows Pending Setup as the status when its servers are working on the setup procedure.*

The Pending Setup status generally lasts about 15 minutes, but it can take up to several hours on a busy day. Click the MySQL link in the left menu to refresh the MySQL Databases page. Once setup is complete, the Status column will change to read Setup (see Figure 2-13) and the Open Manager button will be available to open the phpMyAdmin application.

The basic setup on Go Daddy is complete. The remainder of the setup is performed in the same manner as any Joomla installation: through the Joomla Installation Wizard.

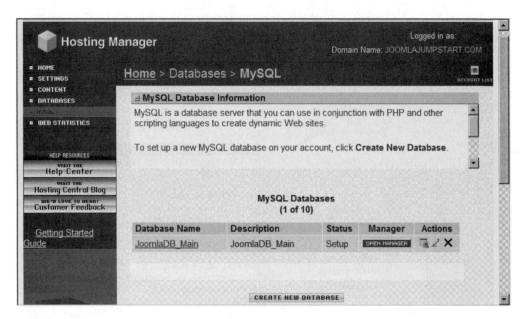

Figure 2-13. *When database setup is complete, the Status column entry will change to Setup and the Open Manager button will activate.*

Using the Joomla! Installation Wizard

With MySQL configured and Joomla uploaded to your web host, you're ready to begin the Joomla Installation Wizard. Open a browser window and enter the URL address of the location of the Joomla files. For example, on a site called "example," you might access the Joomla Installation Wizard with the following URL: `http://www.example.com/index.php`.

The Joomla wizard will load and display the first screen, which presents the language options for the site (see Figure 2-14).

■**Note** If the Joomla application doesn't load, it's difficult to guess what the problem might be. Perhaps your web server isn't executing PHP, or maybe you copied the Joomla installation to a different location than the URL address you entered. If you can't figure out the issue, turn to the "Troubleshooting" section in the next chapter for help.

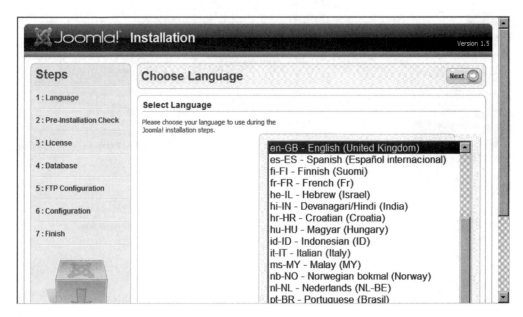

Figure 2-14. *The first screen of the Joomla Installation Wizard allows you to select the language to use for the Joomla installation.*

All of the user interfaces (including front-end, installation, and administration) will be presented in the selected language (if the installer you downloaded includes that language pack). Joomla has significant multilingual support. At the time of this writing, Joomla supports the following languages: Arabic, Bangsamoro, Basque, Bengali (Bangladesh), Bengali (India), Bosnian, Bulgarian, Chinese-Simplified, Chinese-Traditional, Croatian, Czech, Danish, Devanagari/Hindi, Dutch, Estonian, Filipino, Farsi, Finnish, French, German, German (Austrian), Greek, Hebrew, Hungarian, Indonesian, Italian, Japanese, Korean, Kurdish, Lithuanian, Malay, Norwegian, Polish, Portuguese (Portugal), Portuguese (Brazil), Romanian, Russian, Serbian, Spanish, Swedish, Thai, Turkish, and Vietnamese. That's quite a mouthful!

Once you've selected the language in which you intend to use Joomla, click the Next button at the top-right corner of the screen.

Note Joomla isn't limited to a single language. After the installation is complete, you can add additional languages to use for site presentation. Joomla even allows users to select the display language of the site from the installed language packs.

Preinstallation Check

The second step of the Installation Wizard is the preinstallation check. Figure 2-15 shows that first set of Joomla checks confirm that the correct versions of PHP and MySQL are installed and that the configuration.php file is writable.

Figure 2-15. *The preinstallation check queries the web server configuration and reports any problems on the Pre-Installation Check screen.*

If any of these settings do not match the Joomla recommendations, you should consult your service provider for ways to remedy the problem. If your provider offers no way of resolving these problems, you will have to change providers to run Joomla.

The Recommended settings area of the Pre-Installation Check screen displays the settings that will make Joomla function best. Options on the PHP server such as Safe Mode, Display Errors, File Uploads, Magic Quotes Runtime, Register Globals, Output Buffering, and Session auto start are all features that Joomla will use for best execution.

If everything checks out, click the Next button at the top-right corner of the screen.

GNU General Public License

On the screen shown in Figure 2-16, you must accept the GNU General Public License (GPL) to continue with the installation. I recommend you read the license, as it is straightforward and limits the amount of legalese you'll have to dig through to get to actual rights and restrictions.

Figure 2-16. *You must agree to the GNU GPL license terms to use Joomla.*

The most important points of the GNU GPL include the following:

- Grants the right to use the program for any desired purpose

- Grants the right to access the source code and modify it

- Grants the right to redistribute the program and its source code

- Grants the right to release program modifications to the public (but public release is not required; program modifications can be kept private or in-house)

- Stipulates the requirement that derivative works must also be licensed under GPL (meaning you can't take Joomla, repackage it, and sell it as a proprietary application)

If you're OK with the terms of the GNU GPL, and it's likely you are, click the Next button to advance to the database configuration. This screen will likely be the most difficult to get configured properly—depending on your hosting provider.

MICROSOFT AND GNU GPL

It's no secret that Microsoft dislikes GNU GPL licensing. Microsoft reserves special ire for the stipulation in the GNU GPL that requires derivative works of a GPL project to also be licensed under GPL. Microsoft representatives have spoken against it on several occasions and liken this clause to a virus. The provision ensures the product itself and all products derived from it remain firmly in the open source camp.

In the past, Microsoft claimed its strategy with regard to Internet technology was summarized by the slogan "embrace and extend." The company will take an open source solution, fund development to extend it, and at times create a proprietary solution from the results. The GNU GPL is meant as a poison pill to this type of behavior. Opponents of Microsoft in the open source community believe its slogan should be amended to "embrace, extend, and extinguish."

MySQL Database Configuration

The MySQL Database Configuration screen (see Figure 2-17) accepts the parameters to address your (or your web host's) MySQL installation. The first database setting is an options box that allows you to choose your database type. Currently, mysql is the only database option, but there are plans for future versions to include support for Oracle and Microsoft SQL Server.

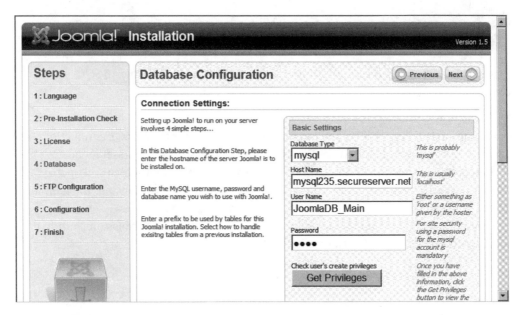

Figure 2-17. *The Database Configuration screen lets you set up Joomla for interaction with the MySQL database.*

If you're running Joomla on your own server, the Host Name setting will nearly always be `localhost`. This means that the database server will be running on the machine that is also hosting the web page.

On a web hosting provider, the procedure is a little different. For Go Daddy, you need to get the MySQL server address where your database is stored. At the main Control Panel in Go Daddy, you will need to click the Connection Settings icon shown in Figure 2-18.

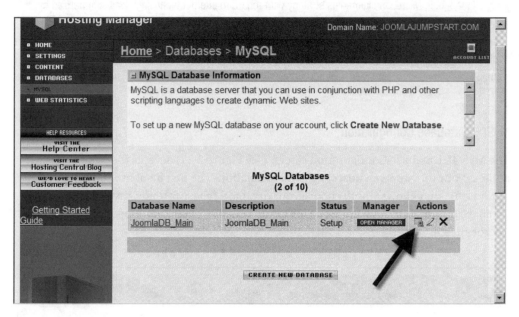

Figure 2-18. *Click the Connection Settings icon for information about the MySQL connection.*

A pop-up will display all of the important information for the MySQL connection. Figure 2-19's arrows indicate where the username, database name, and server address are located in the Connection Settings window. If you have the Joomla screen still open, you can simply copy the information from the Connection Settings window into the Joomla fields.

Enter the username and password now. You can click the Get Permissions button if you have full account administrator privileges.

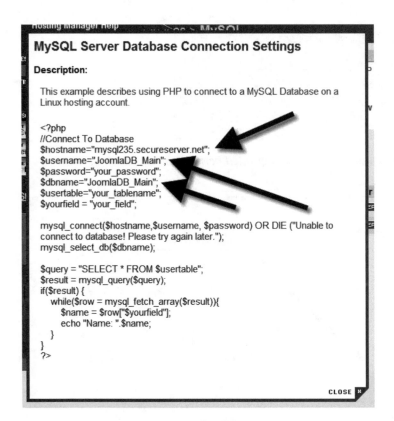

Figure 2-19. *The connection settings you will need for Joomla MySQL configuration*

■**Tip** The Get Permissions button is the first time that Joomla will attempt to connect to your MySQL database server. MySQL is notorious for providing unhelpful error messages. No matter what the problem, you will likely get a simple message that essentially states, "Cannot connect to MySQL." If you have a connection problem, take a look at the next chapter, where the solutions to a number of common MySQL problems are presented.

The installer will query the database to determine if you have account administrator privileges. If you are using a web host or have not given the account the proper security clearance, Joomla will display a message box like the one shown in Figure 2-20.

This message box lets you know that you have not been granted the proper permissions to create a database. Since you've already created the database, you don't need to create a fresh one. Before you can activate your existing database, click the Get Privileges button (see Figure 2-21).

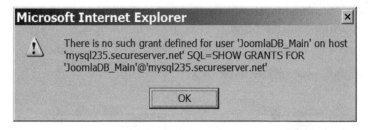

Figure 2-20. *Message box explaining the lack of granted permissions on the server*

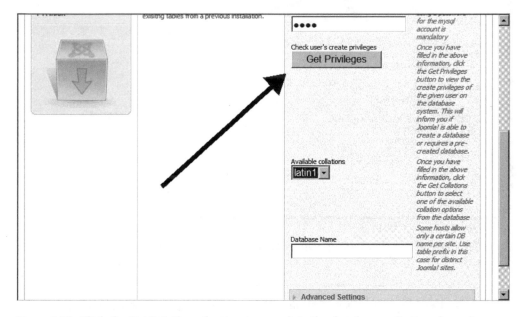

Figure 2-21. *Click the Get Privileges button to populate the database collation drop-down list options.*

You will be presented with a drop-down list of collation options. Depending on your MySQL configuration, you will most likely see a default setting of either latin-1 or utf8-general-ci. You can leave this default setting alone, as changing it is usually necessary only if you will be using a language other than English for Joomla access.

In the next field, Database Name, you'll enter either the existing database name or the name of the database to create if Joomla will be creating the database for you. Enter **JoomlaDB_Main** to match the database you created earlier.

Finally, if you have old Joomla tables already installed that you don't want to write over, you can expand the Advanced Settings tab (see Figure 2-22). The settings here provide the opportunity to either delete (drop) the existing tables or back them up under adjusted table names. In the figure, you can see that I left the selected backup option just in case there is a previous installation.

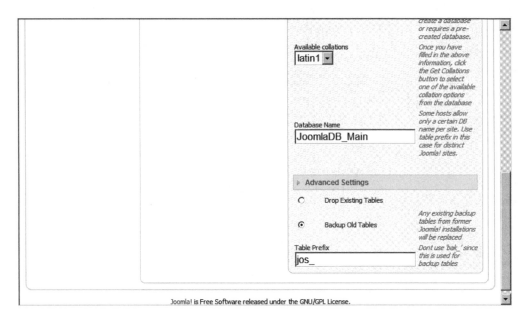

Figure 2-22. *The Advanced Settings tab provides options for handling older Joomla tables.*

FTP Configuration

Depending on your service provider, the FTP Configuration screen may or may not appear as shown in Figure 2-23. The settings on this screen enable Joomla to automatically handle tasks such as installing a template uploaded through the Joomla user interface directly to the proper web site directory. You can fill in this information now if you would like to do the setup. Joomla will allow you to enter it later through the Administrator interface if you prefer to leave it blank for now.

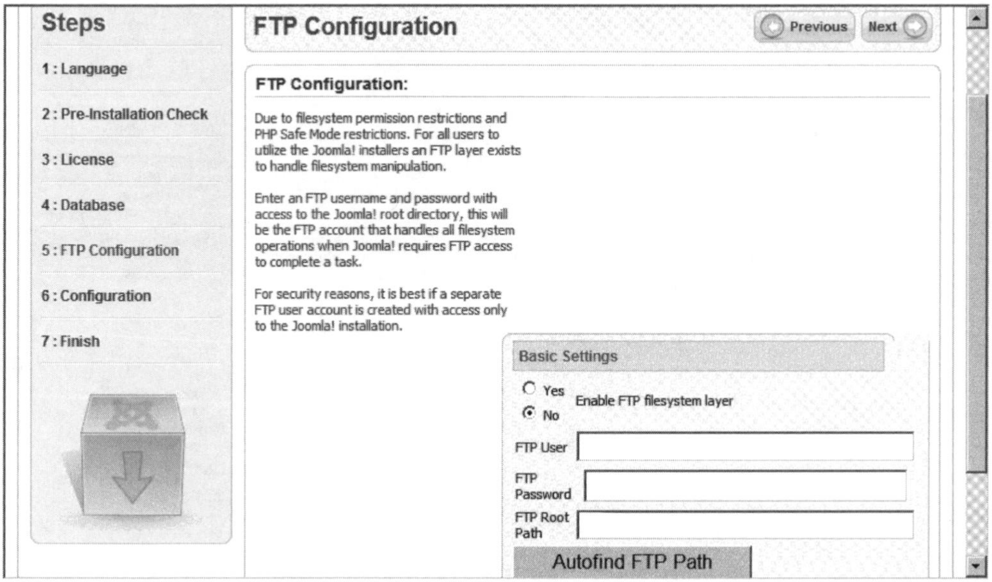

Figure 2-23. *The FTP Configuration screen*

Main Configuration

Click the Next button to move to the Main Configuration screen (see Figure 2-24). On this screen, enter the name of your Joomla web site. Also note the autogenerated administrator password. If you don't modify the password, *write down the autogenerated password*. You will need it to log in to the administration portion of the web site. Right now, enter a custom password in the Admin password and Confirm admin password fields.

If you want to put an administrator e-mail on the site, enter it now in the Your E-mail field. Realize that this e-mail address will be available through the web site, so be careful you don't set it to your main e-mail account. Spammers run programs to harvest e-mail addresses from web sites, and you don't want your e-mail on any more spam lists than necessary.

You're now ready to select where the initial data for the site will originate from. If you have a previous version of Joomla running, you may want to transfer your content from there. For this example, it is assumed this is a new installation. Click the "Install sample data" button shown in Figure 2-25 to write the default site examples into the database.

If the data installs correctly, the button will be replaced by text that reads, "Sample data installed successfully." If an error message is generated, you may have made a mistake with the MySQL configuration a few screens back. You can click the Previous button to return to the MySQL settings screen and try again.

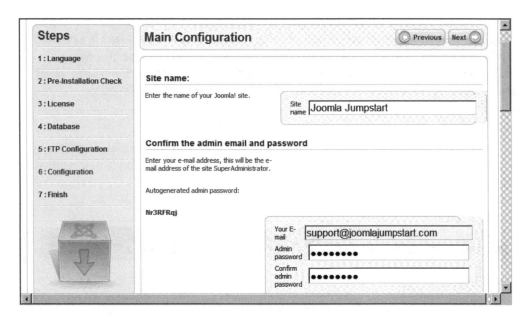

Figure 2-24. *On the Main Configuration screen, you can enter a site name, an admin e-mail, and data loading information.*

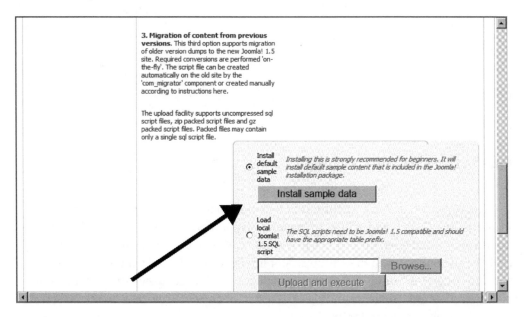

Figure 2-25. *Click the "Install sample data" button to populate the Joomla database with dummy content.*

■**Tip** There's an old acronym known as KISS that is helpful when encountering problems in a situation like this one. A gentle version of this acronym is Keep It Super Simple. Joomla is a complex system. If you're having problems logging in to MySQL through Joomla, go to a direct login for the database server and attempt to use the database from there. The problem may lie outside of Joomla's settings.

With the data installed correctly, click the Next button and you should be greeted by a success screen like the one shown in Figure 2-26. Congratulations! You're now ready to use this installation of Joomla for the first time.

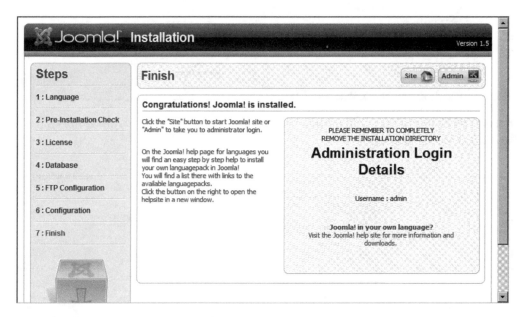

Figure 2-26. *Joomla is correctly installed.*

The Finish screen has two buttons in the upper-right corner: Site, which links to the main site, and Admin, which links to the Administrator portion of the site. Right-click the Admin button and open the link in a new window. Then return to the main window and click the Site button. With the Administrator interface open in one window and the main user interface in the other, you can easily flip back and forth between them. With a simple browser refresh, you'll instantly see the results of any changes made to the main user interface in the Administrator interface.

■**Caution** On older versions of Joomla, you were required to delete the Installation directory before Joomla would run. The new version doesn't require deletion of the Installation directory, although it is recommended. If someone were to either mistakenly or with ill intent can run the installation program, it could write over your existing Joomla site and its content. Be sure to remove this directory and all of the files it contains before you go live with your web site.

Modifying the Joomla! Installation

Now that you have Joomla installed, you probably want to see what it looks like. When you access the web page on your server, a page similar to the one shown in Figure 2-27 displays. I've placed label arrows over the figure to point out the different parts of the interface. You will need to understand the various areas of the screen in order to determine where you need to go in the Administrator interface to make modifications.

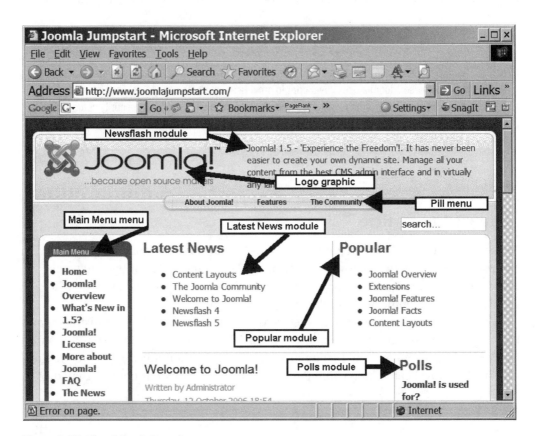

Figure 2-27. *The default Joomla screen*

The areas labeled on the figure are as follows:

- Main Menu menu

- Newsflash module

- Logo graphic

- Pill menu

- Latest News module

- Popular module

- Polls module

In the next section, you'll use the Joomla interface to modify each of these items. With a basic understanding of the fundamental elements of a Joomla page, you can begin editing the site. You will perform all modifications through the Joomla Administrator web interface.

Note If you are having problems using the Joomla Administrator interface, make sure that JavaScript is enabled in your browser. Joomla uses JavaScript to provide an interactive graphical user interface for administration. In the case of Internet Explorer, JavaScript is available if the Medium security setting or less is currently selected. You can check the security setting in the Security tab of the Tools ➤ Internet Options menu.

Adding a New Article

Text is the main type of content managed by a CMS like Joomla. Although a CMS may store other content in the form of pictures, report data, static HTML pages, and media, text is the meat and potatoes of most web sites. In this section, you'll add the text of a simple article to examine how Joomla manages new content.

For now, you will post an article directly as the administrator. An administrator can give permissions to registered users to submit articles and other content items for publication. In later chapters, you'll set up privileges so remote authors can post to the site with final approval before publication reserved for the administrator or designated moderator.

To begin, you'll need to log in to the Joomla Administrator interface. To access the Administrator page, enter your site URL in the address bar of your web browser, followed by the directory reference to the Administrator folder. Most commonly, you will have a URL that reads something like this:

```
http://www.example.com/administrator/index.php
```

You should be presented with a login screen like the one shown in Figure 2-28. I suggest bookmarking this page in your browser so you can quickly and easily get to the administration portion of Joomla.

Figure 2-28. *The Joomla Administration Login screen*

For the login, enter your username and password. Unless you changed it, your username will be **admin** and your password will be the random series of letters that you wrote down when you performed the first installation. When the username and password are accepted, you will be presented with the Control Panel of the Administrator interface. The Control Panel contains buttons for the most commonly used functions of the interface.

If the Administrator interface (see Figure 2-29) seems a little overwhelming when you first see it, don't be alarmed. Soon enough, navigating through it will become second nature. To add an article, click the Add New Article button in the top-left corner.

Figure 2-29. *The Joomla Administrator interface home page*

When Joomla returns the page to you, you should see the article editor, which has a nice What You See Is What You Get (WYSIWYG) interface. To begin a new article, you need to give it a title, select a Section and a Category, and then enter the body text of the content. In Figure 2-30, note that I've filled in a basic article and set the main parameters.

The title for the article will appear in everything from the site map to the contents page, so make it descriptive, but not too long. The *section* and *category* fields are the means of organizing Joomla content. You'll learn about the importance of those for organization in a Chapter 4, but for now, just select News for *section* and Latest News for *category*. For the body, I entered the following simple text:

```
The quickest way to jumpstart a new web site is with Joomla!
Don't be afraid it will be too complicated because with
Joomla, site construction is so simple even a caveman could
do it.

<-- Don't be afraid to use an emotion icon in your article body.
```

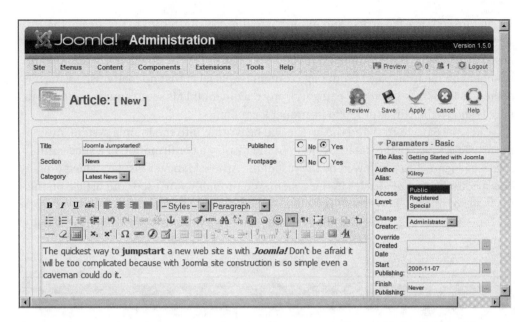

Figure 2-30. *Enter the title, select the section and category, and enter the body text of the article in the article editor.*

After I entered the text, I went back and used the bold icon to highlight the words "jumpstart" and "Joomla", and I threw in italics on the second word for good measure. Then I positioned the cursor in front of the <-- characters, clicked the Emotions button, and added a little icon. From this simple demonstration, you can begin to get a feel for the way in which Joomla can help even a nontechnical person add rich text content to a web site.

When you have the article ready to go, you might add some basic parameters to the fields on the right side of the screen. These are optional settings (Title Alias, Author Alias, etc.) and can be left blank if you desire.

The one basic parameter you will want to change is the Start Publishing date. By default, that date is set to publish the new article the day after posting. You probably want the article to appear right now, so you should change the setting to the current date or earlier. The article will then appear on the front page instantly. You can click the button with the ellipsis (...) to the right of the date to bring up a calendar.

■**Note** You may see an article listed in the Article Manager with a small icon containing an exclamation point in the published column. If you go to the bottom of the table, you'll learn that this icon indicates the article is "Published, but is Pending," meaning that the article is published into the system, but will not appear on the site until the Start Publishing date is reached.

Before you save the article and publish it to the web site, return to the area of the screen where you entered the article title. You'll see a label that reads "Frontpage" followed by two radio buttons marked Yes and No. Click the Yes button to make the content to appear on the front page. Front page content is special in that no matter where the content is filed (by section and category), any document that is set to appear on the front page is shown there in addition to its proper location.

Click the Save button and the article will be written into the Joomla system. After the article is saved to the database, Joomla will display a confirmation of a successful save (see Figure 2-31), followed by the rest of the Article Manager display, which presents a complete list of articles in the system. You probably won't see your article on the first page of this list; however, if you click the Select Section drop-down that sits above the table and choose News, the table will reformat and your article will likely be listed at the top.

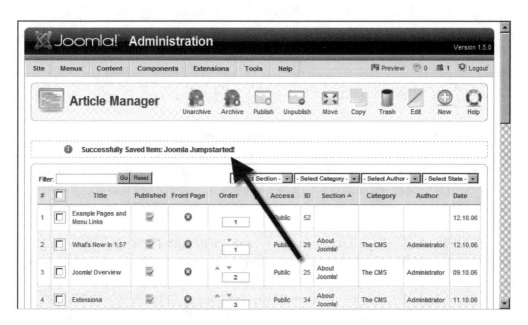

Figure 2-31. *Joomla confirms that an article was saved in the database, and the Article Manager presents a list of articles in the system.*

You've just published your first article! If you switch to the browser window that shows the main Joomla page and click the Refresh button, you should see your new content appear, as shown in Figure 2-32.

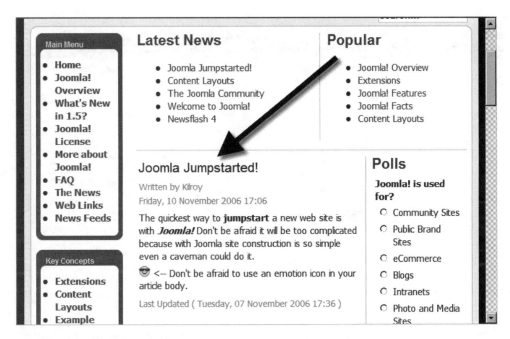

Figure 2-32. *The Joomla front page displays newly published articles.*

That's how easy it is to add content to Joomla. You'll notice that the headline and article citations are formatted using the same style as the other articles. You can also see that the formatting and emotion icon are displayed just as they were chosen in the editor. Before you add more content, you should modify the site itself to reflect the information that will be published here.

Editing the Main Menu

The default Joomla installation has four predefined menus: Top Menu (horizontal menu), Main Menu (vertical menu), Other Menu, and User Menu. Top Menu runs horizontally across the top of the page. Main Menu appears on the left side of the screen and shows the most common site options. The third menu, Other Menu, appears at the bottom left of the screen and includes links to external web sites (Joomla Home, OSM Home, etc.). The fourth menu, User Menu, doesn't appear on the screen until a user has properly logged into the web site. It has links to items such as Your Details and Log-out.

To begin editing the menus on the front page, return to the main page using the Site ➤ Control Panel menu selection. Once at the Control Panel, click the Menu Manager icon (see Figure 2-33).

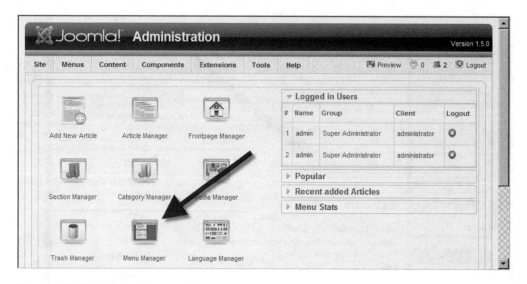

Figure 2-33. *The Menu Manager icon*

The Menu Manager shows a table of all of the menus currently on the site. You can see that the default site has six menus. The table column directly to the right of each menu title lists the type of menu.

Click the Main Menu link to move into the menu editor (see Figure 2-34). You can see the current menu text in the Title field. Change it from Main Menu to Joomla Jumpstart Menu and click the Save button to store the changes.

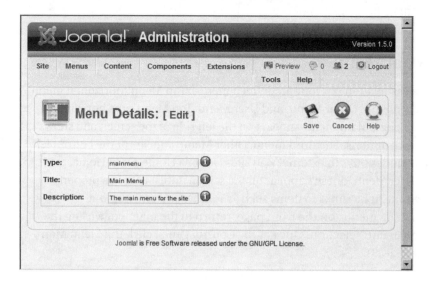

Figure 2-34. *The menu editor's basic fields*

In the Menu Manager, the column labeled Menu items contains an icon for each row. If you click that icon for our Joomla Jumpstart Menu, you will see all of the menu entries for each item that you see on the front page of your web site (see Figure 2-35).

Figure 2-35. *All of the items displayed in the central menu on the front page are listed here.*

You won't need most of the entries for your new web site because they relate directly to the Joomla installation. Like a good administrator, though, you don't want to delete them yet because you haven't completed your web site planning. Therefore, you can simply *unpublish* them so they no longer appear in the Joomla Jumpstart Menu. Click the leftmost check box for each of the following entries:

- Joomla Overview

- What's New in 1.5?

- Joomla License

- More about Joomla

- FAQ

With all of these items selected, click the Unpublish button near the top of the screen. When Joomla returns the updated Menu Manager screen, you should see that all of the checked items now have a small red "X" in the Published column where a green check mark appeared before, as shown in Figure 2-36.

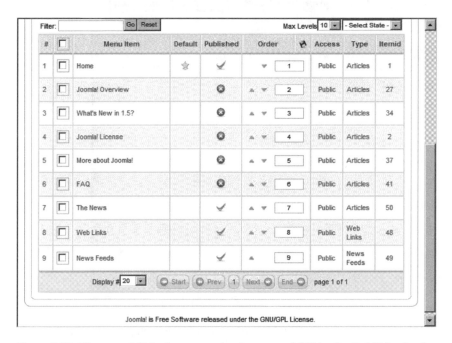

Figure 2-36. *The unpublished menus now have a red "X" in the Published column.*

Return to the browser window showing the current site and click the Refresh button. Look in the menu box on the side of the window and you'll see the unpublished entries are gone! But you're not finished yet—you need to take more action to personalize your Joomla site.

■Tip Menus are some of the most difficult items on a web site to get right. Poor menus hinder a user's navigation through the site. However, most web designers plan the menus at the beginning of the web site creation process and force the content into the preplanned selections, even if the process is akin to creating a round hole before knowing the shape of the pegs to fit in them (which may be square). Since Joomla makes menu modification so painless, do your visitors a favor and revisit the menu options near the end of the creation process, and change them to best represent the content each option describes.

Removing Modules

Most of the display on a Joomla page occurs in small distinct areas called *modules*. The poll on the right side of the main screen shown in Figure 2-32, for example, is the Polls module. The areas titled Latest News and Popular are modules that display the most recent content and the most popular content, respectively.

Currently, Latest News and Popular modules are cluttering up our new, streamlined interface. Let's get rid of them by unpublishing them. Select the Extensions ➤ Module Manager menu option. This takes you to the Module Manager, where you can scroll down until you reach these two modules in the list. Then click the Publish green check mark in the Publish column, and it will turn into the red "X," indicating that the item is being unpublished, as shown in Figure 2-37.

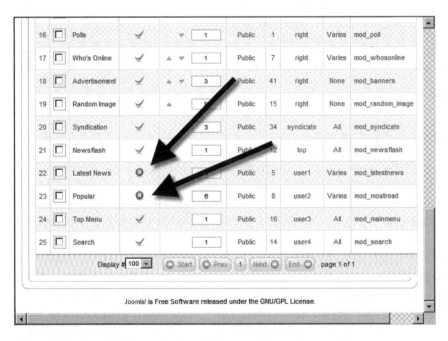

Figure 2-37. *Unpublishing the Latest News and Popular modules*

If you refresh the browser window showing your site, you'll see that those items have now disappeared (see Figure 2-38).

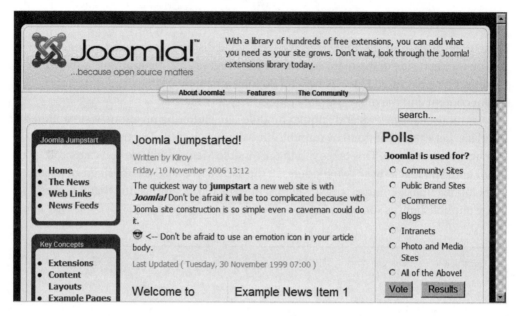

Figure 2-38. *The updated Joomla site has no Latest News or Popular modules.*

Unpublishing Whole Menus

You can also unpublish entire menus through the Module Manager. Each menu in the Joomla system uses a linked module that displays it on the page. If you unpublish the module associated with a menu, although the menu still exists, it has no method of display. The Key Concepts and Resources menus that appear below the main Joomla Jumpstart Menu aren't needed right now. In the Module Manager, locate the entries for these two menus and click the green check marks in the Publish column to unpublish them, as shown in Figure 2-39.

If you refresh the browser window showing your site, you'll see that those items have now disappeared (see Figure 2-40).

Now that you've rid the site of all the items you don't want, it's time to begin modifying the existing items to make the site your own. One of the hallmarks of a web site is the logo graphic that stretches across the top of the screen, so we'll tackle that in the next section. Leave the browser window showing the Administrator interface open; you'll need it after you create and upload your new graphic.

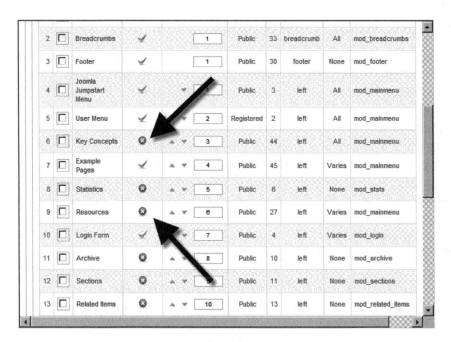

2	☐	Breadcrumbs	✔	1	Public	33	breadcrumb	All	mod_breadcrumbs
3	☐	Footer	✔	1	Public	30	footer	None	mod_footer
4	☐	Joomla Jumpstart Menu	✔	1	Public	3	left	All	mod_mainmenu
5	☐	User Menu	✔	2	Registered	2	left	All	mod_mainmenu
6	☐	Key Concepts	⊗	3	Public	44	left	All	mod_mainmenu
7	☐	Example Pages	✔	4	Public	45	left	Varies	mod_mainmenu
8	☐	Statistics	⊗	5	Public	6	left	None	mod_stats
9	☐	Resources	⊗	6	Public	27	left	Varies	mod_mainmenu
10	☐	Login Form	✔	7	Public	4	left	Varies	mod_login
11	☐	Archive	⊗	8	Public	10	left	None	mod_archive
12	☐	Sections	⊗	11	Public	11	left	None	mod_sections
13	☐	Related Items	⊗	10	Public	13	left	None	mod_related_items

Figure 2-39. *Unpublishing the Key Concepts and Resources menus*

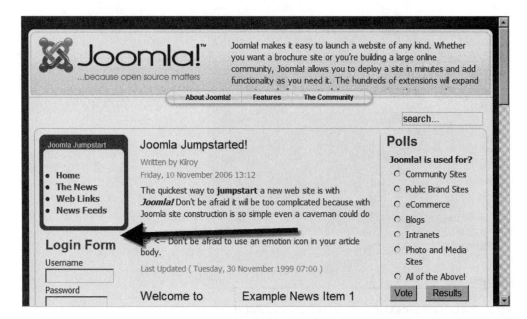

Figure 2-40. *The updated Joomla site has no Key Concepts or Resources menus.*

Changing the Frontpage Logo Graphic

A good logo graphic gives your web site a sense of place. And if you have an e-commerce site, the logo is an important element in establishing your brand. It's time to replace the Joomla logo with a graphic of your own. This logo graphic is generally held within the directory of the current template.

Earlier you extracted the Joomla files to your local drive. You'll use the logo from the original template installation as the foundation for your new logo, and you'll use a painting program to edit the graphic. In this section, you'll learn how to modify the graphic with the simple Paint program included in Windows XP (under Start ➤ All Programs ➤ Accessories ➤ Paint). In later chapters, you'll use Adobe Photoshop and GIMP to do more robust template editing, but to keep things simple, we'll use this primitive little application for now.

Execute Paint and select File ➤ Open to load a new file. You'll have to navigate to the directory where you've stored the Joomla installation files and access the `mw_joomla_logo.png` file in the `\images` folder of the template. The path to this file might be something like this: `C:\ Joomla1_5install\templates\rhuk_milkyway\images\ mw_joomla_logo.png`.

When you load the file into Paint, you should see the graphic that appears in the top-left corner of your Joomla Frontpage (see Figure 2-41).

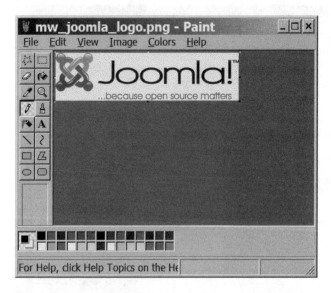

Figure 2-41. *Load the existing Joomla logo into Paint.*

To begin, we need to clear the existing graphic. Select Edit ➤ Select All (Ctrl+A) and press the Delete key to erase the canvas. Now that you have a blank canvas, what are you going to do with it? Anything you want!

Briefly, here is what I did. First, I set the color to dark blue. Then I selected the Fill with Color tool and clicked the background to fill the canvas with this color. Next, I selected a lighter shade of blue and used the Airbrush tool to add some texture. Finally, I needed to add my logo text. I unchecked the Image ➤ Draw Opaque option so the text box wouldn't blot out the background. I used the Text tool to stretch a text area to cover most of the canvas, entered the text **Joomla Jumpstart**, and adjusted the font and size until everything looked decent.

When I was done, I had something that wouldn't win any design awards (see Figure 2-42), but wouldn't embarrass my site either. I selected File ➤ Save As, set the filename as `mw_joomlajumpstart_logo.png`, and saved it into the same folder as the original logo.

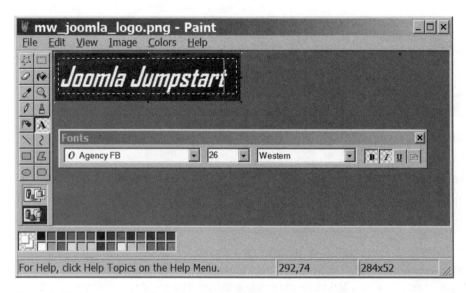

Figure 2-42. *Create a simple logo and store it in the \images directory.*

You may already have a logo graphic that you want to use. If so, copy it to the \images directory for convenience and make a note of the graphic's width and height. You'll need that information later.

Now you need to upload the image you just created so Joomla can use it. Fire up your FTP client program and log in to your FTP server. If you created a site in FileZilla, you can bring up your Joomla directory in a single click. Once the program is logged in to the site, navigate both the local site and the remote site to the \images folder and upload your new logo there, as shown in Figure 2-43.

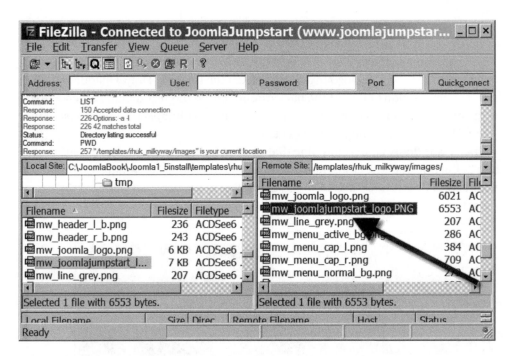

Figure 2-43. *Upload the new logo to the Joomla FTP site.*

You're all done on that front. Now you have to modify the style sheet to point toward your new image.

Caution The `template.css` file that will reference the image is case sensitive. When Paint saves a file, it capitalizes the extension. Therefore, what was `mw_joomlajumpstart_logo.png` becomes `mw_joomlajumpstart_logo.PNG`. Make sure you exactly match the filename when you change it in the CSS file or the new logo won't load.

In the Joomla Administrator interface, select Extensions ➤ Template Manager to bring up the template configuration screen. In the Template Manager, select the default template and then click the Edit button as shown in Figure 2-44.

The Template Parameters screen will display. You're not interested in setting any of the template options. This screen provides the Joomla interface that lets you open the HTML and CSS editors. To adjust the logo graphic, you need to make a small change to the CSS, so click the Edit CSS button (see Figure 2-45).

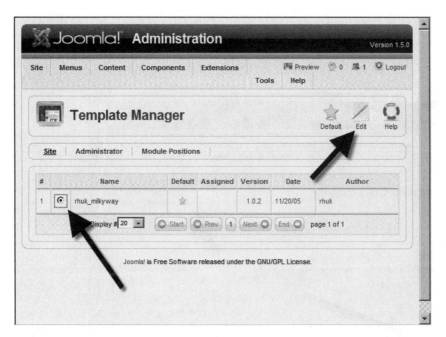

Figure 2-44. *Select the default template and click the Edit button.*

Figure 2-45. *Click the Edit CSS button.*

The template has more than one CSS file, as you can see in Figure 2-46. The main template.css file contains the reference to the logo, so select that file and click the Edit button.

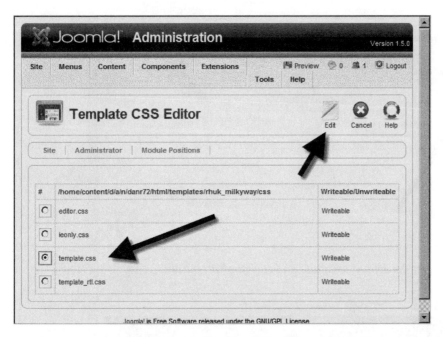

Figure 2-46. *Select the template.css file and click the Edit button.*

The text of the CSS file will be displayed for you. In later chapters, you'll learn how to use a special CSS editor that will make these items more understandable. Right now, you need to locate the CSS element known as div#logo. Scroll down through the text until you locate the entry. Once you find it, you can see that this element specifies a background attribute with the original filename of the logo, as shown in Figure 2-47.

Alter that file reference to reflect the name of your new logo. Remember that the filename is case sensitive, so make it identical to the actual filename. The logo I created was based on the original graphic, so the dimensions of the new graphic were identical. If you're using a different graphic, be sure to modify the width and height attributes of the element to match your graphic.

Figure 2-47. *Scroll down to the div#logo entry and select the existing logo's filename.*

Click the Save button and you're done! Return to the browser window showing your Joomla site and click the Refresh button. You should now see the graphic you created; mine is shown in Figure 2-48.

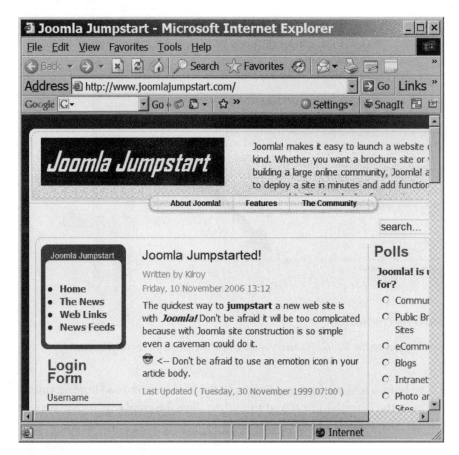

Figure 2-48. *The new graphic will appear in place of the old.*

Personalizing the Newsflash Text

You've changed the logo from the normal Joomla image to one of your own choosing. Still, to the right of the logo is the Joomla boilerplate text. The next step in personalizing the site, then, is to add new text there to match your site's intentions.

The static text that appears to the right of the logo is actually displayed by a Newsflash module. If you create a new article as Newsflash content, your site message can appear there.

On the main Control Panel screen, click the New Article button. Set the title to whatever you want (it won't be seen), and select News from the section drop-down and Newsflash from the category drop-down. Enter some text and perhaps a slogan or two as shown in Figure 2-49.

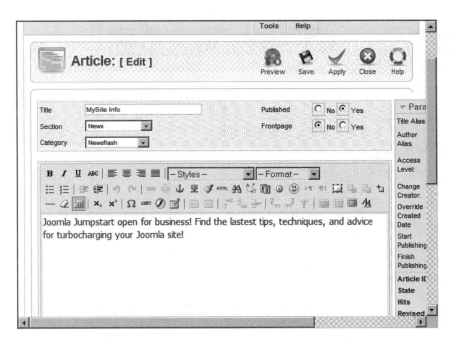

Figure 2-49. *Create Newsflash content that describes your site.*

When you've finished, click the Save button to return to the Article Manager. There are many articles on the default site, so instead of sorting through them for your new addition, click the Select Category filter drop-down and select Newsflash, as shown in Figure 2-50. Only the Newsflash articles will be displayed. In the default installation, there should be only five articles.

Instead of clicking the Published icons on each of the articles to unpublish them, you can use the check boxes to do a group select. Select the check boxes of all articles that aren't your new site description, and then click the Unpublish button as shown in Figure 2-51.

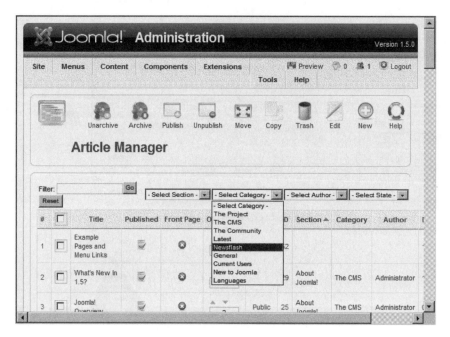

Figure 2-50. *In the Article Manager, select Newsflash from the Select Category filter drop-down.*

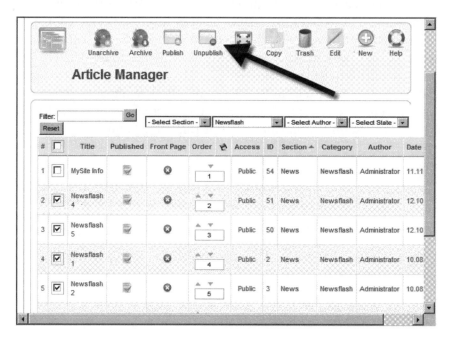

Figure 2-51. *Unpublish all of the Newsflash articles except the one you just created.*

When Joomla refreshes the page, your site description should be the only Newsflash published. Refresh your site browser window, and you should see the new text next to your new logo (see Figure 2-52). Now the site is really beginning to move away from the default presentation.

Figure 2-52. *The new text is displayed in the Newsflash module.*

Creating a Custom Poll

The current Polls module probably doesn't fit your site description either. It's time to create a new poll. Select Components ➤ Polls to display the Poll Manager. You can see the delete "default" poll that is included with the default installation. You'll need a new one that's tailored to your users. Click the New button to create a new poll (see Figure 2-53).

For my page, I wanted to poll visitors about the operating system they use. In Figure 2-54 you can see that I've entered the title "What operating system are you running?" for the poll. To the right, I've entered the options I think are likely to be chosen by my web site visitors. Create any poll you like and click the Save button to store the poll in the Joomla database.

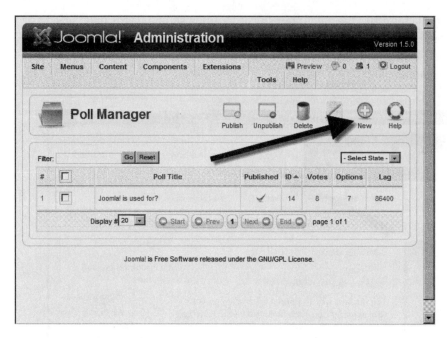

Figure 2-53. *Click the New button to create a new poll.*

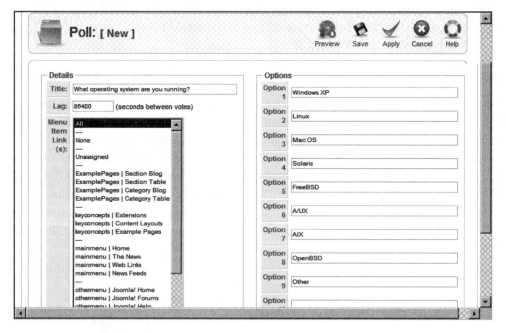

Figure 2-54. *Create a new poll with an appropriate title and well-chosen options.*

Back in the Poll Manager, you will see your new poll, which by default will be unpublished. To display it on the front page, publish your poll and then unpublish the existing one (see Figure 2-55).

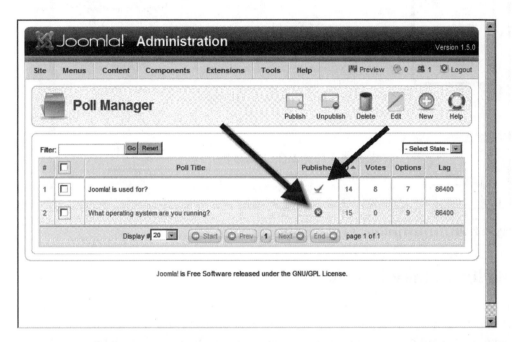

Figure 2-55. *Click the red "X" to publish your poll and the green check mark to unpublish the original poll.*

After refreshing your site page, you'll see your poll display, just like in Figure 2-56.

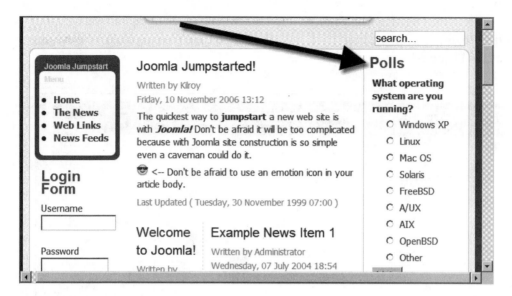

Figure 2-56. *The new poll on the front page*

Modifying the Pill Menu

The site is almost completely yours. Other than the Joomla-specific content in the articles section that you'll gradually replace with your own, only the horizontal pill menu remains to remind you of the default sample data. The *pill menu* is so named because its appearance mirrors that of a gel-cap pill. I don't know if this type of interface originated on Mac OS, but that was the first place I can remember seeing it.

Although the pill menu looks different from any of the other menus, it's merely another menu with a specialty appearance that is defined in the CSS of the template. You don't need to alter the style sheet, however, to change the options presented on it.

Go directly to the Top Menu definition by selecting Menus ➤ Top Menu. Click the About Joomla menu item to bring up the item editor. Change the title of the menu to **About Joomla Jumpstart** as shown in Figure 2-57. Now all you have to do is redirect the target of the link.

On the right side of page, you'll see a Select Article section. If you click the Select button, a pop-up will display a list of article titles. Look through the articles until you find the "Joomla Jumpstarted!" article you created earlier (see Figure 2-58).

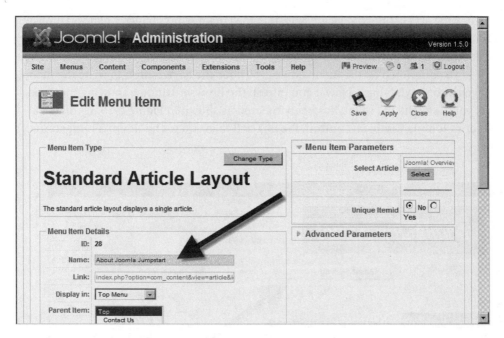

Figure 2-57. *Change the title of the menu to About Joomla Jumpstart.*

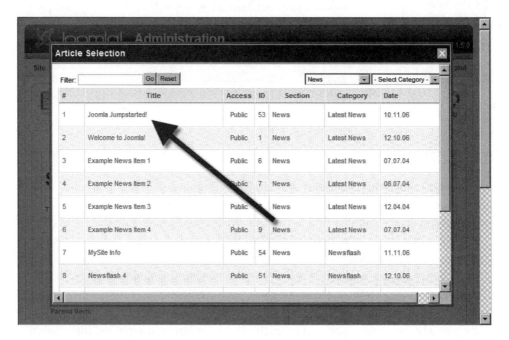

Figure 2-58. *Find the "Joomla Jumpstarted!" article and click the title.*

Click the article title to select it. Note that the cursor won't change when you mouse over the title, but clicking it will select it nonetheless. The pop-up will disappear and you'll return to the Edit Menu Item screen.

You've completed all the menu editing, so click the Save button to write the menu changes into the database. Now if you refresh the browser window showing the main page, you'll see the pill menu has been updated as shown in Figure 2-59. If you click the About Joomla Jumpstart button, the link will take you to the "Joomla Jumpstarted!" article.

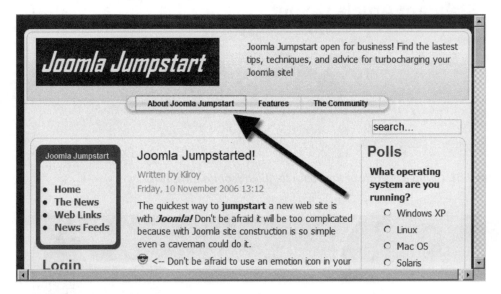

Figure 2-59. *The pill menu has been updated to show the new menu setting.*

Conclusion

After working through this Quickstart tutorial, you know how to install, set up, and run Joomla. You can add articles, make basic modifications to the template style sheet, change the logo display, publish and unpublish articles, and even set up your own poll.

As you can imagine, you've barely scratched the surface of Joomla's capabilities, but in approximately 20 minutes you've learned how to set up and manage a basic site. You could stop here and you would still know enough to run a respectable bloglike web site with a professional appearance. However, you undoubtedly want to squeeze every ounce of power from the Joomla CMS.

The next chapter guides you to a more thorough understanding of the installation and configuration process. After that, you'll learn all of the ways you can master the Joomla system and have a good time doing it. Now that you know the basics, it's a downhill ride from here.

■■■

## CHAPTER 3

Installation and Configuration

In the last chapter, you performed a rapid installation and configuration. If everything worked fine, you have the foundation of a site up and running. You may want to begin customizing your site and skip this chapter for now. However, be sure to return to it so you can get a clear understanding of the core Joomla installation structure. This knowledge will benefit you greatly as you begin to do more advanced Joomla modification.

If the installation from the last chapter didn't go perfectly and you hit a few speed bumps, this chapter is for you. In addition to providing extensive installation instructions on each piece of the technology suite (Apache, Microsoft Internet Information Server [IIS], PHP, and MySQL) that Joomla uses, it also shows you how to install Joomla on your own server rather than a commercial host.

Even if you plan on using a commercial host for final deployment, it's still generally more convenient to perform testing and development on a desktop machine. Generally, the configuration settings that are best for the experimentation phase of a server are not desirable on a deployment server. Your desktop machine can provide the advantages of local testing (such as direct access to files and server settings) without the security threats that exist in a deployment environment.

The multiple programs employed by a Joomla site have to integrate properly and "play nice" for the CMS to function properly. Figure 3-1 shows a general layer diagram of the two different installation options that will be presented in this chapter.

Because of the multiple technologies involved in Joomla, it can sometimes be extremely frustrating to track down the source of a problem. In this chapter, I provide troubleshooting guides that should help you to locate and remedy problems you might encounter. The guides solve most of the more common problems that I've come across. If the presented solutions don't directly eliminate the trouble, they should put you on the right track to solving it yourself.

Before you begin an installation, however, examining the organization of a Joomla site will help you recognize the directory structure for later configuration.

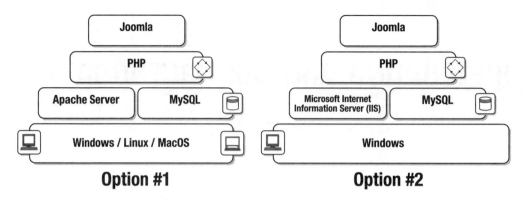

Figure 3-1. *Joomla runs atop three other layers of technology.*

File and Directory Overview

The Joomla system consists of approximately 3,200 files, so the system is too large to describe file by file. Nonetheless, now that you have an understanding of Joomla from an administrator perspective from the last chapter, it's useful to examine the directory structure so you'll know where to look when you want to make a direct modification.

Figure 3-2 shows the basic directory structure and the primary files located at the root. This figure shows the files of a virgin installation. Once you've installed Joomla on a web host, it's a good idea to eliminate the installation directory, even though it's shown here.

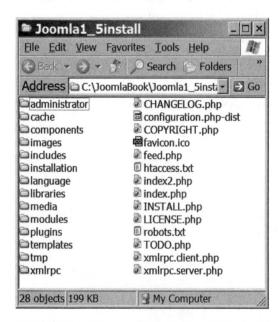

Figure 3-2. *Fourteen primary folders hold the Joomla system.*

The directories of the Joomla system are well named, and you can guess the contents of most of them. Nonetheless, the following list provides a summary explanation of the contents of each folder. Note that any directory in the following list with an asterisk (*) following its name is new to Joomla version 1.5. The directory either didn't exist in a previous version or was named differently.

- root: When you first place Joomla on your web site, the \root directory contains an index.php file that will launch the Joomla installer. Once installation is complete, index.php will detect the settings in the configuration.php file and execute the main Joomla engine. To make the system run the installer again, you need only delete the configuration.php file.

- administrator: This directory holds folders that closely mirror those of the \root directory, because the Administrator interface itself is essentially a Joomla web site. The Administrator has a complete user interface that can be augmented by administrative extensions.

- cache: You will most likely never need to examine the contents of this directory. To accelerate performance, Joomla will cache popular prerendered pages here, so they don't have to be rerendered by PHP and MySQL for each page request. The cached pages will simply be loaded from the directory and sent to the browser.

- components: Components are stored in this directory. You may notice that the default Joomla system includes a number of components, such as login, newsfeeds, poll, registration, search, and others, with functionality that is often displayed on the front-end using associated modules.

- images: This folder contains all of the bitmaps used by the Administrator interface as well as images that have been uploaded to present within article content. Within the \images folder, the \smilies folder contains emoticons that can be used in articles, the \stories folder has images for use within articles, and the \banners folder contains some sample banner files.

- includes: The \includes folder contains PHP execution files that automate inclusion of content. You may notice a couple of files here with the prefix "mambo"— these are included for backward compatibility. Joomla 1.5 can be run in *legacy* mode, making these files necessary. Expect the legacy mode as well as the Mambo files to disappear with the next major upgrade.

- installation: The \installation folder contains all of the files needed for configuration during initial installation. This folder and its contents should be deleted following initial configuration. Older versions required deletion before the main Joomla site would function. Now deletion is optional but highly recommended.

- `language`: This folder holds the site translation files. Joomla stores translations in a simple INI-based file format. All files are saved in the UTF-8 encoding format (see the sidebar titled "UTF-8 Character Encoding" later in the chapter). The file-names indicate the language using a standardized naming convention of a three-letter language code followed by a two-letter country code. The language code complies with the ISO-639-2 standard, while the country code complies with the ISO-3166 standard. For example, the English template from the country Great Britain has a folder name of `eng-GB`. All of the files contained in the folder have a filename prefix that matches the folder name.

- `libraries*`: The `\libraries` folder contains the framework or programming foundation of the entire Joomla system. A Joomla web site is actually a web application that uses the core libraries contained inside the `\libraries` folder for execution. If you look in the library folder named `\joomla`, you will see the various implementation areas (such as application, database, file system, etc.) that make up the functional parts of the application. Third-party libraries are also stored in the `\libraries` folder. Each library has its own subfolder in this folder to aid in organization.

- `media`: Media may be stored here for Joomla to access.

- `modules`: The modules available for display by a template are contained in this folder. Some of the standard modules include banners, breadcrumbs, latest news, login, newsflash, poll, random image, and others. Modules are placed like panels into a Joomla template. They often encapsulate or provide the front-end display for a related component. A module, like a component, is a type of add-on grouped under the general term "Extensions."

- `plugins*`: Plug-ins are located in the `\plugins` directory. In past versions, these were called *mambots*, short for *Mambo robot*. (Mambo was the precursor application to Joomla.) Plug-ins are framework extensions, so they operate at a lower level than components. A plug-in, like a component, is a type of add-on grouped under the general term "Extensions."

- `templates`: This folder holds the folders of any templates installed on the Joomla site. Note that the name of each template subfolder must match the template it contains. With the default installation, the default template is called `\rhuk_milkyway`. You will find a folder of that name within the `\templates` directory.

- `tmp*`: The `\tmp` directory stores temporary files and cookies that are used by both the Administrator and user interface portions of Joomla.

- `xmlrpc*`: This folder signifies perhaps the most powerful new feature of Joomla: eXtensible Markup Language Remote Procedure Call (XML-RPC) interface code. The XML-RPC interface allows remote procedure calls to be encoded in an XML wrapper. This means that a procedure call can be sent into the Joomla server for on-server execution.

What does XML-RPC mean to a Joomla administrator? Potentially multiple Joomla servers could be administered from a single server. More directly, XML-RPC can be used to allow client applications to talk to the Joomla server. In particular, blog applications such as w.bloggar provide support for XML-RPC posting of content. The w.bloggar software has an advanced Windows interface for blogging. Users can maintain their blog in the program, and then the application can directly upload blog content into Joomla as articles. Since the w.bloggar application handles the server interface, the blogger never has to go through the Joomla interface to add content. Support for other blog interfaces such as MetaWebBlog and Movable Type API are planned for future plug-ins.

■**Note** Even if you haven't heard of XML-RPC, you may be familiar with Simple Object Access Protocol (SOAP). SOAP was derived from XML-RPC and has evolved to become essentially a bigger, stronger, younger brother (with features such as Web Services Description Language [WSDL] generation, client proxy generation, WS-Security, etc.). The Joomla team decided to stick with XML-RPC because it is leaner and faster, and the additional SOAP features didn't seem necessary for Joomla applications given the extra overhead they demanded. The Joomla team also realized that if a developer needed the extra SOAP functionality, it could be addressed directly through PHP 5's built-in SOAP extension.

Most of the time, you will have no need to access these directories yourself. The majority of the configuration and modification of a Joomla web site can be accomplished through the web-based administrative interface. However, there are some actions such as modifying a template with a third-party text editor where you may want to directly access the source files.

Installing with XAMPP

As I mentioned earlier, installing and configuring all of the different server programs so they run together properly can be very difficult. Unless you're an accomplished system administrator, you may want to take a shortcut with XAMPP. Known as the "lazy man's installer," XAMPP combines all of the primary web server applications (Apache, PHP, and MySQL) into a single installation binary.

The XAMPP package was created to ensure that all server versions in the installer are compatible with each other and properly configured to work together. The "X" in XAMPP stands for the variety of operating systems for which this superinstaller is available. The other letters of the acronym stand for *Apache MySQL PHP Perl*. Although Joomla doesn't need Perl for execution, it won't interfere with Joomla functionality.

XAMPP installers are available for Windows, Linux, Sun Solaris, and Mac OS. You can download the appropriate installer from the official XAMPP site: www.apachefriends.org/en/xampp.html.

When you download and install XAMPP, there should be no need to edit any configuration files or struggle with incompatibilities. After installation is complete, you should be able to install Joomla immediately without any further work.

Note If you want an even simpler method of installing Joomla, you could choose Joomla! Stand Alone Server (JSAS; available from http://jsas.joomlasolutions.com). However, if you intend to use Joomla beyond the most basic implementation, I suggest you perform the Joomla installation yourself and separately. It will help you learn and understand the system.

XAMPP Components by Operating System

Each operating system (OS) installer contains its own set of applications, some of which are unique to that specific platform. Many of these applications aren't required for basic Joomla execution, but they can help you administer the web server. Others, like the FileZilla FTP server, can add functionality to Joomla for file upload.

The capabilities included in the XAMPP installer vary with the OS:

- *Windows*: Tested to run on Windows 98, NT, 2000, XP, and Vista. At the time of this writing, the installer includes Apache, MySQL, PHP and PEAR, Perl, mod_php, mod_perl, mod_ssl, OpenSSL, phpMyAdmin, Webalizer, Mercury Mail Transport System for Win32 and NetWare Systems v3.32, JpGraph, FileZilla FTP server, MCrypt, eAccelerator, SQLite, and WebDAV and mod_auth_mysql.

- *Linux systems*: Tested to run on SUSE, Red Hat, Mandrake, and Debian. At the time of this writing, the installer includes Apache, MySQL, PHP and PEAR, Perl, ProFTPD, phpMyAdmin, OpenSSL, GD, FreeType2, libjpeg, libpng, gdbm, zlib, expat, Sablotron, libxml, Ming, Webalizer, PDF Class, ncurses, mod_perl, FreeTDS, gettext, MCrypt, mhash, eAccelerator, SQLite, and IMAP c-client.

- *Mac OS X*: Tested to run on version 10.4 and higher. At the time of this writing, the installer includes Apache, MySQL, PHP and PEAR, SQLite, Perl, ProFTPD, phpMyAdmin, OpenSSL, GD, FreeType2, libjpeg, libpng, zlib, Ming, Webalizer, mod_perl, eAccelerator, and phpSQLiteAdmin.

- *Solaris*: Tested to run on Solaris 8 and Solaris 9. At the time of this writing, the installer includes Apache, MySQL, PHP and PEAR, Perl, ProFTPD, phpMyAdmin, OpenSSL, FreeType2, libjpeg, libpng, zlib, expat, Ming, Webalizer, and PDF Class.

Before you install XAMPP, recognize that it was created for use as a development platform, not for deployment. While many people do use it for deployment, the system is set up for ease of use rather than security. That means that there are many areas where the security is left wide open. These insecure areas include (but are not limited to) the following:

- The MySQL administrator account has no password.

- The MySQL daemon is open to the network.

- The PHP web administrative interface (phpMyAdmin) is open to the network.

- Standard default users of FileZilla and Mercury are well known.

If you are thinking of using the XAMPP installation as a server platform, be sure to close all of these security holes before you even consider deployment. Check the XAMPP web site for the latest list of security settings that should be configured before deployment.

The sections that follow describe the installation procedure for each OS.

Installing on Windows

After you've downloaded the installer, installation is as simple as double-clicking the executable file (.exe) or Microsoft installer file (.msi). The first screen (see Figure 3-3) prompts you for the installation language. In most cases you can leave the default language of English and click the OK button.

You will be presented with a splash screen that has no options, so click the Next button. The Install Location screen will ask for a directory in which to place the XAMPP files. The space requirements (around 220MB) will be displayed as well as the available disk space. Click the Next button to accept the default Program Files directory.

XAMPP will proceed to extract all the necessary files into the installation folder. When complete, it will begin presenting you with a series of message box prompts. Each prompt will ask if a separate application in the XAMPP suite (Apache, PHP, MySQL, etc.) can be run as a service. Figure 3-4 shows an example of the primary message box.

Figure 3-3. *Select a language to use for the XAMPP installer.*

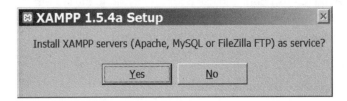

Figure 3-4. *Message boxes will ask whether you want the various applications to run as services.*

You want these servers to execute as services in the background, so click the Yes button on each message box. When installation is complete, you will be asked whether to run the XAMPP Control Panel. Click the Yes button and the Control Panel window will appear as shown in Figure 3-5. From the Control Panel, you can start and stop services, check the status of each application, and access the individual administrative applications.

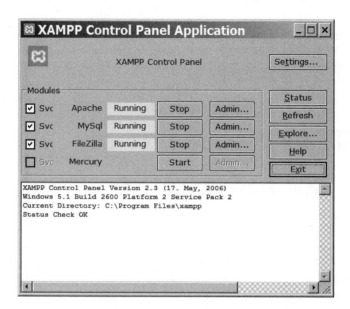

Figure 3-5. *The XAMPP Control Panel centralizes the basic administration of the applications.*

Click the Admin button to the right of the Apache entry. A browser window appears to show the central XAMPP default page (see Figure 3-6). Along the left side of the window, you'll notice there are various options to administer the server through this interface. It's a good idea to bookmark this page so you can get back to it easily.

To get Joomla running, it won't be necessary for you to use any of these links. However, the Security link on the left panel is very useful, as it shows you the current security settings on the web server. I suggest you take a brief look at the page so you may understand what aspects of the new server system are open to others.

You should be all ready for a Joomla install! Note that the default directory for web content is in the \htdocs subfolder of the XAMPP folder. You can copy the Joomla files into this folder for activation and installation. With a traditional installation, the path to the content directory is C:\Program Files\xampp\htdocs.

■**Note** If you're having a problem accessing the web server under Windows XP Service Pack 2, it could be that the default XP installation included a firewall that is blocking one or more of the needed IP ports. See the "Troubleshooting" section later in this chapter for more information.

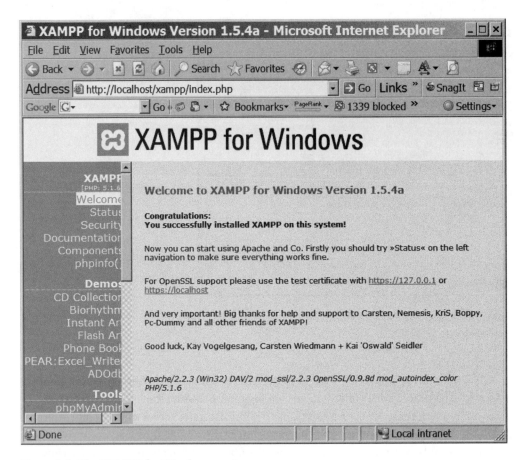

Figure 3-6. *The XAMPP for Windows main page*

Installing on Linux

To install XAMPP, you'll need to download the `tar.gz` archive to your local drive. Once the archive is downloaded, log in to the Linux system with the system administrator root command:

```
su
```

Now you can extract the XAMPP installation into the `/opt` directory. Use the following command, modifying the filename (here shown as `xampp-linux-1.5.tar.gz`) to match the name of the archive you downloaded:

```
tar xvfz xampp-linux-1.5.tar.gz -C /opt
```

This will install XAMPP to the `/opt/lampp` directory. To start the XAMPP system from the shell, type

```
/opt/lampp/lampp start
```

To access the main XAMPP page, just access the default directory of the server from a web browser with the following URL:

```
http://localhost
```

The default directory where web content will be stored is `/opt/lampp/htdocs/`.

■**Caution** XAMPP is intended to be installed as a developer platform; it's not meant to be run as a deployment server. If you do use it as a deployment server, be sure to configure the security properly, as XAMPP installs with no passwords and your system is wide open. To properly configure XAMPP for security, the installation includes a security check application. Consult the online manual for more information.

On many Linux implementations, after you reboot the system following the initial installation, the XAMPP system will no longer be running. You will have to configure your OS bootup sequence to execute XAMPP. The general procedure for configuring your system involves some diagnostic work.

First, you need to determine the default runlevel. Run `egrep` with the following parameters:

```
egrep :initdefault /etc/inittab
```

You should see a line like this:

```
id:3:initdefault
```

The `id` number will likely be 3 or 5. If you're running a Debian installation, the number will be 2. Move to the runlevel directory by typing the following command (substituting the runlevel number `egrep` revealed for X):

```
/etc/rc.d/rcX.d
```

If that doesn't work, try moving into the directory `/etc/init.d/rcX.d` or `/etc/rcX.d`. Set the startup initialization by executing the file link command:

```
ln -s /opt/lampp/lampp S99lampp
```

Link in the shutdown process by typing this:

```
ln -s /opt/lampp/lampp K01lampp
```

That should do it! Your OS should initialize XAMPP on boot.

■**Tip** openSUSE 10.0 has a special bootup procedure. Check the XAMPP web site (`www.apachefriends.`
`org/en/xampp.html`) for instructions.

Installing on the Mac OS

XAMPP installation on the Mac OS is likely the simplest of all. You need to download
the XAMPP package, which is available in both StuffIt (`.sit`) and tar archives. I recommend using the StuffIt archive, as the Mac OS includes the StuffIt Expander natively
and it has a friendly user interface.

Extract the `PKG` file to a scratch directory on your local drive. Double-click to execute
the file, and the installer will take you through the installation steps and install XAMPP
to the `/Applications/xampp` directory.

To start XAMPP, go to the Terminal shell and activate the system administrator
account using the `sudo` command:

```
sudo su
```

You should be able to start Apache, MySQL, and PHP from the shell with this command:

```
/Applications/xampp/xamppfiles/mampp start
```

That should do it!

Installing the Individual Servers of WAMP/LAMP/MAMP

You may decide that XAMPP is more technology than you need installed. Because of the
"everything and the kitchen sink" approach of the XAMPP installation, its footprint on
the local drive is more than three times larger than that of the individual servers Joomla
requires. You can separately install and configure each of these servers. The suite of technologies involved is summarized with one of a variety of acronyms. The first letter of the

acronym typically represents the target OS, so the acronym WAMP refers to the platform that uses **W**indows **A**pache **M**ySQL **P**HP. Likewise, LAMP and MAMP represent Linux and the Mac OS, respectively.

When installing the various servers, you may run into configuration conflicts. I have included some of the most common installation problems in the "Troubleshooting" section, so look there if you have a problem. Although I've tried to cover most of the common obstacles in this chapter, be sure to check the ReadMe files included with the installers to understand the most recent remedies.

■**Tip** If you're going to do your own individual installation, I suggest that you check the version numbers of the various servers that make up each suite in the XAMPP installers. By downloading the versions of each server that match those contained in a XAMPP package (which are known to work together), you can minimize potential problems.

The sections that follow take you step by step through installing the individual servers.

Installing and Configuring Apache Server

Installing an Apache web server is only difficult if the vanilla installation doesn't work. Debugging a failing Apache service can be time consuming because the server itself will often return vague or misleading error messages. For example, if you install a MySQL plug-in that is incompatible with the installed version of Apache, the error doesn't state this incompatibility. Instead it declares that the plug-in was not found with an error such as the following:

```
Cannot load...into server: No such file or directory
```

Like many such errors, this initially led me on a wild goose chase thinking that the configuration parameter pointing to the plug-in was set incorrectly. Figuring out the real problem is usually a combination of guesswork and searching the user forums for answers to similar problems. That said, let's get Apache up and running.

You can download the Apache web server at `www.apache.org`. Click the HTTP Server link for download instructions. I advise against downloading the installation of the very latest, bleeding-edge version of the server. It sometimes takes a while for the Apache developers to work out the kinks in the beta releases. Look for a stable package installation to minimize potential problems.

■**Note** The Mac OS comes with the Apache server preinstalled, so you don't need to download the installation package unless you want to use a version newer than the one already available. Instructions for activating Apache on Macintosh (which Apple calls "web sharing") are provided in the "Mac OS Installation" section.

You will have the opportunity to download either a binary file or the source code for the server. If you know how to compile the source code, you don't need any help from me. If you are a new Joomla user, simply download the binary installation. The following binaries are available: aix, cygwin, darwin, freebsd, hpux, linux, macosx, netware, os2, os390, reliantunix, rpm, sinix, solaris, and win32.

You'll want to download Apache version 1.13 or greater for use with Joomla. At the time of this writing, I recommend that you use a build of version 2.2 or greater.

Windows Installation

When you execute the Windows installer, you will be presented with an introductory screen that describes the Apache server. There are very few steps in the installation. Chiefly you will be asked for the configuration of the network domain, the server name, the administrator's e-mail address, and the selected port (as shown in Figure 3-7).

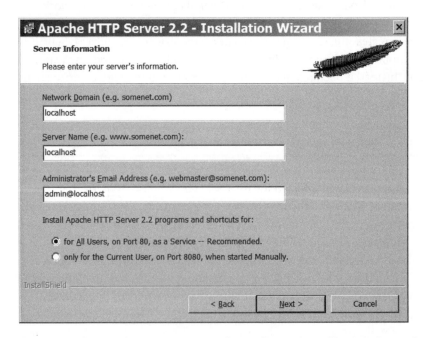

Figure 3-7. *The Apache server requires the configuration of basic information before installation.*

If you are installing Apache on a private server, laptop, or desktop machine, you probably don't have a DNS server that provides a domain URL (such as www.example.com). Therefore, for the Network Domain field, enter **localhost**. Enter **localhost** in the Server Name field as well to keep everything simple. For the administrator's e-mail, enter **admin@localhost**.

■**Note**　If you want your web server accessible on your local area network and don't have a DNS, you can enter the IP address in the first two fields (Network Domain and Server Name). If you run a DNS, you will likely already know how you want these settings configured.

Leave the port set at 80 (the default) if you don't have another web server (such as IIS) already running on the machine. If you do, I suggest setting the port to the "only for the Current User" option, which selects port 8080 to address the web server.

■**Note**　If you install for All Users, the server will run as a Windows service (this is preferable if you're doing a lot of development),), while the "only for the Current User" option will require you to manually run the server every time you reboot. It might be useful to install for all users even if you plan to run the server on a different port than 80. You can reconfigure the port as needed through the configuration file. Alternately, you can select the manual installation option and later add Apache as a service by executing the apache.exe application with the -k install switch. Check the Apache manual for more details.

Click the Next button and you will be asked to select Typical or Custom installation. Unless you already have a good understanding of the Apache server, stick with the typical installation.

Finally, the installer asks for a directory in which to place Apache. The default directory is fine for a Joomla installation. At the time of this writing, the default directory offered by the installer is C:\Program Files\Apache Software Foundation\Apache2.2\.

Take note of the directory where Apache will be installed. You'll need to access the folders within this directory for proper setup of PHP, MySQL, and later Joomla. Click the Next button to move to the final installation screen and click the Install button. Installation should occur without any problems. To get Apache working properly, however, you may have to tweak some of the configuration settings after the installation is complete.

On Windows, the Apache service will be run as the system user on the LocalSystem account. The first time you run Apache on Windows XP, your Windows Firewall may show a prompt asking whether to block the application, as shown in Figure 3-8. The firewall detected Apache attempting to open a port (port 80) for communication. You must click the Unblock button to allow Apache to execute properly.

Figure 3-8. *Click the Unblock button to allow access to the Apache server through the firewall.*

If you open a browser window and type in the address **http://localhost**, you should see the simple welcome Apache message shown in Figure 3-9. If you didn't install Apache to the standard port, you may have to add the port number to the web address like this: http://localhost:8080. In the preceding case, port 8080 was set for the Apache server.

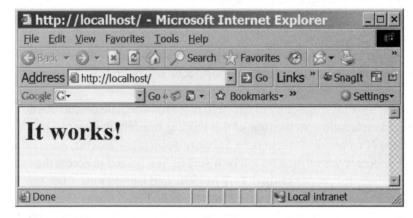

Figure 3-9. *If Apache is working, you should see this simple welcome message.*

If you received any errors during installation, you can look in the logs directory of the Apache folder for files that describe the errors. With a default installation, you will find the logs directory here: C:\Apache Software Foundation\Apache2.2\logs.

In that directory you will find several log files. The most important files for locating your errors are error.log (which contains any Apache execute errors) and install.log (which contains a list of operations performed during the installation). Both are standard text files and may be opened in a text editor such as Notepad.

■**Tip** If you encountered issues during the Apache server installation (aside from the firewall blocking), it may be a good idea to correct the problems, and then uninstall and reinstall Apache. This process can save you headaches later, as a repaired installation can sometimes introduce little flaws in the Apache server such that it doesn't execute quite right.

Linux Installation

Apache installation on Linux will vary greatly depending on your version of Linux. In fact, the recommended procedure for installing on Linux requires downloading the source code files and using a C++ compiler to compile an executable for your flavor of Linux. Such an involved and variable process is beyond the scope of this book, so you'll need to go to the Apache web site (http://httpd.apache.org) for specific instructions to address your needs.

Mac OS Installation

There is rarely a need to install Apache server on the Mac OS since it comes with a copy of Apache built into the operating system! To activate it, simply go to System Preferences under the Apple menu. Select Sharing and you'll see the File & Web tab. In the Web Sharing section of the tab, click the Start button and the Apache server will be activated.

You should note the IP address that appears under Network Identity (something like 172.128.62.114) of your web server. You'll use it in a moment to look at your default page.

To display the default display, bring up a browser window and enter your IP address: **http://172.128.62.114/**. You can locate the root files of your web server by using the file browser to look at the directory: /Library/Webserver/Documents/.

Configuring Apache Server

Configuration of Apache after the installation is generally the most difficult step of running the Apache server. Because of the available features and the powerful technology included with the web server, there are numerous settings that can be modified to resolve a bad condition.

The configuration settings are stored in the \conf directory at the root folder of the Apache installation. On the Windows platform, use Windows Explorer to open the \conf folder now. The main configuration file is named httpd.conf. Open it in a text editor and you will likely be slightly overwhelmed. At the time of this writing, the file was over 530 lines in length.

Listing 3-1 shows a small excerpt of the configuration file for a snapshot of how Apache settings are determined. You can see that each directive in the file is followed by a space and then the setting. Some settings are numeric, whereas others consist of text, URLs, and other character-based options.

Listing 3-1. *Portion of the httpd.conf File Showing Directives to the Apache Server*

```
## httpd.conf -- Apache HTTP server configuration file
##
#
# Based upon the NCSA server configuration files originally by Rob McCool.
#
### Section 1: Global Environment
#
# ServerType is either inetd, or standalone.  Inetd mode is only supported on
# Unix platforms.
#
ServerType standalone
#
# ServerRoot: The top of the directory tree under which the server's
# configuration, error, and log files are kept.
ServerRoot "/usr/local/apache_t3.1b1"
#
# Timeout: The number of seconds before receives and sends time out.
#
Timeout 300

#
# KeepAlive: Whether or not to allow persistent connections (more than
# one request per connection). Set to "Off" to deactivate.
#
KeepAlive On
```

You will need a search function in whatever text editor you use to load the file. Even the simplest of editors (such as Notepad) have a Find command, so you shouldn't have much difficulty.

It's likely that the only edits you'll need to make at the beginning will be related to problems. If you can't get PHP to run after it's installed, you should check the following Apache settings:

```
#BEGIN PHP INSTALLER EDITS
PHPIniDir "C:\Program Files\Apache Software Foundation\Apache2.2\"
LoadModule php5_module "C:\Program Files\Apache Software Foundation\
    Apache2.2\php5apache2_2.dll"
#END PHP INSTALLER EDITS
```

If these lines are missing after you install PHP, you will likely have to add them to guide Apache to the PHP execution engine.

Testing Apache Server

There are two standard ways to address a web server on a local machine. In most cases, the following address in a web browser displays the default web page:

```
http://localhost/
```

If that doesn't work or an error is generated, try the default IP loopback for a local machine:

```
http://127.0.0.1
```

If that doesn't work or an error is generated, make sure you installed Apache to the default port. Open the httpd.conf file in a text editor and search for the Listen directive. The default should read Listen 80 to indicate that port 80 is being used. If the Listen directive specifies another port (such as port 8080), you can use the following URL to access the web server at that port:

```
http://127.0.0.1:8080
```

Setting Up the .htaccess File

The Hypertext Access file, with a default name of .htaccess, is used by the Apache server to determine directory-level security access. If an .htaccess file exists in a directory addressed by the web server, it can modify configuration directives that reside in the main Apache configuration file.

These directives can do many things, including govern the user permissions to that directory or change the error page returned to the web browser when a requested file is not found. Other directives can enable server-side includes, deny users by IP address, change the default directory page, set up page redirects, prevent *hotlinking* (i.e., retrieving files such as images within the HTML from another site), prevent hotlinking from specific domains, and offer standardizing web access.

An .htaccess file controls the directory where it exists as well as any child directories below it in the hierarchy. However, .htaccess files in subdirectories can override the parent directives.

Joomla includes a sample .htaccess file that can be used to provide the proper Joomla configurations for the Joomla directory if search engine–friendly (SEF) URLs are needed (see Chapter 12 for a complete explanation). The installation includes the filename set to htaccess.txt, so it needs to be renamed to .htaccess for use.

Tip On the Windows platform, Windows Explorer will not let you rename the file to .htaccess because Windows sees this as an extension with no filename (like .txt). You can, however, use the rename or ren command from the Command Prompt window and the file will be renamed with no error generated.

Listing 3-2 shows the settings included in the htaccess.txt file that ships with Joomla. The Joomla manual recommends not using this file unless there are permission errors after Joomla installation. If an .htaccess file exists in the directory already, you can compare its settings with the ones shown here to help you determine the differences.

Listing 3-2. *The Joomla .htaccess File Settings*

```
##
# @version $Id: htaccess.txt 4094 2006-06-21 18:35:46Z stingrey $
# @package Joomla
# @copyright Copyright (C) 2005 - 2006 Open Source Matters.
# All rights reserved.
# @license GNU/GPL


#####################################################
#   READ THIS COMPLETELY IF YOU CHOOSE TO USE THIS FILE
#
# The line just below this section: 'Options FollowSymLinks' may
# cause problems
# with some server configurations.  It is required for use of
# mod_rewrite, but may already
# be set by your server administrator in a way that disallows
# changing it in
# your .htaccess file.  If using it causes your server to error
```

```
# out, comment it out (add # to
# beginning of line), reload your site in your browser and
# test your sef urls.  If they work,
# it has been set by your server administrator and you do
# not need it set here.
#
# Only use one of the two SEF sections that follow.  Lines
that can be uncommented
# (and thus used) have only one #.  Lines with two #s should
# not be uncommented
# In the section that you don't use, all lines should start with #
#
######################################################
###   SOLVING PROBLEMS WITH COMPONENT URLs that don't work ###
# SPECIAL NOTE FOR SMF USERS WHEN SMF IS INTEGRATED AND BRIDGED
# OR ANY SITUATION WHERE A COMPONENT's URL's AREN't WORKING
#
# In both the 'Standard SEF', and '3rd Party or Core SEF'
sections the line:
# RewriteCond %{REQUEST_URI} ^(/component/option,com) [NC,OR]
##optional - see notes##
# May need to be uncommented.  If you are running your
# Joomla/Mambo from
# a subdirectory the name of the subdirectory will need to be
# inserted into this
# line.  For example, if your Joomla/Mambo is in a subdirectory
# called '/test/',
# change this:
# RewriteCond %{REQUEST_URI} ^(/component/option,com) [NC,OR]
##optional - see notes##
# to this:
# RewriteCond %{REQUEST_URI} ^(/test/component/option,com)
# [NC,OR] ##optional - see notes##
#
######################################################
## Can be commented out if causes errors, see notes above.
Options FollowSymLinks

#
# mod_rewrite in use
RewriteEngine On
```

```
# Uncomment following line if your webserver's URL
# is not directly related to physical file paths.
# Update Your Joomla/MamboDirectory (just / for root)
# RewriteBase /

### Begin - Joomla! core SEF Section
###### Use this section if you are using a 3rd party
# (Non Joomla! core) SEF extension - e.g. OpenSEF, 404_SEF,
# 404SEFx, SEF Advance, etc
#
#RewriteCond %{REQUEST_URI} ^(/component/option,com) [NC,OR]
##optional - see notes##
RewriteCond %{REQUEST_URI} (/|\.htm|\.php|\.html|/[^.]*)$  [NC]
RewriteCond %{REQUEST_FILENAME} !-f
RewriteCond %{REQUEST_FILENAME} !-d
RewriteRule (.*) index.php
########## End - Joomla! core SEF Section
```

Installing and Configuring PHP

Once you have the Apache server running properly, you'll need to install and configure PHP. Whereas the Apache server is a web server, PHP is a programming language that runs on top of the Apache server (or Microsoft IIS) to provide dynamic web content. Joomla is written in the PHP language, so PHP must be installed for Joomla to execute on the server machine. Conveniently, if you're running the Windows OS, you can install PHP on the Apache server or even Microsoft IIS if that is your web server of choice. You'll need to download PHP from www.php.net.

Apache can process PHP files by two methods: direct module interface (known as Server Application Programming Interface, or SAPI) or through the CGI interface. Since the CGI interface is much slower and more resource intensive than SAPI, only the direct module will be covered here.

Installing PHP on Windows Apache Server

There is a precompiled installer for Windows that you can download and install. For PHP to work properly with Apache, you need to add the PHP directory path to your Windows Path variable. Once you have installed PHP, the full directory path to the folder should be something like this: C:\Program Files\Apache Software Foundation\Apache2.2\.

To add the PHP directory to the Windows Path variable, go to Start ➤ Control Panel ➤ System. The System Properties window will be displayed. Click the Advanced tab and then click the Environment Variables button as shown in Figure 3-10.

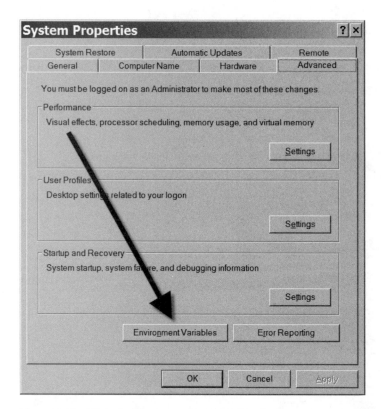

Figure 3-10. *Click the Environment Variables button to access the path field.*

Scroll down the System Variables list until you see the Path variable shown in Figure 3-11. Click the Edit button to display the Edit Variable box. Most likely the Path variable is already very long. Use the down arrow key to reach the end (or press the End key).

You'll need to add a semicolon (;) character and then enter the full PHP directory path. Once you've entered the path, click the OK button to accept the setting. Click the OK on the Environment Variables window, and then click OK on the System Properties window. This new Path variable setting will not be active until you reboot your machine—do that now, so you can test PHP on the Apache server. After the server has restarted, skip to the "Testing PHP" section.

█Caution At the time of this writing, the PHP 5 to Apache interface file (php5apache2.dll) that ships with the most recent version of PHP 5 doesn't work. You can go to the Apache Lounge web site (www.apachelounge.com) to get a newer version that is compatible with PHP 5. This issue will most likely be resolved by the time you read this, but I had expected it to be resolved by the time I wrote this—and it isn't. If you're having trouble getting the interface to work properly, this may be the problem.

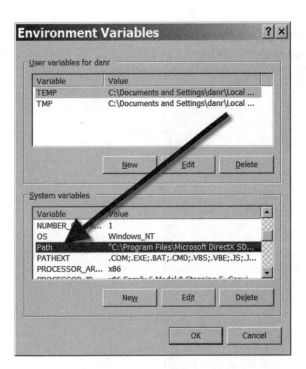

Figure 3-11. *Select the Path variable in the System Variables list.*

Installing PHP on Linux Apache Server

On Linux, like the Apache server itself, it is recommended that you compile the PHP code yourself and then perform the installation. Given the range of platforms, such a technical process is beyond the scope of this book. You can find instruction on the PHP site here: www.php.net/manual/en/install.unix.apache2.php.

Installing PHP on Mac OS Apache Server

There is a precompiled installer for the Mac OS that you can download and install. If you would like Mac OS–specific information on installing or compiling the PHP server, Apple has set up a Developer Connection web page with hints, tips, instructions, and sample code: http://developer.apple.com/internet/opensource/php.html.

Recent versions of the Mac OS have shipped with a free development system called Xcode. Xcode can host a number of different languages and PHP is one of them. You can find complete development information about using PHP with Xcode here: http://developer.apple.com/internet/scripting/phpappledevtools.html.

Installing PHP on Microsoft Internet Information Server

Many users of the Windows operating system already have Microsoft Internet Information Server (IIS) installed. It would typically be a waste of resources to install another web server on the same machine. Further, IIS is specifically tuned to provide the best performance on the Windows platform. To use Joomla, you will need to add PHP capabilities to IIS.

Download the PHP installer and execute it. On the options screen where you select the type of web server you'll be using, select your IIS version. By default, PHP will install to the C:\PHP\ directory.

When you are prompted about whether you want the installation program added to the system path, select the Yes option so IIS will be able to find the necessary PHP components for execution. Additionally, if the installation displays a warning stating that the script map is not registered and asking you if you want to register it, click the Yes button.

Once installation is complete, a message box will be displayed that provides the following information:

```
NT user may need to set appropriate permissions for the various php files and
directories. Usually IUSR_MachineName (or the user your web server runs as) will
need read writer access to the uploadtmp and session directories, and execute
access for php.exe and php4ts.dll.
```

You'll need to reboot your system to reset the Path variable and activate PHP, but that should do it!

Testing PHP

After you've installed PHP, you can test it by putting together an extremely simple PHP program. Open a text editor (such as Notepad) and enter the following line:

```
<?php phpinfo(); ?>
```

Save the file as phpinfo.php in the root directory of your web server. From your web browser, access it with the following URL:

```
http://localhost/phpinfo.php
```

Your browser should display a PHP information page like the one shown in Figure 3-12. I suggest that for future reference you print the current information and tuck it away in a file. If you have problems in the future, check the general information against the printed copy of the clean installation. More than once, I've been able to spot a change that led to the root of the problem.

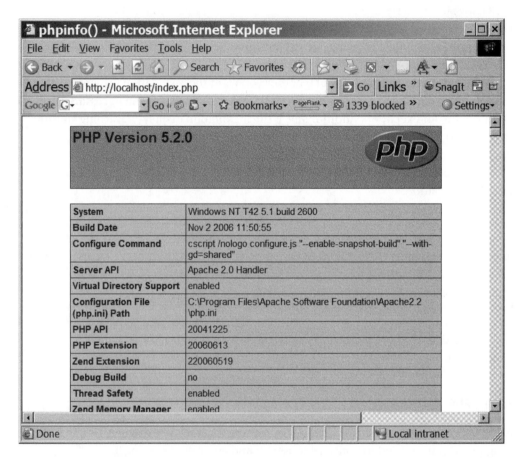

Figure 3-12. *The phpinfo() routine summarizes information about the PHP installation.*

If your browser doesn't execute the function to display the PHP information, and the PHP installation program indicated that everything installed correctly, check out the "Troubleshooting" section of this chapter for help locating the cause of the problem. Always try rebooting the system first to make sure the PHP module is activated.

Installing and Configuring MySQL

MySQL is an amazing open source relational database that has features comparable to database servers costing thousands of dollars. Joomla uses MySQL as the back-end to store for all text content and most configuration settings. Installing MySQL is a simple, short process, whereas configuring the server is a little bit more involved.

You can download MySQL from www.mysql.com. Click the Downloads link on the left side of the page. You will most likely want to install MySQL 5 because it has far more capabilities than previous versions, including stored procedures. If you would like to use the latest update of MySQL version 4, however, Joomla will function perfectly with it.

■**Tip** If you are running the Server Edition of the Mac OS, note that MySQL comes preinstalled. To access the MySQL Manager, look under Applications/Server/MySQL Manager.

There are generally two options when downloading MySQL: the Essentials installer and the Complete installer. You only need the Essentials installer, but I have provided instructions for using the Complete installer here so everything will be covered.

When you go to the MySQL site to download the server, I strongly recommend also downloading the separate MySQL Administrator tool. It provides a GUI for MySQL administration and makes life much easier. It is free and included in the MySQL GUI Tools bundle on the MySQL web site. I will be using it in this chapter.

Once you've downloaded the installer, you will likely have to extract it from a ZIP or tar archive. Extract the installer to your local drive for execution.

Installing MySQL

The MySQL installer works similarly on all platforms. These installation instructions show the Windows MySQL installation process, but other platforms follow a similar path. To begin, extract the MySQL installer onto a local drive and execute it (see Figure 3-13). Click the Next button to advance beyond the splash screen.

For Joomla, you won't need most of the specialty tools that are included with the complete installation. Select the Typical installation and click the Next button.

On the MySQL.com subscription screen, unless you want to receive e-mail and updates from MySQL.com, you can select the Skip Sign-Up for MySQL.com option and click the Next button. The information provided by MySQL.com is useful, but the wizard requires several screens to configure that are unnecessary to go into here.

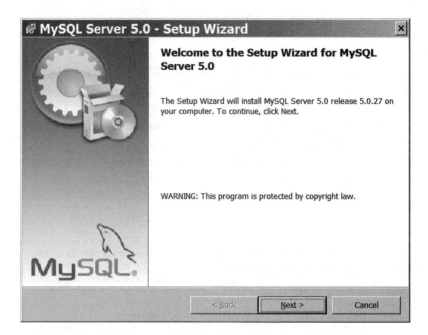

Figure 3-13. *Executing the MySQL installer*

When you click the Next button, MySQL will begin installation. On most machines, complete installation should take less than ten minutes. Although the installation completes, you're not done yet. The installation wizard will give you the option of configuring MySQL. Leave the "Configure the MySQL Server now" option checked and click the Finish button to execute the configuration wizard.

Configuring MySQL

After the MySQL Server Instance Configuration Wizard home screen is displayed, you'll be asked if you want to do a Detailed Configuration or a Standard Configuration (see Figure 3-14). Even though you'll be leaving nearly all of the default options selected, it's a good exercise to go through the detailed configuration so you have an understanding of how MySQL can be configured. Make sure the Detailed Configuration option is selected and click the Next button.

On the server type screen shown in Figure 3-15, you'll see a number of options that ask you to specify how the machine running MySQL will be used. Since this chapter demonstrates how to set up a development machine for Joomla, you can leave the default option, Developer Machine, selected. If the machine being configured was a server or a dedicated MySQL machine, these other options could be selected and MySQL would allocate more of the resources of the target machine.

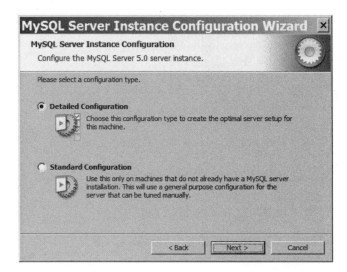

Figure 3-14. *Select Detailed Configuration and click the Next button.*

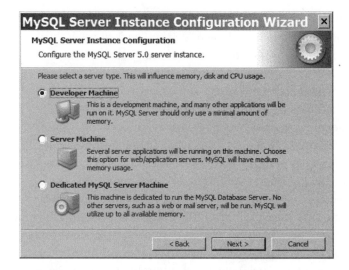

Figure 3-15. *For this Joomla test environment, select the Developer Machine option.*

The next screen allows you to configure the primary usage of the database server. Since Joomla addresses the server in many ways, you can leave the Multifunctional Database option selected and click the Next button (see Figure 3-16). If you were installing MySQL for a point-of-sale Joomla system or a virtual community site that had more transactional operations, the Transactional Database Only option might be a better choice. However, most Joomla installations provide a variety of read-only and interactive situations that are better served by the default selection.

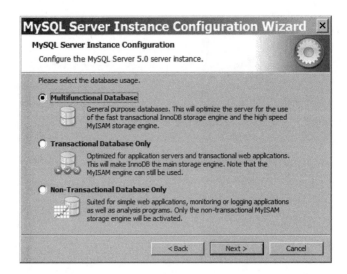

Figure 3-16. *Choose Multifunctional Database and click the Next button.*

The installation path screen allows you to set the location of the MySQL data file. For most development installations, the default will be fine. If you have another location or drive where you want the data file installed, choose it now. Click the Next button when you've finished.

On the concurrent connections screen (see Figure 3-17), you can configure MySQL for optimization to the expected processing load. Since you're performing this installation for a Joomla development server, you can leave the Decision Support (DSS)/OLAP option selected and click the Next button. However, if you're going to be running this MySQL installation as a full Joomla web server, choose the Online Transaction Processing (OLTP) option so the database will be optimized for many concurrent users.

On the networking options screen shown in Figure 3-18, the default options will be effective for most users, so you can click the Next button. The only setting you may have a need to change is the port number. Port 3306 is the default port for MySQL. However, some firewalls restrict this port, so access is impossible. If so, the system administrator should be able to provide you with a generalized database port number that provides a tunnel through the firewall. You can enter it here.

On the language settings screen, you can select the Standard Character Set (the most common UTF-8 character set) as the one to be used by the system and click the Next button. If you are going to be using an alternate character set for your Joomla system, make sure to select it here, as MySQL character recording must match the one to be used by Joomla.

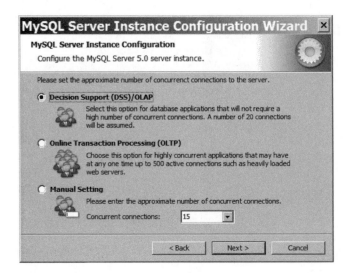

Figure 3-17. *Select Decision Support (DSS)/OLAP and click the Next button.*

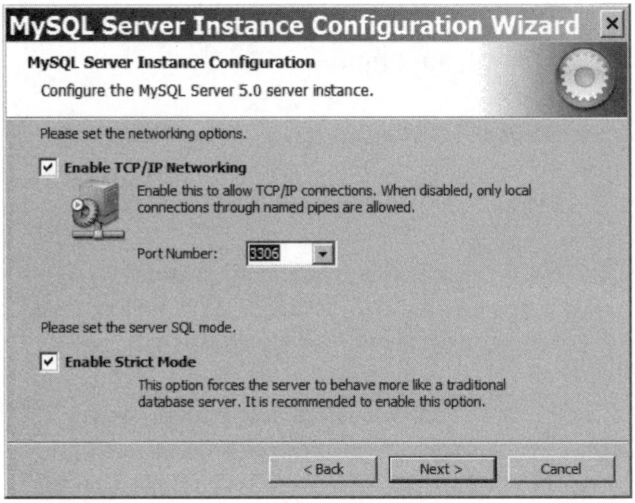

Figure 3-18. *The default TCP/IP settings are fine, so click the Next button.*

You will want to execute MySQL as a service that runs in the background (see Figure 3-19), so leave this option selected and make sure the setting to launch the service automatically is set.

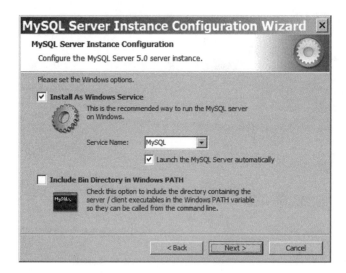

Figure 3-19. *Make sure the Launch the MySQL Server automatically box is checked and click the Next button.*

UTF-8 CHARACTER ENCODING

You may have seen UTF-8 character encoding mentioned in a number of places and wondered what exactly it meant. When computers were first becoming standardized, characters were stored (in memory and on hard drives) and transmitted (to a printer or over a modem) as a 7-bit number. A *bit* is a binary digit that can hold a 1 or a 0.

In the character pattern known as American Standard Code for Information Interchange (ASCII), the numbers were standardized such that the number 65 equaled the letter A, 66 the letter B, and so on. The ASCII standard defined characters for numbers 0 through 127 (the breadth of numbers that can be represented by 7 bits).

While ASCII was an efficient solution at a time when memory, bandwidth, and processing power were in short supply, more recent technology has made these resource scarcity problems secondary to a larger one of internationalization. Having a definition for 128 characters was fine as long as the computers didn't have to store thousands of Chinese characters or numerous other non-Western language symbols.

Enter Unicode, which stores two 8-bit bytes for every character. While Unicode solved the character shortage problem, it doubled the amount of storage and bandwidth required to store every character in every document.

UTF-8 was created to solve this problem. It is a variable-length character-encoding scheme and can use 1 to 4 bytes (a *byte* is an 8-bit number). That means certain characters will take as little space as an ASCII character to store in UTF-8, but when necessary, it can encode full Unicode text (such as a Chinese pictogram).

Joomla provides complete support for UTF-8. There are special considerations you must give to UTF-8 when you're developing a plug-in or otherwise modifying the Joomla system. If you're strictly adding content, however, you won't often be bothered with what character set the system is using.

On the password screen, set the MySQL administrator password. This password can be left blank, but I don't recommend it. You can set it to match the administrative account password on your normal system. If not, make sure you write down your choice and store it somewhere safe. You will need the MySQL password only infrequently, and that means you're more likely to forget it if it isn't recorded somewhere. Just make sure that the *somewhere* you record it is safe and secure.

Click the Execute button to begin the automated configuration process. If you run into any problems during configuration, be sure to check the "Troubleshooting" section at the end of this chapter, where a few of the installation problems are mentioned. When the configuration has completed properly, you will see a screen detailing the steps that were taken, as shown in Figure 3-20.

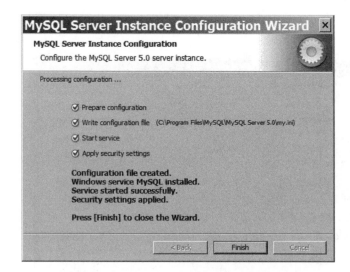

Figure 3-20. *Successful completion of MySQL configuration will give you four blue check marks.*

At this point, MySQL should be running perfectly. If you haven't downloaded the MySQL Administrator program (part of the MySQL GUI Tools package), do that now. Install the Administrator and you can take a look at your new server.

When you first execute MySQL Administrator, you'll be asked for the general configuration settings as shown in Figure 3-21. You'll have to enter this information only once and the program will keep everything except the password for the next execution. In this case, I'm logging directly into the local host. If your MySQL installation is remote, your dialog configuration may appear slightly different from the one shown.

When the Administrator interface opens, it will display all the general information about the server as shown in Figure 3-22. This opening MySQL Administrator screen gives you a general idea of how the system is configured.

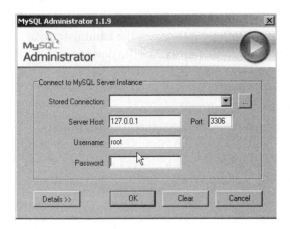

Figure 3-21. *Enter the administrator's username and password, and click the OK button.*

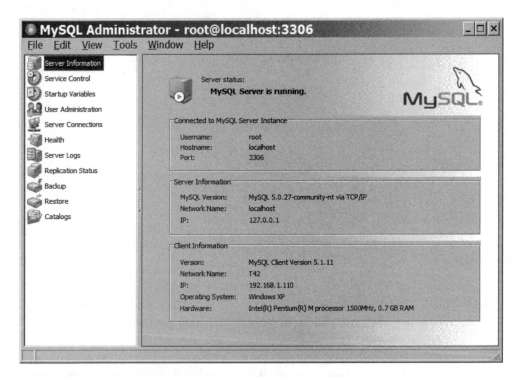

Figure 3-22. *The MySQL Administrator main page shows all the current server status information.*

Creating the Joomla! Database from MySQL Administrator

Security access permissions on a remote web host are generally the most difficult to anticipate and therefore resolve in a book. The next chapter provides an in-depth description of how these authorizations might be configured. One of the difficult configurations (which is unavailable on some web hosts) relates to the ability of a program to create a new database.

Once permission is given to a program to create databases, the potential for security mishaps and hacker malfeasance dramatically increases. Your web host may limit you to manually creating the Joomla database. Therefore, we'll use MySQL to manually create the database to avoid any possible problems.

You can create a database with a single command through MySQL Administrator. Log in to MySQL Administrator, move to the Catalog area, and right-click in the window pane that displays the existing schemas (see Figure 3-23). From the context menu, select the Create New Schema option.

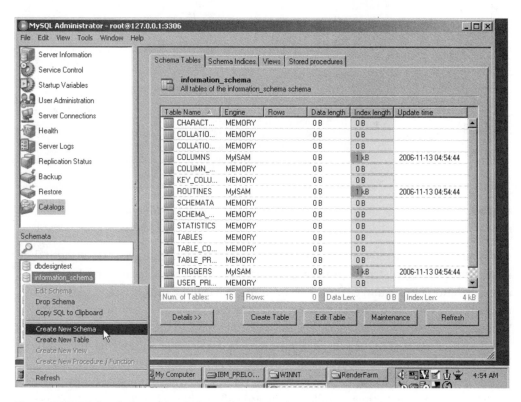

Figure 3-23. *Right-click in the schema pane and select Create New Schema.*

I had an existing Joomla 1.0 database on this server (Joomla 1.0 and 1.5 can coexist on the same server), so I named my new database `joomla15`. You can use the database name `joomla` if you don't have any other installations. Later, after you run the Joomla installer, you can look at the Joomla database with MySQL Administrator and see that it's populated as shown in Figure 3-24.

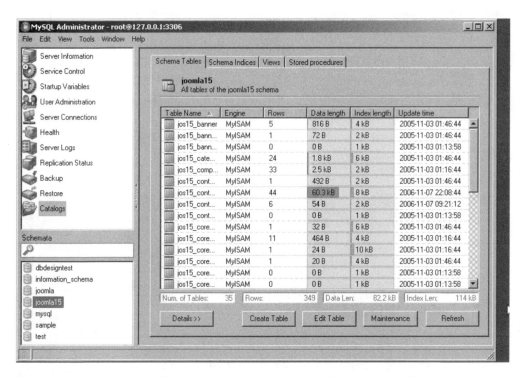

Figure 3-24. *From MySQL Administrator, you can examine the Joomla tables.*

While you're in MySQL Administrator, it's a good idea to create a Joomla account that has the proper administrative privileges to access the Joomla database. Click the User Administration button and create a new user. You can call the user `joomla` or `joomlaAdmin` to keep everything clear. Once you've created this user, select the account and click the Schema Privileges tab. You want to give the user full access to the Joomla database.

In the schema list of the tab, click your Joomla database and then click the double arrows (>>) to move all of the Available Privileges to the Assigned Privileges list as shown in Figure 3-25. Click the Apply changes button to confirm these settings.

That's it! Now the Joomla Installation Wizard will be able to construct the database tables in the `joomla15` database through the `joomla` user account.

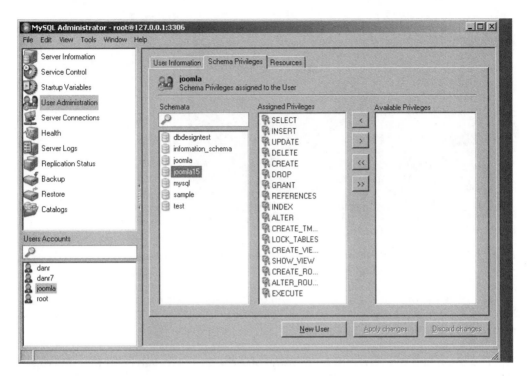

Figure 3-25. *Assign all privileges of the Joomla database to the Joomla user.*

Creating the Joomla! Database from the MySQL Command Line

If your host provides only a command line MySQL interface, these instructions will show you how to create the Joomla database with direct command line statements. If you want to use the command line on a local installation of MySQL, you can access it by selecting Start ➤ MySQL ➤ MySQL Server ➤ MySQL Command Line Client. The command console will ask you for the login password for the root user before you can enter the MySQL system.

Once the password is accepted, you should see a prompt displayed that looks like the one in Figure 3-26. You'll notice that there is MySQL prompt of `mysql >` where you can enter commands.

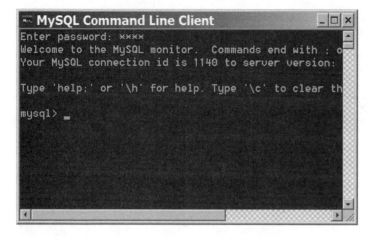

Figure 3-26. *The MySQL command line interface accepts SQL commands.*

To create the Joomla database, you need only enter a single command:

```
mysql> CREATE DATABASE joomla;
```

The command should return notification of Query OK and let you know that one row was affected. If you want to see all of the databases accessible to the current logon, enter the following command at the MySQL command prompt:

```
SHOW DATABASES;
```

You should see the joomla database listed as shown in Figure 3-27.

```
 MySQL Command Line Client                     _ □ ×

mysql> SHOW DATABASES;
+--------------------+
| Database           |
+--------------------+
| information_schema |
| joomla             |
| joomla15           |
| mysql              |
| test               |
+--------------------+
5 rows in set (0.00 sec)

mysql>
```

Figure 3-27. *The joomla database should now appear in the available list.*

Setting Up File and Folder Permissions

If you're running your own web server, then you have administrative access to OS permissions. Properly configuring permissions can be one of the frustrating aspects of setting up the Joomla system. On a UNIX or Linux system, you need to use the chmod command to set up access to file and folder permissions.

You can change the file and folder attributes through most FTP programs. In FileZilla, you can right-click a file or folder and select the File Attributes option. A chmod file attributes screen similar to the one shown in Figure 3-28 will be displayed. From that screen you can make the changes you need. Note that you can enter the numeric value (such as 777) directly into the text field.

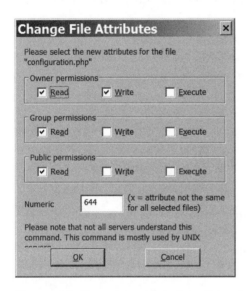

Figure 3-28. *Changing permissions through FileZilla*

Many web hosts provide the online cPanel utility (see Figure 3-29). This cPanel or Control Panel (depending on the installation) can perform a variety of functions, from executing installation scripts (for applications including Joomla, MySQL, Gallery2, etc.) to file management. For setting permissions, the File Manager in cPanel can move, delete, edit, rename, and copy files or folders. Most important for our purposes here, you can use cPanel to change the permissions on files and folders.

Figure 3-29. *Many Linux web hosting services use cPanel to allow for configuration.*

Select the file or folder you want and click the Change Permissions link (see Figure 3-30). You'll be presented with a web interface to the chmod utility, which provides the security settings for User, Group, and World.

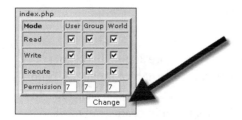

Figure 3-30. *Click the Change Permissions link.*

Set the permission options and click the Change button to save the new settings (see Figure 3-31). If an error is generated, check the permissions policy of your web provider. There may be explicit limits on the level of permissions a customer may set.

Figure 3-31. *Click the Change button to set the new permission settings.*

Installing the Joomla! Files

In this chapter, you saw how each of the servers can be installed separately and configured to work together. Now that you have the servers installed and configured, you can reference the last chapter for a complete description of installing Joomla on your server.

With XAMPP, WAMP, LAMP, or MAMP installed properly, you should be able to use those instructions without much difficulty. If you get an error during Joomla installation (such as a write access error or a connection to MySQL problem), refer to the appropriate section of this chapter to troubleshoot the issue.

Troubleshooting

If you've run into a problem with any of the suite of servers, you may find the solution to your problem here. Technical challenges can be so difficult and varied that is impossible to address all possible situations. In this section, I've tried to collect both the challenges I've encountered and the troubles others have posted about on the Internet. Each problem is described and a solution is proposed to help you navigate even the most treacherous waters of installation.

Keep in mind that when you're troubleshooting, you're often looking for the solution as much as the symptoms. I have often run across an issue that had an answer that I didn't think was relevant to my problem at first. Later I realized that although the error description was different, it was exactly the same problem as my own. Therefore, even if the snag you've hit doesn't exactly fit a problem description presented here, I suggest you skim the solution. It might bring to light an unexpected resolution.

Challenges with Apache Server

In this section, you'll examine some of the common problems with installation and configuration of the Apache server. While an error may lie within Apache, the fault may actually rest in the web server's communication with PHP or MySQL. Be sure to read through the PHP and MySQL sections as well to determine if your problem lies outside of the web server itself.

Accessing Apache Server Remotely

Problem

I can run Apache server on my local Windows XP machine, but I'm unable to access it from anywhere else on the network. What's the problem?

Solution #1

Windows XP Service Pack 2 installs a firewall that defaults to blocking all IP ports, including the http port (80), which Apache needs to communicate with the outside world. With this port blocked, sometimes Apache won't even start!

To test if this might be the problem, go to Start ➤ Control Panel ➤ Windows Firewall. Turn off the firewall for a moment. Try and restart Apache, and then access it from another machine. Do things seem to be working correctly? If not, then the firewall isn't your problem and you'll have to look elsewhere.

If things are working fine, turn the firewall back on. You don't want your machine wide open. Under the Windows firewall control panel, click the Exceptions tab and then click the Add Port button. Start by opening http port 80 as shown in Figure 3-32.

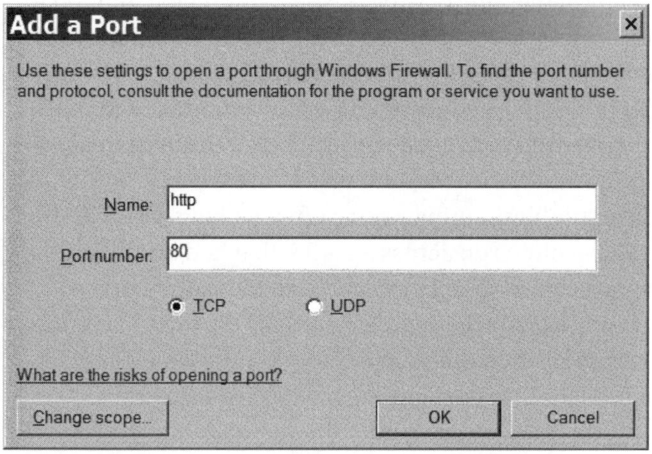

Figure 3-32. *Open http port 80 to allow web service.*

You may need to open a couple more ports for certain Joomla configurations. You can open https through port 443 (SSL) and MySQL through port 3306. You may also want to open the following ports for the other XAMPP servers:

- ftp, port 21

- smtp, port 25

- pop3, port 110

- imap, port 143

- AJP/1.3, port 8009

- http-alt, port 8080 (Tomcat Default Port)

Solution #2

Apache, by default, uses the standard web server port of 80. Only one application can use a port at a time. Sometimes another installed application (such as Skype Internet phone software) can block the port for other applications—most notably your Apache server. First, try shutting down other Internet applications and restart the Apache server.

If that doesn't work, you might try reconfiguring the port used by Apache. To change the port, alter the following directives in the Apache `http.conf` configuration file:

- `Listen`

- `Port`

- `BindAddress`

Note that depending on your version of Apache server, you may not find all of these directives in the default configuration file. You can nonetheless add them to your configuration file and the server will recognize them.

Start with the `Listen` directive. Set it to another value (such as 8080), and restart the Apache server. You can test the server by adding the port to the end of the IP address like this:

`http://127.0.0.1:8080`

.htaccess 404 Problems on Apache Server

Problem

On an Apache/PHP server, if I change the `htaccess.txt` file to `.htaccess`, I get 404 errors on all links.

Solution

On your web server or perhaps on your web host provider, the `.htaccess` file may be cached. Typically the cache reload time is set to one hour. Try waiting for a period of time and trying again. Generally this problem will solve itself.

■**Note** The `configuration.php` Writable feature is changeable on many web hosts via the cPanel utility.

No Server-Side Includes

Problem

Server-side includes aren't working and I get the error "INCLUDES filter removed."

Solution

The `Options +Includes` directive is being overridden by a configuration file. Look in all of the `.conf` files and change the directives that read `AllowOverride None` to `AllowOverride Options`.

Strange Apache Server Behavior

Problem

My Apache server lately has been giving unexplained error messages, cutting off files, and corrupting file downloads.

Solution

You may have installed an add-on into the Apache server that corrupted some of the advanced techniques Apache uses to speed file transfer (such as memory mapping, kernel sendfile support, and Winsock AcceptEx use). If you add the following three directives to your `httpd.conf` file, they will turn off the advanced sending functions:

```
EnableMMAP Off
EnableSendfile Off
Win32DisableAcceptEx
```

Restart the web server. If that doesn't correct the problem, try reinstalling the server.

Challenges with PHP

Some of the most difficult problems with PHP installation occur as a result of the subtleties of the `php.ini` file. The configuration file is fairly long and presents myriad options, some of which conflict with each other.

■**Tip** If you want to understand the initialization backward and forward, check out W. Jason Gilmore's excellent book, *Beginning PHP and MySQL 5: From Novice to Professional, Second Edition* (Apress, 2006), for a directive-by-directive explanation of everything you'll find in `php.ini`.

PHP Not Executing

Problem

When I attempt to access the phpinfo.php page I created, nothing appears in the browser window.

Solution

Whenever you're dealing with PHP and you get a blank browser window, first select the View Source option in your web browser. This option will display the HTML that was received from the server. If the PHP code has not operated as planned, a seemingly blank page may be returned that may in fact have generated some of the header HTML before the code faulted. Looking at the HTML is a way to determine if the PHP code executed *at all*.

If PHP didn't execute, make sure the PHP extensions are in the \ext folder found at the root of the Apache installation. On the other hand, if the source shows some output, an error occurred during script execution. You can check the server log files for the error, or you can turn on the display_errors directive in the php.ini file. Then reset the Apache server and reaccess the page that faulted.

No Input File Error

Problem

When I try to run PHP, I get a "No input file specified" error and it won't start.

Solution

Some installers set the docroot directive to a specific directory and this can cause problems—especially on systems with multiple hosts. Look in the php.ini file and clear the current directory setting.

Changes to php.ini Have No Effect

Problem

When I make changes to the php.ini file, they don't seem to have any effect.

Solution #1

Changes to the `php.ini` file won't take effect until the web server is restarted. For Apache server, use the Restart menu option in the Apache Server Control menu. On Microsoft IIS, you can use the command line to execute the command `iisreset /stop` to stop the service and `net start w3svc` to restart it. Once the web server is rebooted, your modifications should be active.

Solution #2

You may have more than one `php.ini` file installed on the system. Some installers place the `php.ini` file in the Windows directory. If the `php.ini` file is there, those settings will be used in preference to an INI in the central directory. Do a search for `php.ini` on your local drive. Try appending a suffix to the filename such as `_InActive` to the ones you don't think are active. Restart the Apache server and see if your desired `php.ini` file is now used.

IIS Returns a 505 Error and PHP Won't Start

Problem

When I configure IIS to run a PHP script, it doesn't execute and the server gives a 505 error: "The specified module could not be found."

Solution

Sometimes installations of PHP have problems with long filenames (longer than the old DOS eight characters plus three character extensions) or paths with spaces in them. Try relocating the PHP directory and the scripts to a simple directory like `C:\php5`. Locating the PHP directory in the `\Program Files` folder hits both bugs, and this can sometimes cause script execution problems.

Challenges with MySQL

While PHP configuration is generally not that difficult, sometimes getting PHP to work with MySQL leaves you wringing your hands in frustration. As I recommended in the previous chapter, as much as possible think in terms of KISS (Keep It Super Simple).

Try and narrow down the problem to the most basic test that you can execute, and work toward the more complex. When I have a problem, I generally return to the MySQL command line to eliminate even the possible problems introduced by the Administrator interface. From there, I work my way backward to the problem that originally appeared in my PHP code.

Can't Connect to MySQL Server Error

Problem

I get a "Can't connect to MySQL server" error. I've checked and MySQL is running and I have the name and the password entered correctly. What's the problem?

Solution

A great number of things could be preventing the connection. Here are a few of the most common solutions:

- A program will generally connect to MySQL through TCP/IP protocol via a port number. Make sure the port number is configured properly. The default port for MySQL is 3306.

- Try using 127.0.0.1 instead of localhost for the URL in your accessing program (e.g., PHP). On several systems there is a bug that prevents localhost from resolving to the MySQL server.

- At the time of this writing, on Yahoo hosted servers, you need to use mysql instead of localhost for the MySQL address.

- On Linux, a program can also connect to MySQL through a UNIX socket file on the file system. Make sure the filename for connection is correct. The default socket is /tmp/mysql.sock. Also make sure the file exists, as some job executions empty the \tmp directory and the socket file may have been deleted.

- Make sure your accessing program supports the correct MySQL password authentication system. MySQL 4 has a completely different and incompatible password system from MySQL 5. When the accessing program addresses the MySQL database with the wrong system, it will get a "Can't connect" error rather than an invalid password error. See the "Setting MySQL 5 to Use the 4.1 Password Method" section to resolve the interaction when a MySQL 4 accessing program attempts to access a MySQL 5 server.

- The Windows platform opens a number of virtual ports through which it allows TCP traffic. The default installation opens 5,000 virtual ports. While this may seem like a lot, it isn't in the machinery of Internet interaction. Once a port is opened, it remains reserved for 120 seconds of inactivity before allowing reallocation. If you have intermittent connection problems, you can try reducing the time before each port is freed. You'll need to execute the registry editor (regedt32.exe) and locate the HKEY_LOCAL_MACHINE \SYSTEM \CurrentControlSet\Services\Tcpip\Parameters key. Add a value to the key with the following settings: Name= TcpTimedWaitDelay, Data Type=REG_DWORD, and Value=30.

Can't Create MySQL Windows Service

Problem

When I run the installer and get to the MySQL Server Instance Configuration Wizard, I click the Execute button and get the error "Cannot create Windows service for MySQL. Error: 0." How do I correct this?

Solution

You probably have a second, older version of MySQL installed on your machine whether you know it or not (another program may have installed it). You can check by going to the Start ➤ Control Panel ➤ Administration ➤ Services option and looking down the list of services. You may see a MySQL service executing despite the installer telling you the service couldn't start.

To delete the old MySQL service, go to the command line and type

```
sc delete mysql
```

This command runs the Service Control utility and it should respond with

```
[SC] DeleteService SUCCESS
```

Try executing the installation again and it should work fine. Note that the Service Control utility comes standard with Windows XP and later, but for earlier versions of Windows, such as Windows 2000, you'll have to download it from the Microsoft web site.

Connection Error During MySQL Installation

Problem

During the MySQL installation, I get a connection error (see Figure 3-33). How do I get around this?

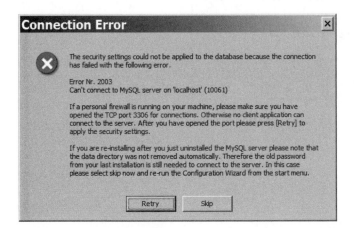

Figure 3-33. *Connection problem during MySQL installation*

Solution

As the error indicates, it's a problem with your firewall. The easiest way to correct this fault is to go to Control Panel ➤ Windows Firewall. Click the Exceptions tab and click the Add Port button. Fill in the MySQL port information (port 3306) as shown in Figure 3-34. Click OK to add the port exception and retry the MySQL installation. It should work fine now.

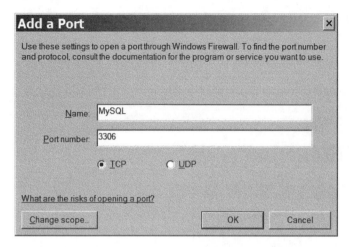

Figure 3-34. *Add a port exception to the firewall.*

MySQL 5 Server Connection Error

Problem

My web host is running MySQL version 5, and I've run into problems when Joomla attempts to log in to MySQL. I get an error message that Joomla cannot connect to my MySQL server.

Solution

MySQL, when moving from version 4 to version 5, modified the method by which passwords were authenticated. While the new password method is more secure, it is also incompatible with many of the applications written prior to the release of version 5. To provide relief from incompatibilities, version 5 includes a method of setting the authentication to the method used by version 4.

■**Note** At the time of this writing, Go Daddy and many other web hosting providers still use version 4 of MySQL. By the time you're reading this section, your web host may have upgraded its server. If you're having connection difficulties, please check the MySQL version.

You can set the password styles for individual accounts using the MySQL command line utility. Execute the command line program and log in to the system. Enter the following command at the MySQL prompt replacing the `joomla` username and `mypass` password with the user and password desired:

```
mysql> SET PASSWORD FOR 'joomla' = OLD_PASSWORD('mypass');
```

If successful, MySQL should respond with the following statement:

```
Query OK, 0 rows affected (0.02 sec)
```

Even though it says that 0 rows were affected, the user password is now set to the older method. Try the application that needed to access the MySQL server again, and you can determine if the password handshake was the problem.

If you want to configure your entire MySQL server to use the older password method, execute the MySQL Administrator program. Select the Security tab of the Startup Variables section. As shown in Figure 3-35, there is a setting that makes MySQL use the older style of MySQL 4 passwords.

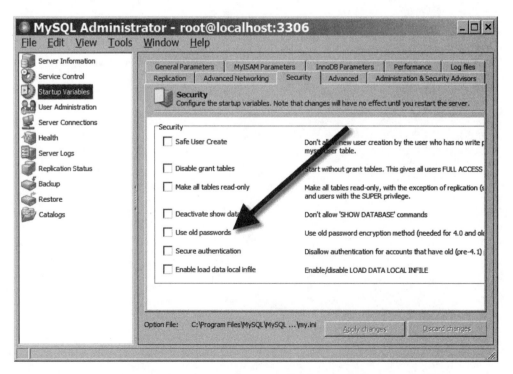

Figure 3-35. *Set the "Use old passwords" option to use MySQL 4–style password access.*

Conclusion

If you're installing a staging server or deploying Joomla on your own server, you now know a variety of ways to set up and configure the system. You can use the XAMPP installer for one-time installation and configuration of all the servers that Joomla needs. Alternately, you can set up each individual server in a LAMP/WAMP/MAMP configuration.

Since Joomla requires essentially four different servers to work together in order to function correctly, you may run into a variety of problems during installation. This chapter presented a basic troubleshooting guide with the most common problems and the solutions to these difficulties. With this information, you should be able to effectively deploy Joomla in most circumstances.

CHAPTER 4

■ ■ ■

Adding Content

Content lies at the heart of any web site. The need to organize that content is the driving force behind the widespread adoption of CMS applications such as Joomla. You will find that adding new content consumes the majority of the time you spend in Joomla after the initial setup. Before you begin putting articles into your Joomla system, however, you should take the time to think about how the site material will be organized and arranged.

You might reasonably ask why you should devote time to organization before you've added any articles to the system. After all, since Joomla lets you reorganize items quickly and easily, you could always perform the clerical tasks later. Like any task delayed, the problem grows quickly out of control and then requires a major effort for proper article categorization.

A disorganized Joomla site is like a computer drive where all the files are located in a single directory—it becomes impossible to find anything! By setting up appropriate categories initially so content is organized hierarchically (like a directory structure), you will be able to rapidly locate items and so will your users. Well-arranged categories make it easy to properly file a newly created article, preventing the chore of later revisiting and refiling a large number of documents.

Planning Your Content

Before you begin planning, you need to understand how Joomla organizes content. Joomla doesn't use an open system like a directory structure that may have unlimited levels (folders within folders within folders), but instead restricts the article hierarchy to two levels. These hierarchical levels, called *sections* and *categories*, should be enough for all but the largest of content sites.

Joomla also offers the designation of uncategorized content for static content. Static content includes articles that don't fit within the site hierarchy (such as a Terms and Conditions page) and therefore are not aggregated (like blog entries are) with other similar content. Uncategorized content can also be used as a catchall designation when the desired location for an article hasn't been determined. You will learn more about uncategorized content later in the chapter.

Joomla! Sections and Categories

Joomla is an advanced CMS, so articles are not organized in static directories on the web server. Instead, each article is stored in a database table and its location is specified within the hierarchy with an attribution field. This makes it easy to reorganize content since, unlike files that must be moved from one directory to another, changing the location of an article simply requires setting a new attribution.

All content in a Joomla web site is organized into a two-level (and only two-level) hierarchy. The top level is known as *sections*, the second level is *categories*. Some users new to Joomla have a hard time remembering the difference between sections and categories, and don't know how best to organize them.

One helpful method of simplifying Joomla site organization is to think of a web site as a small newspaper company. Each department or section (News, Classifieds, Help Desk, Advertising, etc.) has its own room in the building. Within each room/section are many filing cabinets. A Joomla category is a like a filing cabinet, with each filing cabinet containing one or more *articles*. If described like a directory hierarchy, the Joomla content structure might look like this:

```
Section\Category\Article
```

Using the same path notation, the "Joomla License Guidelines" article that's included in the sample data could be located via a path like this:

```
About Joomla...\The Project\Joomla! License Guidelines
```

Figure 4-1 shows the organization of the default Joomla web page. The highest level contains sections (such as About Joomla). Under each section are a number of categories. Categories separate the content into topic areas such as FAQs, News, and so on. All sections and categories are modifiable and new types of each can be freely added by the administrator.

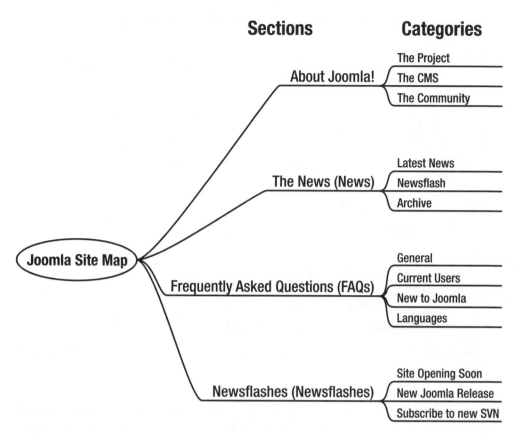

Figure 4-1. *The organization of the default Joomla site*

You can locate a content item in the Administrator interface by working down the tree from section to category and finally to the desired item. For this example, and because there are not many existing items in the default site, you'll view all of the content on the site in a single list.

Start by opening the Article Manager. By default, only 20 list items are displayed at a time. Scroll to the bottom of the screen, click the Display # drop-down list, and select 100, as shown in Figure 4-2.

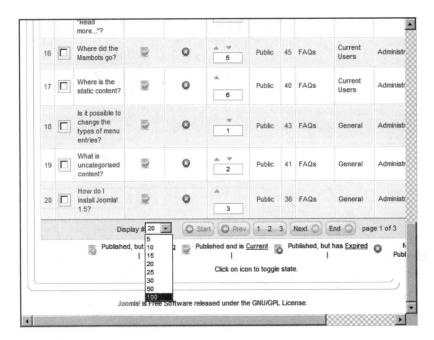

Figure 4-2. *Set the number of displayed articles to 100 to view an unabridged list of items on the site.*

You should see a list of around 43 entries. Scroll down until you locate an entry titled "Joomla Features." If you look at the columns for this article, you can see the items of data associated with it: name of the content, state of publication, flag for Frontpage status, access designation, ID, section, category, author, date of last modification, and total number of hits.

Joomla can sort content in any desired order. Most commonly, Joomla displays content in reverse chronological order, so the most recent article will be displayed first. While this sort order will often be useful, just as often you will want to view only the articles contained in a particular section or category. The "Joomla Features" article is located in the About Joomla section, in the category titled The CMS. At the top of the article list table, select the About Joomla section from the Select Section drop-down list as shown in Figure 4-3. You will see that the list instantly updates to show only articles listed in that section.

Additional selections may be used to filter the content list by category, author, and publication status. The Filter box is also available to search for text within an article title or to specify an article ID. There is a selection on the Select Section drop-down list for Uncategorised content that will show you the static content stored in the system.

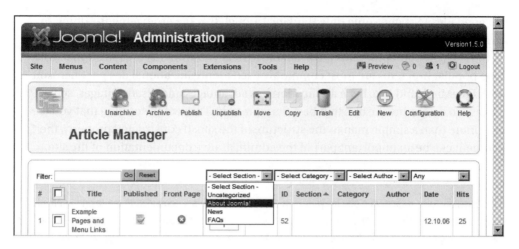

Figure 4-3. *Select the About Joomla! section from the drop-down list.*

Uncategorized or Static Content

If you want to add content in a quick and dirty fashion, you can add an article and set it as *uncategorized* or static content. Static content means that the article won't be compiled into a list (e.g., as a blog shows multiple subject items) and will appear as a separate static page.

Many webmasters begin their Joomla pages as a series of uncategorized articles so they can get the site up and running as soon as possible. This is generally not a good idea. Constructing a Joomla site from the top down (by first defining sections, then defining categories, and finally adding content) rather than the bottom up means your site will be more organized from the start and will likely grow more organically. That translates into planning out the top level of organization and then deciding which branches sprout from the central topic hubs. The small amount of time invested up front to determine how content should be filed will reap great rewards as the site grows in size.

■**Note** In previous versions of Joomla, a separate manager in the interface, the Static Content Manager, was used to track and administer static content not dynamically aggregated by the Joomla CMS. Beginning with version 1.5, this manager was eliminated and static content is managed with all the other articles in the Article Manager interface.

Documenting Your Organization Plan

With a clear understanding of the Joomla content structure, you can begin to determine what sections and categories will provide the best fit for the information on your site.

It's a good idea to spend some time thinking through this site arrangement—doing so can make the difference between a clean, useful site and a cluttered, exasperating one.

Several computer programs are available to help you with this organizational task. Three popular programs are most commonly used for organizational design: Microsoft Word, FreeMind, and Leo. Each application has advantages and disadvantages, so you will have to determine the one that best fits your style. Think of the outline that you create as more than a simple map to the structure of the site. If constructed properly, the document can be an important part of the administrative documentation of the site.

■**Tip** Even if you're setting up a site for your own administration, it is a good idea to make and keep site documentation. Often this documentation material is extremely useful for later reference when time has passed and original design considerations have been forgotten—but not lost. If the site grows dramatically and you have additional volunteers or hired help, documentation can also provide a good map of the territory to bring the new workers up to speed.

Microsoft Word's Outline View

Many web designers and developers perform the initial layout and categorization of a web site using Microsoft Word's Outline view mode. The Outline view lets you lay out ideas in a simple hierarchical fashion, as shown in Figure 4-4. I've used the popular CNN.com web site for this example because it provides an excellent skeleton for any news-based site. The main site is broken into subject areas such as Programs, Health, Education, Law, Local, Politics, and so on.

Word's Outline view has several significant advantages. Most Windows users have Word installed on their machine, so availability is widespread. Word's drag-and-drop editing capabilities allow you to reorganize content quickly and easily. You can use simple shortcut keys such as Tab and Shift+Tab to demote or promote headings, respectively.

Additionally, if you are creating a simple HTML web site (instead of using an advanced CMS), you can save the final outline as an HTML document and all of the specified headings are automatically converted into their HTML style tag equivalent (Heading1, Heading2, etc.). The saved document can provide a rudimentary foundation for your web site.

The disadvantages to this method are many, however. Word's ability to translate an outline into any sort of effective site documentation is surprisingly poor. For a writing tool, the Outline view has terrible formatting problems when you attempt to print or even integrate the outline into a standard document. Further, the presentation of the individual outline levels in their full-sized font styles appear in an unattractive, large node presentation. There are several better alternatives that are free, open source, and cross-platform.

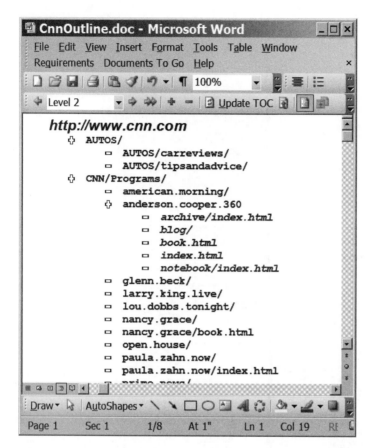

Figure 4-4. *Microsoft Word's Outline view can aid in planning the structure of a web site.*

FreeMind Mind Mapping

You may be unfamiliar with the concept of mind mapping. A technique formalized by educator Tony Buzan, *mind mapping* is a method of visual information organization that mirrors the way the human mind can most easily understand and remember information. Rather than forcing ideas, concepts, and information into the visually restrictive tree structure that most outlines adopt, a mind map spreads across the page like a tree.

In Figure 4-5, the basic organization of the CNN.com structure is presented as a mind map. This mind map was created with the Java-based Freemind application available for download at http://freemind.sourceforge.net. You can see a number of visual elements that help focus the information on the page, including icons, arrow connectors, and area clouds. Although you can't tell from this black-and-white reproduction, the mind map is in full color, making recognition and recall even easier.

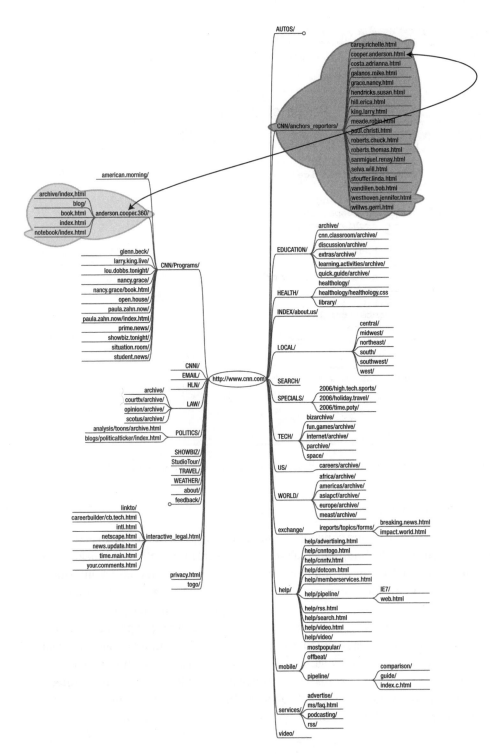

Figure 4-5. *A mind map of CNN.com shows the visual power of organization using this method.*

For web site organization, this is a fantastic free-form method of seeing an intended layout's strengths and weaknesses. For example, I created a simple mind map of a real estate site. Figure 4-6 shows a facsimile of the mind map for the site. Notice how unbalanced the initial organization turned out. The lopsided mind map shows most of the topics clustered in one area. A well-organized site would have a more balanced appearance.

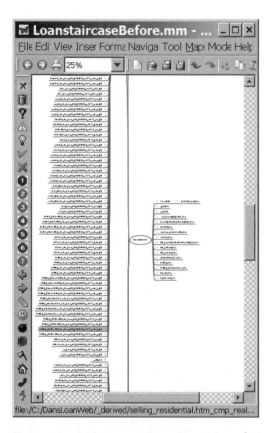

Figure 4-6. *The large number of branches on the left shows how unbalanced the initial site organization can be.*

After some revision, the updated mind map in Figure 4-7 shows an excellent balance of topics and categories. I even put in the titles of a few articles that would be needed by the site to make sure the content fit properly. This sort of testing makes organization and layout simple and helps ensure the right balance of sections and categories.

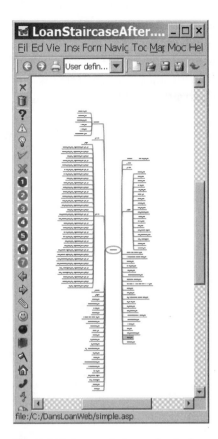

Figure 4-7. *A more balanced mind map has the symmetry of a tree.*

Mind maps seem to be the ideal method of drafting a web site—particularly a Joomla site. By creating such a map, you should be able to visually understand how your intended content can be divided among sections and categories. However, if you want to add any actual information to the structure (such as a draft of an article or further notes), a mind map has limitations. For those features, you could use a professional outlining tool such as Leo.

Leo Outliner

The tool I use most when designing or maintaining a Joomla site is Leo (Literate Editor with Outlines). Leo is a free, open source outliner and general hierarchical information organizer. Leo is written in Python, so it runs on most platforms that support the language (including Linux, Windows, and Mac OS). You can download Leo from SourceForge at http://sourceforge.net/project/?group_id=3458.

Three core aspects of Leo set it apart from other outlining applications: file tangling, cloning, and node body text. File tangling is a slightly complex topic and is used primarily when dealing with code, so I'll save a description of that for Chapter 13, where you'll learn to create and code a Joomla extension. Leo also allows a node within the outline to be cloned so it can appear elsewhere in the outline. Any changes to a clone are immediately reflected in the connected clone nodes. This feature enables multiple ways of organizing the same information in an outline.

■**Note** Leo has many other significant features than the three mentioned in this section. In fact, it has a complete Python interpreter accessible from within an outline (so scripts can be written inside nodes), and the entire Leo framework is exposed as an object model. You can write complete Python scripts, buttons, and plug-ins to perform any macro function. Although the features of Leo that are not relevant to Joomla implementation are beyond the scope of this book, if you're interested in learning more, be sure to check out the wiki devoted to Leo at `http://leo.zwiki.org`.

For web developers, the significant feature of node body text is extremely simple in concept. In Figure 4-8, you can see that the Leo screen is divided into three panes: the outliner or headlines pane (top left), the log pane (top right), and the body pane. The outliner pane shows the same outline of CNN.com that you saw previously as a FreeMind mind map. Instead of a mind map display, the outline is displayed in a standard tree view.

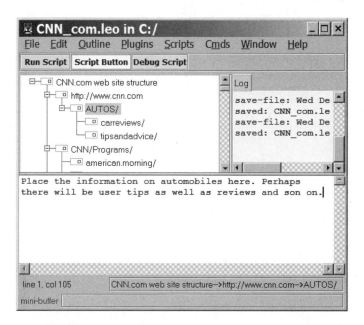

Figure 4-8. *The Leo outliner application displays the CNN.com web site structure.*

In the figure, did you notice how one node is selected? In the body pane along the bottom, you can see text stored in that node that describes the topic. Every node in the outline can have body text attached. Once you begin to use this feature for organization, you'll be astounded at how much functionality it provides.

For the initial installation of a web site, I've found Leo invaluable in drafting not only the outlined structure of a site, but also much of the initial content. Leo has plug-ins that provide spell checking, export of an outline to HTML/RTF/Microsoft Word, inclusion of URL links within the outline (that can launch a browser window), and code syntax coloring (including HTML, PHP, CSS, XML, and many other computer languages). The export functionality means that all of the work you do within Leo can be converted in two steps into your Joomla site.

Further, since additional child nodes can be added at any time, you can include things such as HTML code, PHP scripts, CSS items, and any other text-based information to the outline. As with any outliner, you can move nodes up, down, left, and right, and you can reorganize the tree with drag-and-drop functionality.

One powerful feature of an advanced outliner like Leo is the *hoist* function. If you want to focus on a particular aspect of the outline, you can select Outline ➤ Hoist, and the selected node and its child nodes will be isolated as if they were the complete outline, as shown in Figure 4-9.

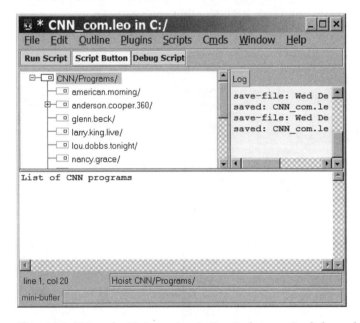

Figure 4-9. *Using the Hoist option in Leo isolates a single branch of the outline tree.*

Once you have completed the draft of your web site structure, you can either manually re-create it within Joomla or use the Leo to HTML plug-in for export. This plug-in generates HTML code of the outline that can then be read into any HTML or text editor. The Leo to Microsoft Word export plug-in can generate an indented outline of the Leo file, so you can use it within the Outline view in Word if you need it.

Using Leo, Microsoft Word, or FreeMind (or any combination of the three) can help you draft your Joomla site to make sure that it will fill all of your needs. With a site plan in hand, you'll be ready to begin actual site construction.

Reincarnating a Web Site (LoanStaircase) in Joomla!

Long ago I had an idea to create a web site where homebuyers, real estate agents, loan officers, and refinanciers could track the progress of their loans. I created a draft of this site with Microsoft Active Server Pages (ASP) code that would store all of the loan information in a Microsoft SQL Server database. It was free for use to anyone who wanted to track his or her loan through the system. One unexpectedly popular aspect of the site was the forum, where real estate professionals could exchange tips, offer advice, and review material such as training books and videos.

Although I shut down the initial site some time ago because of the cost of development, it provides a useful exercise for this book to reincarnate the web site into a Joomla site. The web site offers a good foundation for everything from a custom template to a database access. Additionally, the virtual community that was growing on the site provides an excellent model of what type of interaction is possible through Joomla components.

Therefore, starting in this chapter, I'll use the structure of the LoanStaircase web site as an example of how the functionality of Joomla can be used to create a real-world web presence. To start, Figure 4-10 shows the basic outline of the site I intend to create. I generated the outline in Leo and then began harvesting some of the original site articles for entry into Joomla.

I'll use this outline dynamically with my Joomla site creation. Since Leo can store everything from text to URL links to formatted content, I intend to use this Leo file as living documentation. I'll include the MySQL code for any custom tables I create to store information and documentation for the design choices I make along the way.

When complete, the Leo file will mirror the published site and allow me to archive a complete web site design document. With the basic sections and categories outlined in the document, I'll need to re-create the structure in the Joomla system.

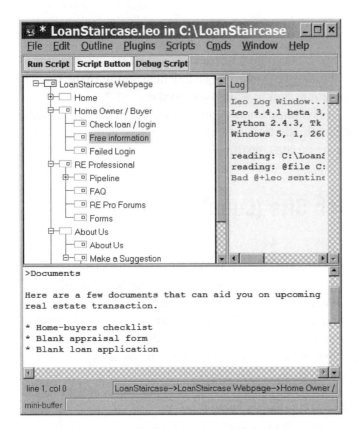

Figure 4-10. *A draft of the LoanStaircase organization is first created in Leo.*

Creating Sections and Categories

I hope you've created some type of plan to organize the site you want to create in Joomla—you'll need that plan right now. Most Joomla sites begin with constructing the sections and categories needed to organize content, so that's what you'll do in this section. Open the Administrator page of your Joomla site so you can begin to implement the necessary hierarchy.

Deleting the Sample Articles, Categories, and Sections

Before you can begin creating your new site, however, you must delete the sample content so you can start from scratch. A section can't be deleted until all of the categories it holds are deleted first. A category can't be deleted until all of the articles it holds are deleted. Therefore, you'll have to start the cleaning process at the article level.

■**Tip** If you see an article, category, or section that has a small padlock in the selection column instead of a check box, that means the item is checked out and is being edited by you or another user. If you clicked the item in the past (which automatically checks it out) and then left the web page or closed the browser window without clicking the Close button, the item remains checked out. You need the item checked in before it can be deleted. Select Tools ➤ Global Checkin to check in all items on the Joomla site.

Bring up the Article Manager and set the Display # setting at the bottom of the page to show 100 articles. All the articles should now be displayed in a single list. In the column that holds the check boxes, you might have noticed that there is a check box in the column header. Click the check box and every item in the table will be selected as shown in Figure 4-11.

Figure 4-11. *Check the box in the column header to select all items.*

With all of the articles selected, clicking the Trash icon will send the articles to the trash. You still can't delete the container categories until the trash has been emptied, so select Content ➤ Article Trash to display the articles in the trash can (see Figure 4-12), and once again select all of the items.

Figure 4-12. *Select all of the items in the Trash Manager.*

Click the Delete button. You will receive a delete screen summarizing the items about to be permanently erased. Confirm that you want to continue, and another warning box displays to make sure you want to delete the content. When you confirm the second deletion command, the articles will be removed and you should see an empty trash can.

Next you need to delete all of the categories. Go to the Content Manager and delete the categories using the same basic procedure you just followed to eliminate the articles. You won't need to take the extra step of going to the trashcan because categories can be instantly deleted. After the category deletion is complete, delete all of the existing sections. Your Joomla site should now be a clean slate with regard to content!

■**Tip** One problem most administrators encounter after running a popular Joomla site is loads and loads of unpublished content. Loathe to delete valid content from an archive even if the content is no longer relevant, they simply unpublish it. This type of moribund content can grow explosively like the insidious kudzu weed and slowly but surely overwhelm a previously efficient Joomla installation. Be sure to back up older articles and then remove them from the site, or your site may become sluggish to visit and difficult to manage.

Adding New Categories and Sections

You should begin the creation of the new content structure at the top of the hierarchy by selecting Content ➤ Section Manager. The Section Manager allows you to add, delete, reorder, and modify sections on the Joomla site.

Start by adding a new section by clicking the New button (see Figure 4-13). For the LoanStaircase site, I'm going to begin by adding a section for Home Owner/Buyer. Take whatever is the first section of your hierarchical plan and enter it into the Title field. Title field text should be brief since it will appear in the menus. In my case, I set the Title to **Home Owner Section**.

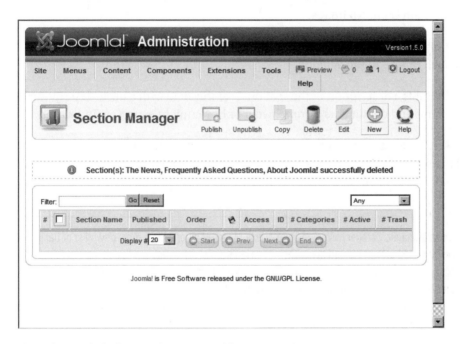

Figure 4-13. *Click the New button to add a new section.*

After the title are the following fields:

- *Section Name*: Holds the name of the current section. Unlike the Title field text, which should be brief as just mentioned, the name will appear at the top of the section when it's selected and can be as long as needed. I set this field to **Home Owner/Buyer Section**.

- *Published*: Determines whether or not the current section is published. This is a very powerful feature, because the system administrator can take a whole topic offline by simply unpublishing the section. Set this field to Yes.

- *Ordering*: Allows the placement of the current section to be set within the overall list. The exact position may be specified (from the drop-down list of sections), or the first or last directive may be selected to make the current item appear at either the beginning or the end of the list, respectively. Since this article is a new item, by default it will be placed at the end of the single item list.

- *Access Level*: Sets the access level of the section and the articles the section contains as Public, Registered, or Special. Set this field to Public.

- *Image*: Sets the iconic image for the section. This drop-down list shows the titles of all of the images currently located in the \stories folder in the Joomla system. I left this item set to No Image.

- *Image Position*: Determines the location of the section image as left, center, or right. I left this set to the default.

- *Details*: Holds a description of the section. I set this field with a basic description of the items and documents a homeowner or buyer might expect to find within.

Once you're done, click the Save button to write the section into the database. Congratulations! You just created your first section. Continue adding sections until you have all the sections listed in your site plan.

Tip   The Section Manager, Category Manager, and Article Manager all provide a drop-down list of basic images that can be added to the selected item. The images in this list are located in the \stories folder in the Joomla \images directory. The Upload button in the Media Manager can be used to upload or transfer additional images into the \stories folder for use from any of the managers.

To create a new category in the Category Manager, you'll use an interface identical to that used to add a new section, so there is no need for step-by-step instructions. There is one additional option for a new category, however: the section name. Since a category is a hierarchical child of a section, a section drop-down list is provided to let you choose which section will be the parent of the category being edited.

Open the Category Manager and add all of the categories from your site plan. Once you've finished, you can begin adding your articles.

Selecting a Text Editor

Before you begin adding articles, you should choose the What You See Is What You Get (WYSIWYG) editor that will be used for editing article content. Each user on the Joomla system can select from among the available editors, but the administrator can choose the default editor using a global configuration setting.

You can select from the editors installed on the system through the Configuration ➤ Site menu. In the Site Settings frame, the Default WYSIWYG Editor drop-down list contains the available editors. With the standard installation, Joomla includes two editors: TinyMCE and XStandard Lite.

A Tale of Two Editors: TinyMCE and XStandard Lite

Joomla comes equipped with two editors with WYSIWYG functionality: TinyMCE and XStandard Lite. TinyMCE has historically been the editor of choice because of the excellent editing features it provides. With the introduction of Joomla 1.5, XStandard Lite has added some capabilities (such as strict XHTML compatibility and accessibility features) that make it a good option.

You should try both editors and see which one you prefer. While the creators of both editors strive to make them compatible with most browsers, there are sometimes limitations within certain browsers that inhibit some functionality. If you are going to have content contributors for your web site, it is a good idea to test the WYSIWYG editor with the browser the contributors will use to prevent any difficulty during posting.

■**Tip** Although the TinyMCE and XStandard Lite editors are included with the standard Joomla installation, additional editors are available for use within Joomla. At the time of this writing, there are nine editors for Joomla that tout features such as Textile compatibility, advanced media management, and XML support. Check the WYSIWYG Editors category in the Extensions section of the Joomla site (`extensions.joomla.org`) for more information.

TinyMCE

TinyMCE (Tiny MoxieCodeEditor) has long been the standard editor for Joomla. It is written entirely in JavaScript and provides complete WYSIWYG functionality. TinyMCE is actually more like a small word processor than a text editor (see Figure 4-14). It even allows direct editing of the HTML source code of the posted content.

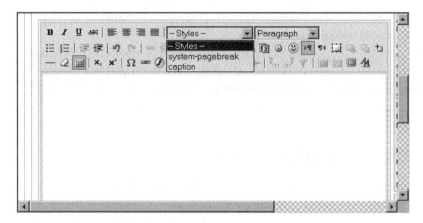

Figure 4-14. *TinyMCE has many features that are generally found only in word processors.*

The substantial editing features include the following:

- Multiple fonts, styles (including subscript and superscript), and font sizes

- Left, center, right, and full paragraph alignment

- Cut, copy, and paste (including options such as Paste as Plain Text and Paste from Word)

- Find and replace capabilities

- Lists (ordered and unordered) and indent settings

- Multiple undoes and redoes

- Insertion of date, time, hyperlinks, HTML anchors, horizontal ruler, symbol characters, smilies, embedded media (including Flash), and images

- Text and background coloring

- Table insertion with full column and row manipulation capabilities

- Complete Cascading Style Sheets (CSS) support

TinyMCE also has excellent interface features, including the following:

- Spell checking

- Printing

- Support for international characters and left-to-right or right-to-left editing

- Full-screen editing mode

- Layers

- Absolute positioning

- Display of visual control characters

The current TinyMCE compatibility chart shows the editor to be functional with the following browsers: Microsoft Internet Explorer 5.5 SP2 and above (not compatible with Internet Explorer 5.0), Mozilla SeaMonkey 1.0.5 and above, Firefox 1.5.x and above, Safari 1.2 and above, and Opera 9 and above. It is likely that all new JavaScript-enabled browsers will be able to use TinyMCE without complication.

Caution One limitation of TinyMCE is article size. Although there should be no problem with most online postings (since they tend to be brief), if your text gets into the 200KB–300KB range, the editor will bog down. This is more a constraint of JavaScript than the application itself. Nonetheless, this can be a limitation if you plan on using Joomla as a document repository.

XStandard Lite

New to Joomla 1.5, the XStandard editor has been added to provide extra capabilities in the area of accessibility and XHTML support. It requires the installation of a plug-in on the client side, which is handled automatically. Unfortunately, at the time of this writing, the client-side plug-in is available only on the Windows platform.

XSTANDARD REGULAR?

The XStandard Lite editor that ships with Joomla version 1.5 is not the widely available (but feature-slim) version of XStandard known as XStandard Lite. The one included with Joomla is a special version created as a collaboration between the XStandard team and the Joomla development team. Joomla's XStandard Lite has many of the features of XStandard Professional (a fully commercial version), but it is free for Joomla users. The professional version is available at the XStandard web site (www.xstandard.com).

Joomla's XStandard Lite includes a number of unique features:

- CSS layout compatibility, XHTML-compliant code, and enhanced accessibility

- An image library from which images can be inserted

- A link library for hyperlinks

- The ability to insert markup snippets from a library

- Functionality to resize images in the editor

- Controls to change table settings (such as column widths) with the mouse

The biggest single disadvantage of XStandard is its limited platform availability. Because it is a client-side plug-in, it runs only on Windows 98, ME, NT, 2000, and XP. This limitation is in stark contrast to TinyMCE, which functions on nearly every platform with a JavaScript-capable browser. However, the native execution of the plug-in does give XStandard Lite a great performance advantage over script-based editors such as TinyMCE.

No Editor

When the selection of No Editor is made in the site configuration, it doesn't literally mean no editing of content is possible. When an editor such as TinyMCE is selected in the configuration, it essentially takes over the HTML text box area where the content of an article is modified. That means that any rendering of fonts, styles, images, and so on within the text area is performed by the selected editor.

When No Editor is selected, a standard scrolling text area displays the contents of the article. Since Joomla articles are HTML based, all of the HTML-encoded text is displayed in the text area with this option. Therefore, a simple message with a single heading and a single line of body text might appear like this when No Editor is selected:

```
<h1>MyHeading</h1><p>MyBody text.</p>
```

The No Editor selection is best used for sites that anticipate that advanced users will be the content contributors or when users need to cut and paste HTML-rich content directly into the body of an article. On more general sites, beginners may be confused about the purpose and function of the HTML tags. Even if they understand how to use HTML, many will find it awkward and difficult to use in an authoring situation.

Adding Articles

In Chapter 2, the initial Quickstart chapter, you learned how simple it is to add article content in Joomla. This time around you'll look more closely at some of the options provided. Not only will you learn about the article settings and how they relate to content display, but you will also discover how you can embed rich content media (such as Flash animations, images, and sounds) directly into an article.

Setting the Basic Article Parameters

The basic parameters of an article are those that can be set every time a new piece of content is added to the site. These are parameters such as publication date, title and author aliases, and so on. They determine the presentation and publication information for the article.

For every article placed on the system, the following basic parameters may be set:

- *Title Alias*: Provides an alternate title for the article that can be used by dynamic title scripts and also as a search engine–friendly name. For example, the Title Alias of the article "What's New in 1.5?" is "whats-new-in-15" to make it more code-friendly.

- *Author Alias*: Provides the option of displaying an alias or pseudonym (if the author's name is configured to be shown with the article).

- *Access Level*: Sets the access rights for the three groups of users (Public, Registered, or Special).

- *Created Date*: Allows the creation date as it appears to web visitors to be overridden. This feature is used to future-date content that will not appear on the site until later or to republish older content that has a newer reformatting or revision date.

- *Start Publishing*: Specifies the date when the article will automatically appear on the Joomla site. This is useful for perennial content, event-related content, and columns that feature a scheduled release, such as "Tuesday Cooking Corner." Columnists can upload an article that is published every Tuesday at any time before that. In military parlance, they can simply "fire and forget." After setting the publication date (and time if desired), the article will automatically appear on the site on the scheduled date.

- *Finish Publishing*: Specifies the date when the article will no longer appear on the site. If this parameter is left empty, the article will remain published until manually unpublished or deleted.

All date fields (such as Created Date, Start Publishing, and Finish Publishing) feature an ellipsis (...) button to the right of the editing area. Clicking the ellipsis button displays a graphic calendar that allows selection of a date from a calendar page.

■**Tip** The Start and Finish Publishing dates provide an excellent opportunity to automatically activate seasonal content. You can create some information that is useful every year (e.g., instructions on how to wrap a gift) and set the Start and Finish dates so that the article appears between December 1 and December 26 of the year. Such an article can be created in the height of summer and then require no further attention. When Christmas rolls around, the article will automatically appear on the site at the proper time. At the end of the year, you can simply reset the dates on this perennial content and your site will always have a timely feel to it.

Setting the Advanced Article Parameters

The Advanced Parameters tab (see Figure 4-15) configures the presentation settings of an article when the article is fully displayed (after the web visitor clicks on Read More link at the bottom of the article summary). A majority of articles have no advanced parameter modifications and are left with default settings.

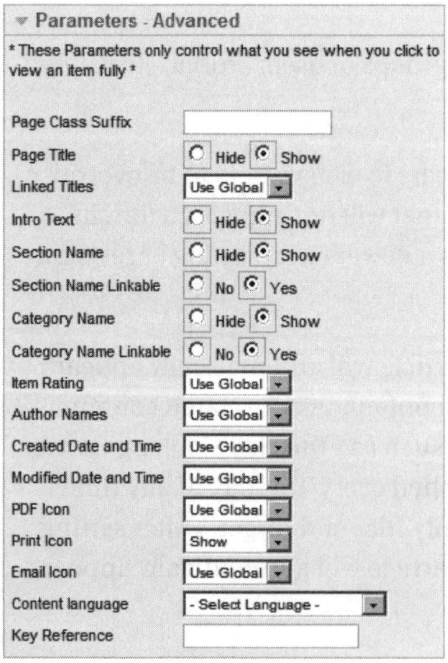

Figure 4-15. *The Advanced Parameters tab contains the options for the article when it is viewed individually.*

Many of the advanced parameters will override global settings. The default setting of Use Global will, in special cases, need to be changed for a particular article. In most cases, leaving the global setting is a good idea, so that any changes in policy on a particular setting can be made once in the Administrator interface, and the alterations will automatically propagate to all articles that don't have custom override settings.

The Advanced Parameters tab features the following settings:

- *Page Class Suffix*: Specifies a suffix to be used for the CSS of this article. Adding a suffix allows a custom style sheet to be used with this particular article. You'll use this feature later in the book to provide your site with a theme that uses styles for different pages, yet maintains a unified brand image.

- *Page Title*: Hides or shows the title of the article.

- *Linked Titles*: Allows the title of the article to be a link. If title is a link, when the visitor clicks on it, the browser jumps to the same location as the Read More link.

- *Intro Text*: Shows the introductory text above the article. The intro text is the abbreviated article shown in an article aggregate (such as a listing of articles in a category) with the Read More link. Use the Read More button at the bottom of the editor window to insert a horizontal rule to separate Intro text from Read More text in the body of the article.

- *Section Name and Section Name Linkable*: Shows the Section Name at the top of the article. The Linkable option specifies whether the displayed Section Name is a link that will take the visitor to the section for other similarly filed articles.

- *Category Name and Category Name Linkable*: Shows the Category Name at the top of the article. The Linkable option specifies whether the displayed Category Name is a link that will take the visitor to the category for other similarly filed articles.

- *Item Rating*: Overrides to show this item's rating (from user selections). Note that a change from the Use Global setting should be carefully considered. If only one article on a site full of rated content doesn't have a rating, it may hint at censorship. Likewise if a single article shows a user rating while others do not, it will appear odd to the user.

- *Author Names*: Overrides to show this item's author name(s).

- *Created Date and Time*: Overrides to show this item's created date and time.

- *Modified Date and Time*: Overrides to show this item's modification date and time.

- *PDF Icon*: Overrides to show this item's PDF icon.

- *Print Icon*: Overrides to show this item's print icon.

- *Email Icon*: Overrides to show this item's e-mail icon.

- *Content language*: Overrides to select a language for this article.

- *Key Reference*: A text key that may be used to reference this article within the Joomla system (e.g., to link to a help topic).

While the advanced article settings are useful in rare instances, the Page Class Suffix and Key Reference fields are the only settings you are likely to change for a given article.

Setting the Article Metadata Information

Metadata is information about information. In this case, it is information about the article that is, while invisible to the user, accessible to web search engines and used for purposes of indexing, filing, and description. The metadata is important for making sure your content is represented properly on the Web, and you'll learn more about it in Chapter 12 when search engine optimization techniques are explained.

The following metadata fields are supported natively in Joomla:

- *Description*: Provides a summary description of the article content. This description will be displayed by some search engines (such as Google) directly under the site title on their search results page.

- *Keywords*: Shows any keywords that relate to the article.

- *Add Sect/Cat/Title button*: Inserts the section, category, and title information into the Keywords text box. Having this information in the keywords will help the article be found and categorized by search engines when they index the page's content.

- *Change Creator*: Sets the creator of the article to a different user. This feature is most useful when an administrator needs to post content from another contributor (such as an article that was submitted via e-mail).

▪Tip Most search engines don't place much emphasis on keywords since spammers have abused this metadata to camouflage the true nature of their sites. Therefore, don't spend too much time working on the keywords. Instead, make sure that any desired keywords are included in the site description and somewhere in the article itself. Generally, that strategy will have much better results in terms of the site being found. If you want to streamline this process, you can use one of several online automatic metatag generators (e.g., www.see-search.com/webdesign/seeMetaTag.htm) to extract keywords from your tags.

With every article you post, try to add this metadata at the time of original publication. It's unlikely you will ever return to fill in the information, so it is best to do it when you have the chance.

Adding an Article to Your Site

You should now have a much clearer idea of the settings and parameters available for each article, which will allow you to make better decisions about which publishing parameters to select. Now is the time to add a new article to your site structure.

Bring up the Article Manager or simply click the Add New Article button on the Administrator Control Panel screen. Enter the title of the article and a machine-friendly version of the title in the Title Alias field. Select a section and a category, and set the article for publication to the Frontpage. You can see the article I will be publishing in Figure 4-16.

Figure 4-16. *Enter the title, alias, section, category, and body of a new article.*

Before I'm finished, I want to change a few settings in the Advanced Parameters. First, I set the section and category names so that they are visible and linkable. Then I turn on the Print icon so visitors can print the article if they want (even if most items don't have a Print icon because the global setting is different). The parameters pane now appears as shown in Figure 4-17.

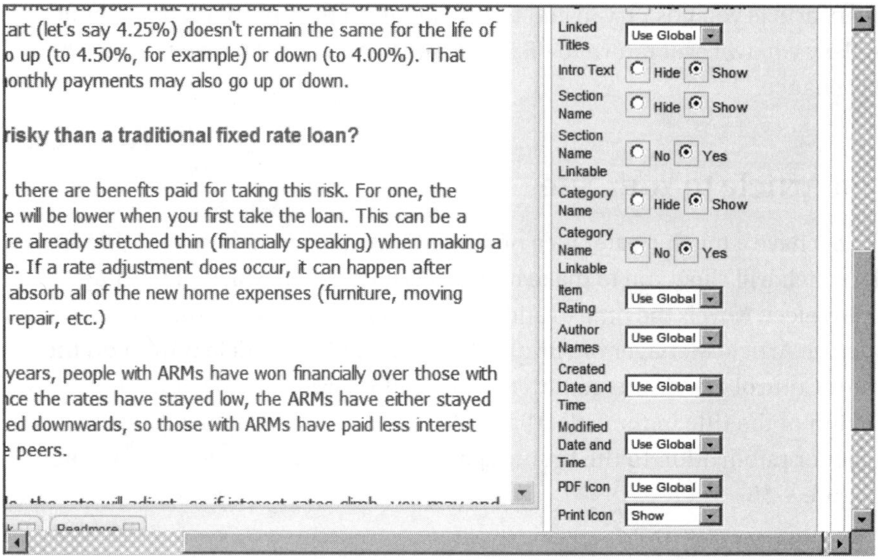

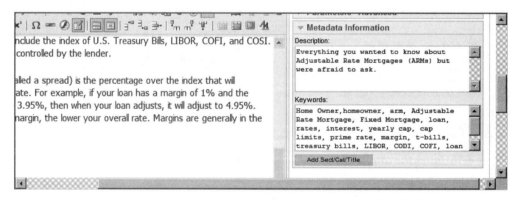

Figure 4-17. *Change the advanced parameters to match the needs of the article.*

Be sure to set the metadata for the article. I wrote up a brief description of the article, making sure all of the most important keywords were in the description. I also put together a list of keywords that I thought would properly reflect the article (see Figure 4-18).

Figure 4-18. *Be sure to add metadata so search engines can properly catalog the site content.*

Before I save the article for publication, I'll add some media to it. First, I upload a small PNG image of a home icon that should appear in the text. Later I'll add an introductory audio file to complete the media experience. You can alternatively add a Flash file or other media.

Place the text cursor at the place within your article text where you want an image to appear. Before you can add the media to the article, however, you have to upload it. Scroll to the bottom of the screen and you will see an Image button. Click the button and the Insert Image window will display. This window shows thumbnails of all of the current media stored in the default media folder on the site.

Tip If you have a number of content items or items that will be shared among several articles, you can upload them easily in the Media Manager.

I want to upload a custom icon, so I expand the Upload section at the bottom of the window and click the Browse button (see Figure 4-19). I select my houseicon.png file and click the Upload button. A thumbnail of the new graphic automatically appears in the images contact sheet.

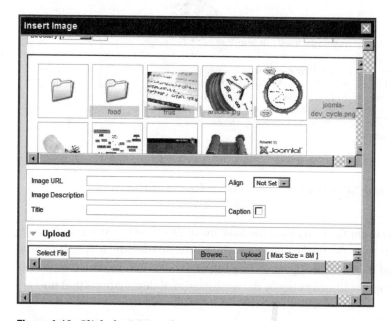

Figure 4-19. *Click the Browse button at the bottom of the window to select an image file for upload.*

Click your new image to select it for insertion. The Image URL field should be automatically filled with the path to the selected graphic. For my graphic, the path is images/stories/houseicon.png.

I entered an image description, which is very important for search engines and accessibility. Search engines can't "see" the content of a graphic, but they can read the HTML `alt` attribute for a text description of the item. The image description sets the `alt` attribute. Additionally, accessibility software (such as screen readers for the visually impaired) needs a text description to communicate to the user what is displayed on the screen.

For the title of the image, I simply duplicate the description field. I also want it captioned on the page, so I check the Caption box. Finally, I click the Insert button at the top-right corner of the screen to insert the image at my cursor position. Now the diagram is inserted directly into my article (see Figure 4-20).

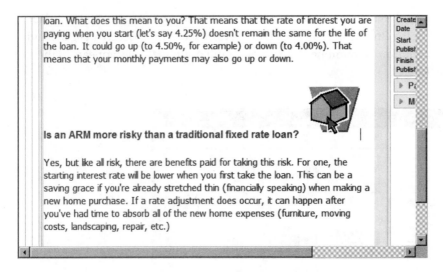

Figure 4-20. *The image now appears where it was inserted in the article.*

The article is ready to publish, so I click the Save button to store the article in the Joomla database. If you go to the home page now, you won't see the article. Why is this? Earlier when you wiped the slate clean, you deleted all of the old sections and categories. The Frontpage was set to specifically display the organizational designations that no longer exist.

To show the new content, you'll need to add the new sections and categories to the Frontpage. Before you do that, however, why not add one more article to test out the uncategorized content functionality?

Adding a Second Article

To understand the various types of Joomla filing, you should add a new article that will be uncategorized. With uncategorized content, you can test a direct link menu that takes the visitor to the specific article rather than a list of items in a section or category. An example of the type of document that would be uncategorized is a Terms and Conditions page of a web site.

Since the sections and categories are specifically organized around the subject area of the site, often documents such as terms and conditions, licensing, and use restrictions don't have a clear place in the hierarchical structure. Of course, you could create a catchall category if you wanted, but for this example you'll leave the article uncategorized.

Create a new article with any parameters and content you want. Be sure to leave the Section and Category drop-down lists set to Uncategorized (see Figure 4-21). Here I've placed text for the site's general terms and conditions as well as limitations of liability, and so on.

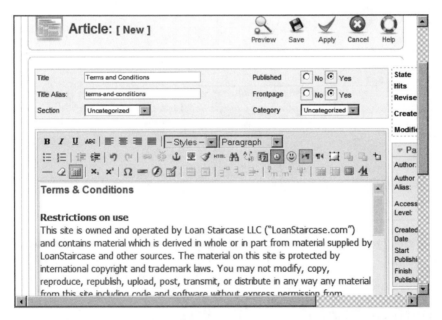

Figure 4-21. *Post an uncategorized article that will be used for a direct link demonstration.*

Unlike the last article, don't use the advanced parameters to set the display of a linkable section or category. However, you can use the advanced parameters to override the global settings for Author Names and Created Date and Time. I recommend you select the Hide option for both of these parameters, as there is no need for a system document such as this article to display such data (even if all other site articles do provide this information).

Once you've finished, click the Save button to publish the article into the database. You're ready now to create menus that can address these items.

■Tip The home page of your Joomla site is called the Frontpage by the Joomla system. The Frontpage Manager is a shorthand way of examining the content that will be displayed on the Frontpage. If you want to do a quick check of the home screen contents, you can easily jump to the manager through the Frontpage Manager menu option or the Frontpage button on the Control Panel. All of the Frontpage material also remains available through the Article Manager.

Upon returning to the Article Manager, if the Published column for either article holds the pending icon (which displays an exclamation point), as shown in Figure 4-22, you'll have to change the publication date for the articles to display. Occasionally, Joomla takes the server date and time and then assigns a future time for publication to a new article. To publish the article now, simply edit the article and change the Start Publishing date to the present date.

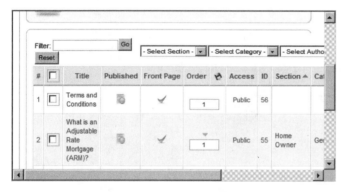

Figure 4-22. *If the exclamation point pending icon is displayed, the publication date is set sometime in the future.*

Adding Menus to Point to Content

Joomla is organized around articles, but to access and display articles, the menu system takes center stage. Every section, category, or individual document needs to be linked in one way or another to a menu for the user to access it. Menus in Joomla aren't always defined in the straightforward manner they are in a desktop application.

In Joomla, a menu may appear as a traditional desktop menu and show options either horizontally across the top of the screen or vertically running down the side. A menu may also look like a simple list of article summaries used by the visitor to navigate to the complete content of the article. Or a menu may contain articles listed in blog format.

The next chapter provides a complete explanation of each type of menu system. For now, you need to use one direct menu and one menu category to display the articles that you've added to Joomla.

Creating a Direct Menu to the Uncategorized Article

For the uncategorized article, you can create a menu that takes the visitor directly to that article. This direct menu will be created as a single menu item within the Main Menu.

To begin, open the Menu Manager and click the Edit Menu Items icon in the Menu items column of the Main Menu. Click the New icon to create a new menu item.

You will be presented with a screen like the one shown in Figure 4-23. This screen contains a list of all of the available types of content that may be linked to a menu items. To expand the possible article choices, click the Articles item under the Internal Link subject.

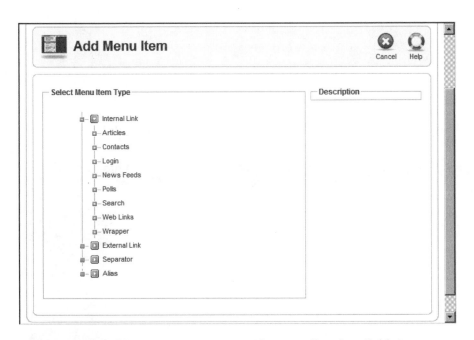

Figure 4-23. *The Add Menu Item screen provides a tree list of available item types.*

Select the Standard Article Layout option for the menu type to create a direct menu link. Set the name of the menu item to **Terms and Conditions** or the title of your uncategorized article. Leave the Display in and Parent Item settings at their defaults (Main Menu and Top, respectively, as shown in Figure 4-24).

At the top-right of the screen is a button titled Select Article. Click the Select button and an article selection window pop-up will display (see Figure 4-25). Click the name of your uncategorized article to select it and you will be returned to the article window with the article title now appearing in the Select Article text field.

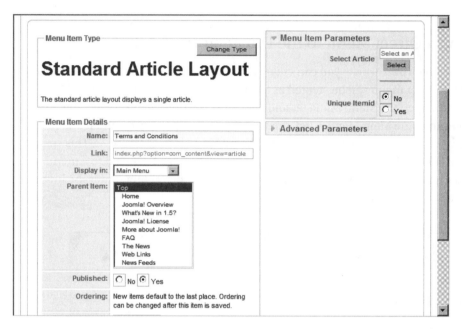

Figure 4-24. *Leave the Display in and Parent Item parameters at their defaults.*

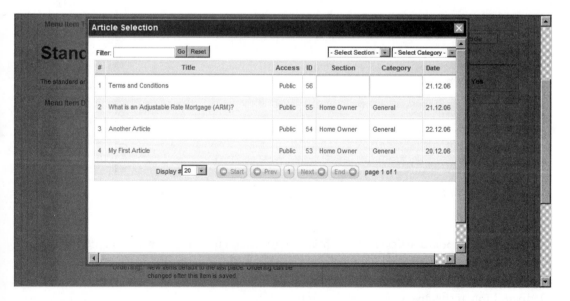

Figure 4-25. *Click the article name to link this article to the current menu.*

For this article, you don't need to change any of the advanced parameters, so click the Save button to store your new menu item.

If you bring up the Frontpage of your Joomla site, you will now see the Terms and Conditions menu item at the bottom of the Main Menu, as shown in Figure 4-26. If you click the link to the article, you will see that it appears as an independent page without any section or category references.

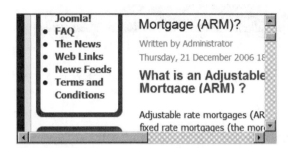

Figure 4-26. *The Terms and Conditions menu item is now part of the Main Menu.*

You can easily add any other direct menu items in this fashion. However, a CMS isn't very useful if you need to create a new menu each time an additional article is contributed to the site. Therefore, most of the menus you create will aggregate content so that Joomla can dynamically handle the presentation of new articles. The most common form of dynamic menu is the Category menu.

Displaying the Category Menu

In this section of the chapter, you can add a menu item that will display all of the articles in a specified category. Before you add the new menu, however, now is a good time to clear out the Main Menu references to all of the sample data content items since they no longer exist.

Start by opening the Menu Manager and clicking the Menu Items icon for the Main Menu. When the list of current items is displayed, select all of the menu items except Home and Terms and Conditions (this includes Joomla! Overview, What's New in 1.5?, Joomla! License, More about Joomla!, FAQ, The News, Web Links, and News Feeds). Click the Trash icon to remove them. Since you're not deleting the menu, you don't have to go immediately to empty the trash; you can leave the deleted items in the trash for the moment.

If you refresh the browser window showing your site's Frontpage, you will see only the two remaining menu items. Now that you've cleaned the broken-link menu items off the site, it's time to add a new menu. While still within the Main Menu items screen, click the New button to begin a new menu entry.

In the same way you created the direct link menu, click the Internal Link ➤ Articles headline in the outline interface. This time, choose the Standard Category Layout option. You'll see a screen that's a bit different from the single article form of the last section. On the right side of the screen (see Figure 4-27), the Menu Item Parameters area lets you set up the configuration for the article display.

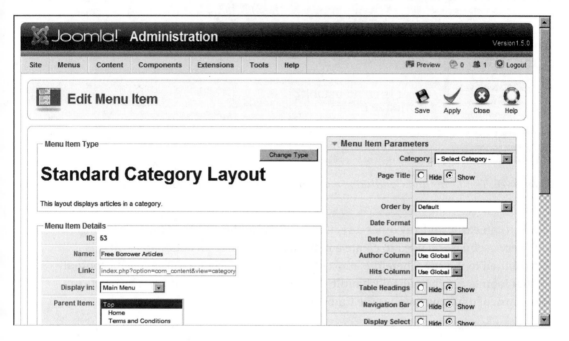

Figure 4-27. *The Menu Item Parameters area contains settings that govern the display of the Standard Category Layout.*

You will need to begin by giving the menu item a title. For the LoanStaircase site, I want all of the visitor documents from the General category to be displayed by this menu; therefore, I give the menu item the title **Free Borrower Articles**. In the Menu Item Parameters area, I also set the category to **Free Borrower Articles**, which is where I placed the main article I created.

When you've completed any other adjustments you want to make to the menu, click the Save button. The screen displaying the current menu items will display, showing your new menu at the bottom of the list. You actually want this menu to appear above your direct menu, so click the up arrow in the Order column, as shown in Figure 4-28.

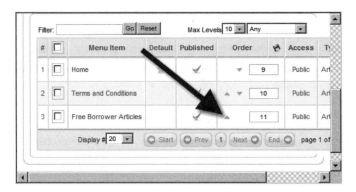

Figure 4-28. *Click the up arrow to move the current menu above the Terms and Conditions direct menu.*

Refresh the browser window of the user display and you should see not only the menu items correctly ordered, but also the article you posted on the Frontpage. The template is configured to display the content of the Main Menu, so your recent addition is automatically displayed. Now that you've begun to customize the content of your site, it's time to alter the appearance as well.

Installing a New Template

The most common method of changing the look of a Joomla site is downloading and installing a custom template. There are many wonderful freeware and commercial sites that can provide a new, high-quality skin for your web site. In this section, you'll learn to download and install a new template that can give a site a more targeted look and feel to enhance the site's brand image.

The theme of your Joomla web site is determined by the default site template. With a standard installation, the `rhuk_milkyway` template is selected. To give you an idea of the power of the template system, you'll be able to see the dramatic recasting of your web site by simply selecting a new template. The entire appearance of the site transforms instantly.

Before you begin, you'll need to locate a new template and download it. There are numerous excellent commercial sites where you can buy a subscription to gain access to all of the templates the site contains. For free templates, check out `www.joomla24.com` and `www.joomlahut.com`.

■Tip Unfortunately, when you attempt to find free Joomla templates on search engines such as Google, you'll often get links to commercial sites that misrepresent themselves. Either the sites have the free templates buried so that they're difficult to find, or they really don't have any free templates at all. Don't give up, though—many free Joomla templates are available.

The template you'll download will most often be a stored as a ZIP or GZIP archive. Since Joomla can internally decode these types of archives, you won't need to extract the files from the archive onto your local drive. Joomla will let you simply upload the archive, and the system will expand the template files and put them in their appropriate locations.

USING LEGACY MODE FOR JOOMLA! 1.0 COMPATIBILITY

Vast numbers of existing Joomla 1.0 templates are available on the Web. The developers of Joomla 1.5 understood that even though the template system needed a complete overhaul, it was important to maintain backward compatibility in case the older templates were never upgraded. Enter *Legacy Mode*.

You can activate legacy mode in Joomla 1.5 by opening the Plugin Manager and publishing the System - Legacy extension. If you are using 1.5 templates, though, be sure to disabled the Legacy extension so the newer template can take advantage of the performance and features improvements of the new system.

The programming interfaces from version 1.0 have been deprecated (set for termination in the future), so if you can upgrade to a version 1.5 of the template you're using, be sure to do so. The Joomla team made a substantial revision to the template system, and it is likely that 1.5 templates will be compatible far into the future, while the sun is already going down on 1.0 templates.

A template typically consists of an assortment of files, including PHP code, style sheets (in CSS files), and images. In Figure 4-29, you can see the screen on the Joomla24 site where I downloaded the Moz Dev v2 template in ZIP format. Find a template on this web site or another, download it, and save it to your local drive.

To change the template, you'll first need to upload it into the system via the Extension Manager. You can find the Extension Manager by selecting the Install/Uninstall option under the Extension menu. Select the file with the Browse button and then click the Upload File & Install button, as shown in Figure 4-30.

After the template upload has completed successfully, open the Template Manager screen. Currently the `rhuk_milkyway` template is selected. To change the site template, click the radio button to the left of the desired template. In this case, select the new template and click the Default button in the menu bar.

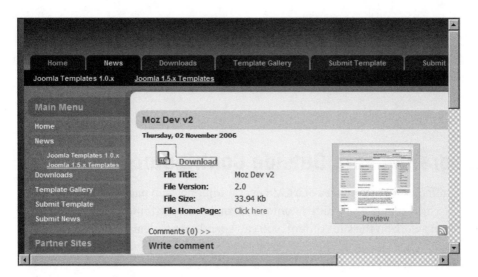

Figure 4-29. *Click the Download link to download the archive of the new template.*

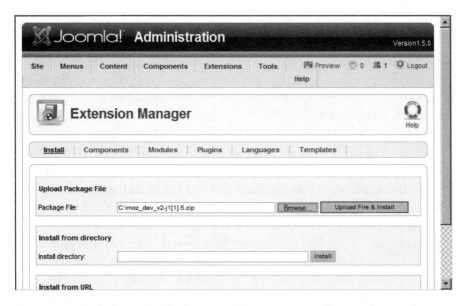

Figure 4-30. *Click the Upload File & Install button to put the template on the site.*

Open a browser window of the user's view of the site. When you click the Refresh button, the new look should be quite a change. Congratulations! You've just made a significant alteration to the look and feel of your new Joomla site. If you want to download some commercial templates, there are numerous sites that sell subscriptions to new templates, which you can download as they become available. You could even change the look and feel of your Joomla site every month!

■**Tip**   In the Template Manager, you can get a preview of any of the templates currently installed on your system by moving your mouse over the name of the template. A thumbnail of the main screen of the template will appear in a pop-up.

Collaborating with Outside Contributors

One of the tremendous advantages of a CMS over traditional web page construction is the ability to easily manage submitted content. If you have contributors, editors, or moderators who will work on the site content, you can spend a great deal more time on site promotion and other management tasks. Joomla allows you to assign registered users various roles that grant privileges to edit or modify your web site.

Even more powerful is the fact that you can allow contributors to submit their additions or changes to the site, but you can reserve final publishing approval for yourself. You can be the final arbiter of all site content.

■**Tip**   Joomla has the rudiments of a web personal information manager (PIM) included with the default installation. Any user added to the Joomla system can be linked to the more robust information store saved with each contact in the PIM. By selecting Components ➤ Contact ➤ Manage Contacts, you can create a new record and link it to the user record.

When you set up a new account for a contributor, there are three categories into which the user will likely fit: Registered Author, Registered Editor, or Registered Publisher. You can add the user yourself or you can modify an existing registered user. As an example, open the User Manager and click the New button to create a new user.

For the sample login, I've entered the name of **John Doe**, the user name of **jdoe**, and an e-mail address. In the Group list box, I've selected Author as shown in Figure 4-31. That group designation will allow the new user to contribute content.

Open a browser window and access the user front-end of your Joomla site. On the left side of the screen, scroll down to the login form, where a registered user can enter his or her username and password. Enter these text fields for the user you just created and click the Login button. When the system has logged you in, the browser will return to the home page. If you scroll down the screen to the place where the login fields had been, you'll find they've been replaced by a personalized greeting and a Logout button.

User Manager

Save   Apply   Cancel   Help

- Add

User Details

Name	John Doe
Username	jdoe
Email	jdoe@yahoo.com
New Password	••••
Verify Password	••••

Group	Public Frontend
	  . - Registered
	       - Author
	         - Editor
	           - Publisher
	- Public Backend
	      - Manager
	        - Administrator
	          - Super Administrator

Figure 4-31. *Select the Author designation in the Group list box.*

To add a new article, the contributor has to select an existing category or section where articles are already located. Since you've created only a single category that has a menu selection, click that now (in my case, the menu is Free Borrower Articles). When you scroll to the bottom of the article list, you'll see a link titled New as shown in Figure 4-32.

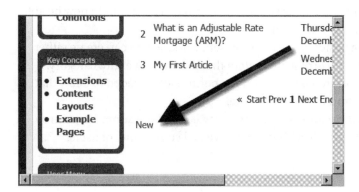

Figure 4-32. *Click the New link to add an article to the current category.*

Click on the New link and the screen should display the WYSIWYG editor you've selected as the default. Below the text editor area, you'll find panels for most of the basic parameters and also an entry space for the article metadata.

Enter a sample article and fill out the article parameters as if you were a third-party contributor to the site. Once the article is complete, click the Save button. The article will be submitted into the site. Once a contributor has posted a new article, it is up to the administrator or moderator to decide if it should be published on the site.

Log in again as the administrator and open the Article Manager in the Administrator interface. You will see the article that was just submitted into the system. In the Published column is a red *X* signifying that the article is not presently published. Only the administrator or a user with Editor or Publisher permissions can accept the article for publication on the site.

Conclusion

You should now have a pretty solid grasp on publishing content on the Joomla system. In this chapter, you not only performed the preplanning of the site with a third-party application (such as Microsoft Word, FreeMind, or Leo), but also implemented your site plan by creating a structure of sections and categories that could be used to file each article properly.

The two editors included with the default Joomla installation (TinyMCE and XStandard Lite) for creating and modifying articles both offer robust features. TinyMCE has an excellent user interface and, being written in JavaScript, will run on nearly any browser. XStandard Lite, with a client component only available on the Windows platform, provides XHTML features as well as superior performance. You should now be able to choose the editor that best fits your needs.

You also learned how the basics of the menu system work, so you can create either a direct menu item link to an article or a menu item that presents an entire category. Finally, you created a new registered user and set the permissions needed to allow that user to contribute article content to the Joomla site.

In the next chapter, you'll greatly expand your knowledge of site administration so you can maintain not only the site itself, but also the virtual community of users.

CHAPTER 5

■ ■ ■

Administering Joomla!

One of the great benefits of using Joomla is the ease of site management that the CMS offers. Nearly all site administration functions are available through the web browser interface, making it possible to alter content and system configuration from anywhere you have access to the Web. When maintenance is required outside of the Administrator interface, it can usually be handled by industry standard MySQL tools.

The Joomla Administrator interface is structured so that each area of responsibility has a separate manager screen. For example, the Template Manager provides the interface for the configuration of all templates, while the User Manager is used to set up and administer user accounts. The Joomla managers can be divided into roughly three categories: presentation administration, content administration, and system administration.

Presentation Administration

The appearance of a Joomla site is governed by various facets of content display. The primary determinant of the look and feel of a site is the template or templates. The template selection will determine the graphics, color scheme, and fonts of all site pages—although some extensions, such as Simple Machines Forum (SMF), have their own theme settings. Therefore, the Template Manager will control most of the site appearance.

In addition to the template choice, the selected display language plays a key role in determining the presentation of the site. While Roman-based languages only slightly alter the appearance, the selection of a pictogram language (such as Chinese) or a language that reads right to left (RTL) can significantly affect the look and feel of the site. The Language Manager offers the configuration for languages options.

Template Manager

The Template Manager (see Figure 5-1) allows the administrator to select the default template, but also provides editing capabilities for both the main index file of the template and the style sheet file or files. That means that you don't need access to a text editor or FTP capabilities to make simple edits to a template.

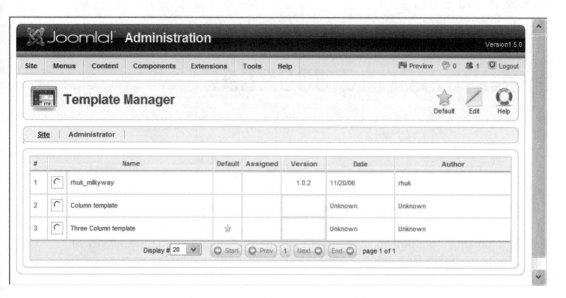

Figure 5-1. *The Template Manager allows you to set a template default or edit it.*

Hovering over the name of a template will display a thumbnail image of the general graphic appearance of that template. Clicking the template name will present the template configuration screen, as shown in Figure 5-2. This screen provides all of the basic details of the template, including a short template description that is retrieved from the template's XML descriptor file. Most commercial templates use the description to include both a summary and an enumeration of the screen/module positions that the template supports.

Any parameters available for configuration of the template are shown in the Parameters pane. A template may be assigned to particular menu items using the list box on the right side of the screen. You can assign a template to be used for an individual menu item, multiple menu items, all unassigned articles, or none. To assign the template to all items, you need to set the template as the site default on the main Template Manager screen.

Clicking the Edit HTML button will display the basic text editor (see Figure 5-3). This text editor doesn't have any advanced features like syntax highlighting or even search and replace. It was designed to allow minor adjustments and touch-ups when more direct editing is not convenient.

Figure 5-2. *The template configuration screen displays general settings as well as template-specific parameters.*

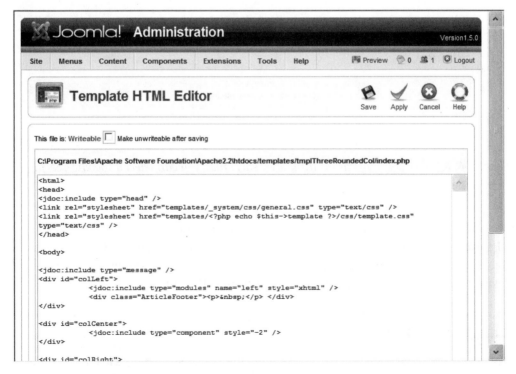

Figure 5-3. *You can edit the HTML of the template from the Joomla Administrator interface.*

Clicking the Edit CSS button on the template screen will open the text editor with the style sheet file of the template. For a template with multiple style sheets, you can select which one to edit (see Figure 5-4). The list will display all style sheet files located in the template's \css folder—it does not display only the files listed in the template's XML descriptor file. Therefore, the list may contain files that are not actually used by the template.

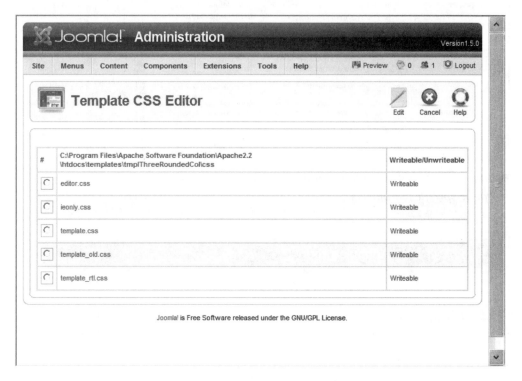

Figure 5-4. *When a template has multiple style sheet files, you can select a specific CSS file for editing.*

Most administrators don't spend a great amount of time working in the Template Manager. Once you set up the site template, there is only occasional need to change it. Since you can select another template to be used by the site with two mouse clicks, even revising the look and feel of the site requires little time investment.

Language Manager

The Language Manager allows you to configure the available languages installed on the Joomla CMS. Joomla provides support for interface capabilities in over 40 languages. In fact, a single Joomla installation can support many languages at the same time. Although the default language set for the site is the language displayed to new users, Joomla allows each individual registered user to select a preferred language for presentation.

Joomla is one of the most robust multilingual applications available. The international focus of Joomla drives the development team to make certain that all of the different languages work properly. The development team has an entire group of people devoted to updating and correcting the various plug-in language extensions.

In fact, one of the most popular extensions is Joom!Fish (www.joomfish.net), which helps manage multi-language content. It provides manual translation capabilities and the ability to hold translations for all dynamically generated content in a single database. It even makes it possible to translate static text used by third-party extensions so the entire site (including add-ons) can appear in the selected language.

The Language Manager will help you administer a multilingual site, but new languages are installed via the Extension Manager. Once installed, the language will appear in the Language Manager for configuration (see Figure 5-5). The pane under the Language Manager banner allows you to select either Site or Administrator to display the language selections for these interfaces. Joomla provides the flexibility of setting the site presentation in one language and administering it in another.

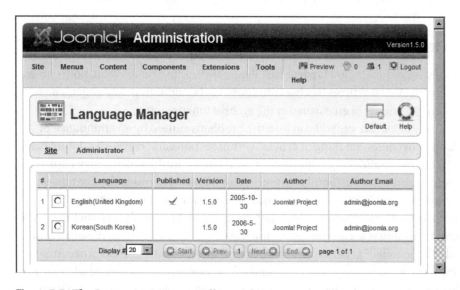

Figure 5-5. *The Language Manager allows selection and configuration of the site and Administrator interface languages.*

Keep in mind that in addition to the flexibility of allowing language settings for particular users, the site, and the Administrator interface, individual articles can also be configured to use a different language. In the Advanced Parameter pane, which is displayed when an article is being edited, a contributor may select the use of any language currently available on the Joomla system from the Content Language drop-down list.

Content Administration

Content administration is at the heart of most of the work an administrator will do on the site. Sections, categories, articles, and media need to be organized, managed, and archived. Since content management is the primary function of the Joomla CMS, the interface has been streamlined and optimized from earlier versions.

Most content management will be performed within the Article Manager after the Section Manager and Category Manager have been used to configure the areas where the articles will be filed. The Frontpage Manager provides a shortcut method of seeing all of the content that will be combined for a sort of "super category" display on the home page of the site. The Media Manager supports uploads and management of media (images, sounds, Flash files, etc.) used within the articles. Finally, the Trash Manager works much like a desktop trashcan as a holding place of "trashed" content before final deletion.

Article Manager

You've already used the Article Manager (see Figure 5-6) quite a bit to create both catego-rized and uncategorized articles (such as the Terms and Condition policy page). The only central feature that hasn't been covered is the archive functionality.

Any successful Joomla site will run into the problems caused by an abundance of articles. Even with consistent filing of articles within sections and categories, Joomla can become like an overabundant garden where a profusion of healthy plants may choke the walking path. In this case, the Joomla administrator will need to prune the content on the site so that neither the visitor nor the administrator becomes lost in the chaos.

Joomla provides a mechanism to prevent the site from becoming overwhelmed with older content. Pruning is accomplished by the use of the Archive button. When an article is archived, it is no longer generally available on the site, it doesn't take up processing time during a site search, and it won't clutter the query results. If you ever need to return the article to the site, simply view the list of archived items, selecting the desired item, and click the Unarchive button and the document will be restored to general publication.

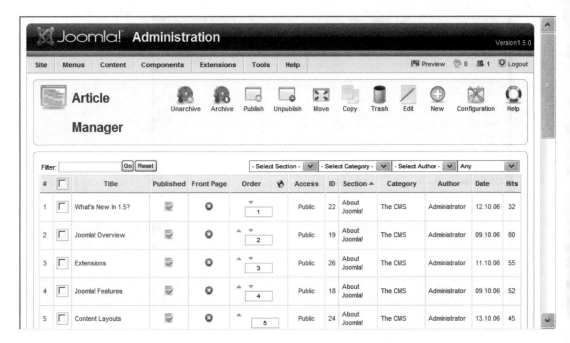

Figure 5-6. *The Article Manager displays all of the published and unpublished articles on the system.*

■Note In previous Joomla versions, archiving was accomplished through a separate Archive Manager. Now that functionality exists in the Article Manager. To view only archived articles as the Archive Manager previously displayed, simply select the drop-down list filter at the far right of the screen and select the Archived option.

There are a number of global settings that apply to articles that can be accessed by clicking the Preferences button in the Article Manager. Parameters such as linked titles, author names display, and so on are available in the Edit Configuration window, as shown in Figure 5-7. These options should already be familiar to you from when you created site articles. When an article parameter is set to the Use Global option, the selection in this configuration window is the one that is used for that parameter.

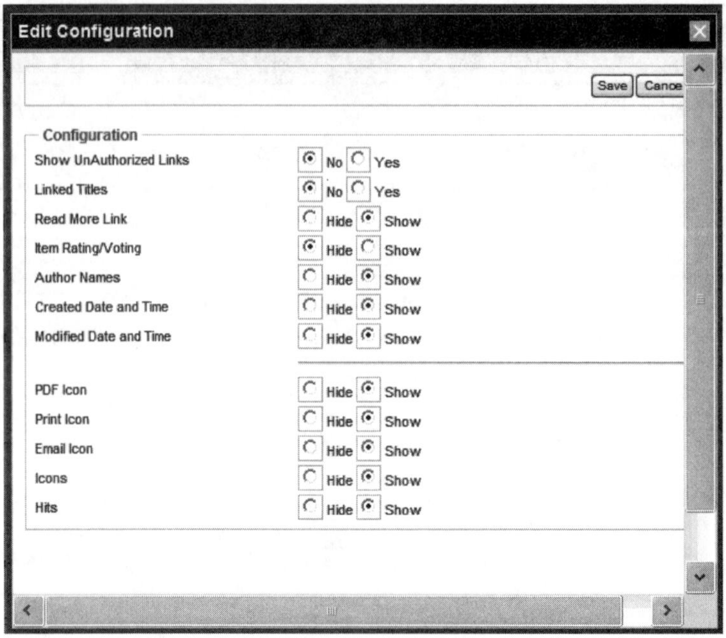

Figure 5-7. *The Article Manager configuration lets you configure the global article settings.*

Section and Category Managers

Since you just worked with the Section Manager and Category Manager extensively in the last chapter, a complete review would be largely redundant. These two managers are used to create the filing sections that determine where an article will be displayed. Content is always presented within the section or category where it was filed—except when it is set for Frontpage display.

Frontpage Manager

While most of the site content is displayed through menus that access sections and categories, there is one page that is entirely unique: the Frontpage. The Frontpage is the home page of the site, and content from any section, category, or uncategorized article can be displayed there. For that reason, the Frontpage has a dedicated manager, as shown in Figure 5-8.

The Frontpage Manager is a catch all that acts in much the same way as the Article Manager. It allows articles to be published, unpublished, reordered, and archived. Think of the Frontpage Manager as a shortcut that acts the same as an Article Manager filter, only it does so for the content that appears on the home page.

Figure 5-8. *The Frontpage Manager displays content from any section or category that is displayed on the home page.*

Media Manager

Although the Media Manager (shown in Figure 5-9) handles all types of media (including sound and video), most Joomla administrators use it primarily to administer images. The Media Manager allows media files of numerous types to be uploaded, including files with the following extensions: .bmp, .csv, .doc, .epg, .gif, .ico, .jpg, .odg, .odp, .ods, .odt, .pdf, .png, .ppt, .swf, .txt, .xcf, and .xls. The types allowed for upload may be customized by adding or removing a file extension type in the Legal Extensions parameter of the System tab in the Global Configuration Manager.

By default, newly uploaded files are placed into the \images directory. On a Linux server, the path to this directory will appear something like this:

```
/home/username/public_html/images/.
```

On a Windows staging server, the path to this directory will appear something like this:

```
C:/Program Files/Apache Software Foundation/Apache2.2/htdocs/images/
```

Figure 5-9. *The Media Manager provides access to the media folders.*

Images inserted into a story are generally held in the \stories subdirectory. Therefore, the path to an image used in a store will have a path something like this:

```
C:/Program Files/Apache Software Foundation/Apache2.2/
    htdocs/images/stories/houseicon.png
```

The Media Manager will allow you to create a new folder by entering the name of the desired folder in the text box that appears to the right of the current path and clicking the New Folder button.

Any of the media uploaded through this interface is accessible for insertion into article content. You may have noticed the Image button that appears at the bottom of the Joomla editor window. The relative path of the selected image will be stored with the article. Therefore, the HTML reference to use the previously mentioned image might look like this:

```
<img src="http://www.example.com/images/stories/houseicon.png">
```

Trash Manager

Like most desktop operating systems, deleted content is not immediately deleted from the Joomla system. When the delete function on an item is selected, that item is relocated to the trash receptacle. From the Trash Manager, you can delete all items, select specific items that are to be permanently deleted, or restore individual items to their predeletion location. It is very easy to forget to perform this necessary function of regularly emptying the system trash, so be sure to add it to your administrative to-do list. Emptying content that was placed in the trash will free up valuable resources and can be a good idea from a security standpoint.

Frequent emptying will also promote "discerning disposal." When there are 700 items in the trash, an administrator will tend to simply empty the trash without even examining the contents. If there are only ten items, however, the administrator will be more likely to glance at those items and determine if they should be actually deleted or if one or more items should be restored to the system (because of mistaken deletion or simple rethinking).

System Administration

There are more settings related to system administration than there are for the other managers. Since a Joomla site may have literally tens of thousands of simultaneous visitors, proper understanding of the configuration settings is critical for the site to function at maximum capacity.

The Global Configuration Manager holds most of the global settings for the site, system, and server. The User Manager is used for administration of the user accounts. The Menu Manager allows for creation and editing of menus as well as the menu items used by each menu. The Extension Manager supports installation and removal of new extensions and languages. The Module Manager, Plugin Manager, and Template Manager provide management functionality for each of their specific add-on types. The Mass Mail Manager lets the administrator create a bulk mail transmission to either selected user groups or all users of the system.

The Control Panel acts as a home page for the administrator portion of the Joomla site and provides a good launching point for examining the system options.

Control Panel

The Control Panel is a centralized panel where the administrator can jump to the most common parts of the site. This page is essentially the home page of the Administrator interface. While at first glance the page may reveal only a number of navigation buttons, there are three useful items on the right side of the Control Panel that are often over-looked by Joomla webmasters—the Preview button, introductory text removal instructions, and the administrative panels.

As you can see in Figure 5-10, the Preview button is available on the toolbar (and active from most locations in the Administrator interface). It provides a hyperlink to the Frontpage of the Joomla site for quick access. You can use this Preview hyperlink to open the home page in another window so that any changes made through the Administrator interface can be quickly evaluated.

Figure 5-10. *The Preview button will take you out of the Administrator interface and to the site Frontpage.*

At the bottom of the page, you'll see that there are instructions showing how to delete the introductory message (see Figure 5-11). You will probably want to delete the message to make the panels that appear below it easier to access. The administrative panels (also shown in the figure) provide helpful information such as the identities of logged-in users, the most popular articles on the site, a list of newly added articles, and general menu statistics (the number of items present on each menu).

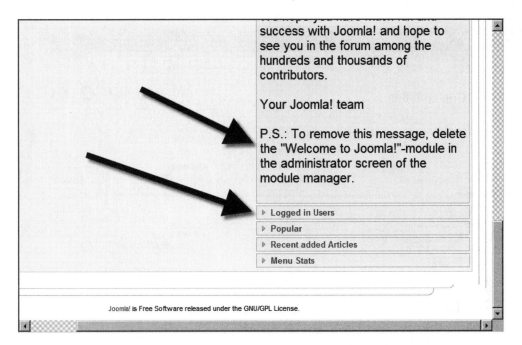

success with Joomla! and hope to
see you in the forum among the
hundreds and thousands of
contributors.

Your Joomla! team

P.S.: To remove this message, delete
the "Welcome to Joomla!"-module in
the administrator screen of the
module manager.

▷ Logged in Users

▷ Popular

▷ Recent added Articles

▷ Menu Stats

Joomla! is Free Software released under the GNU/GPL License.

Figure 5-11. *Instructions on how to delete the Hello Message appears directly above the administrative panels.*

Global Configuration Manager

The Global Configuration Manager, accessed under the Configuration option of the
Site menu, holds general sitewide settings. These settings will let you set up everything
from the administrator password to the FTP upload capabilities. Global configuration
is actually divided into three areas: Site, System, and Server. These panels are displayed
by clicking the appropriate link under the Global Configuration banner. By default, the
Site settings are displayed when the manager is initially presented.

Site Settings

The Site screen includes many of the options you configured during initial installation.
Other settings include metadata for the site, search engine optimization (SEO) settings,
and feed settings (as shown in Figure 5-12). The Site Settings panel allows you to take the
server offline and set the message sent to the visiting browser when the site is inopera-
tive. This option is very useful if you have to shut down the database server for maintenance, since the message will ensure visitors that your site hasn't disappeared when they
attempt to access it.

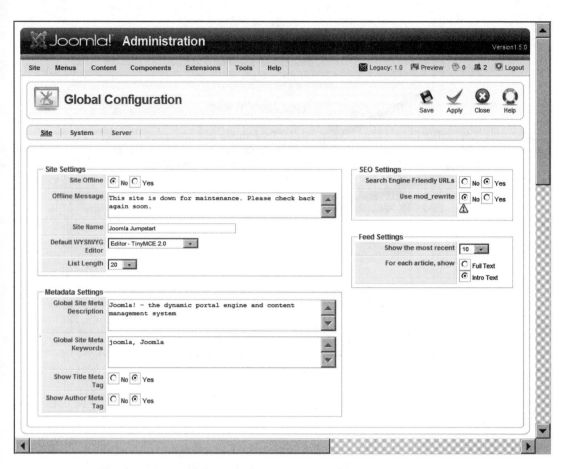

Figure 5-12. *The Site screen within the Global Configuration Manager*

Two of the more useful options is listed in the SEO Settings frame. The discipline of Search Engine Optimization (SEO) is complicated and will be discussed at length in Chapter 12. Briefly, these settings create virtual folders for various sections and categories so that when the web browser (or search engine spider) looks at the site, the URL doesn't hold a list of parameters (which search engines don't like). For example, without this option, the URL to access a particular section might appear like this:

```
http://www.joomla.org/index.php?option=com_content&
    view=category&id=33&Itemid=53
```

All of these parameters—the items following the question mark (?)—confuse the search engine. It doesn't have a clear understanding of them simply because they aren't standardized and are used differently by every PHP-based system. In contrast, a URL with a standard folder-based structure is easy for a machine to understand:

```
http://www.joomla.org/content/view/12/26/
```

You would, of course, want to enable these options. If you're running your own web server, that won't be a problem. If you're running your Joomla site on a remote server, things may be more complicated. For a complete explanation, see Chapter 12.

System Settings

The Site configuration determines how the site functions on the system, while the System configuration screen (see Figure 5-13) holds settings that affect the system itself. Many of these parameters affect performance, so the system should be monitored closely after any modification.

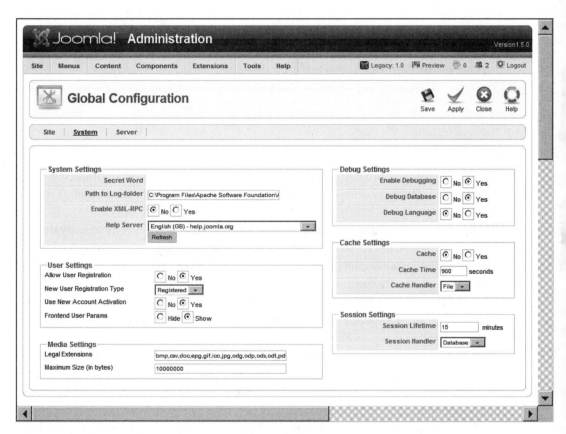

Figure 5-13. *The System Settings panel within the Global Configuration Manager*

A majority of the system settings are self-explanatory, but a few may be puzzling to the beginning Joomla user. The Debug settings have major performance and security consequences for a Joomla site and are rarely activated on a deployment server. The functionality these settings afford is generally beyond the scope of anyone not doing advanced Joomla development.

The Cache settings allow you to turn on the page cache, which streamlines the execution process so that the database is not constantly queried to generate the page to send to the user's browser. If a page is requested that has already been generated for another user in the last 900 seconds (or whatever cache time value has been set), the existing cached page is simply read from the cache and sent to the user. Caching can produce significant performance increases on a popular site.

The central drawback with enabling caching is the requirement that the web server must allow a program to write into the \cache directory. Many web hosts limit this type of functionality, so you'll have to check with your service provider to see if you can enable this setting. The recommended value that can be used with the chmod directory permissions tool for the cache folder (located at the root Joomla directory) is 755.

Caution Making a directory writable can have serious security ramifications if not done properly. Be sure to read the "Writable Directories" section later in the chapter before you make these changes.

Server Settings

The final pane of the Global Configuration Manager shows the Server settings (see Figure 5-14) that help you configure the functionality of the Joomla server and its relation to other servers.

One of the most useful options provided on this panel is the ability to activate GZIP page compression if your PHP server has the feature available. During Joomla installation, the installer checks for it and flags you if it isn't active. The GZIP function will perform on-the-fly compression of the page requested by the browser and send the file to browsers capable of decompressing it. The whole process is transparent to the visitor and simply speeds transmission—particularly if the visitor is using a dial-up access point.

To allow any mailing from the site (such as registered user confirmation messages or mass mail), you will need to configure the mail settings. When the same service provider that hosts your web site also supplies you with your e-mail account, these options should be easy to obtain. Getting the proper settings may be as easy as taking a look at the configuration settings of your e-mail program (such as Microsoft Outlook) and copying those settings into the Mail Settings panel.

If you don't have e-mail capabilities through a web service provider, enabling this function becomes much more difficult. Most SMTP servers (mail transmission servers) are closed to people not specifically authorized to send messages through them because spammers have abused free e-mail servers to flood the Web with their junk. You may be able to use a personal mail server account to provide the mail capabilities to your Joomla server. Check with your service provider.

Figure 5-14. *The Server Settings panel within the Global Configuration Manager*

User Manager

The User Manager allows the administrator to grant and revoke privileges for individual accounts (see Figure 5-15). Joomla was created with collaboration in mind. For that reason, the Joomla user security is configured to essentially follow the needs of an online publication.

If the Joomla site allows for logins, generally the user will register with the system and be sent a confirmation message. If the account is validated, the user is placed into the Registered user group. When a registered user logs into a Joomla site, every user (including those with the lowest security level) has two options in common: Edit Account Details and Submit Web Link. Users with Author security level and above can also submit new content. If a user clicks on the New link in a category or section, they will be taken to the editor that was chosen in the Your Details area of the Account Settings page.

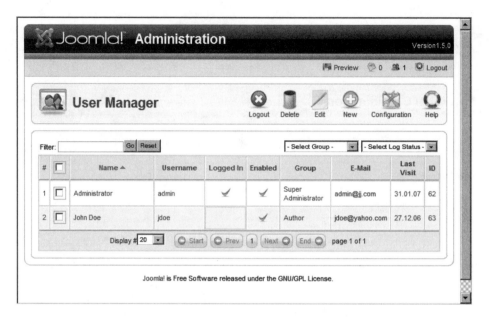

Figure 5-15. *The User Manager maintains the user login accounts.*

Note   User authentication is not limited to the Joomla system. Joomla includes a number of plug-ins that interface with other systems (such as for LDAP and Gmail authentication). If you would like to bridge the user login privileges from another system, particularly if you're unifying Intranet infrastructure, see the Joomla documentation for configuration details for these extensions.

At the lowest security level, on the Your Details screen the user can only modify the name to be used on the site, the e-mail address, the username, the password, and the editor (e.g., TinyMCE) that will be used when content editing is granted.

Registration Configuration

The setting that allows users to register without administrator approval can be set either in the Site panel of the Global Configuration Manager or through the Configuration button in the User Manager. When the Configuration button is clicked, the settings available for the registration system are displayed (see Figure 5-16).

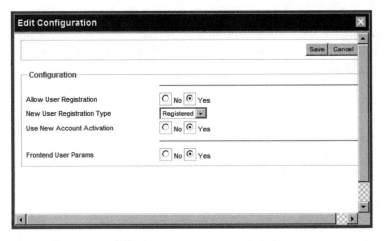

Figure 5-16. *In the User Manager, clicking the Configuration button will display the Edit Configuration window.*

The administrator can freely modify all settings pertaining to the user account, as well as disable or delete the account if necessary. The Filter drop-down lists on the right side of the User Manager let you separate out all but logged-in users or display the users based on the group to which they belong. Note that unlike other security systems, Joomla users may not belong to more than one group at a time.

■Caution If you decide to delete a user record that is linked to a record stored by the Contacts plug-in, you will orphan the contact record. Therefore, after deleting a user record, be sure to check the Contacts list to make sure that there is not a dangling record there.

One of the key aspects of creating a community site is the management of users. Everything from slovenly account request response to malicious cloning of a user's account can lead to distrust from your user base. Be sure that you take user security and responses to authorization requests seriously.

Login Security

Joomla provides anonymous access for everyone and basic login security for registered users. The types of users that will access the Joomla site are broken down into three basic groups:

Unregistered users: These users are simply visitors to the web site who haven't logged in and may not be registered. Most simple web sites don't have a registration system, so all of the users of such a web site would fall into this category. These users are also called *public front-end* users.

Registered front-end users: These are readers of your site who log in to gain access to restricted content. A registered user account may be activated after filling in a simple form, receiving a confirmation e-mail, or being manually confirmed by an administrator. Content on a Joomla site can be restricted to registered users. Some pay sites such as Salon.com provide articles available only to subscribers who pay a monthly fee. Registered users may be authorized to contribute content to the site, but adding new content is the limit of their permissions.

Registered back-end users: These are contributors, system administrators, or moderators who have the ability to log in and modify core portions of the site itself. Their ability to make changes to the site is determined by the permissions granted. These users have access to the administrator back-end.

When you edit a user account in the User Manager, as shown in Figure 5-17, you can see these three categories present in the Group list box. Two of these general categories (registered front-end and back-end users) have subcategories that further define the privileges of the user account.

Figure 5-17. *Editing a user record from the User Manager allows the administrator to assign the user to a group.*

Registered Front-End Users

When registered front-end users are given modification privileges, they can access the WYSIWYG editor to post or edit articles. The four subgroups that are held under the registered front-end users category have varying submission capabilities. The four types of front-end users are as follows:

- *Registered*: Simple registered users have the ability to read restricted content (if available on the site). They have no capabilities to submit new content articles, although they may submit web links.

- *Author*: Members of the author group can post and modify their own articles. They can even determine when the article will be published (limited by the administrator's ability to have a moderator set up who must clear any posted content before it appears).

- *Editor*: Like an author, a user in the editor group can post and modify their content. An editor also has the ability to edit other contributors' content.

- *Publisher*: A user with publisher status can perform any operation available to an editor, but may also publish or unpublish content on the site.

If the user account was created through the front-end Joomla interface (rather than by an administrator or super-administrator) by the user filling out a registration form, Joomla can be set to send a confirmation e-mail to the user to ensure that the e-mail address is valid. Joomla handles all of this work, and this feature is enabled by default.

Registered Back-End Users

Registered back-end user groups contain the various administrative users of the site. Administrators have the ability to change access and permissions, alter the site template, create new sections and categories, install new components, and other functions. The three groups for back-end users are as follows:

- *Manager*: The manager group has the lowest authority in the administrative pyramid. Members of this group have limited access to the administrator Control Panel, and can confirm registration for users and perform basic maintenance such as categorizing an article or managing sections and categories.

- *Administrator*: The administrator can install and uninstall extensions to the Joomla system, change the selected template, change the layout of a page, and modify the permissions of any user lower than their access level. An administrator does not have the power to edit a super-administrator user record (obviously), edit the global configuration, access the mass mail capabilities, or install templates or languages. The administrator level and above are the only groups that can create or authorize new registered users. The Joomla system can be configured to allow a user's automatic registration into the system, but the limits on a user-registered account are determined by administrator settings.

- *Super-administrator (SA)*: The SA is the king of the web site. Like the administrator level on Windows and the root or sa user level on Linux, the SA has no restrictions on the system. The SA account is the one created during the initial Joomla installation. This account traditionally has a username of admin.

When accessing the Joomla Administrator interface, the user's group designation will determine how the interface appears. The interfaces for the lower-level groups (such as manager) are missing many of the buttons and menu items that are present when an SA is logged into the system.

Lost Password

If a user loses their password, the Joomla interface can request a reminder be sent to the registered account's e-mail. Passwords are stored in MD5 format, so they cannot be recovered easily. If a password is lost, it should be reset by an administrator.

The new password will only be sent to the e-mail address that was registered with the account. If the user has closed down that account or is no longer able to access it, the SA must be contacted to do a special individual reset.

Menu Manager

In Joomla, menus are not the simple drop-down menus found in most desktop user interfaces—Joomla menus essentially *are* the user interface. Generally speaking, every piece of content that is accessible through the Joomla system has to be connected to a menu. In most cases, content is inaccessible to the web visitor if a menu hasn't been created to link to it.

The Menu Manager (see Figure 5-18) is truly the core of the Joomla system. Second only to the Article Manager, proper configuration of the Menu Manager is critical to your site's user appeal. If visitors can't find and access the content they're looking to read, then that content doesn't exist for them. If the preplanned hierarchical structure you designed in Chapter 4 was thorough, you may not have to spend very much time in the Menu Manager. After all, if the categories are well set to represent the content of your site, new content will be filed properly as it is created, and visitors will have easy access to the categories and sections that lead to that content.

Figure 5-18. *The Menu Manager shows all of the menu "categories" that hold menu items.*

Every menu in the Menu Manager represents the top level of that menu. A menu is much like a section or a category: it organizes items but does not hold the items itself. Instead, the individual entries in a menu (which are presented on the display as links to content) are stored as menu items connected to the menu.

To access the items held by a menu, click the Menu items icon for any menu row in the Menu Manager. The Menu Item Manager list will display the items attached to that menu. In Figure 5-19, you can see the menu items associated with the Main Menu (mainmenu). From the Menu Item Manager, the administrator can set the default menu item, publish or unpublish an item, and change the item order using the Order column.

One of the features that makes Joomla particularly user-friendly is the ability to disable features rather than remove them from the system. If you don't need a feature at the moment, you can simply unpublish it. That way if you later decide that it really *does* belong on your site, you don't have to reconstruct it—you merely enable it again. On the other hand, if you're sure that it isn't needed, you can delete it at that time. Since menus are essentially filing categories, it is very easy to move one or more items to another menu.

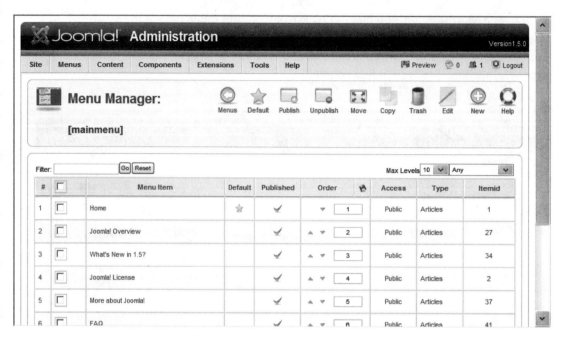

Figure 5-19. *From the Menu Item Manager, you can edit or move menu items.*

If you click the Move icon with one or more items selected, the Move Menu Items window is displayed (see Figure 5-20). In this window, select a destination menu and click the Move icon to transfer the items to the new menu.

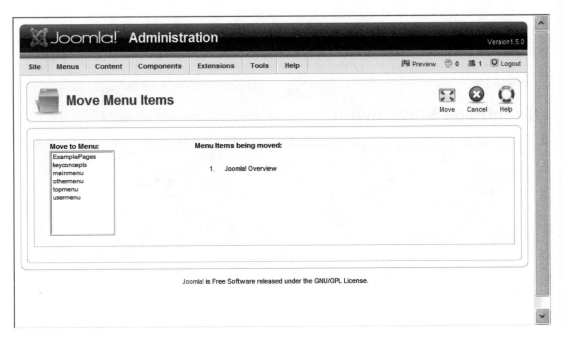

Figure 5-20. *The Move Menu Items window can move items from one menu to another.*

To edit a menu item, click the name of the menu item or check the box next to the name, and then click the Edit icon. The menu item editor (see Figure 5-21) will display the parameters for that item. This editing screen will vary depending on the type of menu item being edited. The one displayed in the figure is a Frontpage blog layout; a standard section layout, for example, will have different options.

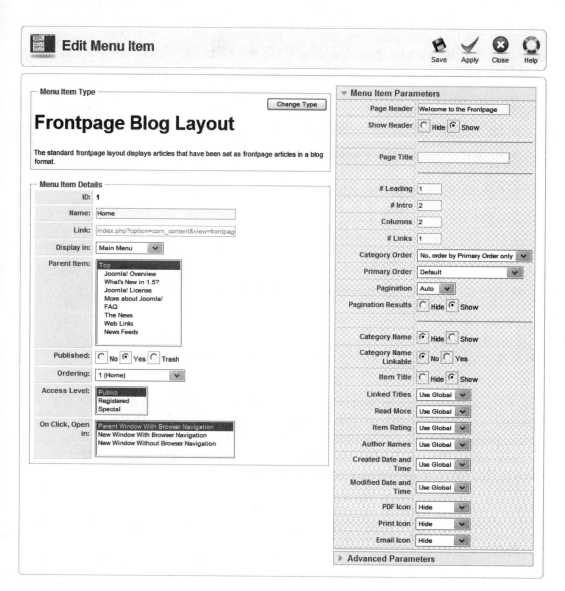

Figure 5-21. *The menu item editor display will vary depending on the type of menu item selected.*

Extension Manager

The Extension Manager (see Figure 5-22) provides a centralized place where you can install new extensions or examine the extensions that have already been installed on the system. This manager is used to administer components, modules, plug-ins, languages, and templates. It also allows you to uninstall any of these items.

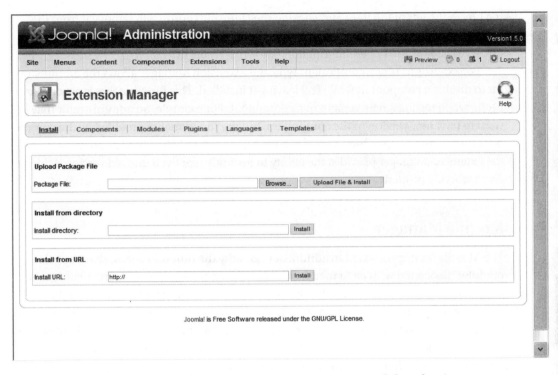

Figure 5-22. *The Extension Manager lets you install components, modules, plug-ins, languages, and templates.*

There are three possible methods that Joomla can use to access and retrieve items for installation:

- *Upload Package File*: Joomla includes the Browse feature to allow you to locate the archive file for the package that holds the extension to be installed. Joomla can extract files from either ZIP archives or tarball archives.

- *Install from directory*: Joomla allows the selection of a local directory where the extension can be read. Note that the web server must have permissions to access this directory or Joomla will return an error.

- *Install from URL*: This option is very convenient—especially if you are managing the Joomla system from a remote client (such as an access point terminal). If you have the URL of a remote component or template, you can simply point the Joomla system at it and the CMS itself will download and install the component.

Once the extension is installed, it can be managed by the appropriate Administrator interface manager (e.g., modules are configured in the Module Manager). The Extension Manager will let you to remove anything that you've installed through it. Simply checking the box to the left of the item and clicking the Uninstall button will remove it from the Joomla system. Joomla has error checking to prevent you from removing extensions that are necessary for the system to function (known as a *core extensions*).

For extensions of the component type, the Extension Manager allows the administrator to disable a component while still leaving it installed. This functionality is especially useful when testing a new version of a component. For example, an administrator may want to try a new version of the component, but the functionality provided by the component is site critical. Since the old component can be unpublished but left on the system, the Extension Manager provides the ability to instantly reactivate the old version if things aren't working properly.

Module Manager

The Module Manager is used to administer not only the modules themselves, but also modules associated with each menu. In Joomla, a menu represents an organizational element, much like a category, that holds the list of menu items. However, a menu doesn't actually display anything—the presentation is left to a module associated with it. When a new menu is created, a module for menu display is automatically created and linked to the menu. When you open the Module Manager, you will see a display list of all of the modules activated in the system, as shown in Figure 5-23.

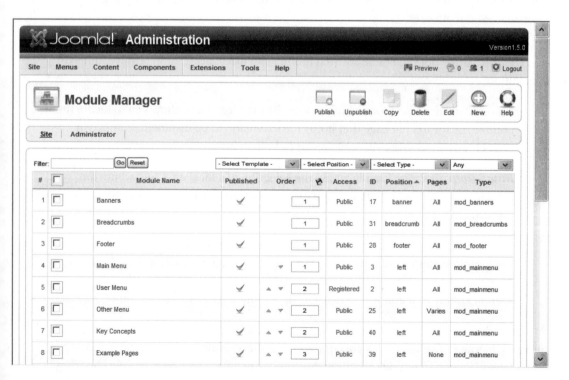

Figure 5-23. *The Module Manager can be used to manage or delete active modules.*

Clicking the name of a module will display the configuration screen for it. In the case of many modules, the configuration screen offers more than the standard details settings. As you can see in Figure 5-24, the Banners module has almost a dozen specialized parameters (shown in the Parameters frame) that apply specifically to it.

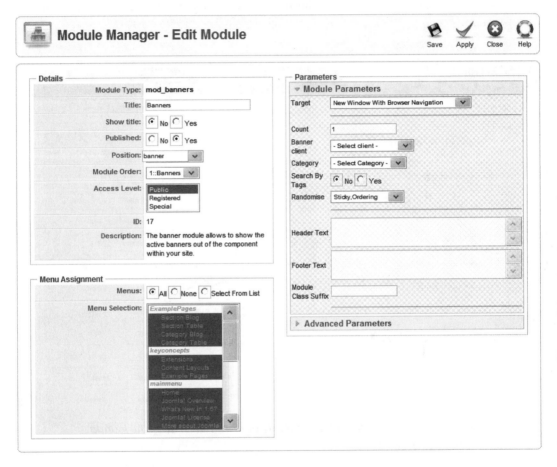

Figure 5-24. *The Banners module has numerous custom settings available that govern its behavior.*

Modules generally appear at predefined places within a template. However, Joomla allows the administrator to configure modules so that they only appear when particular menus are displayed. In the Menu Assignment frame of the configuration screen, you can set the pages where the module can appear. For example, you could configure a poll module so that the voting form only appears when either the Frontpage or the Visitor Input category is active.

Plugin Manager

Plug-ins have the lowest-level interface into the Joomla system, so they have the most
power to change how the CMS functions. Plug-ins are designed to sit between the Joomla
system and the user/browser. The Plugin Manager (see Figure 5-25) provides the administrative interface to publish, unpublish, organize, and edit the plug-ins installed on the
system.

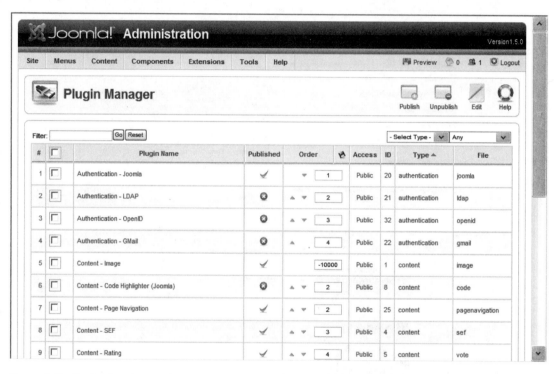

Figure 5-25. *Each plug-in can intercept and/or modify information sent by the Joomla
system before it reaches the user.*

The most comprehensible plug-ins are perhaps the text editors used for modifying
content. The TinyMCE editor is actually a plug-in named `tinymce`. In Joomla, all articles
are stored in the database as HTML text content. An editor plug-in sits between the
Joomla system output and the user.

When a user edits an article, Joomla retrieves the article from the database and
prepares to display the raw HTML code that represents the article in a text-editing box.
TinyMCE intercepts this HTML code and converts it into WYSIWYG content, so, for
example, bold text is displayed as bold text and inserted pictures actually appear in the
user's browser.

Likewise, in the opposite direction, when a user clicks the Apply or Save buttons, TinyMCE takes the displayed content, converts it back to raw HTML, and hands the HTML text to Joomla for proper article storage.

The user interacts a great deal with most editor plug-ins. Most plug-ins, unlike editor plug-ins, don't provide user interface functionality but instead provide background logic, such as various methods of user authentication for foundation-level interaction with the CMS.

From the Plugin Manager, you can edit many of the parameters that define how a plug-in governs user interaction and behind-the-screens execution. TinyMCE provides a large number of parameters (see Figure 5-26) that can be set by the administrator to modify everything from the text direction to the background code cleanup process.

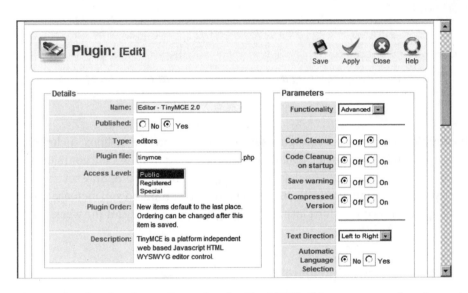

Figure 5-26. *The plug-in configuration for TinyMCE holds parameters that determine both display and back-end processing.*

Mail Manager

Joomla contains a small back-end mail system so that users can send messages to the administrator users. The mailbox can be examined through the Private Messaging screen, as shown in Figure 5-27. This primitive mail system will not take the place of a standard e-mail account, but can help centralize site-specific communication.

Figure 5-27. *The Private Messaging screen displays the Administrator interface for receiving messages.*

Each administrative user can configure settings for their private mailbox, including whether to lock the inbox or provide a mail forwarding setting (through the configuration screen shown in Figure 5-28). By default, messages are purged after only seven days. Unless you have a high-traffic/high-message site, I recommend you increase this value to around 30 days so you don't lose any messages if you're away for the week.

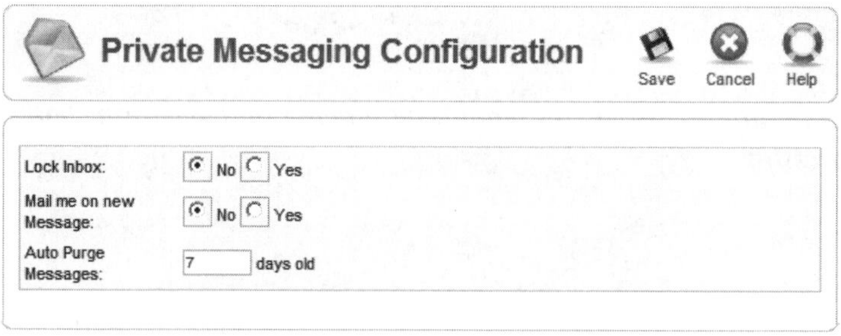

Figure 5-28. *The Private Messaging Configuration screen allows you to set auto-purge and other options.*

Mass Mail Manager

A Joomla administrator may need to send a bulk e-mail to all of the site users for a site-related occasion, a maintenance shutdown, a security alert, or another event. The Mass Mail Manager (see Figure 5-29) lets the administrator send a bulk message to all members of a particular group. These messages are sent through the Joomla mail system, so if no SMTP server is set up in the Global Configuration Manager, they will only be sent within the site mail system.

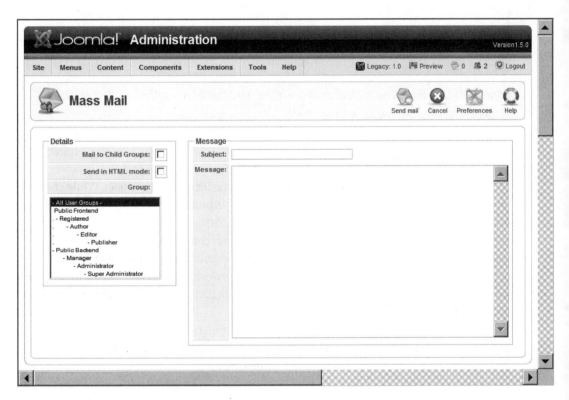

Figure 5-29. *The Mass Mail Manager allows a mass message to be sent to a group of users.*

If you would like to add a subject prefix or body suffix (such as a site signature), you can click the Preferences button and set these parameters in the Edit Configuration panel (see Figure 5-30).

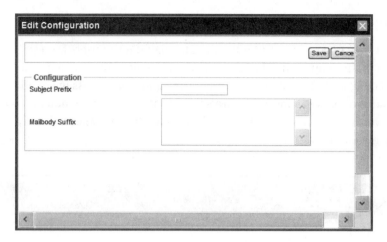

Figure 5-30. *The Edit Configuration window for the Mass Mail preferences lets you add a subject prefix or body suffix to the e-mail.*

Global Check-In

When an article is being edited, it is automatically checked out to the user. While checked out, no other user can edit it until it's checked in. This prevents conflicts of two users trying to make changes to the same document.

On a discontinuous system like the Web, however, connections will often be lost or users will close their browser window without checking in the currently displayed document. For that reason, the Administrator interface provides the Global Check-in function, which, when selected from the Tools menu, checks in all items that are currently checked out (see Figure 5-31).

Make sure that all users are logged off of the system before you execute this option. If a legitimate user is editing content and this routine is run, when they attempt to save the changes they've made, those changes will be discarded.

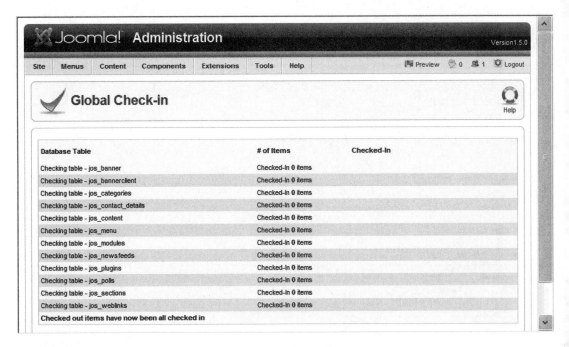

Figure 5-31. *The Global Check-in function will check in all user items.*

System Info

A small but useful screen is the System Info screen (see Figure 5-32), which can be accessed by the like-named option in the Help menu. System Info lists all of the configuration data accessible to the server that is not available for simple modification through the Global Configuration Manager.

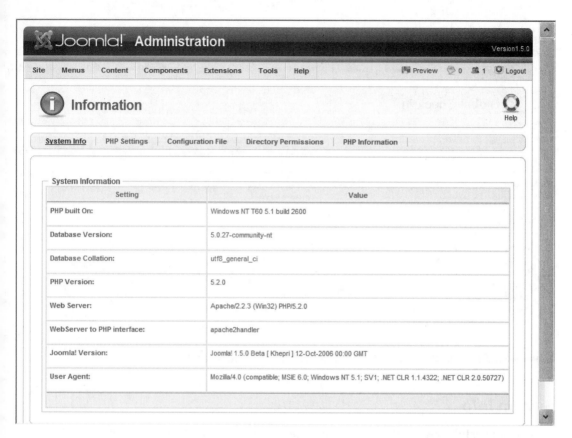

Figure 5-32. *The System Info screen displays system configuration and status information.*

System Info actually consists of five different panels, as follows:

- *System Info*: This panel gives a variety of information, including the current version details of the web server; information on MySQL, the database, and the PHP engine; collation settings; and even the details of the Joomla revision.

- *PHP Settings*: This panel shows the PHP directives that are relevant to Joomla and their current settings.

- *Configuration File*: This panel displays the current Joomla settings that are stored in the configuration.php file traditionally found in the Joomla root directory.

- *Directory Permissions*: This panel indicates the write permissions on directories important to Joomla, including the directories that hold plug-ins, modules, templates, and cache files.

- *PHP Information*: This screen presents information supplied by the `PHPinfo()` function call—the same one demonstrated in Chapter 3 to confirm that the PHP installation was running properly.

Backing Up the Joomla! Installation

All of the content and many of the Joomla settings are held in the various tables in the Joomla database. However, all of the installed extensions and the site configuration data are stored in files within the Joomla folder hierarchy. To perform a complete Joomla site backup, you'll need a method of saving the Joomla files in addition to the data.

One mistake many new Joomla administrators make is forgetting to back up the Joomla database. While it is important to back up the files on the FTP server, all of the real content of a Joomla site is stored in the MySQL database. Therefore, you will need to use MySQL to back up your data store. In Figure 5-33, you can see a list of all of the tables used by the Joomla system.

Despite the number of tables in the database, the database backup is considerably easier than the file backup in most circumstances. Depending on the size of the site, there is generally less data in the database, in terms of total number of bytes, than in the files that make up the site. Additionally, there are several methods of backing up a MySQL database. Most depend on the type of server on which the MySQL database is stored. There are also a number of plug-ins available for performing backups of the Joomla database. You can find many of them at `http://extensions.Joomla.org`.

■**Tip** Whenever you run a database backup, make sure you enable the Quote Names option so that quotation marks are put around all of the string content. This will prevent potential conflicts when restoring the database in case some of the fields have keywords stored in them.

---

jos_banner	MyISAM	5
jos_bannerclient	MyISAM	1
jos_bannertrack	MyISAM	0
jos_categories	MyISAM	15
jos_components	MyISAM	33
jos_contact_details	MyISAM	1
jos_content	MyISAM	6
jos_content_frontpage	MyISAM	4
jos_content_rating	MyISAM	0
jos_core_acl_aro	MyISAM	2
jos_core_acl_aro_groups	MyISAM	11
jos_core_acl_aro_sections	MyISAM	1
jos_core_acl_groups_aro_map	MyISAM	2
jos_core_log_items	MyISAM	0
jos_core_log_searches	MyISAM	3
jos_groups	MyISAM	3
jos_menu	MyISAM	33
jos_menu_types	MyISAM	8
jos_messages	MyISAM	2
jos_messages_cfg	MyISAM	0
jos_modules	MyISAM	43
jos_modules_menu	MyISAM	26
jos_newsfeeds	MyISAM	9
jos_plugins	MyISAM	27
jos_polls	MyISAM	1
jos_poll_data	MyISAM	12
jos_poll_date	MyISAM	8
jos_poll_menu	MyISAM	1
jos_sections	MyISAM	1
jos_session	MyISAM	1
jos_stats_agents	MyISAM	0
jos_templates_menu	MyISAM	2
jos_template_positions	MyISAM	34
jos_users	MyISAM	2
jos_weblinks	MyISAM	5

Figure 5-33. *There are many tables used by the Joomla system.*

Backing Up Through phpMyAdmin

GoDaddy (www.godaddy.com), like many web host providers, uses the online phpMyAdmin utility to allow user configuration of the shared MySQL database. Through the web interface, the utility offers complete administration capabilities, including full database and table creation, MySQL configuration, querying, and even table data editing.

Importantly for Joomla users, phpMyAdmin also provides database export capabilities, so it is possible to back up a remote site. The utility can export the complete database along with all contained tables and data.

■Note The phpMyAdmin application is free and open source. If you have set up your own web server and would like to be able to administer your MySQL database server via the Web, you can install it on your server. You can find the latest version on SourceForge (https://sf.net/projects/phpmyadmin) or go to the phpMyAdmin home page (www.phpmyadmin.net).

In Figure 5-34, you can see the Export screen with all of the options set up for best Joomla configuration. When you click the Go button, the utility will create a ZIP archive with all of the SQL definitions to reconstruct the tables and data they contain, which can be saved or e-mailed to a specified address. If you can perform a site backup every week, you will be pretty well set to recover from a catastrophic site failure.

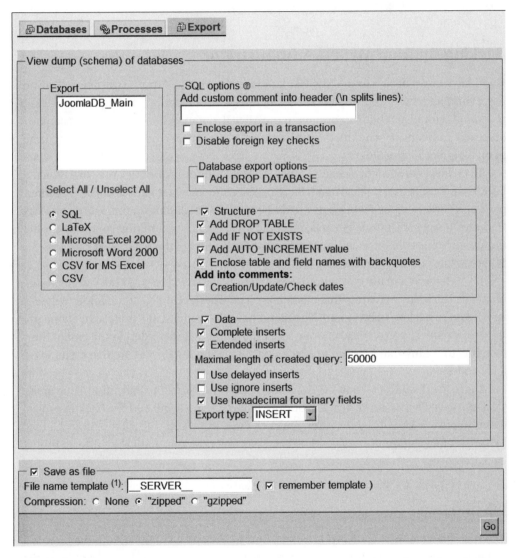

Figure 5-34. *Set your Export settings from phpMyAdmin to match those shown here for best Joomla backup.*

Restoring the Backup

To restore the backup, you need only open the phpMyAdmin interface, select the database where you'll restore the Joomla data, and click the SQL tab. Click the Browse button to select your file, and click the Go button to execute the SQL code contained in the file. This SQL code will recreate the structure or schema of the Joomla database exactly as it was backed up and restore the data contained in it.

Backing Up from MySQL Administrator

If you have direct access to the MySQL database, the MySQL Administrator application has a complete interface available for easily setting up a database backup. Each backup scenario is stored as a backup project in the MySQL database. Backup projects can be executed manually or scheduled to automatically execute at a particular date and time or on a periodic schedule.

To create a new backup scenario, open MySQL Administrator, click the New Project button, and name the project WeeklyBackup. Select the `joomla` database in the Schemata pane and click the right-facing arrow to add it to the list of databases that will be archived. Click the Advanced Options tab and select the ANSI Quotes option (this is equivalent to the Quote Names option mentioned earlier) at the bottom of the page. Next click the Schedule tab.

If you haven't already configured a connection, you need to go to the Connection Manager. Click the "Schedule this backup project" check box. Select the folder where you want the backup to be stored. The filename will automatically match the name of the project unless you want to change it. A time stamp will be added to the end of the filename to ensure that it's unique and to make locating the proper archive easier when it is needed.

Leave the default selection of "Execute backup weekly" in the Execution Time area. Click the Save Backup button on the bottom of the screen. It will add the backup project definition to the MySQL server. After you click the button, you will see the project added to the list of backup projects. The MySQL system will now automatically perform this backup process each week.

File Backup

Although bandwidth intensive, it is usually best to back up all of the files in the Joomla installation. Since Joomla is revised constantly, it is possible that backing up only particular files will cause compatibility issues if you install a newer version.

For a Joomla installation on a local server, you can simply use your operating system's built-in archiving capabilities to create a ZIP or tarball file of the entire web site folder. Alternatively, you can use an automated backup utility such as DriveImage XML (there's a free download at www.runtime.org/dixml.htm) or Areca Backup (written in Java and available free from http://sourceforge.net/projects/areca).

When the Joomla installation is remote, you can simply use the FTP client to copy the installation to your local drive. You can also use an FTP-based backup utility such as Backup Easy (http://sourceforge.net/projects/bueasy) to archive the files for you. FTP-based backup utilities generally feature the same type of scheduled backup features available through the MySQL Administrator application.

If you want to keep your backup to a bare minimum, be sure at least to archive the following files and folders:

- configuration.php: Holds all of the key administrative parameters of the Joomla site, such as database access settings and site metadata information. This file should always be backed up.

- templates *folder*: If you have installed a new template for your site, back up all of the templates in the folder.

- administration/templates *folder*: Some administrators change the template that determines the presentation of the Administrator interface. If you've added administrative templates, you'll find them in the folder.

- modules *folder*: If you've added any new or custom modules, they will be stored in this folder. Also stored in this folder will be any configuration settings that have be made for any of the modules. Archiving the folder will ensure you didn't miss anything.

- components *folder*: Like the modules folder, this folder contains any custom installations and all of the user settings that apply to the components.

- administration/components *folder*: Components may have installed an administration component for managing the execution of the extension. It will be stored in this folder.

- language *folder*: If you installed any additional language packs, they will be stored here.

- plugins *folder*: Any added plug-ins will be stored in this folder. Additionally, plug-in settings are stored in the folder.

Backing up these folders (in addition to the database) should preserve the core of your site should anything happen to it. After you reinstall the Joomla image on a revived server, copy the files back to their appropriate locations.

Security

Joomla's low barrier to entry makes it ideal for almost anyone with a foundation level of technical expertise (or willingness to learn). The drawback to Joomla's ease of installation and administration is the possibility that the site will be left wide open from a security standpoint. I have tried to cover some of the most obvious security loopholes in the installation and configuration chapters.

While, a complete bullet-proofing of your site is beyond the scope of this book, there are a few guidelines that an administrator can follow to minimize the chance of a security breach. Remember that security is a moving target and hackers always find new ways into new technology. Therefore, be sure to watch the Joomla web site (www.joomla.org) for upgrades to the Joomla CMS. Often these upgrades will close discovered security holes, so you want to make sure you stay current.

To maximize your Joomla security, follow these general suggestions:

- Remove any phpInfo() file from your web server since a hacker could execute it and gain a great deal of site configuration information.

- Delete installation files from the server once installation is complete.

- Move the configuration.php file outside the public access area. This file contains your database access account *and* password, so if accessed could provide a hacker with the keys to the kingdom.

- Change the default names of the administrator accounts, both for Joomla and the MySQL database.

- Password protect directories with .htaccess files (if you're running Joomla on Apache).

- Restrict access to IPs with .htaccess.

- Configure PHP filters mod_security and mod_rewrite to block attacks.

- Restrict MySQL accounts.

By making sure that these basic security barriers are in place, you dramatically reduce the chances that your site will be hacked or destroyed by outsiders. Performing a security spot-check periodically (view the Joomla security checklist at http://forum.joomla.org/index.php/topic,81058.0.html) becomes more important the longer a site remains on the net. The longer a site operates, the more buildup there is of obsolete, unused user accounts (perhaps with significant privileges) and antiquated security settings (sometimes made temporarily for an extension installation and then forgotten).

And remember that one of the most powerful tools in preventing disaster if hacking does occur is a solid backup of the site. If someone does penetrate your site and unfortunately manages to bring it down or alter it in some unpleasant way, a secure up-to-date backup can make all the difference in the world.

Writable Directories

Making a directory writable, as you may have to do for search engine–friendly (SEF) folders and cache capabilities, can potentially create security vulnerabilities. The easiest setting for the directory is a chmod value of 755 (read/write/execute for owner, read/execute for group, and no access for others).

One method of minimizing potential danger is changing the owner group of the directory to the web server account and setting the directory's permissions to a chmod value of 770 (read/write/execute for owner and group; no access for others). That will seal off general users from having any access to the folder. Only the account with full permissions—the web server account—will have access.

■**Caution** You should never have a directory set to a chmod of 777, which gives everyone write access. If you can control the security, even a temporary account with write access should be password protected.

Conclusion

Administration of a Joomla site is made much easier by the Administrator web interface, which is not only easy to use, but can be accessed from almost anywhere. The various managers in Joomla (Template Manager, User Manager, etc.) effectively divide the tasks by the various administrative roles, such as managing the presentation, administering content, and configuring the actual site.

Although Joomla runs very well after the initial installation, it is important that a web master consider site administration a task to be performed at regular intervals. Backups, content reorganization, content archival, and security administration are just a few of the jobs that should be carried out periodically to keep the site running smoothly. One of the joys of using Joomla is the ease at which the site can be administered, since complex tasks such as content management and filing take only a few mouse clicks.

Much of the administrative interface you've already experienced. In this chapter, you examined each area of the Administrator interface (represented by the manager screens) in depth, so you can now understand the complete system. Proper administration is critical not just to good site functioning, but also to the presentation and organization of the site for visitors. In the next chapter, you're going to do something most Joomla site operators would like to do: created a personalized site template.

CHAPTER 6

■ ■ ■

Creating Your Own Templates

A key reason that Joomla has been able to thrive in the CMS space despite the numerous excellent competitors is its ability to be extended by users. For instance, the ease with which it's possible to design a new template puts customization within the reach of the average Joomla user. You won't be using Joomla long before you will want to either create your own templates or make substantial modifications to an existing template.

On a word processor, a resume template has the general layout and basic content items that should be present in the document. The job applicant then fills in the personal information such as name, contact information, and work history. A Joomla template works in the same fashion, except that the Joomla CMS retrieves content from the database and fills in the blanks of the template.

The template (or presentation) is completely separate from the content. By selecting a new template, you can change the look of a site from the presentation shown in Figure 6-1 to the one shown in Figure 6-2 with a single click in the Template Manager.

In this chapter, you'll learn how to create a new template that reflects the identity of your web site. The creation of the graphics for the template will be demonstrated in program called GIMP. If you're unfamiliar with GIMP, you'll be glad to discover that it is a free, open source equivalent of Adobe Photoshop. GIMP is available for all the major operating system platforms (Windows, Mac OS, and Linux).

Since the structure of a template can be confusing at first, you can begin down the road of template knowledge by following the instructions in the Quickstart section to create a simple Hello Joomla template. Hello Joomla is a template of the most rudimentary kind. Once the Quickstart template basics have been covered, you can advance to creating a substantial style sheet–based template.

Latest News

- Another Article
- What is an Adjustable Rate Mortgage (ARM)?
- My First Article

What is an Adjustable Rate Mortgage (ARM)?

What is an Adjustable Rate Mortgage (ARM) ?

Adjustable rate mortgages (ARMs) differ from fixed rate mortgages (the more traditional mortgage) in that the rate of the loan changes over the life of the loan. What does this mean to you? That means that the rate of interest you are paying when you start (let's say 4.25%) doesn't remain the same for the life of the loan. It could go up (to 4.50%, for example) or down (to 4.00%). That means that your monthly payments may also go up or down.

Joomla! is used for?

- ○ Community Sites
- ○ Public Brand Sites
- ○ eCommerce
- ○ Blogs
- ○ Intranets
- ○ Photo and Media Sites
- ○ All of the Above!

[Vote]

[Results]

We have 2

Figure 6-1. *A site using a text-based template*

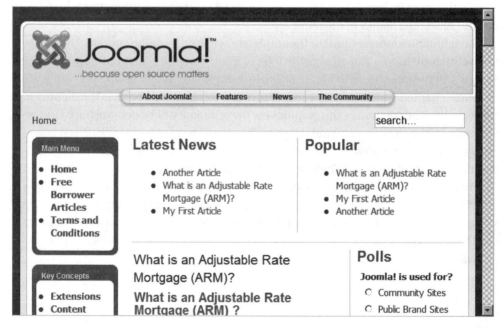

Figure 6-2. *A site using a graphics-heavy template*

Quickstart to Creating a Hello Joomla! Template

A Joomla template is made up of a number of files that work together to display the content held in the database. A template depends on at least two main files:

- `templateDetails.xml`: An XML metadata file used by Joomla to retrieve information about the template (name of the template, author, creation date, etc.). It also contains a list of the files that make up the template itself. The file list must include all index files, style sheets, images, media, and any other files used by the template.

- `index.php`: A file that contains the presentation code to display text, components, and modules. It is the central file that loads modules, parses the Joomla template data, and handles the primary display.

Joomla templates are located on the web server in the `\templates` directory. Each template has its own directory and that directory must exactly match the name of the template. For example, the template `rhuk_milkyway` must be located in a directory named `rhuk_milkyway`. Joomla is case-sensitive, so if the template is named `rhuk_milkyway`, a directory named `RHUK_MILKYWAY` won't be recognized as holding the template.

The `\templates` directory holds a separate folder for each template that you currently have installed. It may be helpful for you to examine the contents of one or more of these folders. You'll see that no matter how different the templates appear when presenting content, the type and number of files used to create them are very similar.

■Note Templates have changed tremendously from Joomla version 1.0 to 1.5. While many older templates used the patTemplate engine as the core technology to render their output, Joomla 1.5 has done away with patTemplate and includes it only for backward compatibility. The object framework has also been rewritten from the ground up. Therefore, if you have experience with designing older templates, the implementation and structure have changed almost entirely. Examine the sample templates in this chapter as well as the site default template to understand the workings of the new template engine. If you simply want to use a Joomla 1.0 template with a 1.5 deployment, you will need to turn on the System - Legacy plug-in in the Plugin Manager.

Creating the Hello Joomla! Template Files

You'll create the two Hello Joomla template files using your text editor of choice (anything from Windows Notepad to a sophisticated program editor). To begin, you will need a new folder to hold these files.

Create a folder named \tmplHelloJoomla in the \templates folder. If you're developing on a staging server, the path to the folder may look like this:

```
C:/Program Files/Apache Software Foundation/
    Apache2.2/htdocs/templates/tmplHelloJoomla
```

Note In an attempt to keep things simple, these instructions will have you manually installing the template files and folders. Templates are generally stored as a ZIP archive, and an administrator uses the Extensions ➤ Install/Uninstall option to insert the template into the system. For development, creating a new ZIP archive each time you make a change to a file, particularly when frequent changes are likely, is impractical. Instead, you can either create the template directory manually if you're running Joomla on a staging server or upload it via FTP if a remote host is being used.

Create the following basic index.php file in your text editor and save it to the \tmplHelloJoomla folder:

```
<html>
<head>
<jdoc:include type="head" />
</head>

<body>
<jdoc:include type="message" />
<div class="center" align="center">Hello World!</div>
<jdoc:include type="modules" name="debug" />
</body>
</html>
```

This index.php file is simplified to the point where it doesn't even comply with simple HTML rules, such as including a DOCTYPE parameter. When you create a full template later in this chapter, you will see all of the bells and whistles that should be included with even a basic template. For the purposes of the Hello Joomla template, however, you can forego them to make the code as straightforward as possible.

In the index.php file, the first Joomla code is the <jdoc:include type="head" /> statement, which inserts the site-specific information into the header. This directive will even insert the metadata used by search engines. For the home page of my web site, for example, the following information is sent to the visiting browser by the header include directive:

```
<title>LoanStaircase.com</title>
<meta name="generator" content="Joomla! 1.5" />
<meta name="description" content="Loan Staircase -- Track your loan or loans" />
<meta http-equiv="Content-Type" content="text/html; charset=utf-8" />
<meta name="robots" content="index, follow" />
<meta name="keywords" content="Loans, Mortgage" />
<link href="http://localhost/favicon.ico"
      rel="shortcut icon" type="image/x-icon" />
```

This header information will change depending on the page that the template is rendering (for example, the Frontpage will be different from article pages). The header information will be drawn from the menu or article that is being presented.

■**Note** Many beginning Joomla users want to change the title of the Frontpage and they look in vain at the template code. As you can see, all titles are generated dynamically. So where is the title obtained for the Frontpage? Go to the items held in the Main Menu (through Menus ➤ Main Menu). Edit the first item in the menu (generally named "Home") to show the Page Title parameter. Set that parameter to the text you want as the title of your Joomla home page.

The second Joomla statement is <jdoc:include type="message" />, which simply includes any server messages in the post. In most cases, no messages will exist, so no extra content will be added.

The final Joomla statement, <jdoc:include type="modules" name="debug" />, references the debug module. Normally, this doesn't display anything. However, if you turn on the Enable Debugging option in the Global Configuration screen (available under the Site ➤ Configuration menu), the debugging information will be displayed below the page. This information can be extremely helpful, as it will describe the execution of the template page. For example, the Frontpage debug information may appear like this:

```
Application 0.156 afterLoadFramework
Application 0.233 afterStartFramework
Application 0.268 afterDisplayOutput
```

The numbers that follow the Application denotation describe the page-rendering time for each step in the sequence. If your page is slow to load, you can begin to determine the cause of the delay by checking where the slowdown occurred.

To complete the template, you need to create the XML details file that directs the Joomla system to the template files. Enter the following code into your text editor and save the file as templateDetails.xml to your \tmplHelloJoomla directory:

```xml
<?xml version="1.0" encoding="utf-8"?>
<install version="1.5" type="template">
    <name>Hello Joomla template</name>
    <description>
    Simplest template in the Joomla world.
    </description>
    <files>
    <filename>index.php</filename>
    <filename>templateDetails.xml</filename>
    </files>
</install>
```

That's it! Go to the Template Manager (under the Extensions menu) in the Joomla Administrator interface. You will see your new template listed there. Click the radio button to the left of the template name to select it, and then click the Default button, as shown in Figure 6-3.

Figure 6-3. *Select the Hello Joomla template and click the Default button to make it the default template.*

Open a browser window and go to the Frontpage of your site. If the template is working properly, you will see the "Hello World!" greeting, as shown in Figure 6-4. Congratulations, you've just created your first template!

Figure 6-4. *The browser displays the "Hello World!" greeting from the template.*

I know this template isn't very impressive. However, you now know the basic structure of a template and how Joomla PHP directives are included within the file.

The first problem with the Hello Joomla template is that it doesn't display any of the content from the site. Before you abandon this template for a more advanced template implementation, it would be a good idea to add a Joomla component to display some basic content.

Adding a Module and a Component to Hello Joomla!

With your primitive template working, it's time to add the instructions that would begin to make it a real template. After all, Joomla isn't much of a CMS if it can't display content. With only a couple of lines of code, you can add a single module and a single component to the template. The module will display the latest news items, and the component will display the text of the latest Frontpage article.

Open your Hello Joomla index.php file and add the bolded lines after the Hello World! element:

```
<div class="center" align="center">Hello World!</div>
<jdoc:include type="modules" name="user1" style="xhtml" />
<jdoc:include type="component" />
<jdoc:include type="modules" name="debug" />
```

In the first added line, the module directive adds the user1 module to display the Latest News title and a list of the latest news articles. The second new line adds a component that displays the text of the most recent Frontpage article.

You may notice that unlike the module directive, the component directive does not have a name attribute specified for the component. If there is no name specified, the component held in the system's $option request variable is used, which in most cases is the default content component. This default component, named com_content, will display the main body content for a page.

When you refresh the browser window, you should see the article contents, as shown in Figure 6-5.

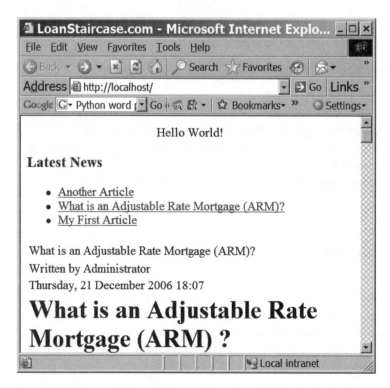

Figure 6-5. *The module and the component will display Joomla system content.*

All Joomla templates match the essential structure of this simple Hello Joomla template. Complete templates use style sheets to more closely control layout, graphics to make the display more robust, and template screenshot thumbnails to make administration easier. They also may feature a number of other enhancements. However, all templates follow the basic pattern of the template you just created.

Note If you are working on your staging server and your text editor program refuses to save over a file, telling you that the index.php or other file is "in use by another process or application," wait a few moments and try again. The PHP engine should release file access after a short time.

Modifying an Existing Template

With a primitive template under your belt, it is time to progress to a more powerful one. On most occasions, when you need a custom template, rather than starting from scratch, you will begin with an existing template as a foundation and tailor it to meet your needs. In this section, you'll make a slight modification to the main default template that ships with Joomla. It will provide your first real exposure to a commercial-grade template.

The default template includes the "Powered by Joomla" link at the bottom of the page, as shown in Figure 6-6. If you don't mind the attribution, please leave it, as it will expose more people to the technical wonder that is Joomla. However, most organizations prefer to give the appearance that their web site is a custom system; they don't want visitors seeing the wizard behind the curtain. This example describes how to remove the "Powered by Joomla" attribution.

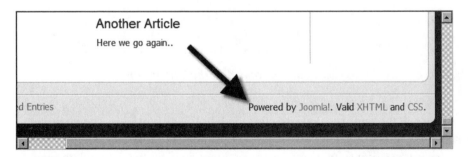

Figure 6-6. *A small "Powered by Joomla" text reference and link appear at the bottom of the template.*

Most of the display options for Joomla may be modified by using one of the tools provided by the graphical user interface. There are some functions, however, that you can control only by directly editing the template file. To remove the "Powered by" attribution, you will need to edit the PHP of the index page.

You may be intimidated when you look at the actual template code because it is much lengthier and more complex than the Hello Joomla template. However, if you look closely, you will see many of the same directives that you've already used.

Open the Template Manager (under the Extensions menu) in the Administrator interface. Select the rhuk_milkyway template and click the Edit button, as shown in Figure 6-7. The Edit function allows you to edit the various characteristics of the template, including setting any parameters the template supports. Template parameters are settings that an administrator can change without needing to edit the template code directly.

Figure 6-7. *Select the rhuk_milkyway template and click the Edit button.*

You need to edit the template code, so click the Edit HTML button, as shown in Figure 6-8, to open the Template HTML Editor. The Joomla Administrator interface provides a very basic text editor so that you can make minor changes to the template, even remotely without needing FTP or direct file access.

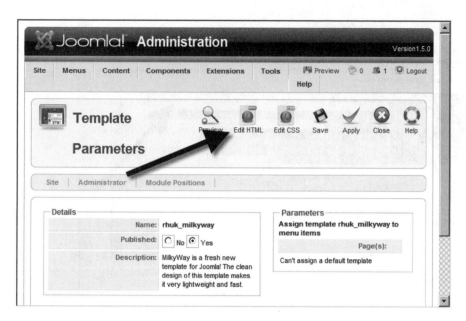

Figure 6-8. *Click the Edit HTML button to edit the index.php code.*

Scroll to the bottom of the template code to see the lines that generate the "Powered by" information, as shown in Figure 6-9 and should read as follows:

```
<p style="float:right; padding-right: 25px;">
    Powered by <a href="http://www.Joomla.org">Joomla!</a>. Valid <a
    href="http://validator.w3.org/check/referer">XHTML</a> and <a
    href="http://jigsaw.w3.org/css-validator/check/referer">CSS</a>.
</p>
```

Select that code and *Cut* (press Ctrl+C on Windows) those lines. It is always a good idea to use the cut option rather than the delete option when modifying a template. If the change results in some problem for the display, you can simply paste the old text back into the template.

If you open a browser window to display your home page, you'll find that the Joomla statement at the bottom is now gone, as shown in Figure 6-10.

While the editor in the Administrator interface is good for minor changes to a template, extensive modifications are best performed with a substantial text editor. In the next section, you'll find an overview of the most popular programs that are used for Joomla development and template creation.

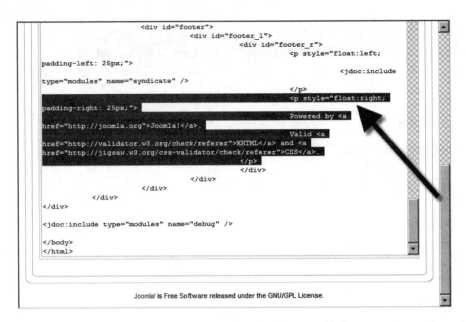

```
                        <div id="footer">
                            <div id="footer_l">
                                <div id="footer_r">
                                    <p style="float:left;
padding-left: 25px;">
                                                <jdoc:include
type="modules" name="syndicate" />
                                    </p>
                                    <p style="float:right;
padding-right: 25px;">
                                                Powered by <a
href="http://joomla.org">Joomla!</a>.
                                                Valid <a
href="http://validator.w3.org/check/referer">XHTML</a> and <a
href="http://jigsaw.w3.org/css-validator/check/referer">CSS</a>.
                                    </p>
                                </div>
                            </div>
                        </div>
                    </div>
                </div>
            </div>

            <jdoc:include type="modules" name="debug" />

        </body>
        </html>
```

Joomla! is Free Software released under the GNU/GPL License.

Figure 6-9. *Select the lines of code relating to the "Powered by" annotation and cut them from the file.*

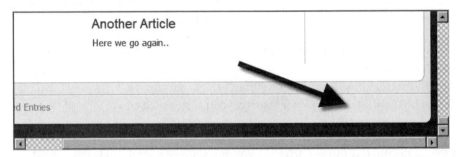

Figure 6-10. *If your edit was successful, the Joomla annotation will be gone.*

Tip Before you edit any source file, I recommend that you make a backup of the original file. For article content creation and parameter configuration, the Joomla user interface provides a sandbox environment that will keep you from making a change that will stop the system from functioning. This is not the case when you make direct file edits—a small change to a file could bring down the whole system. You don't want to need to reinstall Joomla if you can't correct the change that made everything stop functioning. With a backup, you can simply restore the initial file to return the system to functioning order.

Creating Templates with Web Editors

You can use various applications to create a new template. If you only have Windows Notepad, you can still author a suitable template with the bare-bones features available in that application. If you prefer the Emacs text editor, it can provide some powerful features, and the HTML-mode can help you to generate a conforming template. However, most Joomla designers and developers prefer an application that is a little more user-friendly.

There are two primary types of editors: WYSIWYG editors and program editors. Generally, Joomla designers tend to gravitate to WYSIWYG editors for their visual development needs. Joomla developers find the power of direct coding is more accessible in program editors.

WYSIWYG editors—such as Adobe Dreamweaver, Microsoft Expression Web, and Nvu—present an HTML page almost as it would appear in a web browser. These programs cater to designers who need to make visual modifications to page elements (such as tables) by clicking and dragging. While these programs generally have modes where direct source editing is possible, the coding interfaces have limited capabilities.

Program editors—such as Eclipse, jEdit, UltraEdit, and Leo—display the text just like Notepad or Emacs. However, these program editors have many additional features, including color syntax highlighting (especially useful for Joomla PHP coding), style sheet tag editing, advanced search and replace through general expressions, and automatic code formatting. While program editors sometimes offer some page preview capabilities, they are generally best used when performing nonvisual tasks such as PHP code design.

WYSIWYG Editors

Web editors that display a good facsimile of how a page will appear in the browser are excellent tools for creating and editing presentation. Although some sites can be popular despite a plain appearance—for example, the Drudge Report (see www.drudgereport.com)—such sites are definitely in the minority. Most sites will need a combination of looks and substance to meet the expectations of their visitors.

A web editor that can ease the visual design process can be an excellent investment. Joomla designers may choose from Adobe Dreamweaver, Microsoft Expression Web, and the open source Nvu with the Joomla plug-in. The selection you make in this area will have a great deal to do with your personal preferences, so you should evaluate all of the options.

Dummy Files to Aid WYSIWYG Editing

Joomla template design using an editor is inherently difficult because the pages are generated dynamically from the content of the system. This often creates a substantial barrier to WYSIWYG presentation for editing.

For example, simply loading the default Joomla template into Dreamweaver displays a window such as the one shown in Figure 6-11. The screen is blank because without the content that fills a template, there is nothing to display. Since these WYSIWYG programs don't actually execute the PHP code (which would be impractical), the rough tables are all that are displayed.

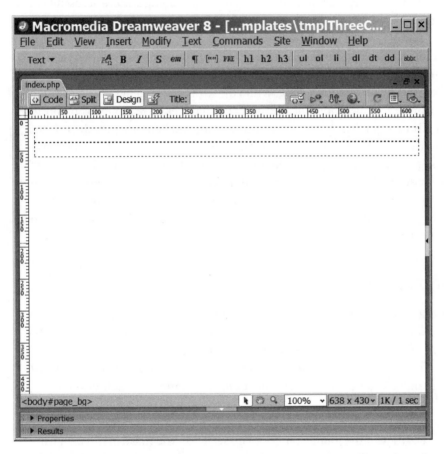

Figure 6-11. *Dreamweaver will not effectively display most templates when they are directly loaded.*

One useful method of overcoming this problem is to have the developer or the programmer of the template create dummy graphics and presentation items (such as style sheets, tables, headings, etc.). When the site is viewed in a browser, use the File ➤ Save As option to store the HTML rendition of the page with all the graphics and support files. Once saved to a local directory, the folder containing the support files will include the style sheets used by the page, as shown in Figure 6-12.

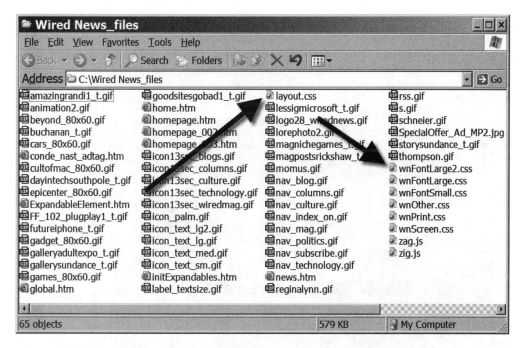

Figure 6-12. *The CSS files of the web page can be found in the support files folder.*

The files can be given to the web designer for editing and formatting. As long as no new styles are added to the CSS files without consulting the developer, the web designer will have fairly free reign to make changes to the presentation, color scheme, graphics, and so on. Once the visuals are complete, the refined files should be returned to the web developer, who can integrate the new presentation items back into the template.

Adobe Dreamweaver

Adobe Dreamweaver is a popular HTML editor, and with good reason. The available features for traditional page editing—particularly the asset library and template functionality—make it second to none in manual site administration. For Joomla template design, you'll be using only a minority of the application's features, since all of the actual content management is handled dynamically by Joomla.

With Dreamweaver's ability to edit style sheets, PHP code, and raw HTML, it is perhaps the dominant web editor for Joomla templates. The program is loaded with features such as FTP upload of modified files that make it a compelling program for Joomla use. Dreamweaver is available for Windows and Macintosh operating systems.

In Figure 6-13, I have loaded the dummy file version of one of my templates into Dreamweaver.

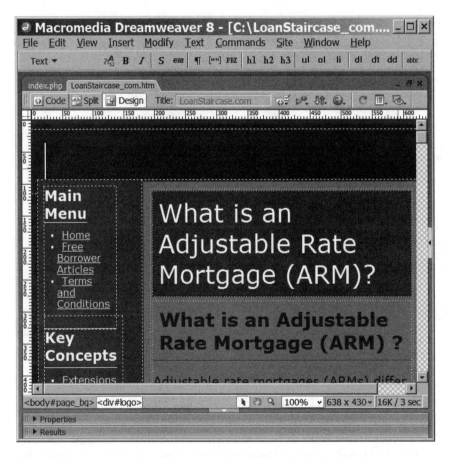

Figure 6-13. *Dreamweaver does an excellent job of displaying a template.*

Microsoft Expression Web

For a number of years, Microsoft FrontPage had been a popular editing option because it was included with the Microsoft Office suite of tools. In features and usability, however, it lagged far behind those offered by Adobe Dreamweaver. Finally, Microsoft replaced FrontPage with a much more powerful web editor called Expression Web, which has features competitive with Dreamweaver. Users may begin returning to Microsoft for web authoring.

Expression Web can do a fair job of displaying a saved Joomla template. It also has extremely powerful editing capabilities in the HTML code editing view, as shown in Figure 6-14. Unfortunately, Expression Web will run only on the Windows platform, leaving out the huge market of Macintosh web designers. Furthermore, the program does not support PHP, but instead focuses on Microsoft's alternative ASP technology. These two drawbacks limit the program's usefulness for Joomla users.

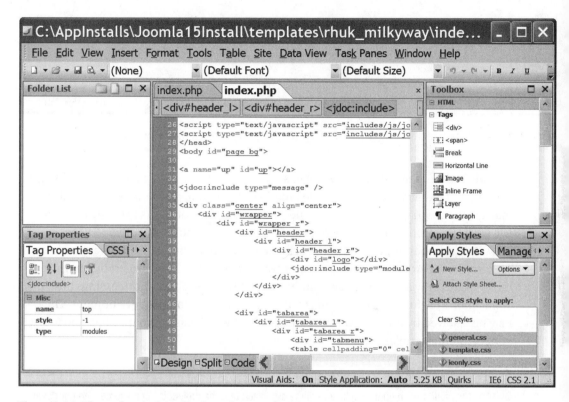

Figure 6-14. *The code window display of a template in Expression Web*

Nvu/KompoZer

Nvu (pronounced "EN-view") is a free, open source alternative to the popular commercial programs, available from www.nvu.com. While not nearly as full featured as the commercial alternatives, Nvu has enough capability to handle basic template design jobs. Nvu is available for all three major platforms (Linux, Windows, and Mac). Best of all, there is a Joomla plug-in for Nvu, called Nvu Template Builder, which can be downloaded for free from www.open4g.com.

Once you've downloaded the plug-in, use the Tools ➤ Extensions menu option in the Nvu interface to install it. After it's installed, it will appear in the Extensions window, as shown in Figure 6-15.

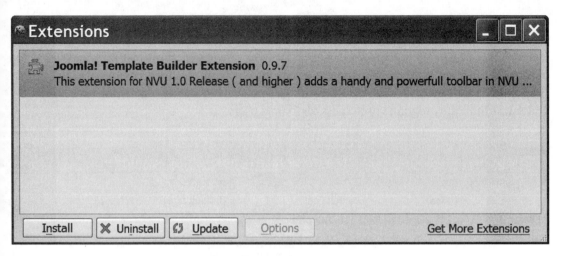

Figure 6-15. *The Extension Manager will display the Nvu Joomla extension once it is added.*

What makes the plug-in so useful to a Joomla developer is the automatic handling of a number of tedious Joomla tasks. The plug-in can generate a prototype of a template, manage the `templateDetails.xml` file, and provide toolbar buttons (see Figure 6-16) that will insert the proper Joomla macro code for common modules and other PHP code.

While this may appear the perfect choice for Joomla editing, the program has several drawbacks. At the time of this writing, the program has many frustrating bugs and incorporates only a limited understanding of style sheets. These shortcomings limit the application's usefulness for any intermediate to advanced Joomla development. They may be resolved by the time you read this book; in which case, Nvu may become the perfect Joomla template tool.

Note Nvu hadn't been upgraded in some time but, given that the project is open source, another developer has picked up the slack and begun remedying the bugs and other problems. The developer dubbed the new bug-fix version KompoZer (`http://kompozer.net`), but little of the foundation implementation has changed. So although the screens may say KompoZer, the application itself is, for the most part, Nvu.

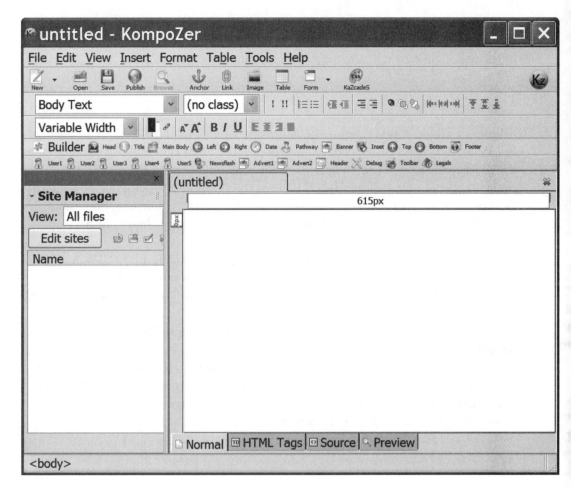

Figure 6-16. *Vanilla Nvu/KompoZer with Joomla toolbar and site manager*

Program Editors

Program editors are designed for coding rather than presentation. While they may offer some presentation capabilities, these editors are intended to provide easy management and editing of a coding project, and that is where their strengths lie. Three program editors useful for Joomla template creation are Eclipse, jEdit, and Leo. All three have unparalleled ability to search and replace (given that they each have an implementation of regular expressions) and manage code or code projects. They provide such capabilities as syntax and matching tag checking, and include extensive plug-in architectures.

Eclipse is the most powerful and robust, but its focus on Java development can make it unwieldy for smaller project development. The editor jEdit is perfect for single-file editing, but isn't built to manage entire projects. Leo has strengths in project organization and documentation, but lacks a robust user interface, which can sometimes make figuring out how to access various functions a challenge.

Eclipse

Eclipse is a project-based *integrated development environment* (IDE) originally created by IBM for its Visual Age line of development products. IBM later transferred the license of Eclipse to the Eclipse Foundation (a not-for-profit foundation) and made the environment open source. Eclipse (`www.eclipse.org`) has become an open-ended IDE that can host development in a number of languages: Java, PHP, Python, C++, Cobol, and others. Eclipse's plug-in architecture allows it to be extended for almost any development need.

Extremely popular among Java developers, Eclipse has a fantastic, full-featured interface that excels at the development of rich web client environments such as Joomla. In fact, many of the Joomla development team members use Eclipse for the development of the Joomla CMS.

Of particular usefulness to a Joomla developer is the Eclipse PHP IDE project manager, shown in Figure 6-17.

Eclipse is most useful for extension development and as such will be covered more extensively in Chapter 13. For most template-creation tasks, it has more complexity than is required by the typical Joomla designer or developer. Designed for multideveloper code-based projects, Eclipse can be cumbersome for single-file editing.

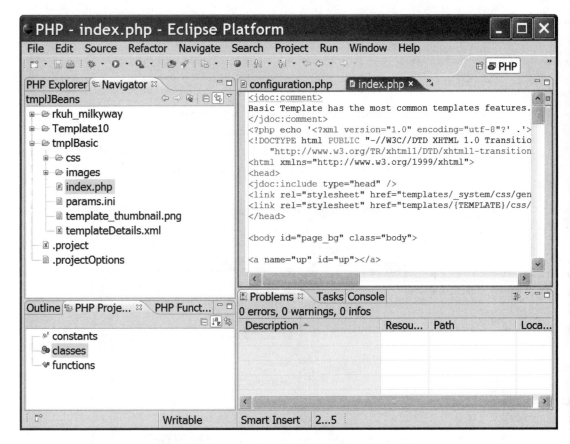

Figure 6-17. *Eclipse provides a rich framework in which the PHP IDE project can run.*

jEdit

Written in Java, jEdit (www.jedit.org) is a powerful open source program editor that is available for all platforms that can execute Java. Although jEdit itself is loaded with features, it is the thriving development community, which frequently releases industrial-grade plug-ins, that makes jEdit one of the strongest editors available. Extremely useful to Joomla developers, there are plug-ins for the following tasks (and many more):

- CSS editing

- PHP syntax checking

- Color-coded, side-by-side, file differencing

- In-program FTP uploading

- Beautifying code formatting

- Tabbed open file access (like Firefox)

- PHP parsing

- XML formatting

For most basic PHP work, I use jEdit because of its numerous features and plug-ins. In Figure 6-18, you can see the default Joomla template style sheet loaded into jEdit. In the figure, the style sheet plug-in is displaying the properties of the currently selected div#logo style, which can be edited with drop-down menu selections.

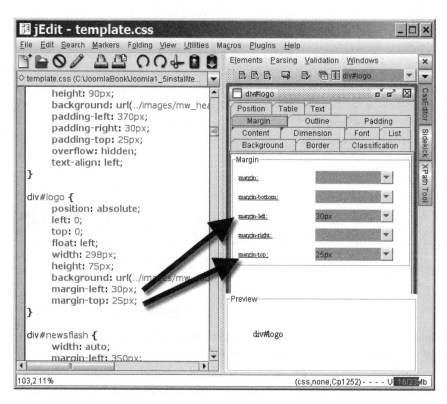

Figure 6-18. *One of the exceptional features of jEdit is the variety of plug-ins, such as this CSS editor.*

jEdit has two primary drawbacks for Joomla development:

- Having been written in Java, it can run on any platform, but many times I've encountered slowdown problems that were not readily explainable. I've noticed this same effect with other Java programs, and I'm not expert enough on the phenomenon to make a guess as to the root cause.

- Its reliance on plug-ins means that some features are not handled as well as they could be. Some functions, such as XML handling, are handled clumsily by the plug-in, while other text editors (such as UltraEdit) handle them natively and elegantly.

These complaints are minor, however, compared to the power and versatility offered by this application.

Leo

You were first introduced to the Leo (Literate Editor with Outlines) tool in Chapter 4, where you saw how to use it for planning the Joomla site structure. Leo is actually much more powerful than just an outlining tool. In fact, it can be used as a combined development and documentation system. Leo has complete capabilities for hosting source code (with full syntax highlighting) and also linking to external files to break them into virtual outlines.

For a simple example, let's say you were trying to develop a complex HTML web page. In an editor like jEdit, you would simply load the file into the editor and proceed with editing. However, what if the source code file were 20 pages long? Although not realistic for an HTML page, long files are not uncommon in complex PHP projects, especially ones that contain client-side JavaScript code.

For a long HTML page, it might be useful to divide the file into various parts, such as header, scripts, column1, column2, column3, and footer. In Leo, you can "virtually" break a file into just this sort of organization. Figure 6-19 shows a sample of such an implementation. I've taken a Joomla template and divided the file into outline headings, which are called *sections*. The arrows in the figure show the sections in the outline and their associated references in the code pane:

- The code begins with a section reference to << License >>. In the outline, I've drawn an arrow to point to the node that actually holds the License section. Any text held in the body of that node is inserted into the file when it is saved!

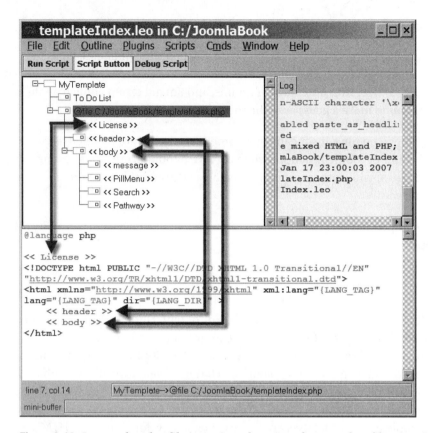

Figure 6-19. *Leo can break a file into virtual sections for complete file organization.*

- << header >> is another section. Clicking that section node of the outline will display the content held in that section, as shown in Figure 6-20. Only the header code is shown in the code pane. That allows you to focus on editing a particular section of a long file and organize it in the manner that makes the most sense.

- Below the header section in the outline is the << body >> section. The body section is further divided into other sections that appear as child nodes.

You may begin to see the power of using Leo to organize a development project. However, this example barely scratches the surface. You may have noticed that the example shows only a single file reference. In fact, all the files of the project can be held in the outline for complete project construction and management. Furthermore, any nodes that are placed in the outline, yet begin with the @ignore directive, will not be stored in the output files. That means you can place complete documentation within the outline without it interfering with the code.

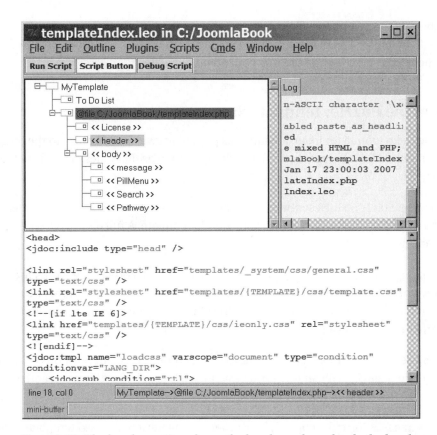

Figure 6-20. *The header section shows the header code and only the header code in the bottom pane.*

As you progress through this book, you will see other examples of Leo for optimizing Joomla projects. The power for development the Leo editor allows cannot be underestimated. And if you know how to program in the Python language, you can access the core Leo framework to automate nearly any task.

Creating a Real Template

While it was useful for learning the basic structure of a template by creating the primitive Hello Joomla template from scratch, most templates are built from an existing foundation or prototype template. It is much easier to use a bare-bones template and add the features you want instead of reinventing the wheel. In this section, I'll detail a core template that you can reuse for most of your future templates.

The bare-bones template will be designed around the LoanStaircase site model introduced in Chapter 4. Feel free to make any modifications that will more directly address the needs of the Joomla site that you intend to create.

Pieces of the Puzzle: Template Structure

To keep the Hello Joomla template as simple as possible, it was boiled down to the minimum two required files. For most templates, though, three primary files define how the site will appear:

- `templateDetails.xml`: Describes the template files to the Joomla system. You created a basic version of this file for the Hello Joomla template. A full details file will use many more parameters.

- `index.php`: Contains all of the primary HTML and PHP code that governs the execution of the site. The Hello Joomla index file was extremely simplistic and contained little of the document description information that is important for proper page rendering.

- `template.css`: Contains the style settings (font, borders, element positions, etc.) of the main page. This file may override existing styles set for sections, categories, or individual articles.

These three files form the core of almost every template; a real-world template must have at least these three files to be used effectively.

■**Tip** When you create a template and want to share it with the public (or sell it for that matter), you should include some type of usage license that defines the way a user can and cannot use the template. I suggest that you read the excellent explanation of the GNU General Public License (GPL) on Wikipedia (`http://en.wikipedia.org/wiki/GNU_Public_License`). It will give you an overview of general software licensing issues and help you to understand which type of license you should reference in your template.

In Figure 6-21, I've created a simple diagram that highlights some parts of the default Joomla installation, with labels pointing out which style sheets are responsible for each piece of the display.

Figure 6-21. *Styles of a Joomla page display*

Beyond the basic three files, most templates also include the following:

- *Thumbnail graphic file:* Located in the root of the template directory, this file is a 140-by-90 image with a filename of `template_thumbnail.png`. This file is displayed by Joomla as a template preview when a mouse-over event occurs over the template name in the Template Manager of the Administrator interface.

- *CSS directory:* A separate directory named `\css` contains any style sheets used by the template. The main style sheet of the template typically has a filename of `template.css`.

- *Images directory:* A separate directory named `\images` contains any graphics used by the template.

The naming and organization for these three items are not rules that the Joomla system enforces, but following these conventions can make a template more comprehensible for later modification. You will find that most existing templates follow these guidelines.

For template distribution, all of the template files are contained within a ZIP or tarball archive. Joomla can read either of these archive types to extract the items they contain and place the files and folders in the `\templates` directory. That allows you to add a new template via the Joomla Administrator interface, instead of needing to manually create the directories and upload the files through FTP software.

Begin your template construction by creating the empty files and folders you need inside the \templates directory. You will need to create a template directory and two directories inside that one. Since this template will be a two-column rendering, I named the main folder \tmplTwoCol. I created the following three paths:

```
\templates\tmplTwoCol
\templates\tmplTwoCol\css
\templates\tmplTwoCol\images
```

Place an empty index.php file and an empty templateDetails.xml at the root of the new template directory. Place an empty template.css file in the \css directory. When you begin your site construction, you can place the code, content, and images in their proper locations.

Step-by-Step Template Creation

A Joomla template is a combination of three key elements: graphics, PHP/HTML code, and one or more style sheets. By methodically working through the process of creating a template, you will have a path to follow when you want to make a new template for your future needs.

You can produce a new template by following these steps:

1. Choose a color scheme for the site.

2. Create style sheets that match the primary color scheme.

3. Choose a font scheme that flatters the content.

4. Create the banner graphic.

5. Create the index.php file.

6. Create the templateDetails.xml file.

Once you have implemented your basic template, you can easily upgrade it in the future. Since all web pages in Joomla are generated dynamically, changes you make to the template will be reflected instantly on every web page of your site. Provided you stay within a few well-defined boundaries, just about any changes can be made to the template, and the web site will still function properly.

Choosing the Color Scheme

Most people without web design experience are either intimidated by the amount of knowledge required to make a site design look professional or simply build the site without paying any attention to aesthetic aspects of the presentation. This section will help you chart a middle course between the two extremes. By following a few basic guidelines, you can have a professional-looking web site without spending years learning graphic design.

One of the most important aspects of site design is choosing a color scheme. Your site may have minimal graphic images and only a few well-chosen fonts, but as long as the color scheme is harmonious and flattering, the site will appear clean and professional.

RGB Color Representation

To begin, you need to understand that there are several basic ways to represent color. The most commonly used method on computers is known as RGB, which stands for Red, Green, Blue.

With RGB, a computer stores the color information for every single dot (or pixel) displayed on the screen using three numbers, each representing the quantity of red, green, or blue that needs to be mixed to show a particular color. Most typically, each number falls within the range of 0 to 255. Therefore, a pixel that is completely red has an RGB value of (255,0,0). The pixel has the maximum amount of red and no green or blue. A green pixel is stored with the values (0,255,0), and a blue pixel is stored as (0,0,255). To get yellow, equal parts of red and green are mixed, for a value of (255,255,0). For any color displayed, the three colors are mixed in various quantities to produce the desired color hue and shade.

While the RGB color model is very useful for computers, it is less useful for humans. It is difficult for humans to think in terms of the color-mixing numbers. To make things simpler for us, programmers have devised color-picker interfaces, such as the one shown in Figure 6-22. Even with a color picker, though, it is difficult to systematize which colors will go well together to provide an attractive interface.

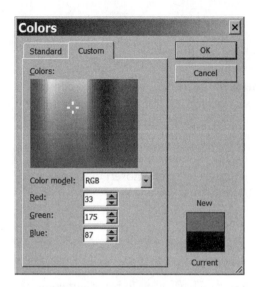

Figure 6-22. *A color-picker interface allows the user to click the color and select an RGB value.*

Choosing Your Primary Site Colors

If you pay close attention to most attractive web sites, you'll notice that the color scheme is generally very simple. In fact, selecting two colors that work together and then using different hues of these colors can make a quick by-the-numbers color scheme. What colors work together? Typically, you want to select a dark color and a light color to provide good contrast. The following are some typical color pairs:

- Black and white

- Black and yellow

- Blue and yellow

- Red and green

- Red and blue

- Purple and yellow

- Red and white

Although you can choose a color pair and use the colors directly on your site, a site rendered in these colors will look very simplistic and unprofessional. You need to use various shades of your color pair to create an integrated color scheme. Selecting shades of the color pair is no easy task in RGB. To solve the problem, you will need to temporarily leave behind the RGB color model.

■Tip Want a great model for choosing effective primary colors? Check out sports logos! Because of the large number of media and materials that are used to reproduce team logos and insignias, professional sports organizations such as the NFL and NBA spend a tremendous amount of energy and expense finding two or three colors that will work together to provide a distinctive team emblem. Checking out the colors of some professional sport teams can help you find your site color pair.

The Hue-Saturation-Brightness (or HSB) Color Model

While the RGB color model is excellent for computers, a web designer will find the Hue, Saturation, Brightness (HSB; also called Hue, Saturation, Value, or HSV) model much more useful. Instead of mixing the three different primary colors, HSB colors are handled in a completely different fashion:

- *Hue* determines the main color, such as blue, green, purple, yellow, orange, and so on. The value stored for the hue is like a location pointer on a rainbow. A low value means red, a little higher value provides a hue of yellow, higher still is blue, and so on.

- *Saturation* indicates how much of the color is present. A completely saturated color will be an extremely bright color, like those used in children's toys or present in Technicolor movies like the *Wizard of Oz*. A completely desaturated color will appear to be gray. Think of leaving a color print out in the sunlight. Slowly but surely, the colors will fade or desaturate.

- *Brightness* or *value* determines how bright the color can be. With no brightness (a value of 0), the color will appear completely black. With a maximum value, the color will appear as bright as the hue and saturation will determine it to be. To understand how brightness works, imagine a colored piece of paper (of whatever hue and saturation values) sitting in a dark room. With the lowest brightness, the room is completely black and the sheet will appear black. As you turn the knob to increase the light in the room, you see the color with more and more clarity, until you reach the highest value where you can see the color paper perfectly (even if it is faded or desaturated).

You may be wondering how the HSB color model can help you with your Joomla site design. It's very simple actually. By increasing and decreasing the brightness value of a particular color, you can obtain perfectly complementary shades of your primary colors without any additional work! Therefore, if the banner for your site is a dark blue, you can obtain a lighter tone to use as a background behind the text by simply increasing the brightness.

Choosing a Light or Dark Site Theme

You have presumably chosen your color pair, but now you need to consider how you want to use those two colors on your site. Your two primary choices are a light site theme or a dark site theme. Choosing either light or dark will determine the dominant feel of the site.

Suppose that your two colors are black and white. If you make your text black, it's likely a majority of the display will be white, like black lettering on a sheet of white paper. That means that your site will likely appear shiny, bright, light, or airy to a visitor. Such a scheme might be perfect for a touring bicycle site, a small-town bakery, or a search engine like Google. It might not be the best choice for a site representing a jazz club or a new first-person-shooter videogame.

On the other hand, if you make the text white, the majority of the remaining space will be black. That produces a completely different effect, doesn't it? The site might feel solid, edgy, mysterious, or lush. This theme might be perfect for a hip sunglasses manufacturer or an investment bank. It might not be the best choice for a handicraft or computer dating site.

More realistically, you may have chosen a very light yellow and a very dark blue. With those selections, setting the text in the blue and the background in yellow will produce a light site theme. Doing the opposite, with yellow text on blue background, will produce a dark site theme.

Select how the colors will be used on your site now, so you can more effectively generate the hues that you will need.

Using HSB to Pick Your Site Colors

Now that you've chosen some colors and understand generally how they will be used in your template, you can create a simple HTML page to help you discover the color hues you will need to make your site appear professional. This page will display colors, and convert RGB values to HSB values and vice versa.

Open your text editor and enter the code shown in Listing 6-1.

Listing 6-1. *RGB/HSB Color Converter*

```
<HTML>/
<HEAD>
<SCRIPT LANGUAGE="JavaScript1.2" type="text/javascript">
<!--
function rgbChange () {
    updateSample();
}

function testVal(testField) {
    if(isNaN(testField)) { testField = 0; }
    if(testField<0) { testField = 0; }
    if(testField>255) { testField = 255; }
    return (testField);
}

function toHexStr(decVal) {
    if(decVal<16) strVal="0";
    else strVal="";
    strVal += (decVal-0).toString(16);
    return(strVal);
}

function updateSample() {
    r = testVal(document.frmRGB.R.value)
    g = testVal(document.frmRGB.G.value)
    b = testVal(document.frmRGB.B.value)
    hexStr = "#" + toHexStr(r) + toHexStr(g) + toHexStr(b);
    document.frmHex.hexVal.value = hexStr;
    document.bgColor=hexStr;
}

function convertHSB() {
    h = document.frmHSB.H.value/360
    s = document.frmHSB.S.value/100
    v = document.frmHSB.B.value/100
    hi = parseInt(h*6);
    f=1;
    var_h = h * 6;
    var_i = Math.floor(hi);
```

```
        p = v*(1-s);
        q = v*(1-s*(var_h - var_i));
        t = v*(1-s*(1 - (var_h - var_i)));

        switch(hi){
            case 0: r=v; g=t; b=p; break;
            case 1: r=q; g=v; b=p; break;
            case 2:    r=p; g=v; b=t; break;
            case 3: r=p; g=q; b=v; break;
            case 4: r=t; g=p; b=v; break;
            case 5: r=v; g=p; b=q; break;
        }
        document.frmRGB.R.value = Math.round(r*255);
        document.frmRGB.G.value = Math.round(g*255);
        document.frmRGB.B.value = Math.round(b*255);
        updateSample();
}

function convertRGB() {
    r = testVal(document.frmRGB.R.value)/255
    g = testVal(document.frmRGB.G.value)/255
    b = testVal(document.frmRGB.B.value)/255

    v = Math.max(r, g, b);
    myMin = Math.min(r, g, b);
    if(v==0) s=0;
    else s=1-(myMin/v);

    if(v==myMin) h=0;
    else
        switch(v){
            case r:
                if(g>=b) h=60*((g-b)/(v-myMin));
                else h=60*((g-b)/(v-myMin))+360;
                break;
            case g:
                h = 60*((b-r)/(v-myMin))+120;
                break;
            case b:
                h = 60*((r-g)/(v-myMin))+240;
                break;
        }
```

```
        document.frmHSB.H.value = Math.round(h);
        document.frmHSB.S.value = Math.round(s*100);
        document.frmHSB.B.value = Math.round(v*100);
}
-->
</script>

</HEAD>
<BODY>
<H1>RGB/HSB Convert</H1>
<table width="200" border="1" bgcolor="#FFFFFF">
  <tr> <td>
  <form name="frmRGB" id="frmRGB">
      <label>R (0-255)
        <input name="R" type="text" id="R" accesskey="R"
      onKeyUp    =javascript:rgbChange(); value="255" size="5">
      </label><p>
      <label>G (0-255)
        <input name="G" type="text" id="G" accesskey="R"
        onKeyUp    =javascript:rgbChange(); value="0" size="5">
      </label></p><p>
      <label>B (0-255)
        <input name="B" type="text" id="B" accesskey="R"
        onKeyUp    =javascript:rgbChange(); value="0" size="5">
      </label></p><p>
      <label>
        <input name="cmdConvertRGB" TYPE="button"
        value="Convert &gt;" onClick=javascript:convertRGB();>
      </label></p>
  </form></td><td>
  <form name="frmHSB" id="frmHSB">
    <label>H
      <input name="H" type="text" id="H" size="5">
    </label><p>
    <label>S
      <input name="S" type="text" id="S" size="5">
    </label></p><p>
    <label>B
      <input name="B" type="text" id="B" size="5">
    </label></p><p>
```

```
    <label>
      <input name="cmdConvertHSB" TYPE="button"
      value="Convert &lt;" onclick=javascript:convertHSB()>
    </label></p>
  </form></td></tr>
  <tr><td>
  <form action="" method="post" name="frmHex" id="frmHex">
    <label>Hex
      <input name="hexVal" type="text" id="hexVal">
    </label>
  </form></td>
  <td> </td>
  </tr>
</table>
</BODY></HTML>
```

Save the file to your local drive as RGB_HSB_converter.html. Open the page in your browser, and you should see a display like the one shown in Figure 6-23. When you change the red, green, and blue values, the background will automatically change color to match the new entries.

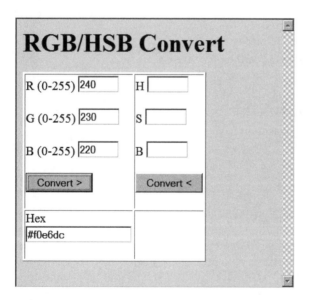

Figure 6-23. *The RGB/HSB color converter lets you enter color values for conversion and display.*

Enter the RGB value of the first color you have chosen for your color scheme. Notice that the Hex text box near the bottom displays the RGB value in hexadecimal notation. That is the notation used by HTML, so you'll need to record that value so you can put the color into the Joomla template.

I've chosen a color close to evergreen for my dark color. It has an RGB value of (88,161,85) with a hex value of #58a155. For my light color, I'm going to go with a simple white.

Click the Convert > button to fill the HSB fields with numbers that are used to represent that color in the HSB color model. In the case of my first theme color, the HSB value generated was (118,47,63). Here is where the magic begins. I know I'm going to need a darker version of this color for backgrounds and shadows. Therefore, I lower the brightness value until I think it looks right. In this case, I set it at 26, for an HSB value of (118,47,26).

Now click the Convert < button to render the color back into RGB and record the new RGB value (along with the associated hex value). For my darker shade, I got an RGB value of (36,66,35) and hex of #244223. Do you see how it would be difficult to find that color using the RGB color model?

Open your text editor or word processor and make a color chart like the one shown in Figure 6-24. Fill in the details for your color scheme. I've included spaces for a bright color for both of your theme colors. The bright color can often be used for highlights.

	Hex	RGB	HSB
Theme Color 1 (background)	#58a155	88,161,85	118,47,63
Theme Color 1 Dark	#244223	36,66,35	118,47,26
Theme Color 1 Bright			
Theme Color 2 (text)	#fafffa	250,255,250	120,2,100
Theme Color 2 Dark			
Theme Color 2 Bright			

Figure 6-24. *A simple color chart for your theme will help you build the template.*

You now have a complete color scheme for your template! You'll use these colors for setting up any graphics on the site. You'll also use it to define the colors within your style sheets.

Creating the Style Sheets

With the basic color scheme of the site decided, you can begin defining the visual presentation of the site. Most of the display is handled by the style sheets loaded by the template. Joomla has been widely embraced because it makes style sheets an integral part in the construction of a template.

Rather than using special template-formatting language for the visual component of a template, Joomla embraces existing and popular web standards. CSS is the standard; it's widely accepted and easy to validate to World Wide Web Consortium (W3C) standards.

If you already know all about CSS technology, you can skip the next section and get right to the special considerations of creating Joomla style sheets. If you don't know much about CSS, you're in for a treat! Browser implementation of style sheets is one of the most powerful and labor-saving technologies available for web site creation. Learning how to use CSS will greatly enhance your web skills.

What Is CSS?

CSS was initially invented to solve problems of uniformity and compatibility for HTML-formatted pages. As web pages became more stylistically complex with multiple fonts, color schemes, and standardized formatting (of tables, line breaks, paragraphs, etc.), the HTML coding for each page grew unwieldy. As web sites grew to encompass hundreds or thousands of pages, maintaining a site-wide visual style became an almost impossible task. Enter CSS.

A CSS file holds definitions of various text and graphical elements (such as heading 1 style, link color, etc.). For example, the style definition of a heading 1 that has a font of Verdana, a size of 18 pixels, and a red color would appear in the style sheet as follows:

```
.h1 {
    font-family: Verdana, Geneva, Arial, Helvetica, sans-serif;
    font-size:18px;
    color: #FF0000;
}
```

Any web page that includes this definition and uses text enclosed by <h1> tags will get this formatting. The period (.) before the name of the style means that the style will override a previous version of the h1 style. Styles can be much more fluid than redefining existing tags. For example, you could create a custom style named mySmall like this:

```
.mySmall {
    font-family: "Times New Roman", Times, serif;
    font-size: 6px;
    vertical-align: top; margin: 3px;
}
```

To format a paragraph with this style, you need only include a `class` attribute within the HTML tag definition:

```
<p class="mySmall">This text is small!</p>
```

Most often, style definitions are not stored within the HTML of a page (although they can be included in a file between `<style>` tags). Instead, they are stored in a separate file with the filename extension of `.css`. With the styles placed in a file, any web page that needs formatting in the styles defined in the CSS file need only include a single line of code in the HTML of the page. The browser will automatically retrieve the style definitions and format the page to match them.

Note If you're not very familiar with HTML coding and the information in this chapter seems slightly confusing, please stick with it. Almost everything you need to do to create a template can be accomplished with tools that will do most of the coding for you. You can use some of these tools (such as the jEdit CSS plug-in) with their simple GUI interfaces to accomplish many tasks.

Common CSS site files are just one of the many advantages provided by using a CSS. At the time the CSS technology was being born, Microsoft and Netscape were engaged in a struggle for dominance of the web browser market. As each company released new versions of their browsers at a lightning pace, capabilities were becoming more robust. However, the platforms where they were being released were sometimes hobbled by technical limitations such as a lack of standard fonts.

To resolve this problem, a CSS file can provide formatting choices that offer one or more options, and the platform could choose an option to best display the content. That means that a site using a CSS file can modify the presentation of the page based on the browser that is accessing it. For example, a CSS file could have explicit styles that are used only when a cell phone browser accesses it. This type of presentation logic is perfectly suited for a CMS, where all content is displayed through a number of site templates.

Using CSS to define a Joomla template allows the content to be completely separate from the presentation. Content articles are stored in the database, while the presentation is contained in the CSS files. One style can be replaced with another (perhaps based on the browser type addressing the page), and instantly, the entire site will take on a new look without any modification of content.

Tip One objective you should set for yourself when creating a new template is to minimize the use of tables for layout. Generally, layout can be controlled much more effectively when stored as elements of a style sheet in a CSS file. Using a CSS file to control layout also promotes cleaner coding for the web site and greater likelihood that search engines will be able to correctly interpret the content of the site.

The CSS standard includes numerous features, such as font alternatives, that make it likely that a browser can properly display a web page, regardless of whether the browser is formatting for a 21-inch flat screen or 3-inch cell phone display.

Search Engine Considerations and CSS

Another reason why implementing CSS can be helpful is that it is machine-readable. For massive search engines such as Google, it would be impossible for individual workers to read and index the tens of millions of web pages that are available for searching. Therefore, search engine companies have technology (called *web spiders*) that reads a web site and creates an internal summary of each web page. These summaries are indexed and filed where the search engine algorithm can find them if they match a user query.

The more machine-readable a web page is to the web spider, the greater chance the search engine algorithm will understand it and can guide visitors to that page. Conversely, the less machine-readable it is, the more "invisible" it will be to search engines. A simple example of search engine invisibility is a web page with a graphic banner that reads *XYZ Company*. The search algorithm won't be able to read the graphic at all; it reads only text. Therefore, even if the graphic shows the company name in letters 5 inches tall, it will be invisible to the web spider. If earnest web searchers typed "XYZ Company" into their browser, they would not find the page.

Let's say that the web designer was a little astute and provided a text alternate to the graphic through the alt attribute defined by the HTML standard. Now the search engine would see that the graphic represented the text *XYZ Company*, but how important would the search algorithm consider this graphic over the other graphics on the page? Other graphics with alternate text of *screen divider*, *home link*, and *CEO photo* would compete with the banner for the web spider's attention.

A much better site, in terms of being found by a search engine, is a CSS-based page. That web page would have a central banner with the text *XYZ Company* defined as a heading 1 style. Immediately, the search program would recognize that this heading is one of the most important parts of the page and rank it appropriately. The heading 1 style could be defined in the CSS file to use a special font, color, horizontal width, and so on to ensure the display would still be impressive.

This example is not very realistic on the surface, since most companies want a central banner graphic that expresses their image exactly. Additionally, there are other ways to make sure the search program knows the important elements of the page, and you'll learn more about these in Chapter 12.

But how about individual articles? Many web sites use custom graphics for the titles of articles or even departmental sections of their web sites. If they instead used CSS formatting, the web spider would be able to much more accurately create a search summary. That means more hits, more traffic, and maybe more money for XYZ Company.

Joomla! Template CSS

With that introduction to the power of CSS out of the way, you can begin to examine the Joomla CSS file to understand what types of alterations you might want to make. The rhuk_milkyway template included with the standard Joomla installation contains two dozen different styles that define the presentation of the template.

In Listing 6-2, you can see a sampling of the styles that define the template page. Notice that each style defines only a small number of parameters. Styles are essentially hierarchical, so when the styles of links are defined in the first style (a:link and a:visited) for the page, all other presentation on the page will use these styles unless explicitly overridden.

Listing 6-2. *With Only a Few Styles, the rhuk_milkyway Template Defines the Primary Pieces of a Page*

```
a:link, a:visited {
    color: #1B57B1; text-decoration: none;
    font-weight: normal;
}

#page_bg {
    height: 100%;
    padding: 10px 0;
    margin-bottom: 1px;
    background: #0C3A6D;
}

div.center {
  text-align: center;
}
```

```css
div#wrapper {
        height: 100%;
        background: #f7f7f7 url(../images/mw_shadow_blue_l.png) 0 0 repeat-y;
        margin-left: auto;
        margin-right: auto;
        min-width: 750px;
        max-width: 1050px;
}

div#wrapper_r {
    background: url(../images/mw_shadow_blue_r.png) 100% 0 repeat-y;
}

div#header {
    background: url(../images/mw_header_blue_t.png) 0 0 repeat-x;
}

div#header_l {
    background: url(../images/mw_header_blue_t_l.png) 0 0 no-repeat;
    position: relative;
}
.ol-foreground {
    background-color: #f6f6f6;
}

.ol-background {
    background-color: #666;
}

.ol-textfont {
    font-family: Arial, Helvetica, sans-serif;
    font-size: 10px;
}
```

As you can see from these styles, you can define almost every aspect of presentation—from text styles to fonts to margins to borders. You can also define the more fundamental parts of layout, including columns, absolute positioned elements (such as images), and float blocks. Unfortunately, many templates (including rhuk_milkyway) don't take advantage of the CSS capabilities for layout.

Instead of using CSS, many templates use tables to perform layout functions. Basic layout might appear like this:

```
<table>
    <tr>
        <td>Column1</td><td>Column2</td><td>Column3</td>
    </tr>
    <tr>
        <td>Home</td><td>ArticleContent</td><td>ItemPrice1</td>
    </tr>
    <tr>
        <td>FAQs</td><td>ItemName2</td><td>ItemPrice1</td>
    </tr>
</table>
```

Using tables is problematic. It requires a great deal of code (especially if spacer images are used) and it is confusing to read. It is also difficult for search engines to understand, and that makes it less likely that your site will be found by people using the search engines. Furthermore, changes to the layout require a significant amount of code revision.

Creating three columns using a style sheet, however, requires simple CSS code, like this:

```
#col1 {float:left;width:20%;}
#col2 {float:left;width:60%;}
#col3 {float:left;width:20%;}
```

The code to place content within each column would look like this:

```
<div id="col1">Column1<br>Home<br>FAQs</div>
<div id="col2">MyArticle</div>
<div id="col3">Column advertisements </div>
```

Isn't that much clearer? Search engines think so. However, the navigation and menu content held in col1 still appears first in the code order, while col2 likely holds the most important content of your site. Since search spiders think the content that appears earlier in a web page is more important, this isn't an optimal way of organizing the site.

There is a method of sorting the columns so that even though the display will match the one created with the preceding code, the col2 content will appear first in the HTML code, making it also the first text the search engine scanning program will see (and therefore on which the search engine will place the most importance). You'll learn about this technique in Chapter 12.

Note When you study CSS technology, you will come across many frustrating implementation choices made by Microsoft for Internet Explorer 6 that defy the CSS standard. You may have noticed that Joomla templates generally include a style sheet called `ieonly.css`. It includes definitions that specifically handle the Internet Explorer way of doing things. I will try to detail as many of the Internet Explorer pitfalls in this book as possible. However, I would recommend that you always test your page with Internet Explorer and at least one other browser so you can have confidence that your style sheets are displayed correctly, no matter which browser is being used. Note that many of these problems have been corrected in Internet Explorer 7.

Modifying the column settings is as simple as changing the single CSS file. You can add an internal column margin to provide some spacing for the content with the `margin` attribute. Unfortunately, Internet Explorer 6 ignores this attribute. Therefore, to include spacing or a "gutter" around each column, you will need to add a `<div>` element that contains the spacing information, like this:

```
<div id="col1">
    <div class="gutter">
        <jdoc:include type="modules" name="left" />
    </div>
</div>
```

Then in the CSS file, include this line:

```
.gutter {padding:8px;}
```

Making a Two-Column Layout with CSS

To create a new template that has a two-column setup, you'll need to configure the CSS file to handle the spacing for the page. If you are already familiar with creating HTML tables, the CSS formatting will be familiar.

A CSS layout can be considered much like the newspaper layout model described in Chapter 4 as it applies to a Joomla page. Each panel is like a box that can hold contents (most often text) and has attributes such as border, border width, padding, and margins. Figure 6-25 shows a simple diagram of a panel and its various attributes.

Margins for a panel are always transparent. A background within the panel will include all of the area inside the borders. For all of the various attributes, different widths may be set for the different sides. For example, a border could have a 1-point top border and a 3-point bottom border.

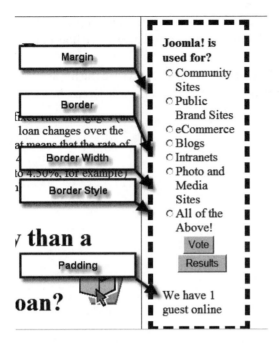

Figure 6-25. *A CSS panel has attributes such as border, border width, padding, and margins.*

Panels can be created within a hierarchy, which means that a set of panels can be held within a panel, which in turn is held in another panel.

There are two primary box types: in-line and block. In-line boxes are treated by layout in the same manner as a piece of text or an image. Block boxes live within formatting tags such as `<p>`, `<div>`, or `<table>`. The `display` attribute of a web page element such as `<div>` will determine what type of box is being used. If the `display` attribute is set to `none`, the box will be hidden from the browser view.

For positioning, CSS supports three different methods: `normal`, `float`, and `absolute`. Normal positioning makes block boxes flow vertically, and it makes in-line boxes flow from left to right. The `float` elements can be placed on the page relative to other elements and `absolute` elements can be located anywhere on the page using absolute coordinates.

■**Note** When one vertical block is followed by another vertical block, the vertical margins are collapsed. If two blocks appeared sequentially in a layout, for example, the bottom margin of the upper box would not be added to the top margin of the lower box. This would create great chasms of white space between content. Instead, the larger of the two margins is selected and used as a shared single vertical margin.

You can also have a box with a relative position in relation to another page element. The box can have a number of offsets that will position the box relative to the flow that came before it.

For your two-column template, enter the code in Listing 6-3 and save the file as template.css in the \css folder in your template folder. The index file will access these styles for displaying the content.

Listing 6-3. *The CSS for the Two-Column Template*

```css
div#logo {
    width: 110%; height: 100px;
    margin-left: -10px;
    background: url(../images/LSlogo.jpg) left no-repeat;
    border: 1px solid #244223 ;
    padding: 20px;
}

#col1 {
    float:left;width:15%;
    background:#244223;
    padding: 10px;
}
#col2 {
    float:left;width:75%;
    border:3px solid #244223;
    background:#58a155;
    padding: 10px;
}

#page_bg {
    font-family: Verdana, Arial, Helvetica, sans-serif;
    height: 100%;
    background: black;
}

.moduletable_menu, .moduletable
{
    color: white;
    border-bottom: 1px solid #fff;
    margin-bottom: -1em;
}
```

```
.moduletable_menu h3 {
    border-bottom: 1px solid #FFFFFF;
    margin-bottom: 0px;
}


.moduletable_menu ul {
    margin-left: 10px;
    margin-top: 0px;
    padding: 10px;
    font-size: 80%;
    list-style-type: square;
}


.moduletable_menu a:link, .moduletable a:link {
    color:yellow;
}


.moduletable_menu a:visited, .moduletable a:visited {
    color:cornsilk;
}


.contentheading {
    border-bottom: 2px solid Black;
    border-right: 2px solid Black;
    border-left: 1px solid LightGreen;
    border-top: 1px solid LightGreen;
    background:#244223;
    color: white;
    padding: 10px;
    font-size:2em;
}


.contentpaneopen h1 {
    font-size:1.5em;
    border-bottom: 1px solid #244223;
    padding: 10px;
}
```

In the style sheet, you can see that the styles like .contentheading are overriding standard Joomla styles. That is an aspect of Joomla that provides the template so much power: content is generated using published style sheet names. That means that any content generated by the system can be formatted using any style sheet attribute included in CSS.

■**Note** Both Mozilla Firefox and Internet Explorer have tools that will display the styles used on a web page that can help you learn which styles you'll want to modify for your template. For Firefox, the Web Developer extension (`https://addons.mozilla.org/en-US/firefox/addon/60`) allows you to examine the styles used on the page and even perform a live modification and application of the changes to see them instantly. For Internet Explorer, go to the Microsoft web site and search the downloads section for the Internet Explorer Developer Toolbar.

Choosing the Font Scheme

Choosing a font scheme is no easy task. The fonts used for your site should be selected for taste as well as availability. If you were to select a font like Smudger LET, the odds are low that a majority of users would have that font on their system. Therefore, if you insisted the text appear in that font, any content that used such a font would need to be rendered as a graphic. Using a lot of rendered text makes maintaining a site onerous with the additional drawback that the technique is not very search-engine friendly, as explained in the "Search Engine Considerations and CSS" section earlier in this chapter.

With CSS definition, the display of a web page is created using styles as a set of guidelines more than a set of rules. A modern browser on a current system will be able to display exactly what the designer intended. However, on a less current system, the web visitor will still get a decent approximation of the design intent.

One of the ways CSS achieves this flexibility is by providing a feature known as *font alternatives*. Font alternatives are a great example of providing power to the web designer and, at the same time, trying to respect the user with the lowest common denominator system. For a cutting-edge web page, a web designer may want to use a font such as Gill Sans MT Condensed to achieve just the right look. However, if the font is unavailable on the visitor's browser (fairly likely if a cell phone browser is used), the site presentation may be ruined, especially if the browser display fails outright or substitutes an inappropriate monospaced font. The designer can minimize this problem by using a CSS file with font alternates. Here is an example of a line using font alternatives:

```
font-family: Gill Sans MT Condensed, Geneva, Arial, Helvetica, sans-serif;
```

When the browser displays the text, it first will attempt to find the Gill Sans MT font on the system and use that font for display. Failing that, it will attempt to use Geneva, and so on, down through the list of options until it reaches the lowest common denominator of sans-serif. For a serif font, the lowest common denominator alternatives might be as follows:

```
font-family: "Times New Roman", Times, serif;
```

Serifs are the little extra lines or curves on characters. For example, the capital letter *T* in a serif font has extra lines drooping down from the top line and another small line on the base. Fonts without these graphic additions are said to be without (or *sans*) serif. Therefore, on the most basic level, fonts can be categorized as one of two types: serif and sans-serif.

You may have noticed my font choices in the #page_bg style, in the template style sheet (Listing 6-3):

```
font-family: Verdana, Arial, Helvetica, sans-serif;
```

I wanted to use a sans-serif font for the site, and Verdana is a very clean and modern sans-serif font. However, not all systems have Verdana, so the style includes substitute fonts that will provide an approximation of the desired look.

Once you choose to make your site a serif or sans-serif presentation (and you can use both on a site), you need to select individual fonts. Selecting typefaces and font families is more of an art than a science. So I have a shortcut: imitate the professionals!

Find a web site that you think looks good and supplies the font look you would like your site to mirror. For an example of contemporary design, I might examine www.wired.com for font choices, since the publishers of that site (and magazine) expend a great deal of effort on the site's graphic design. Once your desired model site is displayed in your browser, choose the option to save the entire page under the File menu and all of the files of the site will be written to your local drive.

■Tip Whenever I want to save a web page and its associated files, I use the Mozilla Firefox browser. For reasons I don't understand, Internet Explorer often has problems saving the site to a local drive, resulting in an abort window that states that the page couldn't be saved. I have never had similar problems with Firefox.

Open the folder that contains the support files (images, advertisements, etc.). You should see one or more style sheets. With a text editor, open the CSS files and determine the font schemes that the site uses. You can now incorporate this scheme into your own site! Most large sites are very aware that they want to reach the broadest audience possible, so they make safe choices in the font lists—fonts that most browsers will be able to display properly.

Creating the Banner Graphic

You have the site color choices and font scheme, so all of the pieces needed to create a good banner graphic are in place.

When discussing graphic web design, one program stands far above the others: Adobe Photoshop. The installed base of Photoshop alone guarantees a tremendous availability of training material, plug-ins, and web support. However, in keeping with the spirit of free and open source, this book will use a program called GIMP to provide graphic editing. GIMP is nearly as powerful as Photoshop, and while it may not have all the bells and whistles, it carries no price tag either. Figure 6-26 shows the GIMP interface.

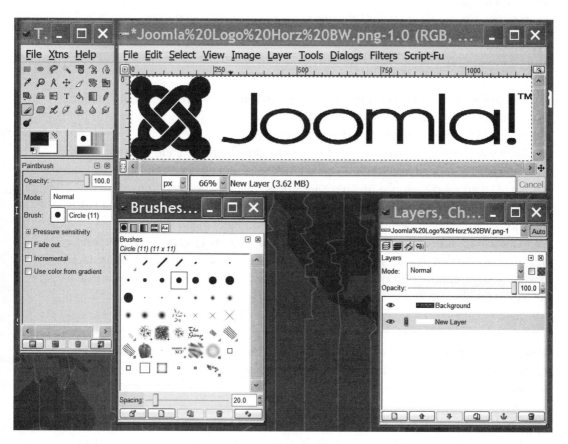

Figure 6-26. *GIMP editing the Joomla logo*

An installer for GIMP (alternately known as The GIMP) is available at www.gimp.org. GIMP requires a graphics toolkit called GTK+ for display. You will most likely need to download and install GTK+ separately. On the GIMP site, you'll find complete installation instructions.

■**Tip** The excellent book *Beginning GIMP: From Novice to Professional*, by Akkana Peck (Apress, 2006), can guide you through all of the ins and outs of this wonderful program.

If you already know how to use Photoshop, you should be able to follow the image-editing instructions without any difficulty because of the functional similarity between GIMP and Photoshop. If you have Adobe Photoshop, you probably already know how to create the banner headline you want. Try to make the banner graphic around 150 pixels tall and around 800 pixels across. That will mean most browsers will be able to view it without a problem.

Feel free to use any of Photoshop's capabilities to throw in some visual flourish to the template graphics. With source code, a detour away from a tutorials detailed path is likely to cause problems. Improvisation in graphics tutorials, in contrast, seldom creates any difficulties.

To create the banner, fire up GIMP and select the Xtns menu. You will see a submenu labeled Script-Fu. This submenu contains a large number of scripted extensions for GIMP that perform macro operations to automate graphic tasks. In the Script-Fu menu, you will see an option for Logos. The Logos menu has numerous scripts for the quick and simple generation of banner logos. In Figure 6-27, you can see that I have selected the Chrome logo to create my banner.

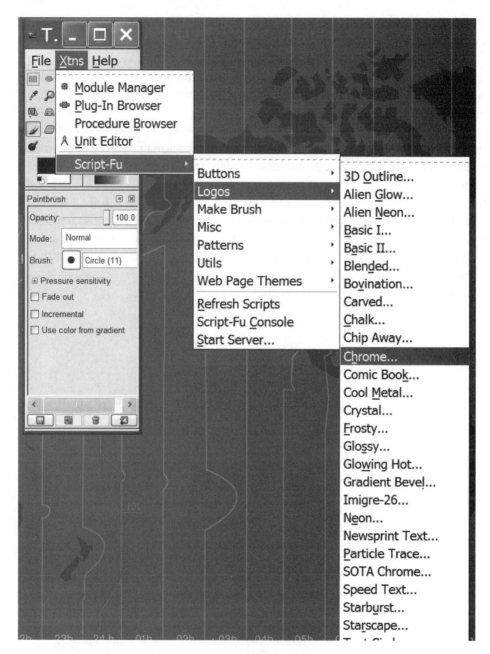

Figure 6-27. *Selecting the Chrome logo for a banner graphic*

The script will display a window with a number of script parameters or arguments that can be set to customize the rendered graphic. For most of the logo scripts, you can select a color or texture and font. In Figure 6-28, I've entered the text that I want for my banner graphic, and I've changed the background color to match the darker color choice from my site scheme.

Figure 6-28. *Selecting the parameters for your banner graphic*

When you click the OK button, the script will execute and generate the requested graphic. That's it! My logo generated as shown in Figure 6-29.

Try a number of the logo scripts, and you will almost certainly find some graphic that appeals to you and fits the look of your web site. When you've chosen the appropriate graphic, save it as a JPG or PNG file and store it in the \images folder of your template.

The most important step is just ahead: creating the index file of your template.

Figure 6-29. *After clicking the OK button, you'll see a window displaying your rendered logo.*

Creating the index.php File

The index.php file is the central file of the template and holds all of the template logic. In most cases, since the presentation is handled by CSS, template index files are very similar. Unless you need to add user interface coded features (or Ajax functionality), most of the templates you create will have an index.php file almost identical to the one you will create here (although they may have more module inserts).

A template PHP file appears very similar to a standard HTML file, with the addition of processing directives. Here is an excerpt of the default template file so you can see the similarity to a traditional HTML page:

```
<?php echo '<?xml version="1.0" encoding="utf-8"?' .'>'; ?>
<!DOCTYPE html PUBLIC "-//W3C//DTD XHTML 1.0 Transitional//EN"
    "http://www.w3.org/TR/xhtml1/DTD/xhtml1-transitional.dtd">
<html xmlns="http://www.w3.org/1999/xhtml"
lang="<?php echo _LANGUAGE; ?>" xml:lang=
    "<?php echo _LANGUAGE; ?>">
<head>
<jdoc:include type="head" />
```

Notice that the page opens with a !DOCTYPE declaration. The DOCTYPE tag describes the standards and schema that will be used by the file. It also tells the browser how to interpret the CSS. While not required, having a proper DOCTYPE can prevent a number of compatibility problems with a browser rendering the page.

■**Caution** When you create a new template file, make sure you duplicate the DOCTYPE given in the Joomla default template file exactly. The DOCTYPE in the file has been well tested. Errors in this tag can cause all sorts of unpredictable and difficult-to-locate problems.

This tag is followed by the html tag. Within the html tag is embedded PHP code that adds the language attribute before the page is sent to the browser.

The jdoc tag is the Joomla include that executes pieces of the Joomla CMS written in PHP. In any version of Joomla from 1.5 forward, the jdoc (JDocument) interface is used to access the Joomla interface framework. JDocument handles the presentation output of the Joomla system. To include a module in a particular location, you need only use the jdoc:include call. For example, to add the left modules at a place in your index.php file code, you could use the following statement:

```
<jdoc:include type="modules" name="left" />
```

■**Note** In older templates and programming items, you may encounter the prefix mos. Joomla was originally based on the Mambo CMS. Mambo often used the prefix mos (for Mambo Open Source). Therefore, you may find Joomla legacy code that still bears the moniker of the predecessor. You'll see it less and less as Joomla moves away from its past. For example, in older Joomla or Mambo templates, functions such as mosLoadModules() and mosCountModules() were used to access the system. These are now replaced by jdoc calls, such as jdoc:include and jdoc:exists, respectively.

It is important to include the head code in the header section of your template, like this:

```
<head>
<jdoc:include type="head" />
</head>
```

This code does more than include the general Joomla header. It also determines whether the current page is an article being edited by a front-end contributor. If the article is being edited, the include will insert the selected Joomla editor code into the page.

Enter the code in Listing 6-4 and save the file as index.php at the root of the directory for this template. This file will be the core of the template.

Listing 6-4. *The Template Code for index.php*

```php
<?php echo '<?xml version="1.0" encoding="utf-8"?' .'>'; ?>
<!DOCTYPE html PUBLIC "-//W3C//DTD XHTML 1.0 Transitional//EN"
    "http://www.w3.org/TR/xhtml1/DTD/xhtml1-transitional.dtd">
<html xmlns="http://www.w3.org/1999/xhtml"
lang="<?php echo _LANGUAGE; ?>" xml:lang=
    "<?php echo _LANGUAGE; ?>">
<head>
<jdoc:include type="head" />
<link rel="stylesheet" href="templates/_system/css/general.css"
    type="text/css" />
<link rel="stylesheet" href="templates/
    <?php echo $this->template ?>/css/template.css"
    type="text/css" />
</head>

<body id="page_bg">

<jdoc:include type="message" />
<div id="logo"> </div>
<div id="col1">
  <jdoc:include type="modules" name="left" style="xhtml" />
</div>
<div id="col2">
  <jdoc:include type="component" />
</div>
```

```
<jdoc:include type="modules" name="debug" />

</body>
</html>
```

While this code is similar to the Hello Joomla template code you created earlier, it includes a number of refinements that make it a true template file. The opening header information including the DOCTYPE and language definitions are critical for proper conformance to the HTML standards. Furthermore, you can see that two style sheet (.css) files are addressed: the Joomla core styles and the custom style sheet you created earlier (Listing 6-3).

The style sheets are important, because the <div> elements are used to specify which content will be displayed in each column. In the left column, the left module will display the selection menus. The right or main column will display the main article component.

That's it. Your template file is simple but clear. Now you need to create the template's metadata file so Joomla can understand which files comprise the template.

Creating the templateDetails.xml File

The final step in deploying the template is the creation of the details metadata file. Enter the code in Listing 6-5 and save the file as templateDetails.xml in the root directory of the template.

You might notice that the file has far more elements than the original details file. The more information you can provide to the Joomla system, the more validity and weight the license denoted by the copyright will hold.

Listing 6-5. *The templateDetails.xml File Holds Pointers to All of the Files Used by the Template*

```
<?xml version="1.0" encoding="utf-8"?>
<install version="1.5" type="template">
    <name>Two Column template</name>
    <version>1.0</version>
    <creationDate>01/18/2007</creationDate>
    <author>Dan Rahmel</author>
    <authorEmail>admin@joomlaJumpstart.com</authorEmail>
    <authorUrl>http://www.joomlaJumpstart.com </authorUrl>
    <copyright>2007</copyright>
    <license>GNU/GPL</license>
```

```
<description>
  Two CSS columns in the Joomla world.
</description>
<files>
        <filename>index.php</filename>
        <filename>templateDetails.xml</filename>
        <filename>images/LSlogo.jpg</filename>
        <filename>css/template.css</filename>
</files>
    <positions>
        <position>left</position>
    </positions>
</install>
```

Template Installation

You have all of the files and folders laid out for proper use. To actually install the template through the Joomla Administrator, you need the files to be collected within a ZIP or tarball archive. If you go to your current template folder, you need only create an archive from the files and folders stored there. For those using WinZip, make sure the "Include folders and paths" option is selected so the directory structure of the template remains intact.

The archive file of your template provides a convenient way for you to distribute a template. You can actually release your custom template for other Joomla administrators to use! To install a template, choose the Extensions ➤ Install/Uninstall option in the Administrator interface, as shown in Figure 6-30.

Figure 6-30. *The Extensions ➤ Install/Uninstall option allows the administrator to upload a new template into the system.*

Template Previews

You can preview any template installed on the system. The preview is an excellent feature because it can show the location of all modules within the layout. That means that an undocumented template will still reveal its layout through the preview.

To see a page preview, open the Template Manager. Click the title of the desired template to display the template parameters. Then click the Preview button near the top of the screen to display the template with the various modules. If you previewed the template you just created, you would only see two modules since that was all that was coded into the template. In contrast, as shown in Figure 6-31, the default template has many page items.

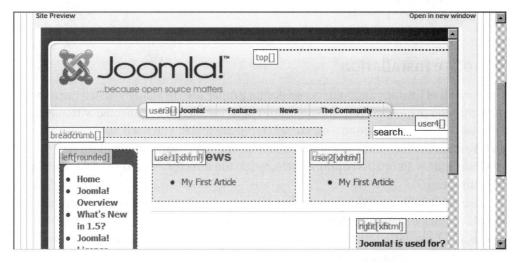

Figure 6-31. *The Preview option will display all of the module and component locations.*

The Preview screen is also a good starting point if you are considering modifying an existing template. It displays the presentation structure of the template. This structure is sometimes difficult to visualize from the template code.

When you look at the final template, as shown in Figure 6-32, you'll see that the template has come a long way since the primitive functionality of the Hello Joomla incarnation. Additionally, you can understand that it is only a small leap between this basic template and a comprehensive template such as the Joomla default rhuk_milkyway. Most of the work lies in the area of tuning style sheets and adding custom graphics. The Joomla display automation through the jdoc interface takes care of most of the heavy lifting in Joomla site display generation.

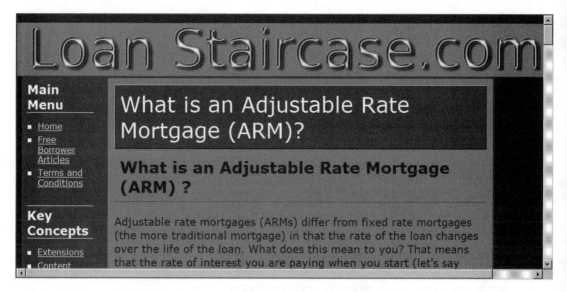

Figure 6-32. *The final template appears mimimalist, but professional.*

Validating Template Code

After you've created a new template, it is always a good idea to validate the HTML code that the template generates to make sure it complies with approved standards. The W3 offers an online tool that will scan a site based on a URL and return a verdict of any problems that might keep you from compliance. You can use your browser to view the following site and enter the URL of your page for validation:

```
http://validator.w3.org/
```

Alternatively, you can use a desktop application such as the CSE HTML Validator. This application provides validation of HTML, XHTML, CSS, accessibility, hyperlinks, and even spelling. A desktop test tool can often be used more easily than a web application to check sites on staging server, as they may not have an access URL outside the intranet. The validator application is available for free download here:

```
http://download8.htmlvalidator.com/cselite.exe
```

Conclusion

Based on what you learned in this chapter, you can produce almost any Joomla template you can imagine, limited only by your graphic design skills, knowledge of PHP, and experience with CSS. You've learned how the template is structured and how to use some of the important Joomla directives. In fact, many Joomla templates use only the directives described in this chapter.

You learned the basics of CSS and saw how tools such as Dreamweaver, jEdit, and Leo can aid in the creation of the files and organize your template projects. By further study of the default templates, you will be able to build on the knowledge you gained from creating your own template from scratch. The RGB/HSB color converter tool constructed here can also be reused for many of your future projects.

Now that your site is attractive enough to attract visitors, it will be important that you understand how to make your site a magnet for web visitors with advanced web site features. In the next chapter, you will learn about the Joomla extension technology that can add capabilities and functionality to your web site.

Joomla! Extensions

One of the undeniable reasons for Joomla's popularity is the broad spectrum of available extensions. Joomla's celebrated extensibility means much more than adding new templates. Through modules, components, and plug-ins, almost any type of web functionality can be incorporated into your site.

Popular additional features include shopping cart technology, RSS aggregation, shoutbox communication, forums, chat rooms, stock tickers, visitor maps, wiki collaborative authoring, inventory management, and customer relationship management (CRM) functionality. Essentially, Joomla can be expanded to fulfill nearly any web-related need. You can check out the broad range of extensions listed on the main Joomla site at `http://extensions.joomla.org`.

Almost 80 percent of the extensions available are released for free use, so simply downloading a small extension from the Web can dramatically increase the power and flexibility of your site. The best way to learn about extensions is to examine the ones that come preinstalled with the initial Joomla setup. By learning to administer the existing extensions, you will be able to grasp the workings of most new extensions you might want to use.

The Difference Between Modules, Components, and Plug-Ins

There seems to be a great deal of confusion among beginning Joomla users as to the difference between the various types of extensions. Since there are three different types of extensions and their functionality can somewhat overlap, it is important to be clear about the range of capabilities and the limitations fundamental to each. Many Joomla packages use more than one type, which can lead to further confusion. For example, the Polling package uses a *module* to display the user interface while the associated *component* allows configuration and administration.

Each extension entry on the Joomla web site extension directory displays the type or types of extension included in the package. Figure 7-1 shows two extension entries in the list. The first, joomlaXplorer, shows a single icon in the right column indicating that the package contains only a component. In contrast, the second entry shows that the Joom!Fish package includes one or more of each type of extension (component, module, plug-in, and language).

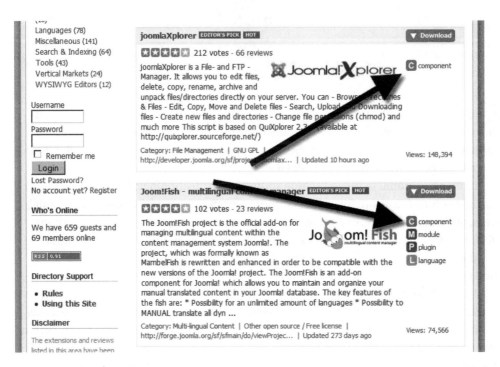

Figure 7-1. *The right column of each entry holds icons indicating the extension types found in the package.*

Many of the extensions available for the Joomla system have at least two different types for each package. To understand how all of these types function together, it is best to begin with the most complicated type of extension: the plug-in.

Plug-Ins: The Most Advanced Extensions

Plug-ins are the most advanced extension types because they integrate with the Joomla foundation at the very lowest level. A plug-in operates between Joomla and the user, as shown in Figure 7-2. Plug-ins are set to be activated by various events from the server (such as system events, user events, editor events, and content events). A plug-in can intercept output from Joomla and make changes to it before the data is sent to the user browser. On the receiving end, it has access to any user feedback or data entry before the data is processed by Joomla. That means a plug-in can modify data both coming and going.

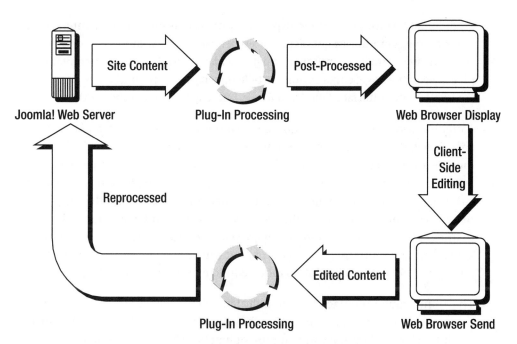

Figure 7-2. *A plug-in is situated between Joomla and the web visitor.*

The most visible type of plug-in is the WYSIWYG text editor. Article content in the Joomla database is stored in pure HTML. If no editor is selected, the HTML will be sent to a text box for editing by the content contributor. However, if an editor plug-in is selected, the HTML is intercepted by the plug-in and converted into a rich text field that displays bold text, color, images, and other presentation elements.

The user can edit the article content in this WYSIWYG environment. When the user clicks the Save button, the data returned to the system is intercepted by the plug-in, which converts it back into HTML and passes it to Joomla for storage. While this is a simplistic explanation of the actual execution of a Joomla editor, it describes the fundamental process of a plug-in.

You may use a number of plug-ins for your site, but unless you are very ambitious, you are unlikely to actually author a new plug-in. In contrast, even an intermediate user can construct a basic module or component.

Components and Modules

The dividing line between the capabilities of components and modules is not black and white. The component type of extension is the more powerful of the two. While a module can do many things a component can do, and a component can do almost anything a module might, here are a few generalizations that might help you understand the difference:

- Traditionally, a module is either display-only or accepts only minimal interaction. For example, a module might display a stock ticker or allow the simple entry of a poll vote. In contrast, a component might display multiple articles, modify the display style of the page, edit a content article (given proper permissions), or provide a complete user interface (such as a forum/message board component).

- A module is located within the module positions (such as top, left, and right) specified in the template. The login module, the search module, and the Banners module are all excellent examples. In contrast, a component generates what is essentially an entire web page within the main page. This operation is seen most easily in the central Frontpage component (named com_frontpage) that displays the intro text of one or more of the most recent articles with complete article formatting. *There can only be a single component per page*, while many modules are generally present on a page. The component can be thought of as a miniature page generator, while a module is more akin to a user interface widget.

- The Administrator interface for a module generally consists of just a few parameter settings. In contrast, components often have an elaborate multitabbed administrative interfaces to allow full configuration of functionality and presentation.

These distinctions between components and modules should provide a baseline from which you can understand the difference. Making the distinction between these types of extensions is not very important in most circumstances except that it affects how a particular extension is deployed. In Figure 7-3, you can see a preview of the Frontpage of a site. The preview shows all of the display positions of the modules (such as user3[], breadcrumb[], left[rounded], etc.). Notice that only at the center of the page where the component is rendering the content is there no labeled module position (although I have included a label to point out the component display).

Modules appear in specific module positions of a page, so a menu link is never connected to a module. With components, however, adding the component to the site interface generally involves creating a menu item link that, when clicked by the user, presents the page with the component output displayed in the center column.

Components and modules often work together with the component handling the configuration or output and the module rendering the display panel. For example, the search module displays the search entry panel—it needs to be a module so it can appear in a specific location on all pages. However, once a search query is entered by the user and submitted, the search component actually performs the query and displays the results. A similar type of connected relationship exists between the Banners module (which displays the banner) and the Banners component, which allows for the creation and administration of a banner campaign.

Since modules are typically the simplest type of extension, a tour of preinstalled Joomla extensions should begin with them.

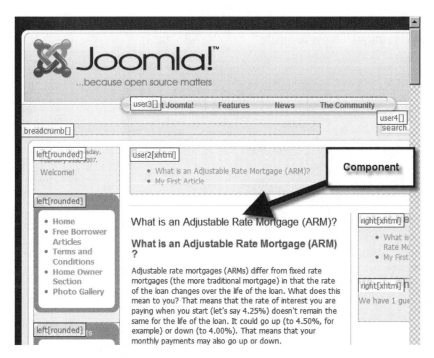

Figure 7-3. *The preview of a page shows the numerous module postions.*

Module Types

To understand how modules work in the Joomla system, you first have to understand the underlying *module type* system. The modules shown in the Module Manager list are actually *instances* created from the various module types. The rightmost column of the module list in the Module Manager shows the type designation for each module listed.

Much like the way a site template is used as an empty form from which a final document is created, module types act as templates atop which the module instance is created. For example, the module list shows many module instances with the type mod_mainmenu. The mod_mainmenu type is the foundation template for the menus on the Joomla system, and the individual instances contain the parameter settings that define the options of each menu.

When you install a module to the system, you are not actually installing a module, but a new module type. The Joomla system automatically creates the first instance of a module from that type—and that instance is the entry listed in the Module Manager.

While the Module Manager lists all of the current module instances on the system, if you click the New button you will see a list of the available module types (see Figure 7-4) from which they were created. Selecting a type will take you to the module creation screen, where you can customize the new instance of the module type.

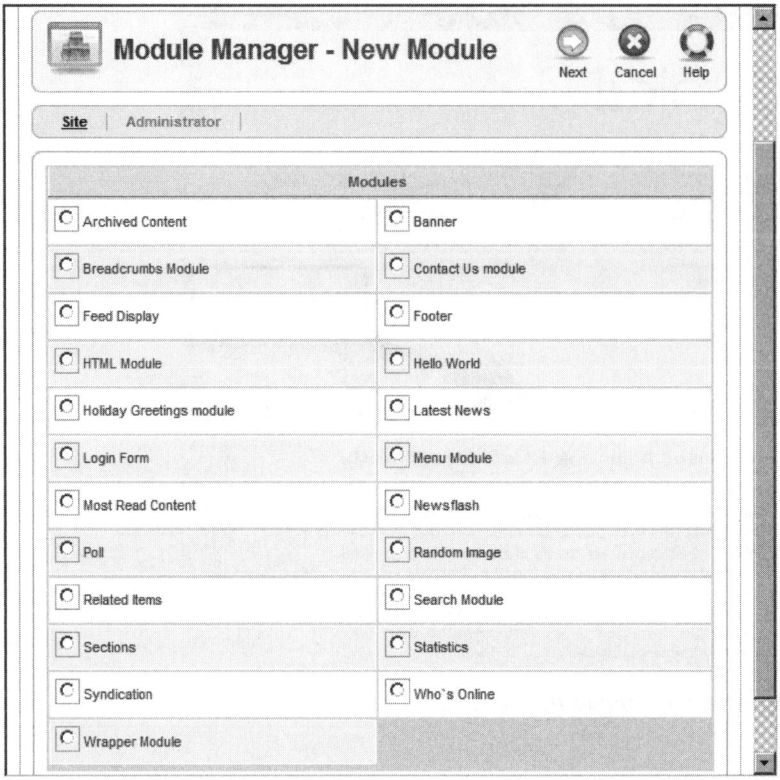

Figure 7-4. *You can create a new module from any of the module types installed on the system.*

Module types follow a standardized naming convention that includes a prefix (mod_) added to the module name, no spaces in the type name, and all letters of the module name in lowercase. In contrast, module instance names include spaces and have a mixture of uppercase and lowercase. Checking the Type column of the Module Manager will reveal the foundation type that defines each module instance.

Default Site Modules

The site modules that are created with the default installation are shown in Table 7-1. Note that each *menu* found on a Joomla site is actually a module instance of a menu module type. Therefore, when you create a new menu, the module that actually handles the configuration and display of that menu will appear in the list.

Table 7-1. *Default Modules Included with the Joomla Install*

Module	Description
All Menus	Provides display of vertical or horizontal menus.
Archive	Presents a dated list of content items that have been moved to the archive.
Banner	Displays an advertising banner that may be configured by specified customer ID or automated display rotation.
Latest News	Presents the latest content items in a specified category.
Login	Offers an area for site login of username and password.
Newsflash	Presents random content items in a specified category.
Polls	Presents an online poll with poll results stored into the MySQL database. Most of the control of this module occurs in the component, and the module features only a single parameter to add a style sheet suffix.
Popular	Presents a list of the most popular content items in a specified category.
Random Image	Displays a random image from a specified folder of images.
Related Items	Suggests other content on the site that is related to the displayed content item.
Search	Provides an input field for the user to enter a search phrase for content on the site.
Sections	Displays the Section area available for the site.
Statistics	Supplies the statistics of the current Joomla server.
Syndication	Allows a web visitor to subscribe to an RSS or Atom feed of the content of this Joomla site.
Weblinks	Provides a linked list of URLs that may be supplemented by user suggestions.
Who's Online	Displays the number of registered guests online and (optionally) the names of those users.
Wrapper	Wraps external HTML content in an iFrame for proper display with a Joomla site.

Many of these modules will typically appear on a single page. Most of these modules are self-explanatory (e.g., the Search module). Some of them include functions that aren't obvious and have features worth examining more closely.

Wrapper (mod_wrapper)

For adapting an existing site to Joomla, the Wrapper module provides a powerful method of including legacy content before it is imported into the Joomla database. This module allows you to set an existing URL and wrap it inside an inline frame (or *iFrame*) for display within the Joomla site. In fact, it can even wrap a remote site so that it appears inside your web page. For example, in Figure 7-5, I have used the Wrapper module to encapsulate the Coherent Visual web site into the user1 column of my Frontpage.

Figure 7-5. *External web pages can be wrapped in an iFrame within the page.*

The Wrapper module only has a few important parameters that need to be set (see Figure 7-6). The URL is obviously the most important, as it determines the location from which the content to be wrapped will be taken. This URL may be a relative address, a completely qualified URL to content on your web server, or a URL that points to a remote site.

The Module Class Suffix parameter allows you to specify a custom style sheet suffix (for a style stored in the CSS file) that will be used for this module. The other parameters (such as Scroll Bars, Width, Height, and Auto Height) determine the presentation of the content on the Joomla page. Setting the Auto Add parameter to Yes will add an http:// or https:// prefix to the URL field unless it already has one. The Target Name parameter sets the name of the iFrame.

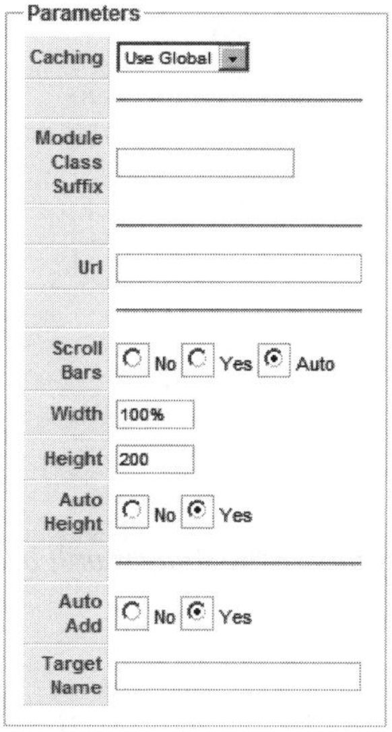

Figure 7-6. *The parameters for a Wrapper module define what content is shown and how it is presented.*

The Wrapper module that is created by the default installation is essentially a blank module instance created from the mod_wrapper module type. You can create other wrapper modules using the New button in the Module Manager and setting the module type to mod_wrapper.

Random Image (mod_random_image)

The Random Image module displays a random image chosen from a specified folder. This module is useful for displaying random banner images that have a similar theme or presentation. The module can essentially impart to frequent visitors that the site is changing and new without requiring the system administrator to do any work beyond the initial setup. This module can also be used for banner advertising, but given the primitive nature of the module, the Banners module would be a better choice for that application.

The parameters for the Random Image module are shown in Figure 7-7. The Image Type and Image Folder settings determine how the images will be retrieved. The Link parameter will attach a hyperlink to the displayed image. The Width and Height parameters will scale the image to fit the corresponding values. Finally, the Module Class Suffix parameter will append a suffix to the style sheet names to access a custom style sheet for this module that has been created in the CSS file.

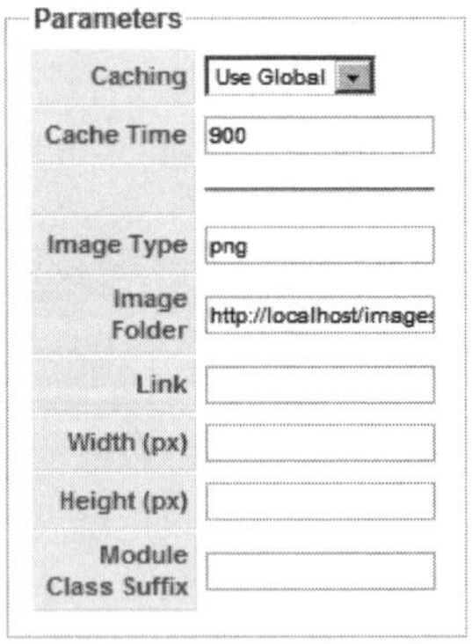

Figure 7-7. *The parameters for the Random Image module specify where the images will be collected and how they will be presented.*

To test the module, you can easily set the Image Folder parameter to reference the /images/stories directory and set the image type to **png**. You will need to select where the module will appear, so for simplicity, set the Location to **right** (for the right-side position of the template). To set the web pages where the module will display, select the All option so every page will feature it. Finally, note the module position and order where the image is set to appear. You need to know where to look when you first test the module. With the settings described, the Frontpage of the Joomla site will show a random image in the proper module position and order.

As with most default modules, the Random Image module instance is provided as an example instance in the default installation of the mod_random_image type. You can create new Random Image modules from the Module Manager.

Banners Module and Advertisement Module (mod_banners)

The Banners and Advertising modules (both of which use the mod_banners type) handle the presentation of banner campaigns created with the Banners component. In the component section, you'll learn how to set up and manage an advertising campaign through this system. For the actual banner display, the Banners module provides a number of options.

Figure 7-8 shows the parameters that affect how the banner is rendered. The Count parameter determines the number of banners to be shown at once. The Banner client and Category parameters allow you to select the campaign that has been created in the Banners component interface. The Search By Tags parameter is a powerful option that matches the banner to the tags or keywords set up for the page or article content. Therefore, you can have baseball banners for pages set with baseball tag words and football banners for those set with football tags.

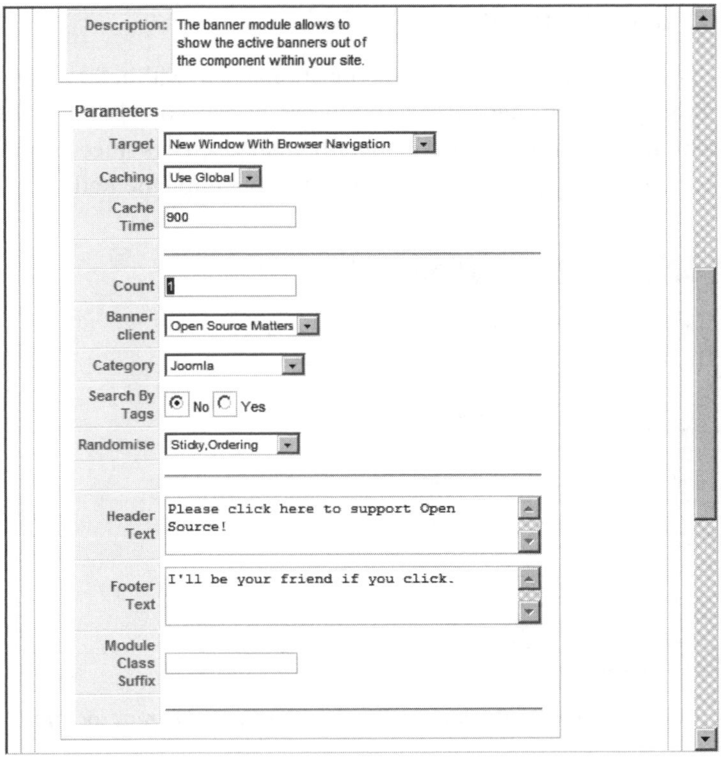

Figure 7-8. *The parameters of the Banners module will determine how it is displayed.*

The Randomise, Header Text, and Footer Text parameters operate as you might expect. In Figure 7-9, I've set the banner to display in the *top* section with special header and footer text. Note that in this template, the footer text has been cut off. The template could be modified, however, to display the entire footer.

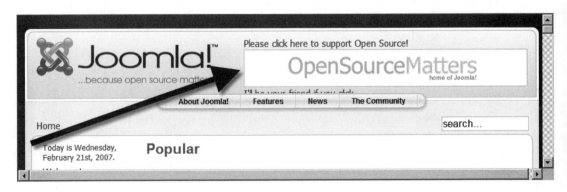

Figure 7-9. *The Banners module is displayed in the top position with header and footer text.*

Breadcrumbs (mod_breadcrumbs)

The Breadcrumbs module (see Figure 7-10) show the organizational path within the web site where the currently viewed page is located. Breadcrumbs can be clicked to jump upward in the page hierarchy. Breadcrumbs are useful to more than just users since search engine spiders can more accurately navigate your web site if these are implemented.

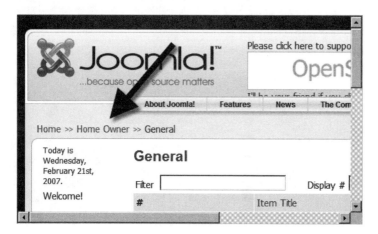

Figure 7-10. *The Breadcrumbs module shows the hierarchical path of your current location in the web site.*

The Breadcrumbs module parameters (see Figure 7-11) are primarily concerned with the path display. The Show Home parameter determines whether the top level (home) is displayed in the hierarchy. The Text Separator parameter lets you override the default double arrow (➤➤) separator.

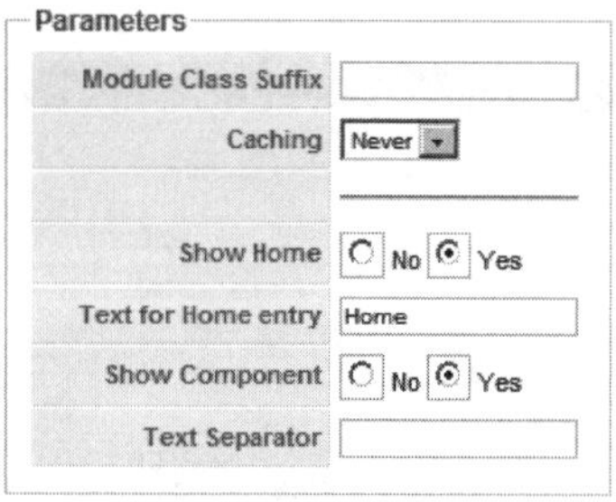

Figure 7-11. *The parameters for the module offer a few simple options.*

Syndication (mod_syndicate)

The Syndication module will create a syndicated feed for the page it is located upon. News feeds (RSS and Atom are the most common) are a technology that provides an automated method of sharing content with other users and other web sites. If a site has a news feed (or syndication), that means a file is stored on the web server that acts essentially like a table of contents file to all of the newest articles on the site.

This file is read by a piece of software called an *aggregator*. The aggregator may be a desktop program that can fetch news features from many different sites and display the newest articles for the user to read. Alternately, the aggregator may retrieve new items and display them within another web site (with proper attribution, of course). Popular aggregators include the web-based Bloglines (`www.bloglines.com`), the news reader built into Internet Explorer 7, the Live Bookmark feature included in Mozilla Firefox, and the New Account ➤ RSS News & Blogs option in Mozilla Thunderbird.

The Syndication module will automatically generate the table of contents news feed file for articles contained in the Joomla site where it is executing. The module display presents a link to the syndication file (see Figure 7-12).

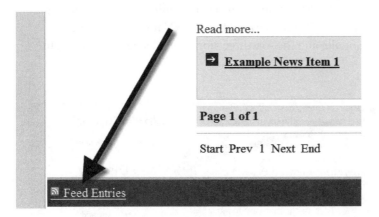

Figure 7-12. *The link to the RSS feed is displayed by the module.*

If you examine the news feed file (see Figure 7-13) that the link targets, you will find the table of contents for your site stored in an XML file using the format of either an RSS or an Atom feed. In the Module Manager, you can specify whether the feed will be generated using the RSS or Atom standard (although I recommend using RSS as it is becoming the dominant standard). There is also a parameter that lets you set up a custom style sheet suffix to use with the module.

```
   <?xml version="1.0" encoding="utf-8" ?>
   <!-- generator="Joomla! 1.5"  -->
 - <rss version="2.0">
   - <channel>
       <title>LoanStaircase.com</title>
       <description />
       <link />
       <lastBuildDate>Thu, 22 Feb 2007 11:57:57 -0800</lastBuildDate>
       <generator>Joomla! 1.5</generator>
       <language>en-gb</language>
     - <item>
         <title>What is an Adjustable Rate Mortgage (ARM)?</title>
         <link>http://localhost/index.php?
```

Figure 7-13. *The RSS format is a specially formatted XML file.*

Feed Display (mod_feed)

While the Syndication module publishes an RSS feed for other sites to subscribe to your content, the Feed Display module allows you to subscribe to other site feeds for display on your Joomla site. In Figure 7-14, I've subscribed to the CNN top stories RSS feed through the Feed Display module, and the top three stories are displayed in the right position of the page.

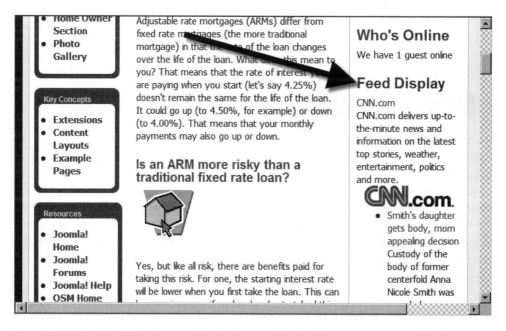

Figure 7-14. *The Feed Display module is shown with the three top stories grafted directly into the Joomla page.*

Setting up a feed is extremely simple. Find a site that provides an RSS or Atom feed of their content (usually indicated by a linked icon on the home page). Copy the link or shortcut that holds the URL to the feed file. In the module parameters (see Figure 7-15), you need only set the Feed URL parameter to begin receiving the feed articles for display on your Joomla site.

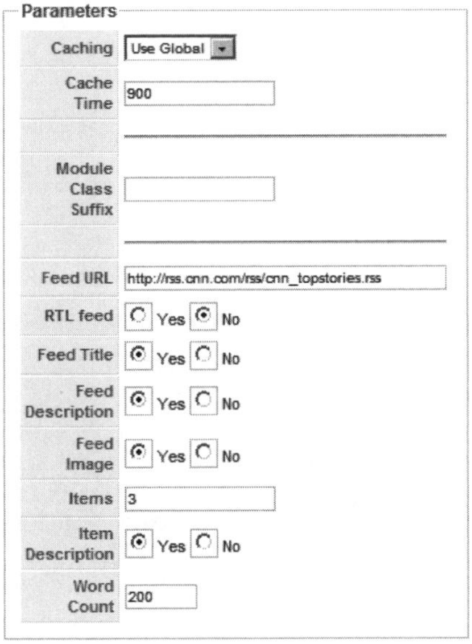

Figure 7-15. *Only the URL is required of the parameters to activate the module to display feed content.*

The RTL feed parameter is used when the feed comes from a non-English language that reads right to left. Display of the feed title, feed description, feed image, and item description can all be turned on or off with the corresponding module parameters. You can also set the number of items to display and the maximum number of words that will be presented for each item.

Main Menu, Key Concepts, User Menu, Example Pages, Top Menu, and Resources Modules (mod_mainmenu)

All menus that are displayed by the Joomla system have an associated module that actually renders the web page menu. The mod_mainmenu type is used as the basis for most of the menus on the system. Installation of Joomla will automatically create a Main Menu module instance from this module type that is the central module used on the Frontpage and cannot be deleted from the system.

There are many parameters for the mod_mainmenu type (see Figure 7-16) that govern how a menu will appear on the page. Several of the parameters relate to hierarchical menus that allow the user to drill down into the site. The default settings are good for most sites, but the available options provide complete control of the menu display without having to modify any code.

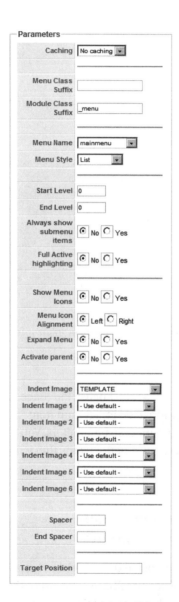

Figure 7-16. *The parameters for mod_mainmenu can change everything from the menu style to the menu hierarchy.*

The parameters for the `mod_mainmenu` type include the following:

- `Menu Class Suffix`: Sets the suffix used for custom menu style sheets.

- `Module Class Suffix`: Sets the suffix used for custom module style sheets.

- `Menu Name`: Specifies the menu record handled by the Menu Manager that is connected to this module.

- `Menu Style`: Sets the style of presentation of the menu to one of four formats: list, vertical, horizontal, or flat list. The list and flat list selections use HTML `<ul>` and `<li>` tags to define the list. The vertical list and horizontal list selections use an HTML table for formatting instead.

- `Start Level`: Specifies the first level of the hierarchy to be displayed.

- `End Level`: Specifies the last level of the hierarchy to be displayed.

- `Always show submenu items`: Sets the presentation to display the submenu items regardless of whether the visitor is in a location that would normally display them.

- `Full Active highlighting`: Supports active highlighting of the links. Selecting this option may render the menu code not entirely complaint with the strict XHTML guidelines.

- `Show Menu Icons`: Displays the icons for the menu if any are specified.

- `Menu Icon Alignment`: If a menu icon is set for display, this parameter specifies whether right or left justification is used for the associated icon.

- `Expand Menu`: With this parameter set to Yes, all of the submenus will always be visible regardless of whether the user expands it.

- `Activate parent`: When set to Yes, activation IDs will be set for all parent menus in the hierarchy.

- `Indent Image`: Provides a drop-down list of choices to determine the indent images. The default selection uses images specified in the template. Other settings include using default images installed with the system, images specified in the parameters section, and no indent images.

- `Indent Image 1` *through* `Indent Image 6`: If the "Use params below" selection is made in the Indent Image parameter, then these six list boxes are used to specify the images to use for the various levels of indentation. All images contained in the `/images` folder will appear in these six lists for selection.

- Spacer: Specifies a character or characters to be used as a spacer between menu items when a horizontal list type is selected.

- End Spacer: Specifies a character or characters to be used before the first item and after the last item in a horizontal menu.

- Target Position: Determines the target of the links (such as a new window or another existing one).

Administrator Modules

Administrator modules work in a similar fashion to site modules, except they augment the Administrator interface. Adding new modules to supply additional functions such as better reporting, relevant statistical information, custom toolbars, and other functionality can make administering the Joomla site more productive. Generally only very large sites need additional administrator capabilities, so in-depth coverage is beyond the scope of this book.

In Table 7-2, you'll find a complete list of the administrative modules that are included with the default install. You can familiarize yourself with the modules of the system if you intend to replace one or more with a third-party control with additional functionality.

Table 7-2. *Administrator Modules Included with the Joomla Default Install*

Module	Description
Components	Shows a list of installed components as a tab in the Control Panel
Full Menu	Regulates the display of the Administrator interface menu
Latest Items	Lists the latest content items added to the site as a tab in the Control Panel
Logged	Displays a list of users currently logged in to the site as a tab in the Control Panel
Menu Stats	Generates the menu statistics shown as the Menu Stats tab at the bottom of the main Control Panel screen
Online Users	Displays the number of users currently logged in to the site in the place header
Pathway	Displays the Administrator pathway
Popular	Lists the most visited pages of the site as a tab in the Control Panel
Quick Icons	Adds fast access icons to the Control Panel
System Message	Controls the messages for system-wide display in warnings, pop-ups, and dialog boxes
Toolbar	Regulates the display of the Administrator icon toolbar
Unread Messages	Displays the number of unread Administrator messages in the queue in the place header

Site Components

Components have many more features than modules and generally have an entire configuration interface. For that reason, components have their own menu on the Joomla Administrator interface menu bar.

There are only five components included with the Joomla installation that have a visible user interface. These are the Banners, Contacts, Newsfeeds, Polls, and Weblinks components. Each of these components has a menu under the Components item in the Adminstrator interface menu. The menu for each component has selections for all of the tab items that will appear in the component configuration window.

Banners Component

The Banners component offers a fairly robust system of banner display that can be used for commercial and noncommercial purposes. Individual banners can be programmed to display a particular number of times (known as *number of impressions*), and the number of times a visitor clicks on the banner (known as *click-through*) can be monitored. The Banners component works in conjunction with the Banner display module described earlier.

A list of all installed banners is displayed by the Banner Manager (see Figure 7-17). Some of the banner statistics are displayed in the columns, such as the number of impressions, the number of impressions left, and the click-through percentage. The banners created in this interface are displayed on the page by the Banners and Advertisement modules described earlier.

You can change the configuration tracking settings by clicking the Configuration button in the Banner Manager. The configuration allows activation or deactivation of daily banner tracking (see Figure 7-18) and the setting of a tag prefix. Daily banner tracking requires more disk space, but provides a more accurate record of banner activity.

Figure 7-17. *The main Banner Manager screen shows all of the individual banners and their statistical information.*

Figure 7-18. *The Configuration window of the Banner Manager lets you change tracking options.*

You can create a new banner by clicking the New button or edit an existing one by clicking the banner name. You can see by the number of available settings (see Figure 7-19) that you can set up a banner to display in nearly any way you might want. Note that you can even include custom banner code if some JavaScript interactivity is needed.

The actual banner graphics should be located in the \images\banners folder of the installation. You can use the Media Manager or an FTP program to transfer the files into the proper folder. Once there, the filenames will appear in the Banner Image Selector drop-down list.

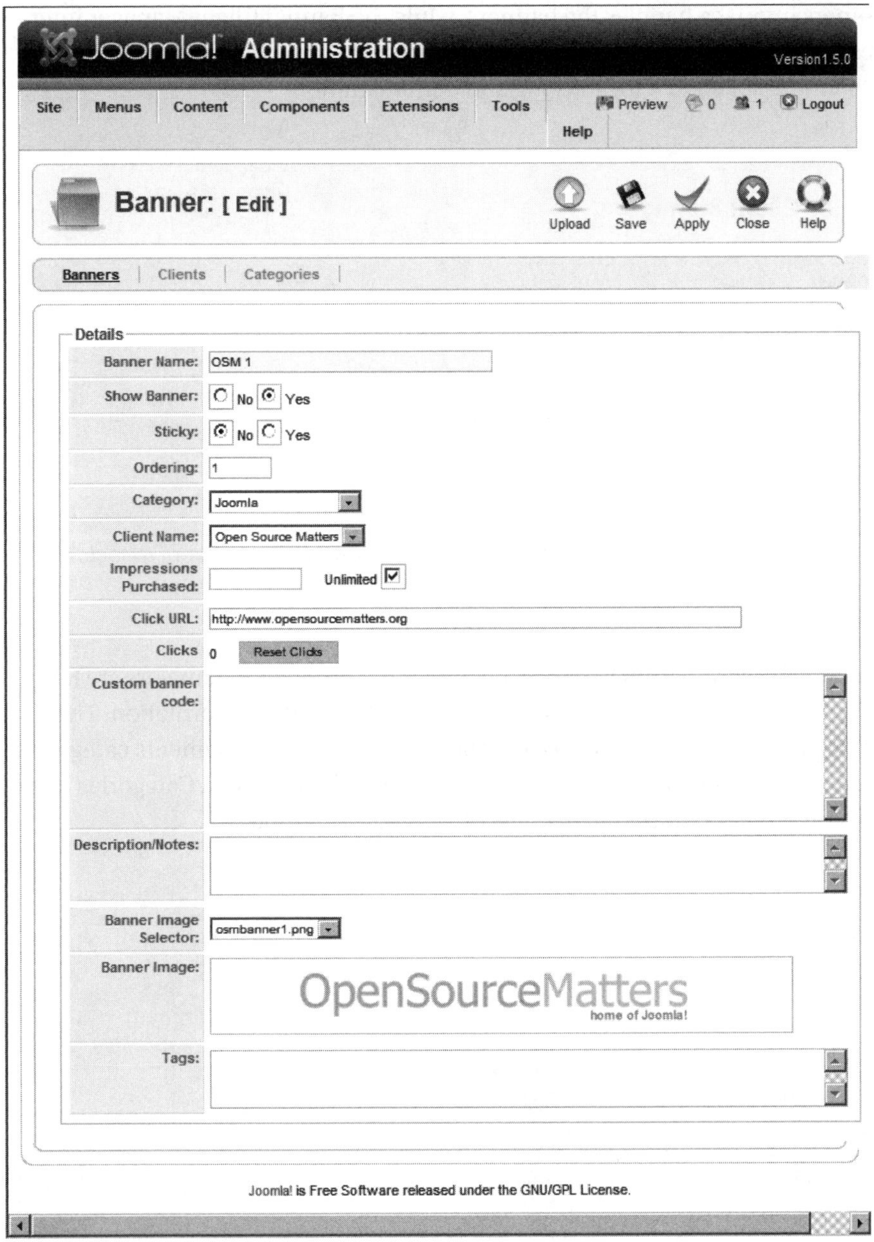

Figure 7-19. *Editing the details of a banner allows setting the presentation of the banner, including the image.*

The Banners interface handles the banners, while the Banner Client Manager interface handles the actual client or campaign (see Figure 7-20). A single client entry may have many banners linked to it for tracking and administration.

Figure 7-20. *The Banner Client Manager shows each client and the number of associated banners.*

You can click the New button to create a new client. The client parameters are fairly basic (see Figure 7-21). You can set the client name and the contact information. The client record is primarily an additional type of organization that supplements categories for banner campaigns. The Banners component additionally provides a Categories interface if you would rather organize the banners through that method.

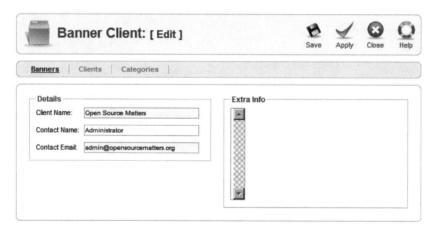

Figure 7-21. *You can create a new client record and organize banner campaigns around it.*

Contacts Component

Joomla includes a small contact management system within the CMS. Contacts stored in this component can be interlinked with the Joomla accounts of registered users, which makes usage, content contribution, and e-mail transmission all trackable through the Joomla interface. Contact entries are displayed in the Contact Manager (see Figure 7-22). Any accounts linked to a registered Joomla user account are shown in the Linked to User column.

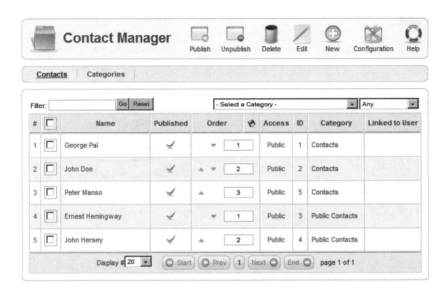

Figure 7-22. *The Contact Manager displays the contact list, including the Linked to User column, which shows when a contact record is linked to a Joomla account.*

Editing an existing contact (see Figure 7-23) or creating a new one provides all of the common parameters (Name, Street Address, Town/Suburb, State, Telephone, etc.) that a traditional standalone personal information manager might have. Since Joomla is entirely web-based, it provides the advantage of having a contact manager accessible wherever a web connection is available.

The Category Manager of the Contacts component presents the same interface that the site Category Manager does for article content. However, the categories you create in the Contact Manager are kept separate from the categories used for articles, users, or other pieces of site information.

Contact: [Edit]

Save   Apply   Close   Help

Contacts | Categories

Details

Name:	Ernest Hemingway
Published:	○ No ⊙ Yes
Category:	Contact records that are shown to the public ▾
Linked to User:	- No User - ▾
Ordering:	1 (Ernest Hemingway) ▾
Access:	Public / Registered / Special
ID:	3

Information

Contact's Position:	Author
E-mail:	ernest@hotmail.com
Street Address:	
Town/Suburb:	
State/County:	
Country:	
Postal Code/ZIP:	
Telephone:	310-555-1234
Mobile:	
Fax:	
Webpage:	
Miscellaneous Info:	
Image:	- Select Image - ▾

Parameters

* These Parameters only control what you see when you click to view a Contact item *

Name	○ Hide	⊙ Show
Position	○ Hide	⊙ Show
Email	⊙ Hide	○ Show
Street Address	○ Hide	⊙ Show
Town/Suburb	○ Hide	⊙ Show
State	○ Hide	⊙ Show
Country	○ Hide	⊙ Show
Post/Zip Code	○ Hide	⊙ Show
Telephone	○ Hide	⊙ Show
Mobile Column	○ Hide	⊙ Show
Fax	○ Hide	⊙ Show
Webpage	○ Hide	⊙ Show
Misc Info	○ Hide	⊙ Show
Image	○ Hide	⊙ Show
Vcard	⊙ Hide	○ Show

Figure 7-23. *The contact-editing screen allows the recording of all basic personal information.*

Newsfeeds Component

Unlike the Feed Display module that appears within a position of the template (such as the right position), the *Newsfeeds component* provides a center column display of the feed content. The feed display can be linked into the menu system to provide menu items for browsing or reading any of the feed articles (in contrast to the module, which provides a static summary). Essentially, you can create a news feed section that can act like an feed aggregator within your Joomla site.

All feeds are defined in the Newsfeed Manager (see Figure 7-24, where the list shows their name, category, ID, maximum number of articles, cache time limit, and order).

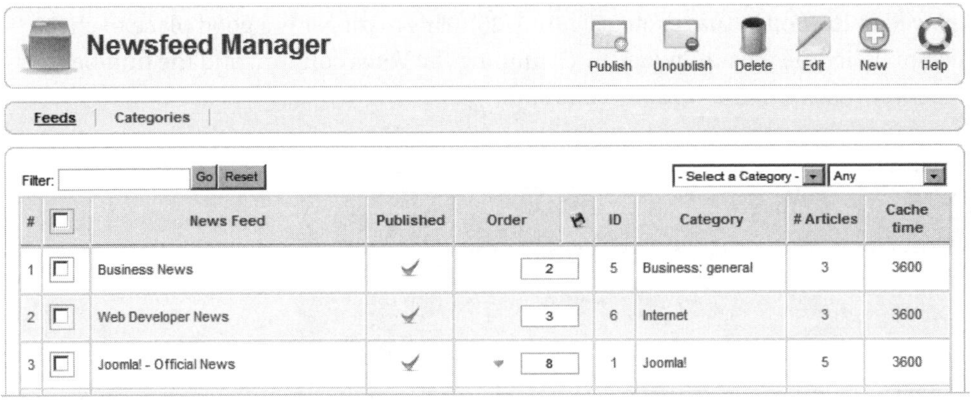

Figure 7-24. *The Newsfeed Manager displays a list of each feed and its parameters.*

When creating a new feed (see Figure 7-25), you need only assign a name, category, and link to get the feed started. The maximum number of articles displayed by the feed and the cache time limit are also available for modification. If the feed is in a non-English language, the right-to-left reading direction of the feed can be specified.

Figure 7-25. *When creating a newsfeed or editing an existing one, Name, Category, and Link are the only necessary parameters.*

Polls Component

The polling interface available through the Polls component allows you to set up and edit an online poll that is then displayed by the Poll module. All of the current polls are displayed in the Poll Manager (see Figure 7-26). This manager is a good place to check which polls are the most popular (by examining the Votes column) and the number of choices for each poll (the Options column).

Figure 7-26. *The Poll Manager lists the existing polls and also provides a summary column of the number of votes per poll.*

The Polls component allows up to 12 options for each poll, as shown in Figure 7-27. It also allows you to set a lag time between when an individual can vote in the same poll again. The default setting, in seconds, is 86,400, which is equivalent to one day. You can increase this value to an extremely high number, such as 31 million (roughly a year), to prevent the voter from participating more than once.

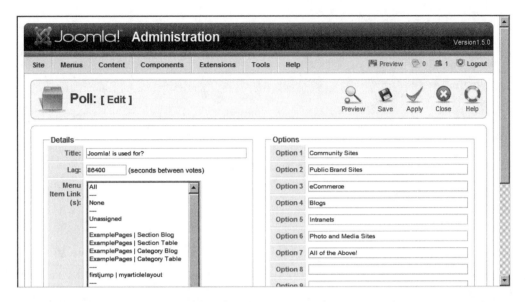

Figure 7-27. *When creating a new poll, you can enter up to 12 choices for the voter to select.*

Weblinks Component

With the Weblinks component, you can allow registered users to suggest links that can become part of the current list. Allowing link suggestions is a double-edged sword. On the one hand, you can take a step toward fostering a virtual community where users contribute and have an investment in the site. On the other hand, you have to monitor these closely for spam links or objectionable content. Luckily, Joomla provides a built-in interface that allows an administrator to approve or decline to add the suggested link to the current list.

For each link, Joomla lets you specify information for the following parameters (see Figure 7-28): Name, Category, URL, Description, Ordering (where it will appear in the link list), Approved, Published, and Target (whether clicking the link should open a new window to display the target page).

■Note When you place an external link on your web site, you should consider if you want your user to leave your web site for another. For example, if a page has a number of footnote links to other sites that support the arguments of the article, you probably don't want a click on the footnote link to take the user to the new site. What if they aren't finished with the article, or they want to click some of the other footnote links as well? By setting the Target parameter of a web link to New Window With Browser Navigation or New Window Without Browser Navigation, you can force the web browser to open a new window and display the destination of the link. This leaves your window still available on the user's system.

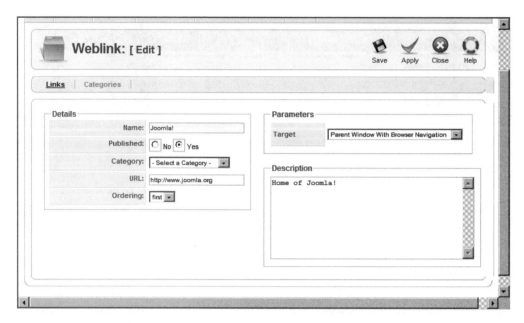

Figure 7-28. *The parameters of a web link let you specify a target for the link.*

Site Plug-Ins

Nearly every site plug-in handles behind-the-scenes functionality. You can examine plug-ins by accessing the Plugin Manager through the Extensions menu (see Figure 7-29). Few of these have configurable parameters that will significantly affect the system functions.

Although plug-ins are the most powerful type of extension, they usually perform a specific function and therefore operate almost transparently within the system. They are generally bundled in a package with a component or module to supply the presentation and user interface aspects.

Since authentication and security play a large role in e-commerce, you'll examine the system plug-ins directly in Chapter 11 when you learn how to set up a virtual store. Until then, the only plug-ins you will likely want to examine in the Plugin Manager are the editor extensions (TinyMCE and XStandard Lite) and the System - Legacy plug-in.

The editor extensions have a few parameters for modifying the content-editing process that you may find useful (e.g., dealing with compression capabilities or the size of the editor window). The System - Legacy plug-in can be activated to allow Joomla 1.5 sites to use Joomla 1.0 modules, components, plug-ins, and templates.

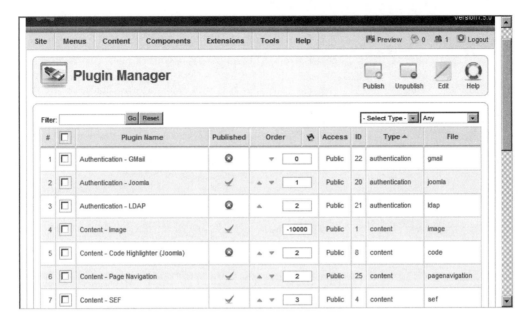

Figure 7-29. *The Plugin Manager will list each plug-in available on the system.*

Conclusion

In this chapter, you saw how Joomla extensions consist of three different types: modules, components, and plug-ins. Each type of extension has particular capabilities that make it useful for implementing a specific sort of task. A module is good for presentation (since it can appear anywhere on a page) and minimal user interaction. A component can support one or more complete user interfaces both for the web visitor and the site administrator. A plug-in sits at the foundation of the Joomla system, allowing it to provide low-level interaction such as supplying a WYSIWYG editor for article content.

Often, an extension will include several types in the same package. The Polls extension, for example, includes a component that is used to create, edit, and manage individual polls. The Poll module displays the polling options and allows the user to cast his or her vote.

While the extensions that have been covered in this chapter are included with the Joomla installation, there is a whole world of third-party extensions that can add all manner of functionality to Joomla. In the next chapter, you'll see how a few of these components can be used to facilitate your site becoming the hub of a virtual community.

■ ■ ■

Web Community Features

In the world of Web 2.0 dynamic content, a web site will sustain a broader audience if it can cultivate an active virtual community. Fortunately, Joomla is an ideal CMS for building such a community. You have already seen some of the built-in extensions (such as the Poll module) that can provide interactive features. In this chapter, you'll examine other Joomla extensions that can offer users significant opportunities to interact with your site. You'll also learn about some of the benefits and problems of deploying the community technologies.

Contrary to the perceptions of many webmasters, adding a virtual community doesn't guarantee traffic increases. You can't simply set up a web site and leave it running as users supply content and increase traffic. In fact, maintaining a virtual community often involves more work than maintaining a static site. However, like the interest paid on a deposit in a bank account, the work you put into the site will be compounded by the contributions of others.

Since you want your efforts to be multiplied, it is important to first define the direction where your Joomla site will be headed. It is vital that you have more than a general idea—you need a specific plan. Creating a site profile is a good way to figure out the role of your virtual community and its eventual destination.

A Site Profile

One of the most intractable problems for webmasters is the difficulty of pinning down exactly what they want their web site to be. That seems like it should be a simple task. For example, if you are shoe manufacturer Nike, the site should focus on shoes, right? Well, not exactly. A quick visit to the Nike site reveals that Nike isn't interested in a simple virtual store to sell shoes. The company is more interested in promoting an image that will lead to bigger payoffs down the line.

On the front page of the Nike web site, two-thirds of the screen is devoted to an expensive video that barely focuses on the shoes. What's on the remaining third of the home page? That space is equally divided among a shop-online image (of merchandise with the Nike logo including a watch, a T-shirt, and a large basketball), a Nike podcast, and a customizable shoe-ordering link.

So is Nike doing anything wrong by dedicating so little actual screen area to selling shoes? I doubt it. Nike understands that people are unlikely to buy shoes often costing exorbitant sums of money just for the sake of having something to wear on their feet. They are selling style. They are selling cool. They are selling the sizzle and not necessarily the steak. And Nike knows that these intangibles are important to its image and should be the focus of the site.

Your Joomla site may not be selling anything but itself, but you still need to recognize exactly what message it should convey to target a specific type of visitor. In fact, choosing the target audience should be key in any site content design.

While these considerations are important to a static web site, to a web site community, they mean the difference between a thriving online metropolis and a virtual ghost town. For instance, a web site for high-end product designers shouldn't communicate a homemade and "cute" atmosphere. On the other hand, appealing to needlepoint aficionados with sleek modern styling could work against creating the online community you desire.

In this section, you'll learn how to put together a site profile to hit the target that you set for your site. The site profile doesn't need to be a formal document. It can be a three-ringed binder filled with notes and outlines. The important part of building a site profile is often not the profile itself, but the time devoted to the thought process that will give you a clear idea of what your community will be about.

Profiling a Site Visitor

The best place to begin any site profile is by thinking about your visitors. Who do you think they will be? Begin by listing general characteristics and then get more specific:

- Are they social or nonsocial in their offline life?

- Do they feel more comfortable communicating over the phone or through e-mail?

- What types of online sites do they already visit?

- What types of information are they looking for, or are they looking for interaction more than information?

If there is a magazine for the topic area that your site will focus on, check out the magazine contents and draw some conclusions about the type of reader interested in this information. Pay particular attention to the advertisements. Advertisers are "putting their money where their mouth is." Looking at the magazine ads will tell you the types of products and services that are purchased enough by your target visitors for advertisers to break even or better.

Your magazine research shouldn't end there. Many magazines do their own extensive market research to know their audience, and you can get some of this information for free. Magazines supply market research to potential advertisers to convince them to spend their advertising dollars. You can contact the magazine advertising department for this information, although increasingly, you can also find it on the magazine's web site.

Nearly as important as your initial site visitor projection is a follow-up after you've launched the site to determine how close your profile matches the real visitors. Only by updating your initial conception to the mirror of reality will you be able to create a nearly self-sustaining community.

Looking at Your Community

One of the most overlooked factors in choosing a community is looking at the financial demographics. Most nonprofessional web developers begin with a topic that interests them and use that as a starting point for their site profile. However, this might not be the best place to start.

Returning to the Nike example, that web site may have begun by targeting professional athletes. After all, for the price and the technical advantages of the shoes, a first glance might suggest that athletic professionals were the market Nike should pursue with its web marketing. However, the financial demographics of professional athletes clearly indicate a fairly niche market. But what about people who dream of being professional athletes? That could be a huge financial demographic.

Presuming that you don't have a market research firm to do an extensive statistical survey, you might do well to check online and see what the membership looks like for groups and associations related to your desired topic area. That may provide some concept of the depth of the market you want to cater to through a virtual community.

Considering How Much Interaction Your Site Requires

Community features can be thought of in much the same way as *leverage* in a real estate investment. If you were to buy $10,000 worth of stock, you would have to pay $10,000 in most cases. For real estate, however, you can put that same $10,000 into a down payment and have control of a $100,000 investment. If the stock doubles, you've made an extra $10,000 from your initial investment. If your real estate investment doubles to $200,000, you pay back the bank for the $90,000 loan, and you've made $110,000 from your $10,000.

Try to look at community features in the same way. If you put in an hour to create content on a standard web site, you now have the content that can be produced in an hour. In contrast, putting in an hour fostering community growth and expanding the ability of others to interact with the site leverages your time. Depending on the volume of visitors, you will gain the cumulative effort of others spending far more than one hour on expanding your site.

You don't need to look any farther than Wikipedia to see this principle at work. I really enjoy reading the work of author Jack Woodford, who wrote a series of how-to-write-a-novel books in the mid-1900s. I must have spent at least a dozen hours of unpaid time researching and creating a Wikipedia entry for him. Tens of thousands of other people are doing the same on topics that interest them.

If you can provide a community platform where people feel passionate about a subject, they will grow the site for you. It's not that there is no work involved; only that the work you do is leveraged by the other members of the community to create a much larger and more robust site than an individual or small organization could afford to do.

Table 8-1 shows common community features with estimates of the setup and maintenance efforts, and typical return value. Note that these features nearly almost always require work and vigilance to obtain a proper payoff.

Table 8-1. *Investment and Return for Joomla Community Features*

Extension	Setup Effort	Maintenance Effort	Community Return
Newsfeed	Low	Very Low	Low
Article rating	Very Low	Very Low	Low
Polls	Low	Low	Low
Suggestion box	Low	Low	Medium
Guestbook	Low	High	Low
Comments	Low	Medium	High
User profile pages/user blogs	Low	Medium	Medium
Event calendar	Low	Medium	High
Wiki	High	High	High
Forum	High	High	High

Take a close look at how the Joomla extensions you're considering might be used to target your site profile and the possibilities of integrating several of them for best effect. Keep in mind that it is never a good idea to throw in everything and the kitchen sink when it comes to added community functionality.

Making Your Site a Home for Other Groups

Once you've incorporated interactive features into the site, you've created a vehicle for promotion. Most web sites lack community features either because the web provider does not offer them or (more likely) the webmaster doesn't know how they might be implemented.

One excellent method of mutually beneficial cross-promotion is to offer the features your Joomla site affords to another web site. For example, if your Joomla site focuses on camping, offer a private forum to a local outdoors group. If your site sells archery supplies, let people from the local archery club post reviews of the various target ranges around the nation. If your site focuses on local environmental issues, offer to host a local conservation group's poll on what people see as the barriers to recycling.

Literally hundreds of special interest groups would love to have an online venue for their area. They don't even need to be an organized group, thanks to modern search engine technology. For example, I enjoy going to library used book sales. Such sales are very poorly advertised, and there is no central list that identifies them in the Los Angeles area. One day in the future, I would like to create a Joomla event calendar where people could post such information. When I attend a sale, I often see about 10 percent of the same people at each event. That's easily a big enough group that if a half dozen people kept the calendar updated, hundreds of other people interested in these events would be attracted to that Joomla site.

Using the Community to Retarget Your Site

If you notice that a particular portion of your site is getting a lot more attention than expected (see Chapter 9 for information about site statistics), focusing the interactivity on that area can help clue you in to exactly who is visiting your site and what interests them.

If most of your visitors are looking at an odd posting on extending the life of a laser printer, wouldn't it be useful to know that those same people are looking for a good place to buy specialty paper (where you may have a web affiliate account)? Put up a forum in the area, and those people will tell you and the world what is on their minds.

Joomla! Technology for Building Web Communities

Once you have established your site profile and general plan, you can begin choosing the extensions that will provide the community features that you want. With Joomla, often a half dozen extensions provide nearly the same functionality, so choosing one can be difficult. The extensions highlighted in this section have been chosen for two reasons:

Availability for free download: In the interest of readers being able to download, test, and deploy extensions that add these features, I have chosen to include only those that are freely available. Some fine commercial components match or surpass the capabilities of the extensions presented here. When possible, I have also mentioned popular commercial extensions that target the same field as the extension being discussed.

High user rating on the Joomla extensions directory site: Most of the selected extensions are the best-of-breed for use with Joomla. However, don't let this stop you from evaluating other extensions that may better cater to your virtual community needs. Application development, particularly open source development, is somewhat like a horse race, with the various contestants constantly jockeying for position. As time goes on, one extension will pull ahead in features and usability, only to fall behind the next month as new versions of other add-ons are released.

The community functionality that can be added to any Joomla site includes newsfeed subscriptions, user article ratings, web poll surveys, guestbooks, user comments, event calendars, and forum/message boards. None of these extensions rely on any other, so there is no reason to read the following sections sequentially. You can read only the sections about the technology that interests you.

Subscribing to Newsfeeds

While you may not want your site to become a portal (due to the high costs of such heavy web traffic), making a few well-chosen newsfeeds available on your web site can increase the amount of information available through your site and give it a sense of up-to-the-minute relevance. While search engine optimization experts argue whether the content will be considered part of your site and contribute to your search engine rating, it certainly can't hurt your search placement.

In the previous chapter, you learned how to use the Feed Display module to show an RSS or Atom feed. However, finding appropriate feeds that provide information your visitors will want to read can be difficult. From your site profile, you should have a basic idea of the topics that will generally interest your target users. Try looking for newsfeeds related to your desired subjects on the following newsfeed search engines:

- `www.syndic8.com`

- `www.2rss.com`

- `www.rss-network.com`

- `www.feedster.com`

You should be able to find a least a few feeds with topics relevant to your site.

One of the best methods of evaluating a feed is to subscribe to it through a feed aggregator. By executing or accessing the aggregator every day, you will quickly get a feel for the level of content available from each feed and whether it will be useful to your visitors. Popular desktop aggregators include Sage (a Firefox newsfeed reader available at `https://addons.mozilla.org/firefox/77`), ThinFeeder Java RSS Aggregator (`http://sourceforge.net/projects/thinfeeder`), and the Windows-based SharpReader (`www.sharpreader.net`). You can also use web-based aggregators, like Google Reader (`www.google.com/reader`) and Bloglines (`www.bloglines.com`), which require only that you set up an account to store the subscriptions you want to monitor.

To find useful feeds, examine web sites that you visit often for RSS or Atom feeds. Newsfeeds for even small web sites are more common than you might think. You may be surprised that a favorite web site offers a feed that can be used for your Joomla site.

Allowing User Rating of Articles

Allowing users to rate articles is perhaps the first step toward allowing community feedback. This functionality is built in to the Joomla system, so using it requires only simple activation.

To enable article rating, in the Article Manager, click the Configuration button and select the Show option for the Item Rating/Voting parameter, as shown in Figure 8-1. Aside from articles that have been set up to specifically exclude article rating, all content on the site will now be available for user opinion.

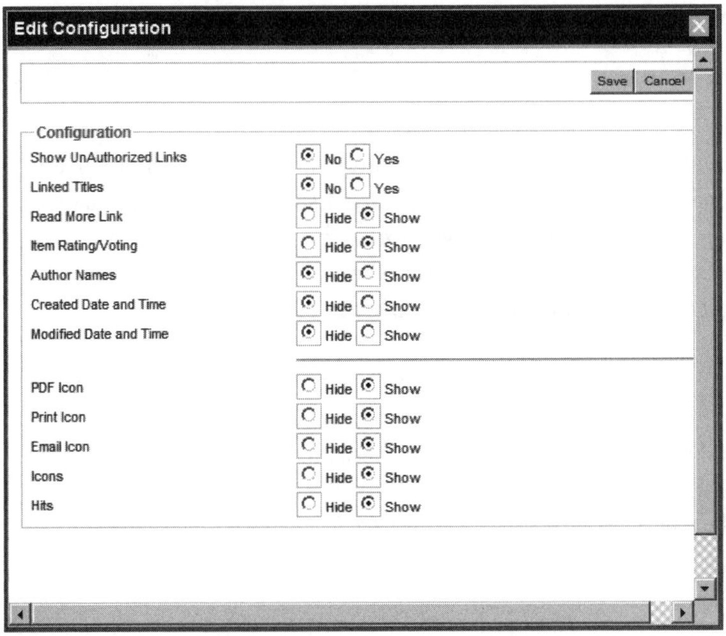

Figure 8-1. *Set the Item Rating/Voting parameter to allow user rating of articles.*

Each article will display a current number of rating votes and the rating average directly under the article title, as shown in Figure 8-2. A small rating submission form will appear directly under the current values, so new users may vote for their preferences. Note that depending on your configuration settings, the voting form may not appear on the articles when they are presented in summary form (such as on the Frontpage), although the current rating is displayed.

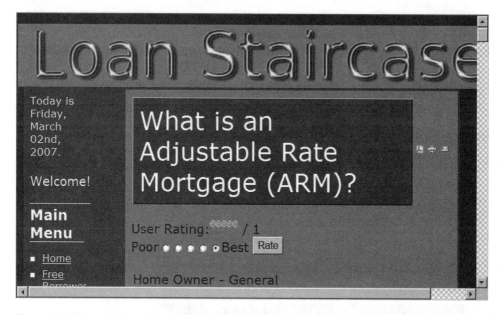

Figure 8-2. *The article rating in filled circles is followed by the number of current votes that generates that average.*

The Joomla article rating setting can also be overridden for individual articles. However, you should avoid allowing rating on most articles and disallowing it on only a few, particularly articles that are controversial. Users will notice the missing rating, and your site may come across as disingenuous or give the users the impression that rather than creating a community, you are building an audience to listen to you preach.

■Note The user rating system (like the polling system) included with Joomla is just a primitive implementation. If these features will be used prominently on your web site, be sure to check out the variety of alternative third-party implementations that are available from the Joomla extensions site (http:// extensions.joomla.org). These offerings generally have many more features and a more powerful interface.

Adding Polls

Polls can be an effective way to get everything from general opinions to feedback on specific site features. Since Joomla makes polling so easy and convenient, you can add a poll to your site within moments of completing the initial installation. The sample poll that appears on the Frontpage of a default installation demonstrates the elegance of this handy community feature.

Chapter 7 provided a general overview of the Polls component and module. While the overview described the basic features, implementing a poll is somewhat counter-intuitive, so I'll walk through a poll setup here.

■**Tip** The Polls component in Joomla automatically shows the current results of a poll. Other polling components available through the extensions site (http://extensions.joomla.org) have a variety of result display options based on user registration and security privileges. You can even make the results available to only the administrator. Except in the most limited cases, you should (at least eventually) exhibit the public results of the poll. Otherwise, visitors will seldom take the time to vote. There is no better way to kill participation in site polling than to never reveal the results to satisfy the curiosity of those who voted.

Creating a New Poll

To create a new poll, you use the Polls component. From the Components menu of the Administrator interface, select the Polls option. Click the New icon to create a new poll. Enter some options for the poll. For the LoanStaircase web site, I wanted to ask some questions about the most attractive loan programs, as shown in Figure 8-3.

Before you leave the parameters screen, you should change the default Lag parameter. There are dangers of individuals attempting to stuff the ballot box, regardless of how trivial the subject matter of the poll. Joomla includes a few methods of guarding against poll rigging, such as preventing the same IP address from voting repeatedly in a certain period of time.

You can also limit the poll's appearance to pages displayed to registered members of the site. Of course, this may drastically limit the number of votes cast, making the poll nearly worthless. Therefore, I suggest setting the Lag parameter to a higher value to cut down on repeat votes. The parameter, set in seconds, has a default value of 86,400, which is equal to one day. That means the same user can vote every 24 hours. By setting the parameter around 30,000,000, you ensure that the same user will not be able to vote more than once a year.

Click the Save button to write your poll into the database, and you will be returned to the Poll Manager. Your new poll will appear in the poll list, but will show a red X icon, indicating that it hasn't been published yet. Click that icon to publish the poll.

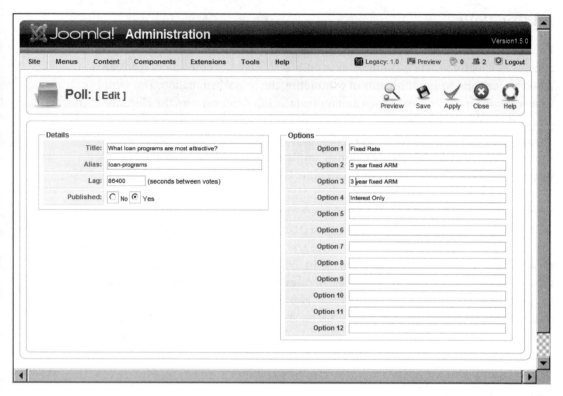

Figure 8-3. *Create a poll that is more useful elsewhere in the site than on the Frontpage.*

If you refresh the Frontpage in your browser, you'll still see the original poll. Although you've set up the poll in the Polls component, you haven't configured the linked Poll module, which actually handles the poll rendering. Open the Module Manager and click the Poll module instance. The module's parameters screen includes the Poll parameter, which is a drop-down list of currently available polls created in the component. Select your new poll from the list, and then click the Apply button to write the parameter setting into the system.

Refreshing the Frontpage now will display the new poll, as shown in Figure 8-4. Each module instance (such as the Poll module instance you just modified) is created from the foundation mod_poll type. You can create another poll for display elsewhere on the site by creating a new instance. Just click the New button in the Module Manager and select the mod_poll module type.

Right now, the Poll module displays only on the Frontpage. You can change the pages on which it appears by modifying the Menu Assignment parameter on the module's parameter screen.

Figure 8-4. *The new poll will be displayed on the Frontpage by the Poll module.*

Setting the Display Menu for the Poll

If you left the parameters screen for the Poll module, return to it now. The bottom-left side of the screen shows a frame labeled Menu Assignment. The Menus options let you select whether the module is displayed in all the menus, none of the menus, or the menus that are selected from a list. The list displayed below these options is set to Home by default, so the poll displays only on the Joomla Frontpage. In the list box, select the Joomla! Overview menu. That will make the poll appear only when the Poll module is displayed by that menu.

If you refresh the Frontpage, you'll see that the poll no longer appears there. However, if you click the Joomla! Overview menu, you will see the new poll rendered on that page.

■**Caution** Information generated by polls can be of questionable real value and is difficult to rely on for authentic reaction. Many site visitors, even your most regular users, will ignore polls. Results can be skewed by casual visitors or zealots and may differ widely from the feelings of your general community. Therefore, the data rendered by an online poll should not be acted upon without careful deliberation.

Adding a Guestbook

Guestbooks are a technology that originated with the very genesis of the Web. When the Web was initially developed, almost every web site was made up of static read-only pages. People quickly realized that having a guestbook where visitors could enter a simple message or compliment made creating and updating a web site far more rewarding.

A guestbook can furnish an excellent way for visitors to contribute to your Joomla site. Most often, you'll find that entries are either complimentary or (even more valuable) suggestions on how the site might be improved. However, be sure to check the guestbook frequently, as spammers will occasionally find some way around the spam-protection measures.

One of the best Joomla guestbook extensions is an open source component called Jambook (www.jxdevelopment.com/jambook). It has the following features:

- Joomla editor interface for rich text posting

- Various configuration options for poster name display

- Preview of page before entry is saved

- E-mail interface for administrator and user notification of new postings

- Administrative specification of allowed HTML tags in post

- Spam blocking through a number of configuration settings (including image render confirmation before entry)

- Capability to ban specific IP addresses (so visitors who graffiti or otherwise deface the guestbook can be prevented from cluttering the text)

- Double-posting checking and prevention

- Automatic culling of expired postings (if a time limit is set)

- Administrator interface for guestbook configuration

You can install Jambook using the Extension Manager, in the same way you add a standard component. Once installed, Jambook will add its own menu to the Components menu of the Administrator interface.

To manage your guestbook, select the Jambook ➤ Control Panel option to display the Control Panel, as shown in Figure 8-5. From this central interface, the administrator can jump to the other Jambook panels. All menu options appear in the Control Panel except the Jambook ➤ De-Install option, which removes Jambook from the Joomla system. The De-Install option will leave existing entries on the server for later Jambook reinstallation and import.

Figure 8-5. *The Jambook Control Panel is the launching point to access the other administrative panels.*

Managing Guestbook Entries

The Guestbook Entries panel provides a list of existing posts for selecting, editing, and deleting multiple posts. As the administrator, you can edit any guestbook entry, or you can create new ones, as shown in Figure 8-6. You can enter the title, author, and message using standard user interface fields. You may want to turn off the e-mail address and home page entries through the configuration screen so that you don't encourage spammers and unwanted site associations.

The entry screen in Figure 8-6 mirrors the one presented to users in the front-end. However, the administrator entry screen has two differences: there is no spam protection image, but there is a Publishing tab that holds security settings for the entry.

When users attempt to post to the guestbook, they are presented with an anti-spam image and asked to enter the letters and characters displayed in the image. For the image to be generated, your web server must have GD2 activated in the PHP installation (see Chapter 10 for additional information about this interface).

The Publishing tab allows the administrator to set options such as the access level of the entry and the publishing start and end dates.

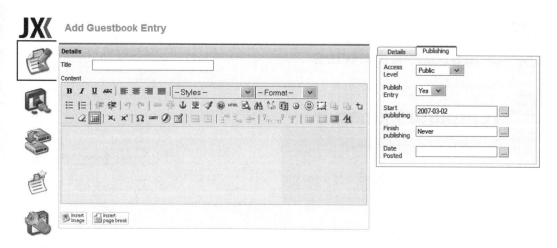

Figure 8-6. *Creating a Guestbook entry is similar to adding a content article to Joomla.*

Managing Templates

The Jambook Template Manager governs all the aspects of display of the guestbook entries. Each part of the guestbook presentation (such as list item, preview, or search) has a separate user-editable template, as shown in Figure 8-7. These templates may be modified directly in the folder with a text editor or through the editor's user interface.

If the template is edited through the user interface, a simple editor window displays the template code, as shown in Figure 8-8. Since the code is written in JavaScript, it is often a much better idea to edit the files directly using a tool such as jEdit (www.jedit.org) or Eclipse (www.eclipse.org). However, the built-in editor does allow you to make small changes remotely and is particularly useful if you are making minor modifications on a remote server.

Figure 8-7. *The available templates for the guestbook presentation are displayed in the templates list.*

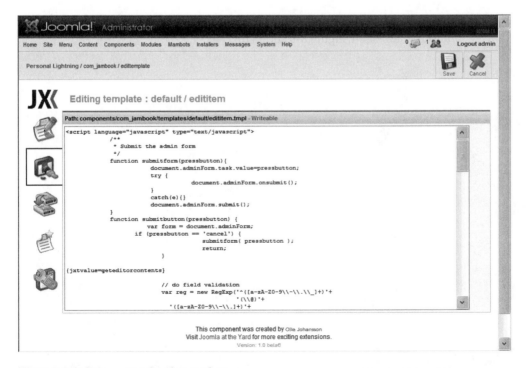

Figure 8-8. *Editing a Jambook template*

Importing Entries

The Import Entries screen is very simple. At the time of this writing, Jambook could import only the entries of the popular Joomla guestbook component AkoBook or Ako-Book+ (a fork of AkoBook available at www.alikonweb.it/451). AkoBook is available for free download from here:

```
http://joomlacode.org/gf/project/akocomment_se
```

Viewing Jambook Information

The Information screen has a good amount of data, including installation requirements, general instructions, license requirements, to-do list for developers, and version history. The screen also has some valuable information about the plug-in directives that can be used with the component.

Configuring Jambook

The Configuration option on the Control Panel takes you to the setup screen for guest-book parameters, including general settings, posting selections, e-mail configuration, spam settings, and import execution parameters. Each set of configuration settings is available from the tabs on this screen:

Settings: This tab offers options that govern entry display, such as Days Kept, Days New, and Days Published. Figure 8-9 shows this tab.

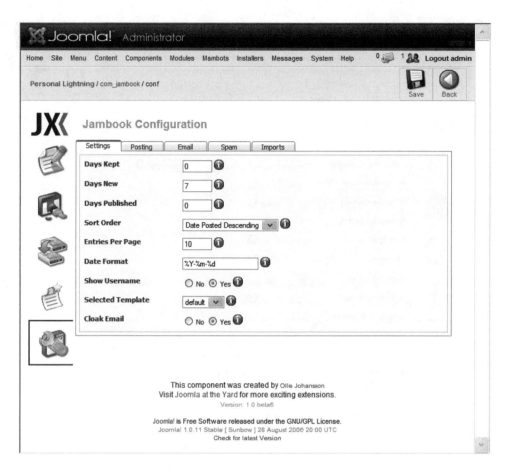

Figure 8-9. *The Settings tab has display settings.*

Posting: This tab, shown in Figure 8-10, supplies the parameters that determine how posting occurs. The following are some of the most important settings:

- When the Auto Approve setting is enabled, all posts are instantly present on the site. Turning this off will require the administrator to approve the display of new entries.

- Flood Protection determines the number of seconds before the same poster can add another message to the book.

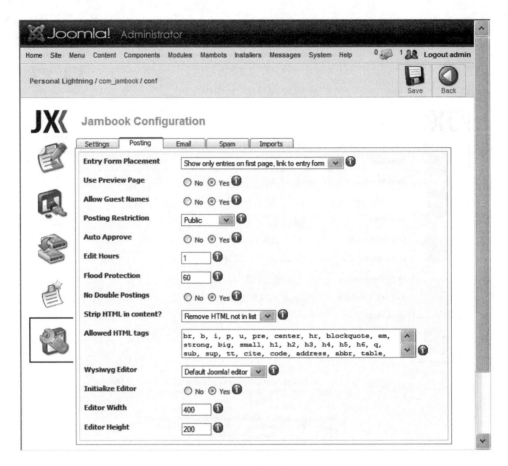

Figure 8-10. *The posting settings determine the rules of posting.*

- The Allowed HTML Tags option lets you list specifically the tags that may be used in a message. By default, table-creation tags are included in the list and allowed for posting. In my experience, tables are used by graffiti artists to mess up the display of the guestbook. Therefore, I always remove the table tags from the posting capabilities.

Email: The settings on this tab, shown in Figure 8-11, determine how automatically e-mail messages are handled. You can configure the address and name that automatic mail (such as new message postings) will be generated under. Note that the automatic e-mail functionality uses the underlying Joomla mail interface. If you don't have the Joomla e-mail settings configured, automatic e-mail will not function properly.

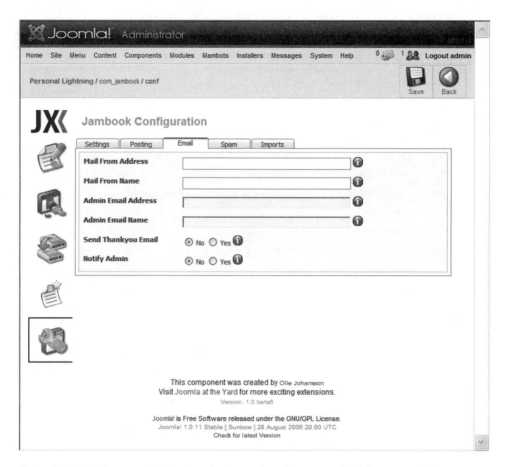

Figure 8-11. *Settings on the Email tab determine the text and addresses used for automatic e-mail.*

Spam: These settings, shown in Figure 8-12, are powerful for a guestbook component. The Use CAPTCHA setting requires the user to interpret a series of letters and numbers and enter them into a text field before their message can be posted. CAPTCHA is an acronym for "completely automated public Turing test to tell computers and humans apart." It represents an image-generation technology that prevents automated bots (used by spammers) from interpreting the image. The other spam settings will depend on how restrictive you want your guestbook to be.

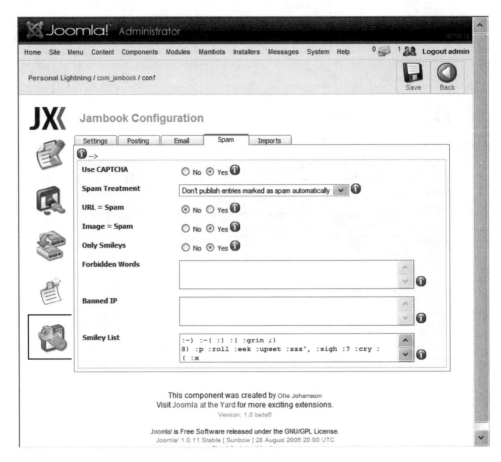

Figure 8-12. *Spam settings can help prevent spammers from using your guestbook for advertisement.*

- The URL = Spam setting will treat any message that includes a URL as spam. A good-willed user may post a suggestion URL, and this would be labeled as spam.

- The Image = Spam setting detects any entry that includes an image tag and labels it as spam.

- The Forbidden Words setting can help you keep cursing from your web site, if desired. Even more useful, you can find a list of words that are used by spammers that can be forbidden to minimize the plague of spam in your guestbook (search for "spam filter word list" on your favorite search engine).

- The Banned IP setting lets you prevent users from posting by blacklisting their IP in this field.

Imports: These settings, shown in Figure 8-13, will determine how entries imported from AkoBook are handled. You can have the importer automatically truncate title text length to a specified number of characters and convert Bulletin Board Code (BBCode) formatting automatically into HTML formatting before the entries are saved into Jambook.

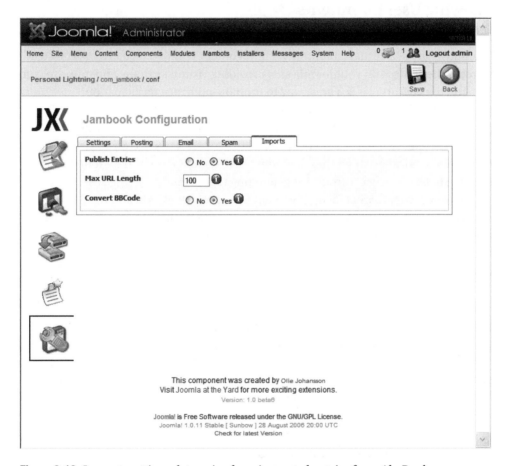

Figure 8-13. *Imports settings determine how imported entries from AkoBook are handled.*

■**Note** The Jambook extension, and many others, allow rich text (fonts, styles, etc.) to be specified in a message with BBCode. BBCode is a lightweight markup language that uses bracketed tags that surround the text to be styled, such as [b]This text will be bold![/b]. BBCode predates HTML tags for text formatting, but it remains in use because it is more difficult to page spoof with it and there is no ability to include dangerous script code (as JavaScript can be embedded in HTML).

Once you have the guestbook configured, you may want to post the first message to set the tone for future posters. You can even create a few entries that remain published for only a limited time (such as "Welcome to our new site!") so the guestbook doesn't seem dated after it has been available for a while.

Allowing User Comments

Allowing users to post comments to site articles is an extraordinarily effective way of retaining users of a virtual community if new content is added regularly. As you steadily increase the content on your Joomla site, providing visitors with the apparatus to comment on the new articles is a great way to promote audience participation.

This model has been used successfully on sites too numerous to mention. The most popular comment-based systems are celebrity gossip sites such as TMZ.com and The Superficial. Sites for niche markets, such as Ain't It Cool News and Slate, also do very well. More merchandise-oriented sites, including CNET and Epinions, have found user commenting to be the magic formula for generating repeat traffic.

Whatever your market focus, if you have a slightly thick skin and regularly post new material (even if your updates are as simple as listing the new camcorders available), adding comment technology is the way to go. It takes simple administrative oversight to ban spammers and people who can't get along with other, so you won't spend a great deal of time managing the comments.

Tip Many of the popular sites that have comment functionality include a document that has clear rules describing what can and cannot be posted. Generally, these site guidelines have evolved over time to handle most of the problems that a comment site encounters. It is a good idea to visit a popular comment-based site and model your own comment guidelines on the battle-tested rules that a popular site has already refined.

The Joomla site offers more than 20 comment extensions for free download. Among the most popular comment extensions is AkoComment. It provides a full-featured comment interface and also allows the administrator quite a bit of control regarding the posting policy. The following are some of AkoComment's more useful features:

- Templates for comment formatting

- Compatibility checking to ensure XHTML compliance

- Optional RSS feed created from comments

- Parameter limits to specify the maximum comments that can be added or displayed for an article

- System alert generated when new comment is added

- Integration with the Community Builder extension (discussed later in this chapter)

- Administrator and user e-mail notification of new comments

Installing AkoComment

Installing the AkoComment package takes several steps. Start by downloading the package archive here:

```
http://joomlacode.org/gf/project/akocomment_se
```

The archive contains a plug-in, a component, and two modules. The modules are optional, but you will need to extract the component and plug-in, and install them via the Extension Manager. By default, when new plug-ins are installed, they remain unpublished. Therefore, to begin AkoComment, open the Plugin Manager and publish the AkoComment component.

Adding Comments

With the component installed and the plug-in published, AkoComment should already be activated. Go to your Frontpage and look at the bottom of any article. You should see the options that allow entry of comments for that article, as shown in Figure 8-14.

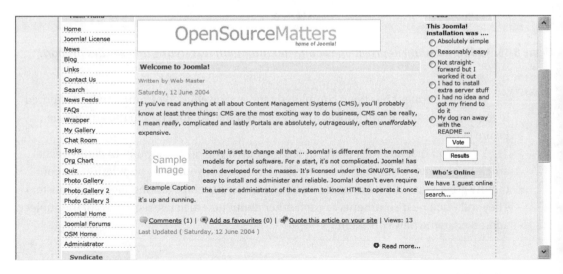

Figure 8-14. *The Comments link will appear at the bottom of the article, along with links for favorites and quoting the article.*

If there are no existing comments, the Comments link will state "Be the first one to comment on this article." Clicking that link will take you directly to the comment editor, as shown in Figure 8-15. You can see that the editor supports basic formatting. Like the Jambook extension, AkoComment supports CAPTCHA image generation to prevent automated spam programs from entering a comment.

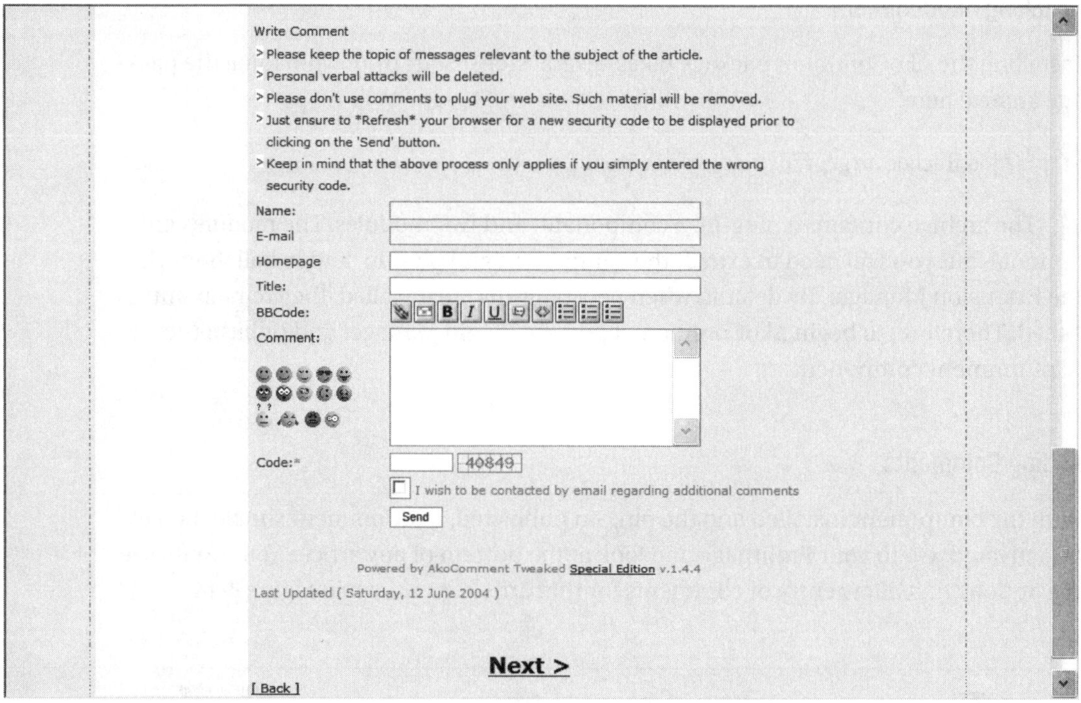

Figure 8-15. *Adding a comment provides a complete editor with text styling and smilies support.*

Once a comment has been completed (and approved, if AkoComment is configured to require approval), it will appear in a speech bubble list attached to the article (see Figure 8-16).

When you first add the comment technology, it will take a popular or controversial article to generate a number of comments. However, as your site's popularity and community grow, you will find an entire subcommunity develops among the regular posters. They will often post comments to each other about new articles, regardless of the subject addressed in the new comment.

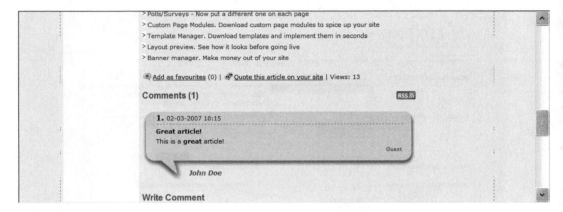

Figure 8-16. *Comments appear as speech bubbles at the bottom of the article.*

Configuring and Managing Comments

One of the great features of AkoComment is the substantial control it gives an administrator to govern how comments and posters are handled. From the Components menu, the AkoComment submenu has three options: View Comments, Edit Settings, and Edit Language. The View Comments option allows editing of any existing comments. You can also reorder comments and publish or unpublish them.

Most of the administration and setup settings are available through the Edit Settings option. When you select that menu option, you see a screen with seven tabs:

General: This tab, shown in Figure 8-17, provides the basic commenting options, including where to allow comments and how usernames are presented.

Layout: The Layout tab, shown in Figure 8-18, has settings that allow you to configure the display of the comments in the order and fashion that you want. You can modify the interface shown below each article. By default, the "Add as favorites" and "Quote this article on your site" links are presented to the right of the Comments link. On the Layout tab, you can choose to hide these links.

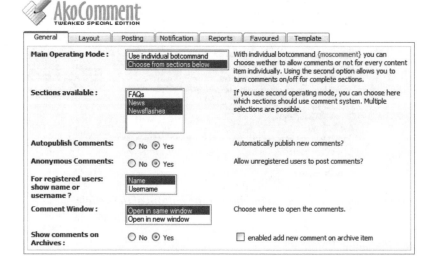

Figure 8-17. *General settings*

Figure 8-18. *The layout settings let you configure both the comments display and the links to comments that appear below the article.*

Posting: The settings on the Posting tab, shown in Figure 8-19, let you configure nearly every aspect of the posting interface. Note that all the settings below the "Disabled security code" option relate to the CAPTCHA image generation. Changing these from the defaults is never a bad idea. If sites with AkoComment become popular enough, you can be sure that spammers will create an algorithm to target the default generation properties in an attempt to bypass the spam security.

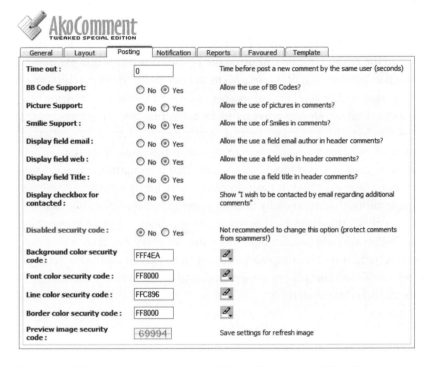

Figure 8-19. *The posting settings control how the posting editor functions.*

Notification: The settings on the Notification tab, shown in Figure 8-20, determine the automatic e-mail sent when a new comment is generated. Like the Jambook extension, these e-mail features rely on the Joomla e-mail system to be correctly configured. You will find the Joomla e-mail setting in the Global Configuration Manager.

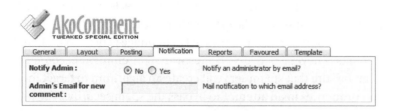

Figure 8-20. *The notification settings control automatic e-mail delivery.*

Reports: The settings on the Reports tab, shown in Figure 8-21, enable users to report a comment to the administrator. Choosing the proper setting for this parameter is perhaps the hardest decision of the setup. On the one hand, users can be some of the best policing agents of posters who abuse the comment sections by posting spam or even illegal information. On the other hand, by activating this reporting capability, you may be flooded with unwanted petty e-mail messages. Particularly when a flame war erupts, users will report each other for various infractions faster than snitches in an overcrowded prison. Handling the problems cited is sometimes no easy matter either. Someone may post their honest opinion, particularly regarding religious or political viewpoints, that others may find very offensive. Still others will take it upon themselves to police the comment boards and report back anything they run across. Consider whether you will be administering your site every day. If so, it isn't much trouble to deal with possible complaints. However, weekly or monthly checks will make it seem as if filed complaints are ignored, and in those circumstances, it is best to leave the feature deactivated.

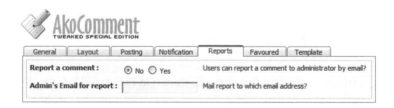

Figure 8-21. *The report settings determine whether users can send a report to the administrator about a particular comment.*

Favoured: The settings on the Favoured tab, shown in Figure 8-22, allow you to create a Favorites menu that users can select. The tab offers instructions on how to create the menu within the Joomla Administrator interface.

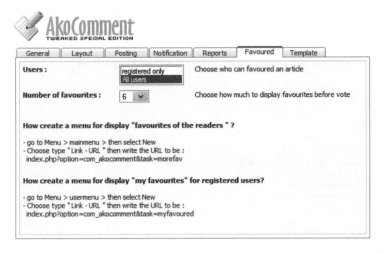

Figure 8-22. *The settings on the Favoured tab determine the presentation of the menu.*

Template: The settings on the Template tab, shown in Figure 8-23, let you set how the visual presentation of the comments will appear. The Style parameter provides six different settings (Table with alternate color, Fieldset, Template bubbles acid/beige/ gray, and Template dashed 2007). The Form position sets the location of the new comment-posting text area. You can even create an RSS feed of the comments by activating the Display RSS Feed option.

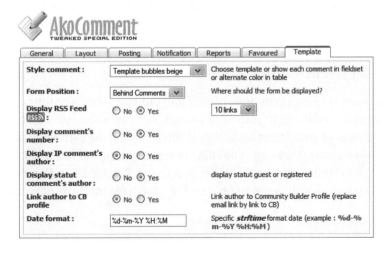

Figure 8-23. *The template settings determine the visual presentation of the comments.*

For international adoption, AkoComment allows most of the text in the user interface to be modified into a native language. This feature is available through the Components ➤ AkoComment ➤ Edit Language option. The editor allows you to set any of the interface text to your desired language text, as shown in Figure 8-24.

Path: C:/Program Files/Apache Software Foundation/Apache2.2/htdocs/Joomla10/components/com_akocomment/languages/english.php

```php
<?php
################################################
# AkoComment - A User Comments Component #
# (C)opyright  2004  by  Arthur  Konze    #
# Homepage : www.mamboportal.com          #
# Version  : 1.0 beta 1                    #
# License  : Copyright, don't distribute #
################################################
# Translation: Arthur Konze               #
# Homepage    : www.konze.de               #
################################################

// Header language definitions
DEFINE("_AKOCOMMENT_WRITECOMMENT","Write Comment");
DEFINE("_AKOCOMMENT_WRITEFIRSTCOMMENT","Be first to comment this article");
DEFINE("_AKOCOMMENT_QUOTETHISARTICLE","Quote this article on your site");
DEFINE("_AKOCOMMENT_CREATELINK","To create link towards this article on your
website,<br />copy and paste the text below in your page.");
DEFINE("_AKOCOMMENT_PREVIEWQUOTE","Preview :");
DEFINE("_AKOCOMMENT_GOBACKITEM","Go back to the article");
```

Please note: The file must be writable to save your changes.

Figure 8-24. *The Edit Language settings allow for localization of the AkoComment interface.*

The AkoComment package also has modules to display the last comments and the most favored comments. You can place them on the Frontpage or another page.

Implementing an Event Calendar

A group or event calendar is an excellent opportunity for your site to become the central source for event information relating to your site's topic. It can also allow you to cater to specific geographic sectors of your target audience. If you've visited the extremely popular Craigslist web site (www.craigslist.org), you may have noticed that all classified and job postings are broken down by geographic area (Los Angeles, Bay Area, San Diego, etc.). Communities that grow within a geographic sector often have the most potential for depth.

■**Tip** If you don't want to host the calendar on your site, Google offers a Calendar service (www.google.com/calendar) that has the advantage of integration with the Gmail user interface, the ability to create and send invitations, track RSVPs, and set up automatic event notifications, including mobile phone messaging. You can use the Wrapper module in Joomla to incorporate Google Calendar into your site.

The chief problem with an event calendar is the danger that it will remain empty. A calendar does no one any good and will attract few visitors if no events are posted. Therefore, when you begin planning your calendar, search out annual events that focus on your topic area. By setting these items up as repeating events, you can ensure that the event calendar always has entries on those days.

A full calendar can also create its own problems—chief among them is the possibility of overwhelming a search engine spider or a sitemap. When a search engine spider visits your web site, it may register the large number of links in the calendar and simply add your site to its slow spider queue. This can hurt the frequency of your site being spidered. Likewise, a sitemap may run into the thousands of links if the calendar is included on multiple pages. Be sure to archive older events and set up exceptions (in the sitemap components and `robots.txt` file) so that this doesn't become a problem.

JCal Pro is one of the most well-regarded Joomla event calendars. It has an excellent CSS-based presentation, as shown in Figure 8-25. It also lets users search for specific events. The component supports native Joomla permissions for event creation and administration.

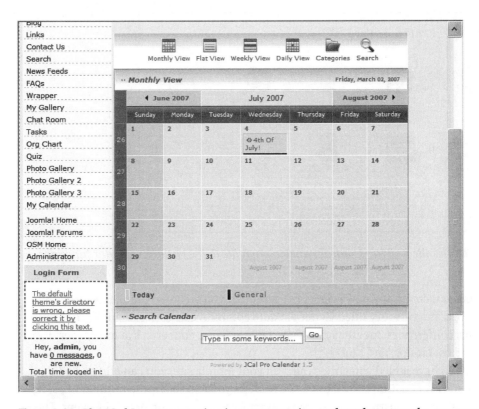

Figure 8-25. *The JCal Pro presentation is very attractive and works across the spectrum of web browsers.*

You can download JCal Pro for free from the Anything-Digital web site:

`http://dev.anything-digital.com/index.php?option=com_content&task=view&id=2&Itemid=3`

JCal Pro is a single component in the package archive, so you can install it through the Extension Manager. To allow access to the component, simply create a menu reference that links to it.

For event listings, JCal Pro uses the Joomla WYSIWYG editor, so event descriptions can be in rich text formats. Events can be configured as repeating events or placed in privately viewable categories to allow complete access control over event viewing. JCal Pro also has a different display option from the general calendar mode, in which events can also be viewed from most recent to least recent.

From the JCal Pro Control Panel in the Administrator interface, shown in Figure 8-26, you can configure the component, set up categories (akin to standard Joomla categories), create events, install and set themes (akin to Joomla templates), and view the documentation.

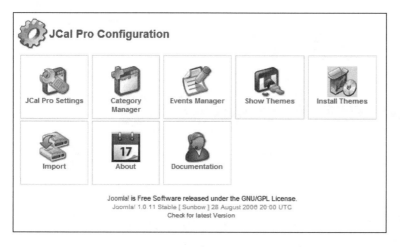

Figure 8-26. *Use the JCal Pro Control Panel to navigate to the various calendar functions.*

Before you create any new events, I suggest that you create relevant categories. By default, there is a category titled General. Some common categories might include holidays, fairs, conferences, meetings, festivals, talks, movies, concerts, live music, performances, interest groups, and tours.

After you have added categories that suit your Joomla site, you can add and edit events in the event editor, shown in Figure 8-27. As you can see by the number of event parameters, an administrator can be fairly exacting in the parameters of the event. The repeat capabilities can set the repetition of an event to occur in subsequent days, weeks, months, or years. The repeat can be set to cease after a certain number of times or after a particular date.

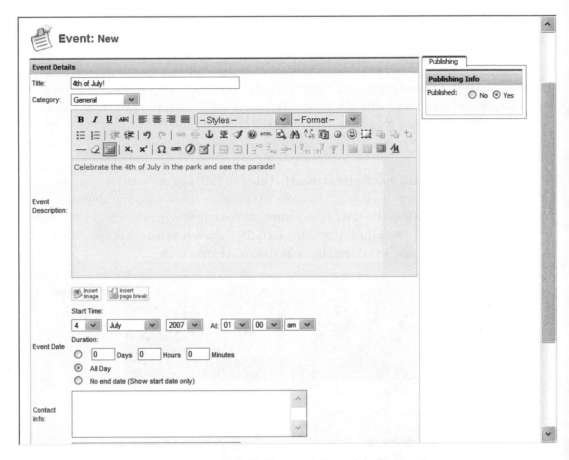

Figure 8-27. *Create a new event and set up the date and time of the happening.*

JCal Pro can import events from only the ExtCalendar component for Mambo. The import occurs automatically if another calendar is found to be installed.

Creating an Active Forum/Discussion Board

Forums are as useful in generating a user community as they are fraught with peril. Anyone who has run a forum knows about the flame war brawls between users, the posting of content that has questionable legality (copyright-wise), the foul language, and the dead boards where no one posts for months. It is often a difficult balancing act trying to keep a forum flourishing and having it stay on message. Nonetheless, if a forum is successful, it can become a large storehouse of self-generated content.

Several forum components are available for Joomla. However, the main Joomla web site uses Simple Machines Forum (SMF), which is a pretty substantial recommendation. While SMF is a PHP-based forum, it is not native to Joomla. Several bridge components are available to allow the SMF to run within the Joomla page.

■**Note** Although SMF is not native to Joomla, there are a number of excellent forum extensions have been customized specifically to Joomla's capabilities. Perhaps most popular is the Fireboard Forum extension (http://joomlacode.org/gf/project/fireboard/frs), which has a designer-friendly template system, support for personal mail systems, capability to add Joomla modules within the forum itself, forum statistics, and much more. Another popular forum extension is Kookaburra (www.thejfactory.com), a Joomla-integrated version of the fast and lightweight PHP forum application PunBB.

Since the Joomla development team has chosen SMF, and this web forum receives more than 1,200 posts per day and has over 60,000 active users, adopting SMF seems to be a wise choice. SMF is free and open source, with many skins and templates are available for use with it. Once the bridge is in place, SMF appears as part of the Joomla interface for fairly seamless integration, as shown in Figure 8-28.

Figure 8-28. *The SMF can be bridged into Joomla.*

In addition to choosing a forum, you must also choose a bridge into Joomla. For SMF, you can choose from commercial and open source bridges. This section will demonstrate the JoomlaHacks Joomla-SMF Bridge.

Installing SMF

Before you begin the installation, make sure that your machine supports all of the prerequisites. If your server is already running Joomla and MySQL, you will very likely be able to install SMF without any trouble. The minimum requirements include the following:

- PHP 4.1.0 or higher (it can be running on Apache or Microsoft IIS)

- MySQL 3.23.4 or higher

- The PHP `engine` directive set to On

- The PHP `magic_quotes_sybase` directive set to Off

- The PHP `session.save_path` parameter set to a valid, writable path

- The PHP `upload_tmp_dir` parameter set to a valid, writable path

- The PHP `file_uploads` directive set to On

Once you have established that your web server can execute SMF, you can download it from the SMF web site, at `www.simplemachines.org`.

Three basic download packages are available: full install, large upgrade, small update, and web install. Since I presume you've never before installed SMF, the full install is probably your best bet. Alternatively, you can do the web install if you feel comfortable with that option.

■**Tip** As a web administrator, I've found it nearly always a good idea to keep the virgin installer of whatever new system I'm implementing. When I was first getting started, I would simply throw away the installer image file once it finished. I thought that the package could always be downloaded again later if I needed it. Several times after having a system fault, however, I found that the version used on the system was no longer available. The package had been upgraded, sometimes making it incompatible with the data and configuration of the older version. Worse still, the developer sometimes would simply evaporate, and I had no way of obtaining a critical installer. For these reasons, I suggest downloading and backing up the virgin installer just in case. Try to avoid web or Internet installers unless you have no choice.

For the SMF-Joomla Bridge, you can find it at `www.joomlahacks.com/joomla/ components/Joomla-SMF_Forum`.

To most effectively use SMF with Joomla, extract the files from the package into a folder within the Joomla hierarchy. For simplicity, create a folder called \forum at the Joomla root directory. On the Windows platform, the path may appear something like this:

```
C:\Program Files\Apache Software Foundation\Apache2.2\htdocs\forum
```

Once you have extracted the files from the archive into this folder, you need to address it through your web server with a web browser window. The index.php file will automatically execute and begin the installation process. This first installer screen accepts all of the basic configuration and MySQL information, as shown in Figure 8-29.

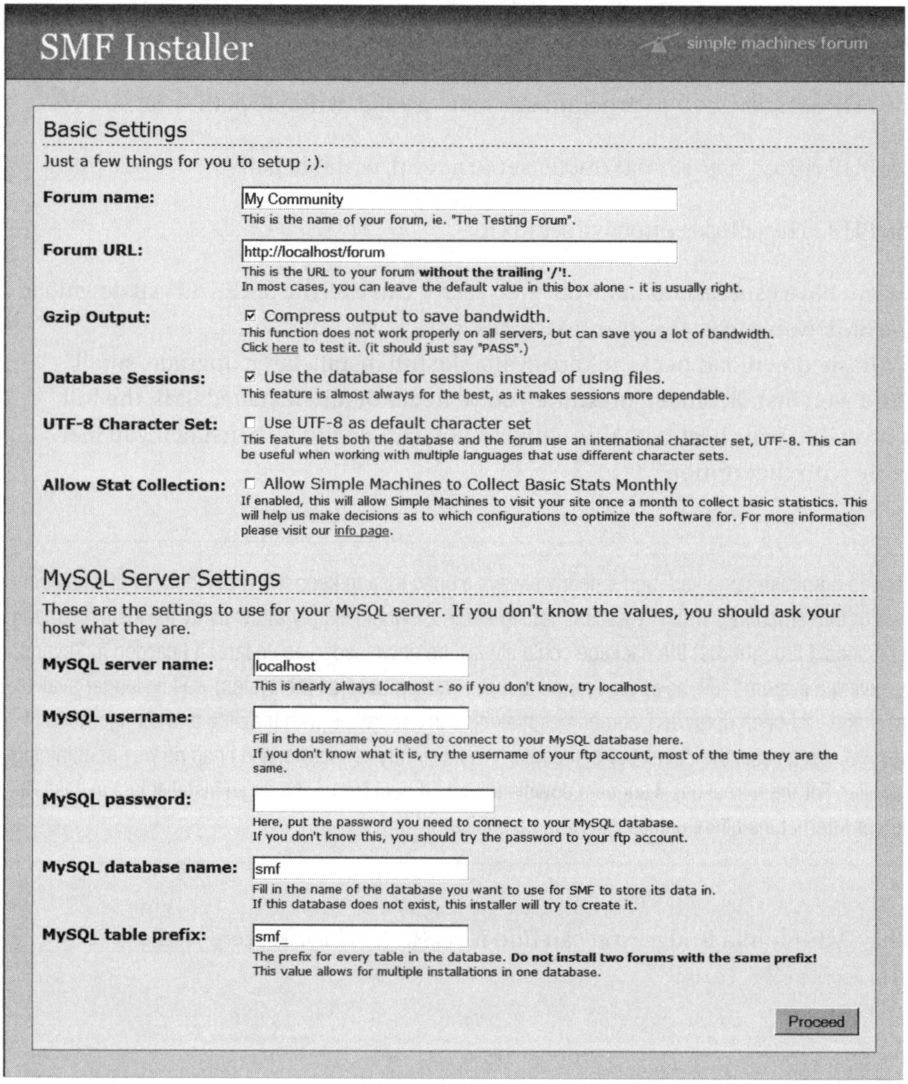

Figure 8-29. *Click the Proceed button once you have set the parameters and MySQL settings.*

The second installer screen allows you to create an administration account for the forum, as shown in Figure 8-30. Use the standard precautions (such as a varied password with numbers and letters) when choosing an administrative password, to make sure hackers won't be able to guess their way inside.

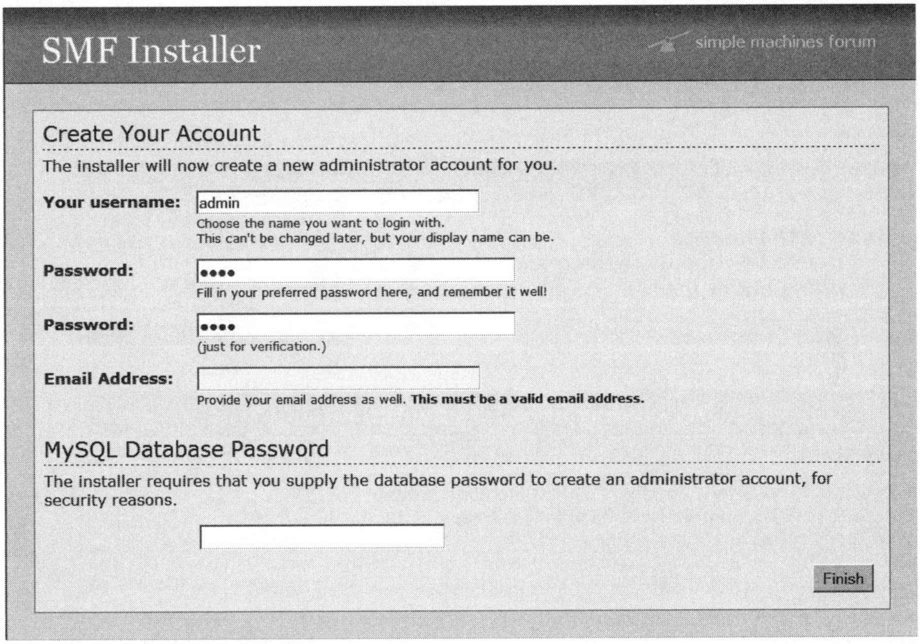

Figure 8-30. *Create a secure administrator account for the forums.*

That's it! Installation is complete.

Running SMF

If you access the URL in a web browser, you can navigate through the forum, as shown in Figure 8-31. SMF is a full-featured forum and can be run by simply creating a link within the Joomla system to this URL. However, you will lose many features, such as site navigation, if you don't bridge SMF into your Joomla site, as described in the next section. Nonetheless, take a few moments to examine SMF so you can have a clear idea of how it works.

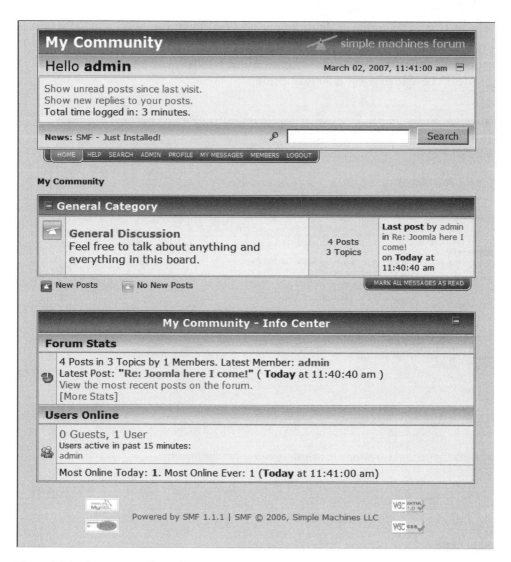

Figure 8-31. *The message board home page shows the available categories and general statistics.*

Clicking General Discussion will display all of the message topics within that category, as shown in Figure 8-32. The display shows each topic along with the user who originated it, how many replies have been made, the number of times the topic was viewed, and when the last posting occurred. If you have spent any time with forum software, you know how useful this information can be to frequent visitors.

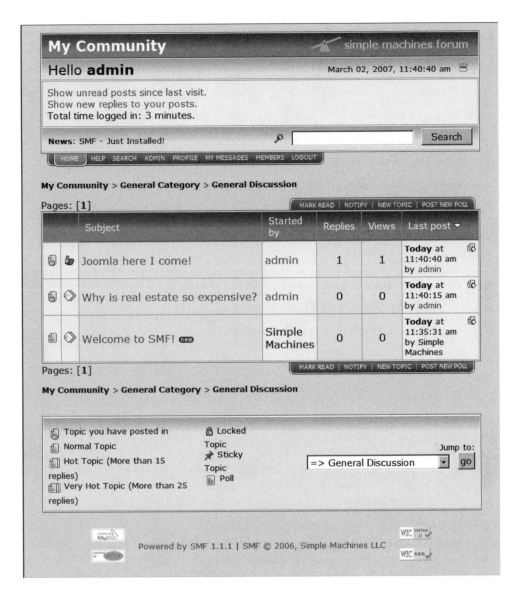

Figure 8-32. *Each topic within the category displays summary information about the activity related to it.*

Choosing to post a new topic displays a standard editing interface, as shown in Figure 8-33. The editor is not an advanced WYSIWYG interface like the ones included with Joomla. However, it can accept rich formatting within the message, displayed as attributes, as shown in the figure.

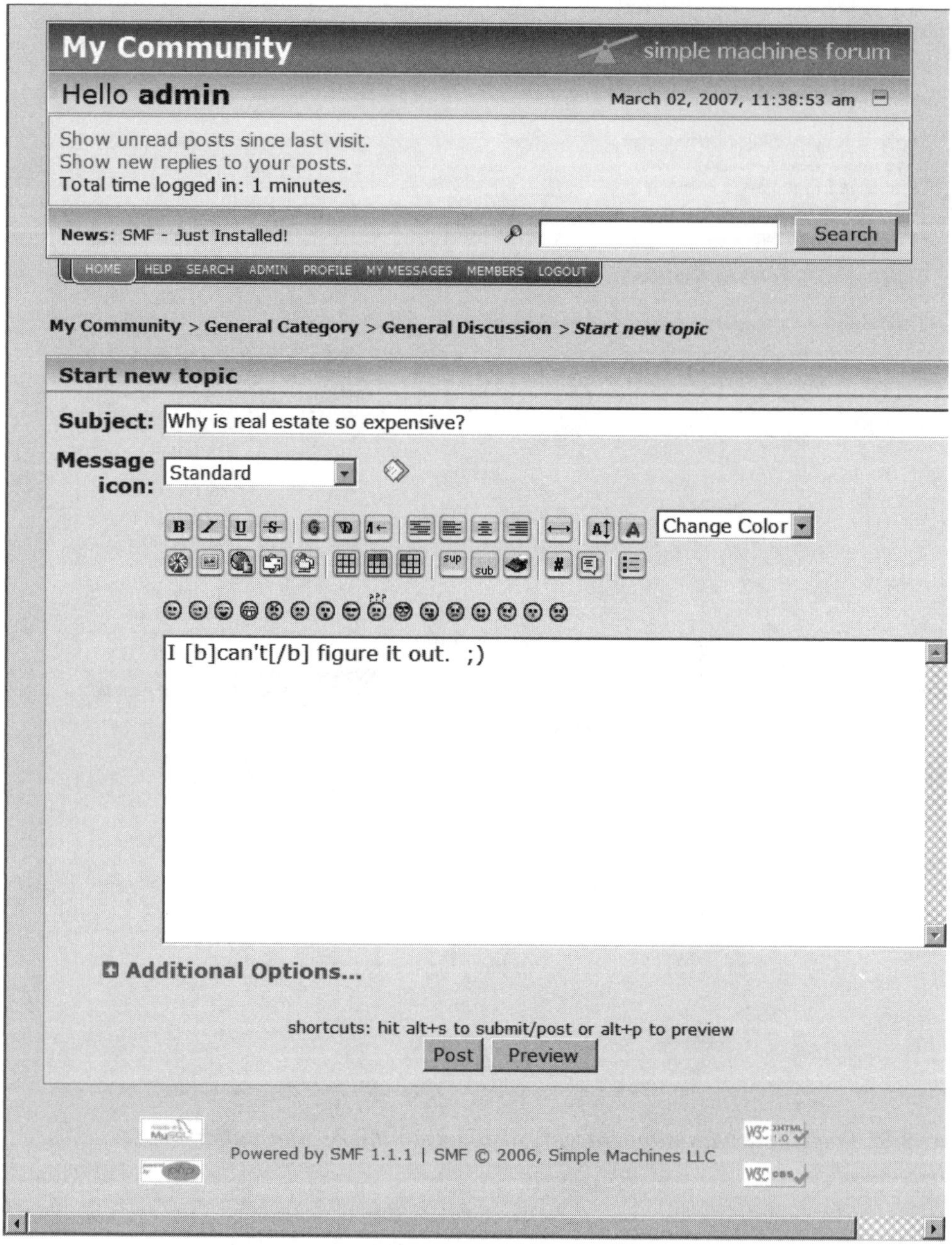

Figure 8-33. *You can post a new topic through the SMF editor.*

You administer SMF through the SMF Administration Center, as shown in Figure 8-34. It is actually fairly complicated, but the SMF site has fairly extensive documentation and tutorials. It will take some time, but it is worth the effort to learn how to configure this robust system to match your exact specifications.

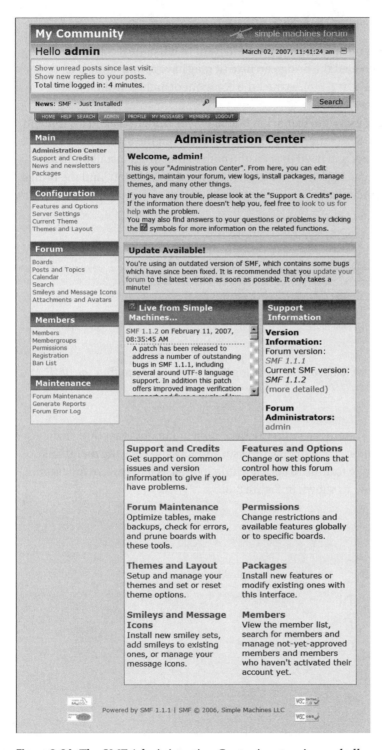

Figure 8-34. *The SMF Administration Center is extensive and allows substantial forum modification.*

Installing JoomlaHacks Joomla-SMF Bridge

Once you have the forums up and running, you will want to integrate it into the Joomla system. If you have downloaded the bridge archive (it may have a long name like `smf_1-1_jsmf_1-0-x_bridge_1-1-7.zip`), extract the component archive from it (likely with a filename like `com_jsmf.zip`).

Install the component using the Extension Manager. The bridge will add a submenu to the Components menu. Select the Configuration option from the SMF Bridge menu. The only essential parameter you need to set is the path to the forum installation, as shown in Figure 8-35. You can click the Create path automatically button, and the bridge will attempt to create it dynamically.

Figure 8-35. *Set the path parameter so that the bridge will know where to find the SMF installation.*

Click the Save button to store the path. Create a main menu item that directs the user to the SMF bridge component. Then open a browser window and click the menu link. You will be able to browse the forums wrapped within Joomla as if they were functioning in the separate SMF window, as shown in Figure 8-36.

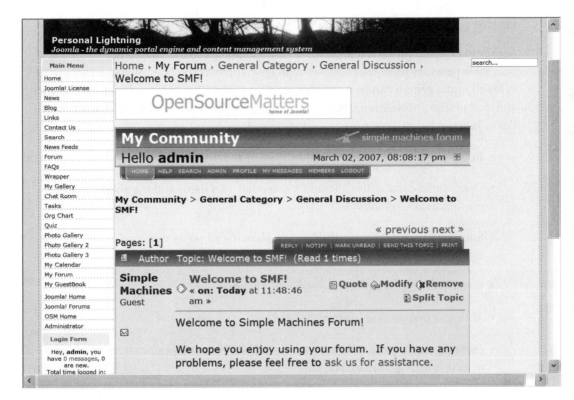

Figure 8-36. *Browse the forums within the Joomla interface.*

Adding a Suggestion Box

One thing I rarely see on web sites is a suggestion box. Visitors often want to make suggestions (and sometimes vent their frustration) when your site doesn't have what they're seeking. Don't you want to know? Surely, for the one person who makes a suggestion, there are literally dozens looking for the same content.

You can easily create a suggestion box by simply repurposing any one of the plug-ins available. For example, the comments or guestbook extension can be easily presented as a suggestion box, much to the advantage of your site. And if you add the suggestions, giving a small credit at the bottom of the page will reinforce site loyalty.

Since a suggestion box is an easy application to build, you will build a component in Chapter 13 to add a suggestion box to your web site.

■**Tip** When any suggestion is made, send a "thank you" message, either automatically or manually. No one likes to take the time to make a suggestion only to feel ignored. You don't have to take the suggestions, but do make sure to thank people for submitting them.

Using Community Builder

Community Builder (CB) is one of the most popular Joomla extensions on the Web because it provides wide-ranging user-management features. User management on the default Joomla system can be somewhat primitive, and CB fills out the user management and user profile information. The open source CB extension adds the following capabilities to Joomla:

- Robust login system with workflow process for authentication

- User profile capabilities, including extended user fields and the ability to add custom fields and tabs

- Summary list on the user profile page, showing all posts and article submissions by the user

- Connection paths between users, including user lists

- Ability to upload user avatars

- Individual user page contributions through blog entries and custom user pages available through bridge plug-ins

- Complete plug-in architecture for adding capabilities such as CAPTCHA, Google Map (through Joogle) functionality, PonyGallery image display, instant message status, and event sessions tracking

CB is so popular in the Joomla world that many other extensions integrate with the login system it provides. Some of the extensions include Fireboard, OpenSEF, Zoom Gallery, and phpBB.

Installing Community Builder

Before you can download CB, you need to register on the Joomlapolis (www.joomlapolis.com) home page. Without registration, you can enter the Downloads area, but the links to the individual download packages will be disabled. After you register, the site will send a confirmation e-mail message with a link that will confirm your user account. Once confirmed, you will be able to download an archive named something like CBuilder1_0_2_unzip1st.zip, which contains the complete CB package.

The CB package consists of several extensions that work in concert. The default installation includes the following:

- *Comprofiler*: The central component retains the name used by CB when it was initially released. This component provides the central user interface and display for CB interaction.

- *CBlogin*: This module replaces the standard Joomla login on your Frontpage to allow users to register, log in, and log out of the CB system.

- *Mod_comprofilermoderator*: This module handles the workflow of user registration and specifies the moderator responsible for individual registration.

- *Mod_comprofileronline*: This module displays a list of CB users that are currently logged into the site.

To install CB, use the Extension Manager to install `comprofiler.zip` and `cblogin.zip`. If you are going to be using the moderator functions, make sure you also install `mod_comprofilermoderator.zip`.

After these extensions have been successfully installed, you will need to disable the standard Joomla login system. Open the Module Manager and unpublish the Login Form module. While still in the Module Manager, publish the CB Login module. If you open a browser window and display your Frontpage, you will see that the CB Login module has transparently replaced the standard login at the bottom of the left column, as shown in Figure 8-37.

Figure 8-37. *The CB Login replaces the standard Joomla login.*

You can log in now and see how the traditional registration process occurs. If you create a menu that connects to the CB component (Comprofiler), clicking the link when you're logged into the system will display your user profile page, as shown in Figure 8-38.

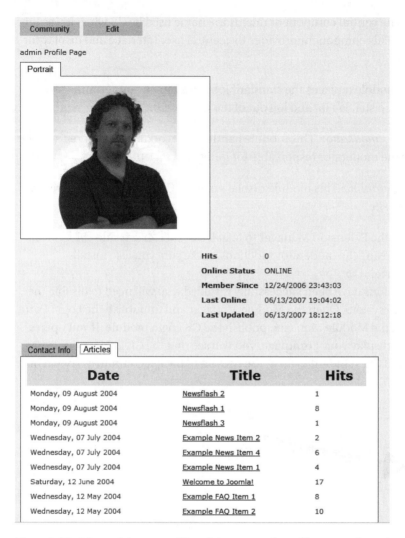

Figure 8-38. *A logged-in user will see his personal profile page when viewing the main CB component.*

Managing Community Builder

In the Administrator interface, the Community Builder submenu provides the following options:

> *User Management*: This displays the User Manager that allows you to perform a number of tasks in relation to user records, including creating, editing, searching, enabling, confirming, and approving.

> *Tab Management and Field Management*: These options allow you to make custom additions to the user profile (perhaps the most popular feature of CB).

List Management: The List Manager interface allows you to create new user lists. Lists can be sorted by one or more of the user fields and can include up to four columns (each column can contain one or more values). List filtering and group access rights can also be defined.

Plugin Management: The Plugin Manager shows the large number of plug-ins that are included with the default installation, as shown in Figure 8-39. You can find a number of additional third-party CB plug-ins for download and installation on the Joomlapolis site, in the Add-ons (3PD) section of the Downloads area.

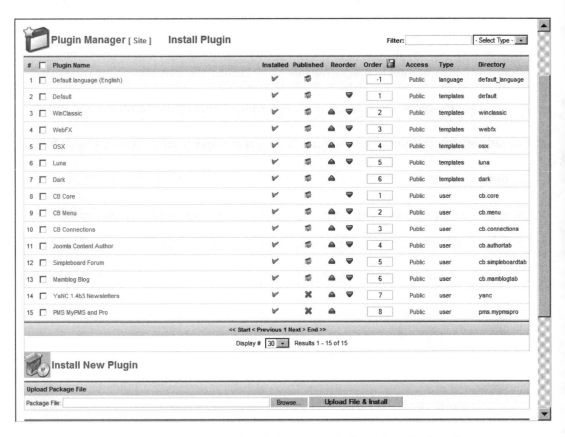

#		Plugin Name	Installed	Published	Reorder	Order	Access	Type	Directory
1	☐	Default language (English)	✔	🗐		-1	Public	language	default_language
2	☐	Default	✔	🗐	▽	1	Public	templates	default
3	☐	WinClassic	✔	🗐	⬥ ▽	2	Public	templates	winclassic
4	☐	WebFX	✔	🗐	⬥ ▽	3	Public	templates	webfx
5	☐	OSX	✔	🗐	⬥ ▽	4	Public	templates	osx
6	☐	Luna	✔	🗐	⬥ ▽	5	Public	templates	luna
7	☐	Dark	✔	🗐	⬥	6	Public	templates	dark
8	☐	CB Core	✔	🗐	▽	1	Public	user	cb.core
9	☐	CB Menu	✔	🗐	⬥ ▽	2	Public	user	cb.menu
10	☐	CB Connections	✔	🗐	⬥ ▽	3	Public	user	cb.connections
11	☐	Joomla Content Author	✔	🗐	⬥ ▽	4	Public	user	cb.authortab
12	☐	Simpleboard Forum	✔	🗐	⬥ ▽	5	Public	user	cb.simpleboardtab
13	☐	Mamblog Blog	✔	🗐	⬥ ▽	6	Public	user	cb.mamblogtab
14	☐	YaNC 1.4b3 Newsletters	✔	✖	⬥ ▽	7	Public	user	yanc
15	☐	PMS MyPMS and Pro	✔	✖	⬥	8	Public	user	pms.mypmspro

<< Start < Previous 1 Next > End >>

Display # [30 ▼]   Results 1 - 15 of 15

Install New Plugin

Upload Package File

Package File: [   ] [Browse...] [**Upload File & Install**]

Figure 8-39. *CB installs a significant number of plug-ins and allows installation of additional ones.*

Tools: The Tools Manager lets you load sample data, synchronize the existing Joomla user table with the CB user table, and test the CB databases for integrity.

Configuration: The Configuration Manager lets you modify parameters for everything from the user profile display, to the registration workflow, to the moderator interface.

If you need more advanced user management than that provided by Joomla (and most community web sites will), you will want to download and install CB. Although the registration system independent of Joomla's standard user table can present some challenges, the extra functionality provided makes it worth the effort.

Conclusion

The extensions you can add to Joomla can enable your web site to host a virtual community. With proper background research and a site profile to guide the site content, you can substantially increase the possibility that your Joomla site will become a real web traffic center.

When you decide to create a web community, you will still need to decide how much interactivity you want to make available to the visitors and how much time you are willing to spend administering the community features.

The content of a traditional site is determined only by the administrator and specially designated contributors. In contrast, a virtual community has the ability to add content, and that renders as much danger as opportunity. Without a watchful eye and proper supervision, a web site can become like an errant child and turn in a dark direction.

Before you deploy the virtual community features, be sure that you are willing to dedicate the time and energy to properly maintain the site. Otherwise, you may one day find that your site has been taken over by distasteful or even illegal content.

■ ■ ■

Site Statistics

The more traffic you draw to your Joomla site, the more you will want to know about your visitors. Fortunately, a web server can capture a vast array of data that can be examined and analyzed to see who is visiting your site, how long they are staying, the technology they're using to access the Web (browser, OS, etc.), and a tremendous quantity of other information. Perhaps most importantly, through site statistics it is possible to determine the most popular pages, as well as the ones no one ever reads.

There are three primary methods of generating site statistics: a standalone web log analyzer, a Joomla extension, and a web-based statistical package. This chapter will detail the workings of two open source standalone packages (Webalizer and AWStats), a few Joomla extensions, and one web-based package (Google Analytics) that can be used to detect web traffic patterns.

The information needed by a webmaster and the format of the presentation is a personal preference. Package A might supply flashy charts and visualizations that may appeal to some developers, while the column-based reporting of Package B may appear superior to others. Therefore, it is important to examine all the available features and determine which appeals most to you.

■**Note** In versions before 1.5, Joomla included a basic site statistics package incorporated into the Administrator interface. The package was removed because the Joomla team decided that there were existing extensions that provided far more functionality. If you see references in articles or online material mentioning Joomla's site statistics, you don't need to waste your time looking for that capability in the current Joomla version—it has been eliminated.

Web Analytics

Studying the pattern of web visitors is known as the field of *web analytics*. By correlating information such as the page used for entrance into the site (known as a *landing page*) with user selections, a webmaster can fine-tune a web site to reach targeted site goals (such as traffic levels or online purchase volume). While the primary analysis in analytics is directed at processing web server information, establishing relationships with other information such as e-mail response rates, advertisements, or lead purchases also comes under the umbrella of web analytics.

To obtain the web server information needed to perform analytic examination, there are two main methods of tracking web site traffic: from web server log files and from active collection of visitor information, known as *page tagging*. Each of these methods has advantages and disadvantages; methods for adopting each for Joomla site analytics are included in this chapter.

■Note You can find a number of resources relating to web analytics on the web site of the Web Analytics Association (www.webanalyticsassociation.org). The organization is devoted to measurement and analysis of web data. It even offers distance learning classes for the study of web analytics.

Parsing Web Logs

Web logs are stored as text files on the web server and record information in one of a variety of standardized formats. Almost every web server on the Internet uses one of the two most common formats (Apache Custom Log format and W3C Extended Log File format). A *log analysis program* can parse the information held in the log and generate a summary report of usage and trends. WebTrends (www.webtrends.com) makes one of the most popular commercial implementations of a log file parser.

Log files hold a great amount of site access data as well as information about the visitor's browser machine, such as browser type, operating system, and browser version. Once the program analyzes the traffic, a log analysis program can generate extensive reports that demonstrate the type of access that has occurred in the past and the trends that will predict traffic in the future.

Web logs also contain information about bots (such as search engine spiders) that access the site. By examining this information, a webmaster can determine how often the page is being spidered and what type of access is being attempted by each bot.

One of the shortcomings of examining log files is the possible under-reporting of page accesses when a remote server caches site pages. Some organizations—particularly those who use proxy servers—implement local caches, so if a page request can be fulfilled from the cache, the page is not drawn from the original web server (which would cause a log entry), but instead read from a cache. To avoid this problem, page tagging was created.

Page Tagging

With page tagging, a small piece of HTML (usually JavaScript) code is inserted into each page. When the visitor's browser displays the page, the tagging reference in the page will force the visitor's browser to access a remote server. When this access occurs, the remote server records information about the user. The reference may be an invisible piece of JavaScript code that is executed or an image retrieved for display.

Page tagging is most visibly used when posting content to a third-party site (such as eBay). Many eBay sellers post auction items that include a small bit of code to display a page counter or ticker. Popular free services such as Easy Counter (`www.easycounter.com`) and Simple Hit Counter (`www.simplehitcounter.com`) provide counters that can be placed on any web site. When the user's browser displays the page, the image for the ticker is retrieved from the remote server—and at the same time the server hosting the counter retrieves and records information about the requester.

A page tag doesn't necessarily access a remote site. Many of the Joomla extensions that provide site statistics use a small tag in the form of a Joomla module to record user information directly into the MySQL database on the server.

Two of the dominant commercial players in the page tagging analytics area are Google and Visual Sciences (`www.visualsciences.com`), formerly known as WebSideStory. While the Google page tagging system is free, Visual Sciences works with an organization to customize analytics and reporting capabilities based on the needs of the concern.

Page tagging has a number of advantages over log file processing. Since the code executes in the browser window, there are few problems with page caching minimizing the visitor counts. Further, since the JavaScript code executes in the browser window, it can collect additional information (such as screen size) from the user's machine.

Page tagging also has a number of drawbacks when compared with log file analysis. Since bots don't execute page, when they reference a code (including JavaScript), page tagging provides no information about bot access to a web site. Additionally, remote page tagging systems collect their raw data in a proprietary format that is inaccessible to a webmaster. Therefore, if a web site adopts a different tagging provider, the past data cannot be integrated with future information.

Most tagging solutions also require cookies to be activated on the client browser or they cannot effectively track a user session. This is usually not a problem since cookie features are generally enabled on most browsers.

Standalone Log Analysis Packages

Standalone packages provide perhaps the most convenient way to perform web analysis—especially if you have direct file access to the server logs. Most standalone packages allow the user to specify one or more log files to examine and select the statistics to be included in the report output. The output reports are generally stored as a series of HTML files for local or online analysis.

As any experienced webmaster knows, web server log files can become huge and require regular backup and pruning. Standalone analysis packages work very well because they can be used even on archived data stored apart from the web server. By analyzing current as well as archived log files it is possible to see historical usage trends.

In this section, two of the more popular packages (Webalizer and AWStats) will be examined. Both are open source programs and therefore freely available. They have also been around for a long time, so over time they've gained the features most needed by webmasters.

■**Note** Web traffic reporting is much more useful if the URLs of your site are formatted in a search engine–friendly (SEF) format. In Chapter 12, there are complete instructions for activating the SEF option on the Joomla system. I would suggest you activate this option as soon as possible to maximize the usefulness of the log information collected by the server.

Webalizer

Created in 1997 by Bradford L. Barrett, Webalizer is one of the oldest and most popular standalone packages. It has international support and is currently available in over two dozen languages. It can process log files no matter their size and the program is available on most platforms (including Windows, Mac OS, and Linux).

Instead of a graphical user interface, it is executed from the command line so that it can be activated with a macro process. The site statistics are output in a series of HTML pages that include tables of information and usage graphs. Webalizer is available for free download at www.mrunix.net/webalizer.

Webalizer can process log files stored in the three most popular formats: CLF (common log format), Apache Custom Log format, and W3C Extended Log File format. By default, Apache uses the Apache Custom Log format and Microsoft IIS uses the W3C Extended Log File format. CLF holds the least amount of traffic information, so a web server should not be configured for this format unless it is needed for a special requirement (e.g., your stastics package only supports this format).

The Webalizer application is run at the command line. The most common method of running an analysis is specifying the log file with a direct path. However, Webalizer can also access a log file via the FTP protocol. That allows the program to process the log files on remote hosts and eliminates the need to transfer the often very large files before analysis can be performed.

On a local drive, Webalizer can be run with an execution statement, like this:

```
webalizer c:\mywebserver\logs\access.log
```

This command will generate a master index.html file that gives a general overview of the site usage, as shown in Figure 9-1. The figure shows three graphs that diagram the total usage summary categorized by month and parallel time graphs showing visits and kilobytes transferred. The data tables beneath the graphs show daily average and monthly total usage in terms of file transfers, page accesses, site visits, and kilobytes transferred.

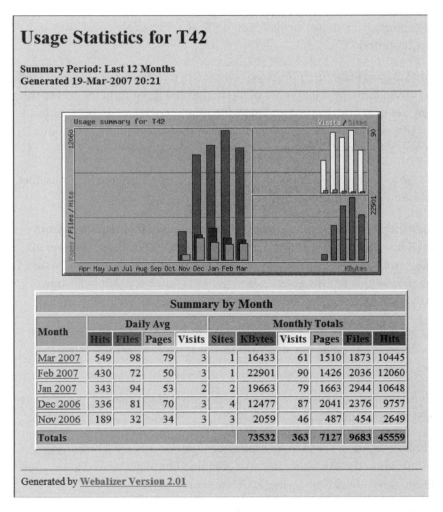

Usage Statistics for T42

Summary Period: Last 12 Months
Generated 19-Mar-2007 20:21

Summary by Month									
Month	Daily Avg				Monthly Totals				
	Hits	Files	Pages	Visits	Sites	KBytes	Visits	Pages	Files	Hits
Mar 2007	549	98	79	3	1	16433	61	1510	1873	10445
Feb 2007	430	72	50	3	1	22901	90	1426	2036	12060
Jan 2007	343	94	53	2	2	19663	79	1663	2944	10648
Dec 2006	336	81	70	3	4	12477	87	2041	2376	9757
Nov 2006	189	32	34	3	3	2059	46	487	454	2649
Totals						73532	363	7127	9683	45559

Generated by Webalizer Version 2.01

Figure 9-1. *The Webalizer central index file displays site overview information.*

The Usage Statistics page is only the summary portion of the Webalizer report. With each Webalizer execution, a usage file is constructed for each month found in the log. The usage files contain the following information:

- *Monthly statistics*: This gives you the total hits, total files, total pages, total visits, total kilobytes, total unique sites, total unique URLs, and so on.

- *Hits by response code*: These two or three character HTTP codes can indicate important status conditions about the web server execution. For example, a large number of 404 codes (the error code for "file not found") can indicate that the site has one or more broken hyperlinks that are regularly accessed.

- *Daily usage graph*: This shows the daily site traffic in terms of hits, files, sites, and kilobytes transferred.

- *Daily statistics in terms of hits, files, pages, visits, sites, and kilobytes*: These are daily statistics broken down by the number of files requested (Hits) from the server, the number of files sent from the server (Files), the number of HTML pages sent from the server (Pages), the number of unique visitors (Visits), the number of unique referring sites (Sites), and the number of kilobytes transferred (KBytes).

- *Hourly usage averages graph*: This shows the hourly site traffic in terms of hits, files, sites, and kilobytes transferred.

- *Hourly statistics*: These are broken down by the number of files requested from the server (Hits), the number of files sent from the server (Files), the number of HTML pages sent from the server (Pages), the number of unique visitors (Visits), the number of unique referring sites (Sites), and the number of kilobytes transferred (KBytes).

- *Top URLs of total URLs*: Perhaps the single most important reported statistic, the top URLs information will help you determine what pages were most requested by visitors.

- *Top URLs by kilobytes downloaded*: These are the top URLs requested from the site in terms of kilobytes downloaded.

- *Top entry and exit pages*: These show the most common entry or "landing pages"— where visitors enter the site—and the most common last pages viewed when users leave the site (since there is no formal HTTP session to close).

- *Usage graph by country*: Shows the countries and kinds of domains (e.g., .edu, .gov, .com) that have accessed the site.

These are the only statistics generated when the program is executed without any special options activated. Options are available for a large number of other reports, such as a ranking of all URLs, comparison with a previous month's statistics, and much more. The ReadMe file contains an extensive list of possible settings. You can also get a list by executing the program with the -h argument to show all available command-line options.

Since Webalizer is open source, it has been adapted to a variety of execution forms, so there are several alternatives to the Webalizer executable that use the same core logic. A few of these Webalizer-based programs include the following:

- *Log Miner*: This is a powerful log analysis package for Apache/IIS (or other web servers using the "combined" or W3C Extended Log File formats). It can extract and present statistics about visits, hits, traffic, navigation paths, browsers, and OSs used by users. Unlike Webalizer, Log Miner generates reporting data into a PostgreSQL database so that many reports can be run quickly from the same data. Unfortunately, PostgreSQL is the only database server supported. Logminer is available on SourceForge at `http://logminer.sourceforge.net`.

- *Wephpalizer*: Known as "The Improved Webalizer," this tool the uses a PHP interface to collate visitor statistics. It has better visualization than Webalizer, MySQL database support, and can process a log file incrementally. It is available on SourceForge at `http://sourceforge.net/projects/wephpalizer`.

- *AWFFull*: This program uses Webalizer as a foundation and adds features such as greater-than-12-month display, implementation of CSS for custom report presentation, resizable graphs, automatic log type detection, and GeoIP support for country detection. It is available free for download from the home page at `www.stedee.id.au/awffull`.

AWStats

AWStats is a full-featured standalone package written in Perl (Webalizer is written in C++). Since Perl is available on almost every known platform and operating system, AWStats can run almost anywhere. The program can process logs in formats including Apache Custom Log format (NCSA combined/XLF/ELF log format or common/CLF log format), WebStar, W3C Extended Log File format (for Microsoft IIS), and numerous other rarer formats. It can even analyze FTP and mail log files.

The AWStats program has many advanced features, such as recognition of "human" vs. bot visitors; unique visitor statistics; technology usage reports that enumerate visitor access to Flash, QuickTime, RealPlayer; and other site media, and personalized reporting. AWStats is available for free download at `http://awstats.sourceforge.net`.

As you can see in Figure 9-2, the application has an extensive browser-based interface that uses a statistics frame (the left column) and a display frame (the right column) for the output.

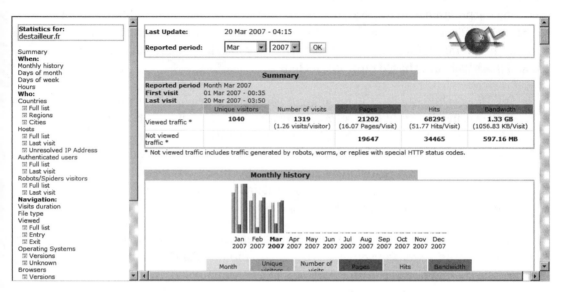

Figure 9-2. *AWStats uses a frame-based layout in the browser window for display.*

There are a number of plug-ins available for AWStats that provide features such as IPv6 format log processing, GeoIP to determine the geography of the access log entries, and ClusterInfo to process logs on server clusters.

Unlike Webalizer, you will have to download and install Perl onto your destination machine. This can be an advantage since many remote hosts allow execution of Perl scripts where they do not allow general executables (such as the binary compilation of Webalizer). On the other hand, if your platform doesn't have Perl installed, it is one more development system that you must run.

Joomla! Extensions

There are a number of extensions that can be installed into Joomla that can provide site statistic analysis. Instead of analyzing the web server log files, these extensions actually execute under the Joomla system and collect statistical information that is particularly relevant to a Joomla administrator. Some of the most popular packages include the following:

- *AstatsPro*: Perhaps the most comprehensive open source Joomla statistics package, astatsPro (`http://astatspro.joom.la`) is available in a number of languages and provides an extensive Administrator interface that allows you to create custom reports. The statistics offered are nearly comparable to those available through the standalone package AWStats.

- *JoomlaStats*: This package (see `www.joomlastats.org`) is the most "user-aware" in that it understands the Joomla user system and allows nearly all statistics to be broken down by user movements. It also records the search keywords that users enter on search engines such as Google to find your site. The package includes a number of modules and an administrative component.

- *Entana Statistics*: This is a very well-reviewed commercial package (see `www.entanacomponents.com`) that can track traffic over multiple Joomla sites and coordinate visitor data with the registered Joomla user database.

- *BSQ Sitestats*: This is a lightweight extension that collects the primary site-usage figures (see `www.bs-squared.com/wp`). It also includes statistics for the search terms entered into the Joomla search engine. On the back-end, it provides a broad number of reports, including graphical visitors chart over time period, top referrers, top pages viewed, top visitors, top users, top daily users, top web browsers, top languages, visitor session tracking, visitor geolocational information, search engine keywords frequency tracking, and summaries by day, week, and month.

The disadvantage of using a package that is installed into Joomla is the performance hit that the system will take gathering the statistics. These packages can put a strain on the web server performance as well as the MySQL database. Most Joomla-centric web providers strongly advise against installing statistic extensions because of these performance drawbacks.

Google Analytics

Google, the web search company, has a fantastic free service for web site tracking. Called *Google Analytics*, the service provides almost every type of statistical site analysis in a user-friendly graphic display (see Figure 9-3). The reporting page is dynamic, so you can easily change the date range examined or even compare two periods of time for differences or patterns. Since Google Analytics is run on Google's servers, all processing of the logs is handled without any performance loss on your web server. Also, since the reporting environment is web-based, it can be accessed from anywhere.

Figure 9-3. *Google Analytics displays graphic analysis of site information on the Dashboard display.*

The reports include everything from page hits to search engine terms used to find your site. All of this information is generated by including a small script that is under a dozen lines on the bottom of your web page.

Page Tag Code

When you sign up with Google Analytics, you are given a user account from which you can manage as many sites as you like. Each site is provided with specific scripting code that is placed just before the final </body> tag. The Google code looks something like this:

```
<script src="http://www.google-analytics.com/urchin.js"
    type="text/javascript">
</script>
<script type="text/javascript">
    uacct = "UA-xxx-xxx";
    urchinTracker();
</script>
```

This code must appear on every page of the web site. For Joomla users, implementing Google Analytics is extremely easy since all access occurs through the same index.php file of the current template. To add the code to a Joomla template, you can simply open the Template Manager in the Administrator interface, select the desired template, and click the Edit HTML button. The code to the template will be displayed. Scroll down to the closing tag for the document body and paste the custom code that was generated for your web site there. All pages that are rendered using that template will automatically be logged into the Google service.

■**Note** Google Analytics obtains information by executing JavaScript code on the visitor's browser. That means that browsers that don't have JavaScript capabilities (including many cell phone browsers), browsers with JavaScript deactivated, and machines with ad-blocking software (such as Adblock) will be invisible to the Google Analytics engine. It is therefore advisable that you perform a log analysis periodically with one of the standalone tools. Comparing the Google Analytics reports with independent reports will give you a measure of how accurately Google Analytics portrays your site traffic.

Instead of modifying a template, you can download a Joomla module called the Google Analytics Tracking Module. It is available at the Estime (www.estime.fi/en/reading-room) web site. It will place the Google script code at the proper location without requiring you to modify the template.

When the code is placed on your site, you can log back into the service and click the Check Status button. The system will access your site and attempt to confirm that the scripting code is in place. Don't worry if you attempt to check the status and it fails in the first few minutes. There seems to be a caching mechanism so that code placed on the page is not immediately seen by the checking routine. Wait a half hour and try checking again.

Once the Google Analytics service is active on your web site, you need only wait a few days for a baseline of data to be established. The longer you run your web site, the more accurate the reporting will be, and you will be able to look at trends over time and modify the site content to cater to your intended audience.

Google Analytics is especially useful if you have an AdWords marketing campaign. It can help you more precisely target your campaign by analyzing the referring site that brought visitors to the page and the geographic locations of those visitors. For a campaign, you can also set up goals such as sales, lead generation, or page visit targets. Then Google Analytics will track which ads are performing best and help determine the sources of the highest-quality visitors.

■**Caution** Whoever said there is no such thing as a free lunch may have had Google Analytics in mind. While the service comes at no charge to you and is incredibly robust, keep in mind that by using the service, you are providing Google with all of the visitor and usage information for your web site. Most hobbyist web sites will have no problem with giving away this information. However, many e-commerce and virtual community sites would like to keep this important data private. If you are implementing a Joomla site for an organization or another individual, make sure they are aware of these privacy aspects of using the service and get their approval before you include it on their site.

Google Analytics Reports

In the Google Analytics interface, the summary display is know as a *dashboard*. There are a great number of more specific reports, and they are divided into four broad categories: visitors, traffic sources, content, and goals. Each set of reports provides statistical information in a way that will be most useful for that particular area. The data of the site is formatted so you can look at it from different perspectives.

Each report area presents its own table or graphical display of the statistical data. For example, the Defined Funnel Navigation (see Figure 9-4) shows the entrance points for various pages that are part of a target "goal" set up within the Google Analytics system. This report will help you track the success of the definite site goals.

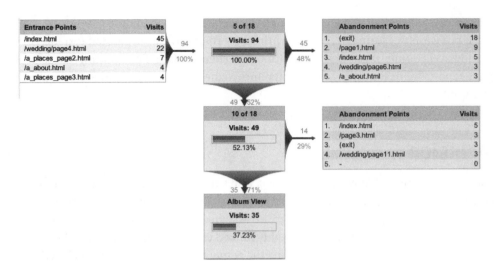

Figure 9-4. *The entrance points relate to the site goals that you have defined in Google Analytics.*

There are many, many reports available through the Google Analytics service. These reports can be selected from the hierarchical listing panel on the left side of the screen. Under the four primary categories, there are the following reports:

- *Visitor Reports*: Map Overlay, New vs. Returning, Languages, Visitor Trending, Visits, Absolute Unique Visitors, Pageviews, Average Pageviews, Time On Site, Bounce Rate, Visitor Loyalty, Loyalty, Recency, Length of Visit, Depth of Visit, Browser Capabilities, Browsers, Operating Systems, Browsers and OS, Screen Colors, Screen Resolutions, Flash Versions, Java Support, Network Properties, Network Location, Hostnames, Connection Speeds, and User Defined

- *Traffic Sources*: Overview, Direct Traffic, Referring Sites, Search Engines, All Traffic Sources, Keywords, AdWords, AdWords Campaigns, Keyword Positions, Campaigns, and Ad Versions

- *Content*: Overview, Top Content, Content by Title, Content Drilldown, Top Landing Pages, Top Exit Pages, and Site Overlay.

- *Goal*: Overview, Total Conversions, Conversion Rate, Abandoned Funnels, and Goal Value

All reports and even dashboard information can be downloaded onto a desktop machine in a variety of formats. The three primary formats are tab-separated text file, XML, and Excel comma-separated values (or CSV). There is also a Print button that reformats the reports for best printing output (it removes the user interface and extraneous information).

Conclusion

A webmaster can't really know who is visiting a web site without hard data. A webmaster may create a site focusing on a topic area he knows very well and expect to can predict what content will be popular. Often enough, an unexpected article will catch the public's attention or gain a link reference from a highly ranked web site that will make it the most popular piece on the site. Only by examining the actual traffic of the site can such activity be ascertained.

There are many more web statistics packages than the ones described in this chapter. Hopefully this overview has provided a foundation by which you can examine the numerous available applications. I would suggest that you try more than one, and by comparing them with each other, you will be able to determine the one that best suits your needs.

CHAPTER 10

■■■

Photo Gallery

Joomla's widespread adoption by individual users as well as substantial organizations has created a gap between the need for a quick-and-easy solution and the requirements of a powerful (and often more complicated) industrial-grade solution. The vast divide between the requirements of basic consumer and professional deployment has caused a torrent of extensions that fill many niches. Nowhere is this more apparent than in the flood of photo gallery extensions for Joomla. At the time of this writing, there are over 75 extensions available to add gallery functionality to Joomla that run the gamut from simple image displays to complete photo-publication services.

In the interest of serving both communities, this chapter will demonstrate one simple gallery display component (Easy Gallery) and one full-featured implementation (Gallery2). Most gallery software falls roughly into one of these two categories, so the information here should be useful regardless of which of the dozens of gallery extensions you finally choose. Whether you want to set up a photo album of your children or launch a web site to compete with the largest digital image licensers, Joomla can be extended to meet your needs.

Before you begin examining the Joomla extensions, think about installing an FTP server to allow better gallery management. You may already have FTP server capabilities activated for use with the Joomla Administrator, in which case you can skip the following section. If not, consider FTP server installation to streamline both upload and download (especially of large photo files) during the creation of a gallery.

FTP Server for Gallery Management

Many gallery extensions allow image upload and maintenance through an FTP server. If you haven't already installed an FTP server, you might consider it now. This section provides FTP server instructions for Linux, Mac OS, and Windows. The basic setup procedures are presented to familiarize you with the server configuration. I recommend that you consult the server documentation for more complete instructions.

Most Linux distributions include an FTP server, although you will likely need to activate it. Likewise, the Mac OS X 10.2 and above comes with a preinstalled FTP server. On Windows, if you are using IIS as your web server, you can easily enable the bundled FTP server and configure it through the IIS Management Console. In case you're running Apache on the Windows platform, I've included instructions for installing and configuring FileZilla—a free, open source FTP server application.

Tip If the FTP servers presented here are not to your liking or lack a critical feature you need, take a look at CrossFTP Server. Written in Java, it can execute on any platform. You can download it at `http://sourceforge.net/projects/crossftpserver`. You can also visit the home page (`www.crossftp.com`), which has a Web Start live installer to help you simplify installation.

Activating a Linux FTP Server

Most Linux distributions have an FTP daemon installed that can serve FTP files. You can search for the FTP service with this statement executed at the command line:

```
chkconfig --list | grep ftpd
```

There are several FTP servers available, so you will have to customize your interaction based on the daemon listed. Some common FTP servers include VSFTPD, ProFTPD, Glftpd, pureftpd, wzdftpd, and wu-ftpd. Most of these FTP servers can be activated with the same commands. For example, if your distribution has VSFTPD installed, you can activate it like this:

```
vsftpd start
```

Alternatively, you can use the `service` command:

```
service vsftpd start
```

To have the FTP server automatically start on boot, with Fedora/Red Hat you can use the `chkconfig` command, like this:

```
chkconfig vsftpd on
```

On Ubuntu or Debian systems, use this command instead:

```
sysv-rc-conf on
```

You can check if the FTP server is running like this:

```
netstat -a | grep ftp
```

If no output is returned, then the service is not running. Try executing it again. You will generally need to add a user for the Joomla extension so you can give the application access to the upload directory. You can create a new user for the /gallery2 directory (if that is the extension you'll use) like this:

```
useradd -d /home/gallery2 galleryadmin
```

The password to the account can be set with this command:

```
passwd galleryadmin
```

The passwd command will prompt you with these three inputs, with the new user password blank by default:

```
Current Password:
New Password:
Confirm New Password:
```

Then you will have to modify the upload directory with chmod:

```
chmod 750 /home/gallery2
```

To give the gallery user the permissioned access to the directory, use the chown command:

```
chown root:galleryadmin /home/gallery2
```

On some Linux firewalls, lower port numbers, including the standard FTP port (port 21), may be blocked. You can either reconfigure the firewall to allow traffic on that port or set your FTP server to address a port within the range allowed by the firewall.

Activating the Mac OS FTP Server

On OS X 10.2 and above, the FTP server is enabled through the system preferences. Double-click the Sharing icon to display the Settings window. On the Services tab, use the FTP Access setting to activate the FTP server. Check the box to the left of the setting to enable the server.

Check your firewall settings to make sure that FTP connections (generally through port 21) are available on the machine. On Mac OS Server, you can activate Internet File Sharing Server, which supports the FTP protocol.

Installing FileZilla Server on Windows

Windows bundles Microsoft IIS with an FTP server that has all the features you will need for a Joomla gallery extension. If you are running Apache on Windows, you can use FileZilla FTP server, which is a free, open source, basic FTP server that uses minimal resources on your machine. It can be downloaded from SourceForge at `http://filezilla.sourceforge.net`.

When you have the FileZilla installer downloaded to your local drive, execute it and choose the options that fit your needs (such as automatic server startup on boot). Make sure you install the administration utility (called the FileZilla Server Interface), which you will need to secure the server to limit access.

To configure the server, execute the FileZilla Server Interface application, and the login window will appear. By default, the administrator has no login password, so you can click the OK button to open the application.

The first thing you'll want to do is secure the site. Select the Settings option under the Edit menu. You should see a window like the one shown in Figure 10-1. Select the "Admin Interface settings" option in the General settings list to set the administrator password. Click the "Change admin password" box and enter a new password in order to secure the site. Click the OK button once you've made all the configuration changes you want.

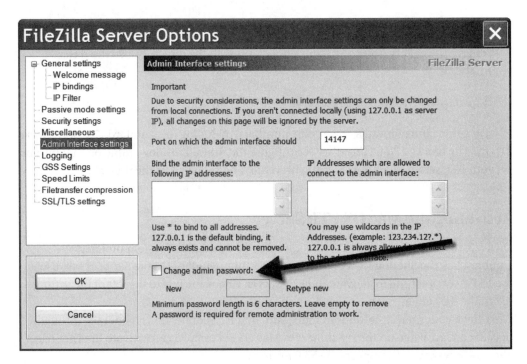

Figure 10-1. *Select the "Admin Interface settings" option in the General settings list.*

After you've set the admin password, it is a good idea to create a user login for the Easy Gallery component. To create a new user, select the Users option from the Settings menu. You will see a configuration window, as shown in Figure 10-2. Click the Add button to set up a new user.

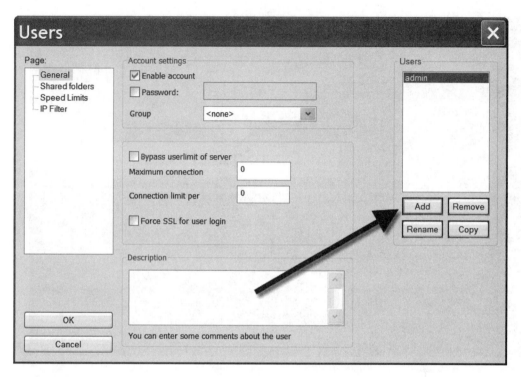

Figure 10-2. *The configuration window for FileZilla Server lets you add users and user permissions.*

Once FileZilla Server is installed and configured, you should be able to access your own site through any basic FTP program (including the free FileZilla client). Both Mozilla Firefox and Microsoft Internet Explorer 6 and above have built-in FTP clients. You can use these to test the configuration of the FTP server and make certain that the Easy Gallery user you created has access to the web directories.

Easy Gallery

Easy Gallery (see Figure 10-3) is a small, nimble component that allows photos to be added to albums for display on the Joomla front-end. The Easy Gallery photo-organizer extension features a complete administrative interface that allows pictures to be uploaded by several methods, and then filed in a number of user-created categories. This extension is meant for display of images and provides no front-end picture upload methods or user privilege designations beyond those included with the standard Joomla interface.

Figure 10-3. *The Easy Gallery presentation can display numerous photographs, filed by category.*

Despite the simplicity of the Easy Gallery interface, the extension includes the following advanced features:

- It understands ZIP file archives, so multiple images can be added to the gallery at once.

- It allows server-side directories to be scanned for multi-image addition.

- It provides upload through FTP for image submission so that ownership and access problems can be avoided.

- It generates automatic thumbnails for images as well as a thumbnail representation for each category.

- It supports server-side resizing and light box effects on images.

Easy Gallery is also very easy to install and manage. So, without further delay . . .

Downloading and Installing Easy Gallery

Easy Gallery is free for use and available for download under the Creative Commons license. This license allows you to distribute, display, and use the component for free. However, you are prohibited from creating a derivative work from it or removing the license text or attribution from the component code (although you can remove the "Powered by" text displayed by the component).

You can download Easy Gallery from `www.joomla-addons.org/components/easy-gallery/easy-gallery.html`.

The download is a small ZIP archive of around 100KB that has all of the files for both the display component and the administrative component. Store the file on your local drive for subsequent upload into the Joomla system.

To install Easy Gallery, open the Extension Manager screen in the Joomla Administrator interface. Browse your local drive for the ZIP component, select it, and click the Upload and Install button. If successful, Joomla should display the component success screen. Note, however, that even if the component installs successfully, you may not yet be done with configuration.

There is only one requirement to run Easy Gallery: the GD2 image manipulation library. Easy Gallery needs to use an image manipulation library in order to generate thumbnails of uploaded images and to allow image-resizing functions. The GD2 library is a library of PHP functions that allow for image manipulation, and is often included with PHP installer binaries and supported by many web providers. Sometimes activating the library is all that is needed to allow it to execute on the server.

To determine if you have GD2 installed on your server, check in your PHP extensions folder, which may be named either \ext or \extensions, depending on the PHP version. On the Windows platform, if the library is installed, you should find a file named php_gd2.dll in that directory. Alternatively, you can execute the phpinfo() function on the PHP server and look in the gd section to make sure GD2 is available (where you should see parameters such as GD Support, GD Version, FreeType Support, JPG Support, and PNG Support).

On Linux, make sure the GD2 library is included with your version of PHP through the phpinfo() call. Near the top of the information returned by phpinfo() (perhaps the third entry), you will see a row titled "Configure Command." If GD2 is available, you should see an entry like this in the right column:

```
cscript /nologo configure.js "--with-gd=shared"
```

If GD2 is not present on your system, you will need to install it to use the Easy Gallery image generation. While GD2 is included with the current PHP installers, it is an optional extension and is not installed by default. To obtain the GD2 file, simply download the entire PHP installation archive (ZIP or TAR) file from www.php.net/downloads.php.

Open the installation archive and browse to the \extensions folder. In this folder, you should see a GD2 file (such as php_gd2). Extract that file and place it in the extensions folder of your active PHP directory.

To allow PHP to use it, you still need to activate it in your PHP configuration file. Open your PHP configuration file (possibly named php.ini) in a text editor and find the following directive:

```
;extension=php_gd2.dll
```

Delete the semicolon (;) from the front of the line and save the file. When PHP is restarted, the GD2 library should load. Be sure to restart the Apache server after this change or the library will not be found.

▓Note If you are using a remote web host and your service provider uses cPanel for configuration, you can activate GD2 from there. Check in the Update Apache section for a GD2 check box. Selecting the check box will activate the GD2 library so the thumbnails can be rendered.

Configuring Easy Gallery

With the Easy Gallery component installed, an FTP server running, and GD2 operational, you are now ready to configure the component. Under the Components menu, you should now see an Easy Gallery menu. Select the Configuration option from the Easy Gallery menu. You should see the configuration settings screen shown in Figure 10-4.

You need to configure the FTP settings to allow pictures to be uploaded. The first setting, FTP host, is simply the URL path to the FTP server. On a staging server, the path will likely be set to localhost.

Figure 10-4. *The Easy Gallery configuration screen lets you set the FTP, thumbnail, and path parameters.*

For the FTP username and password, enter the ones you set for your FTP user login, or your own login information if the FTP is located on a remote server. The default FTP port of 21 is usually correct unless a proxy server is being used or a firewall closes off this port. In either case, you will have to contact your host administrator to determine the possible options.

The FTP path parameter may be different from the normal absolute path URL. For example, if the default path where the FTP logs in to the system is the root directory, but the web server accesses the Joomla directory to display the Joomla site, then the FTP path parameter might be /joomla.

On many remote servers, you will have to enter the prefix /www to select the web root directory on the FTP server. If the files are held in your username directory, you will have to set the FTP path to /username. Note the forward slash (/) at the beginning of the FTP URL must be present for Easy Gallery to use the path properly.

■**Note** When you try to upload pictures for the first time, if you receive an error like "Fatal error: Call to undefined function: ftp_connect()," then your web provider has disabled the FTP services available to PHP. You will need to check if they have any way of enabling FTP.

Managing Easy Gallery

With Easy Gallery configured, you're ready to add images to the system. Like Joomla itself, Easy Gallery files content under user-defined *categories*. Before you begin adding image files, you will need to create one or more categories to hold them.

To create a new category, click the Manage Categories option in the administrative interface of the Easy Gallery component. An empty list of categories will be displayed. Click the New button to create a new category. The "Add a category" screen will be displayed, as shown in Figure 10-5. Enter information relevant to your new category and click the Save button to store it in the gallery. That's it—you're ready to add some photographs.

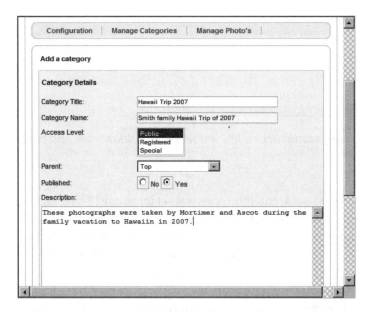

Figure 10-5. *The "Add a category" screen allows entry of category title, name, parent, and description.*

Click the Manage Photos option in the Easy Gallery menu. When the photo manager screen is displayed, click the Upload button to enter the uploading interface. The Upload Photos interface will notify you of the upload size limit when using the HTTP transfer protocol (by default 2MB) and allow you to select a category where the new photos will be filed. There is a name entry field for the title of the uploaded photograph, which if left empty will be set to the filename of the image.

You can choose one of three methods to upload photos (see Figure 10-6): single file, ZIP archive, or directory scan. Adding a single image file or a ZIP archive of files is done in the same manner as adding an extension to the Joomla system. For the directory scan, you will need to manually enter the path on the server where the image files will be located.

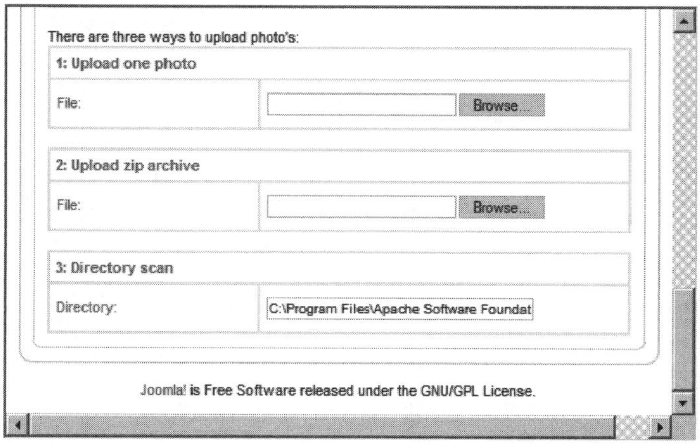

Figure 10-6. *There are three upload options for Easy Gallery.*

Upload a few images right now so a gallery will be visible when you add the gallery display to the Joomla system. If you have a large number of photos or individual images that have large file sizes, it is recommended that you use an FTP server to make the transfer quick and more reliable. The size of the HTTP image upload (performed through the Joomla Administrator interface) is determined by the maximum upload size set in the PHP configuration file. If you want to allow larger uploads, you will have to increase the size of the `upload_max_filesize` parameter to greater than 2MB.

■**Note** If you attempt to upload and receive an error, there may be a configuration parameter that isn't set properly. For example, if you don't have the GD2 plug-in working properly, Easy Gallery will return an error in the server log that states that the create image function wasn't found when it attempted to create the thumbnail for the image. If you encounter such a problem, return to the earlier "Configuring Easy Gallery" section for instructions on making sure that the FTP server is installed and GD2 is functioning properly.

Creating a Menu for the Component

Before you can see the images that you've loaded into Easy Gallery, you will need to create a Joomla menu to access and display the Easy Gallery component. Go to the Menu Manager and open the menu items for the Main Menu by clicking the Edit Menu Items icon. Click the New button to create a new menu.

Select the Easy Gallery internal link, as shown in Figure 10-7. Type a name for the menu (I chose to name my menu **Photo Gallery**) and click the Save button to store it in the Joomla system.

Figure 10-7. *Select the Easy Gallery option to create a connected menu.*

Display the home page of the site in a browser window and you should see the photo gallery option at the bottom of the Main Menu list (see Figure 10-8). When you click the link, the categories will be displayed in the Joomla page.

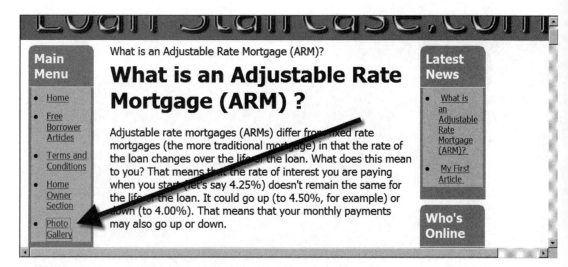

Figure 10-8. *Click the Photo Gallery link to display the gallery in the component space.*

Easy Gallery Front-End

Easy Gallery has a simple user interface (see Figure 10-9). All categories are displayed with a thumbnail of the first image uploaded. Selecting a category will display a table of all of the photos in that gallery. Clicking an image within the category will display it in real size.

You have seen how easy it is to add a gallery to Joomla. However, you might need a more powerful gallery that allows user uploads, better categorization, a shopping cart for ordering, and other advanced features. Gallery2 provides all of those features and more.

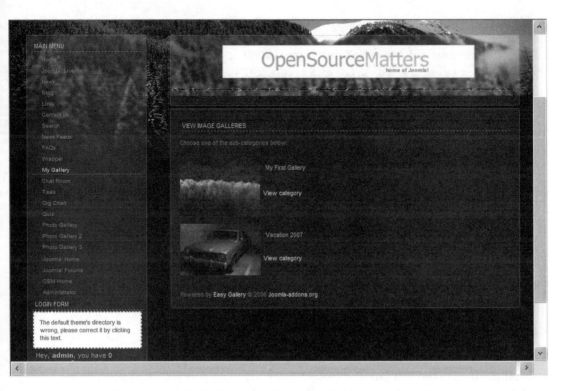

Figure 10-9. *Easy Gallery lets you drill down into the categories for image display.*

Gallery2

Gallery2 (see Figure 10-10) is a full-featured, industrial-strength picture gallery application. Unlike the Easy Gallery component, which was developed expressly for use within Joomla, Gallery2 was written for independent execution in PHP. Like many of the more established photo gallery implementations, Gallery2 was created for the broader web server market.

Fortunately for Joomla users, a *bridge* extension was created to wrap Gallery2 for use within Joomla. The extension makes Gallery2 appear to a Joomla visitor as if it is executing directly within the Joomla web site. On the Joomla web site (http://extensions. joomla.org), you can find many such bridge extensions that wrap PHP software not natively written for Joomla.

Since Gallery2 was written for independent execution, it requires a separate installation and has its own system requirements. While most web providers that host Joomla will be able to support Gallery2, it is important that you check the requirement lists before you attempt to deploy any extension.

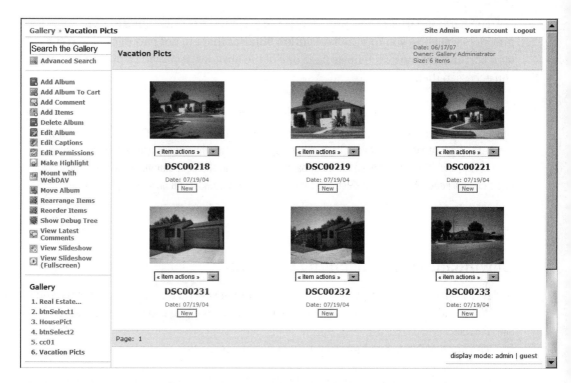

Figure 10-10. *The Gallery2 display when running as a standalone PHP application*

To execute properly, Gallery2 has the following requirements:

- PHP version 4.1.0 or above with safe_mode disabled

- MySQL 3.x or above

- Graphics execution library (such as GD2.x or above, ImageMagick 4.x or above, GraphicsMagick 1.x or above, or Netpbm 9.x or above) for creating the thumbnails and handling image resizing

- Drive space for photo storage (more than you might think)

In contrast to the simple installation of Easy Gallery, you can see that Gallery2 places more demands on the server. However, the trade-off is the substantial functionality that Gallery2 grants both the front-end user and the administrator of the system.

The hardest part for most providers is the graphics execution libraries. Few web providers will allow you to install execution libraries that are not part of their current system. Fortunately, most web hosts have one of the libraries or provide a plan that can give you access to them.

■Tip While you can use GD2 (as you may already have it installed for use with Easy Gallery), it may not be your best option. At the time of this writing, ImageMagick produces thumbnails and resized images much more quickly than GD2. Netpbm, on the other hand, produces the sharpest thumbnails with the most fidelity to the original image. You may consider using one of these extensions if you have the option.

Downloading and Installing Gallery2

Gallery2 is an open source project, so it is available in several downloadable forms. You can download the current version from the Gallery2 home page, at `http://gallery.menalto.com`.

The application is available in four installation versions:

- *Minimal*: Contains the basic application as well as two presentation themes, three graphics toolkits, and the essential functionality modules (similar to Joomla components)

- *Typical*: Contains the basic application as well as six presentation themes and the most popular modules

- *Full*: Contains the basic application as well as six presentation themes and all the available modules (there are 56 at the time of this writing)

- *Developer*: Contains the basic application as well as six presentation themes, all the available modules, and developer tools that allow you to further develop Gallery2 as well as create you own modules

You can also access the Subversion version control system to download the latest development version of the Gallery2 files. However, I don't recommend such a path for your first experience with the application.

I would recommend that you use the typical installation unless space is not precious (as it is on most remote web sites). On a staging server, the full installation is a good choice, as it will demonstrate everything that Gallery2 has to offer.

Create a folder called `gallery2` at the same root where the Joomla system is executing. Joomla will need to access this directory, so it is generally easiest if the folder is located in the same file permissions area as Joomla. On most Linux systems, the path will likely be based on your username and so will be similar to this:

```
/home/username/public_html/gallery2
```

On Windows, the directory path may look like this:

```
C:\Program Files\Apache Software Foundation\Apache2.2\htdocs\gallery2
```

Copy all of the files from whichever of the four installation archives you've chosen into the `gallery2` directory. You will need to execute the setup from within the directory in order to configure that application.

While Gallery2 is optimized for execution on the Apache web server, it can be configured to run on Microsoft IIS. Check out the IIS installation page on the documentation site (`http://codex.gallery2.org/index.php`) for more information.

■**Note** Some web service providers have built-in Gallery2 installation features as part of their service. Some of these hosts include DreamHost, Go Daddy (as a value-added application), PowerWeb, OpenSourceHost, Delphian Internet, HostGo, CirtexHosting, and DownTownHost. Before you do an installation from scratch, check to see if your host provides one that is preconfigured to match its system parameters.

Creating the Gallery2 Database

Before you can install Gallery2, you will need to create the database that will be used by the gallery system since the installer will not do it for you. Although Gallery2 is capable of using several database servers (including PostgreSQL and Oracle), since Joomla already uses MySQL, that is the database server that will be used here.

To create the Gallery2 database, execute the MySQL Administrator application. Once you've logged onto the server, right-click in the Schema pane and select the Create New Schema option (see Figure 10-11). Set the name of the schema to **gallery2** for simplicity.

The schema should be left empty as the Gallery2 installer will populate it with the necessary tables and foundation information. It is a good idea while in the MySQL Administrator application to create a user account that will be used by Gallery2 and has full access privileges to the database. That way you won't need to have the application access the database through a MySQL administrator account.

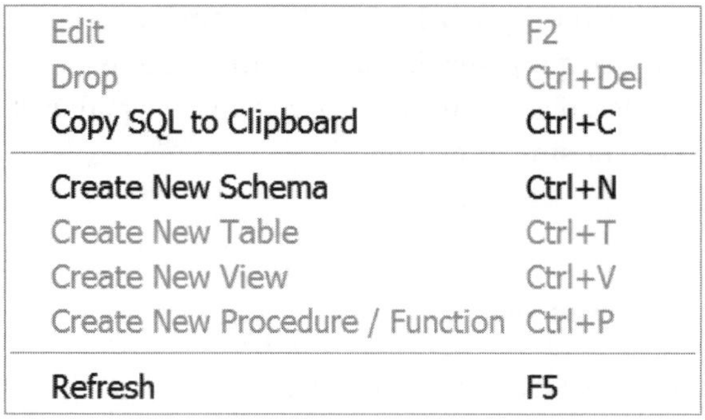

Edit	F2
Drop	Ctrl+Del
Copy SQL to Clipboard	**Ctrl+C**
Create New Schema	**Ctrl+N**
Create New Table	Ctrl+T
Create New View	Ctrl+V
Create New Procedure / Function	Ctrl+P
Refresh	**F5**

Figure 10-11. *Right-click in the Schema area and select the Create New Schema option from the context menu.*

To add the user, select the User Manager. Create the new account with the name **galleryadmin** and set an appropriate password. In the permissions section, give the account all privileges for the gallery2 database. Simply click the left-facing double arrow (<<) button to put all of the permissions in the user permission list, and click the Apply changes button to grant the privileges (see Figure 10-12).

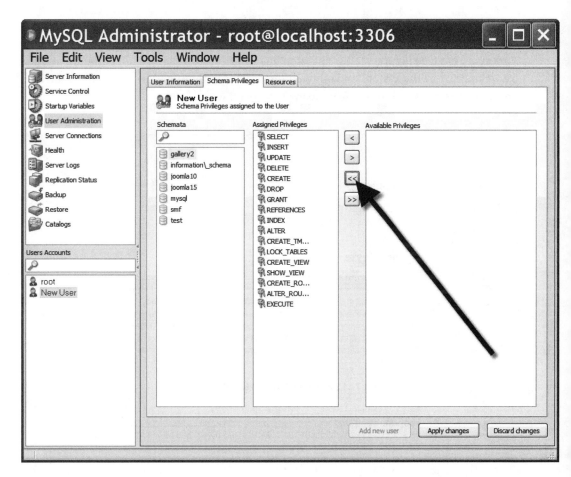

Figure 10-12. *Grant the user all permissions for the gallery2 database to the new user account.*

Configuring Gallery2

With everything in place, you can activate the Gallery2 installation process. Installation is provided by a dozen-step setup wizard that will do most of the work for you. It will configure all of the necessary files, allow selective activation of installed modules, create the necessary database tables, and populate the tables with the foundation data.

You can begin installation of Gallery2 by accessing the index.php file in the \gallery2 directory. On the Windows platform, your URL may look like this:

```
http://localhost/gallery2/index.php
```

The first step of the installation is a simple welcome screen; you can click the Next button to move to the second screen. The second step requires you to create an authentication key file (see Figure 10-13). This step has you to store a file with an authentication key generated by the system on your web server. This authentication key is later used by the system to prevent hackers from using forgery attacks.

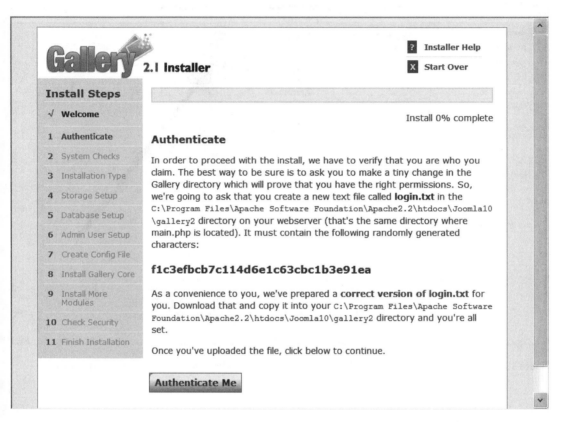

Figure 10-13. *The authentication screen provides a link to an autogenerated file for placement on your server.*

Right-click the link to the authentication file and save it to your local drive. On a staging server, you can save it directly into your \gallery2 directory. If you're using a remote web host, save it on your local drive and then use your FTP software to upload the file to the proper directory.

Once the file is in place, click the Authenticate Me button to check the file. If there are problems with authentication, go to the Gallery2 home page, which is often updated to detail resolutions to problems users have with authentication on various web providers.

If the authentication is successful, the installer will proceed to the system check execution, as shown in Figure 10-14. You can see from the figure that my web host has several items that generate warnings in this verification phase. If you encounter any failures in the system check, most can be remedied with changes to the PHP configuration file.

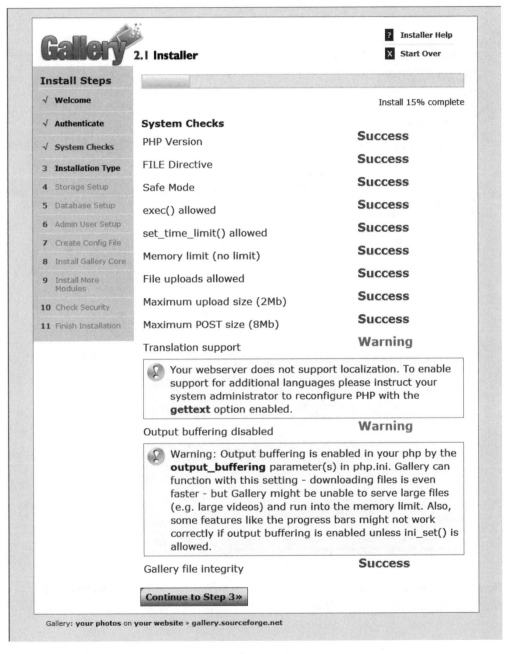

Figure 10-14. *The system check attempts to validate the functionality of the web server for proper Gallery2 execution.*

The next screen allows you to choose whether there will be multiple installations of Gallery2 running on a single web server (see Figure 10-15). In most cases, you will want to select the Standard installation option and continue.

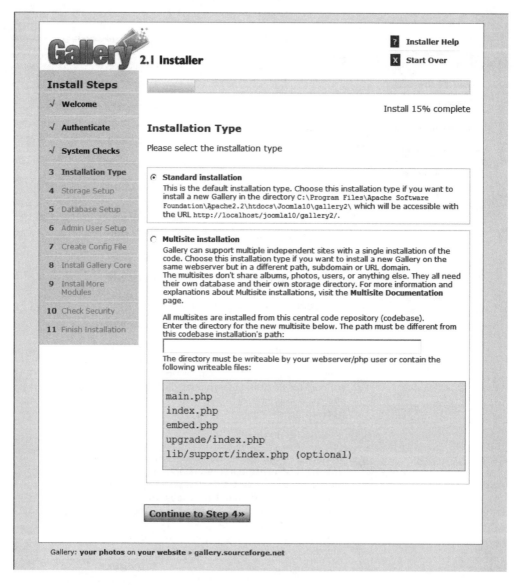

Figure 10-15. *This screen allows configuration of a standard installation (normal for a single site) or a multisite installation.*

Storage of your pictures is important. For greatest security, it is best to locate the \images folder so that it is available to the Gallery2 system, but not accessible directly through the web server. For this reason, the Storage Setup screen (see Figure 10-16) will request that you create a folder outside the standard web server path and also make the directory name nonstandard so that it cannot be easily guessed by hackers. Therefore, if possible on your Apache server installation, try to locate the folder outside the \htdocs folder.

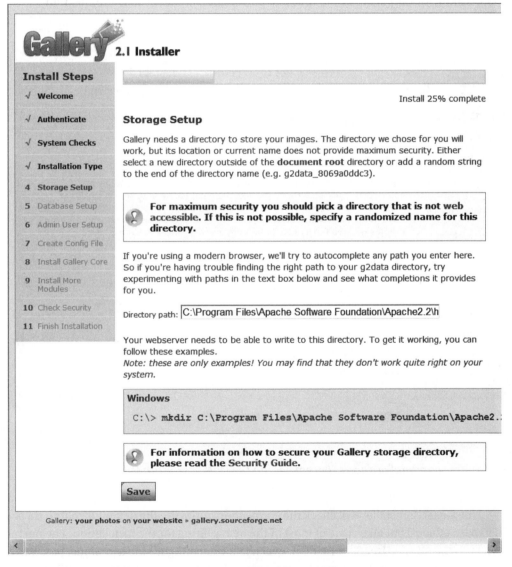

Figure 10-16. *If possible, locate your image storage folder outside the general web server path.*

You will need to create this directory for the images before you click the Continue button. When you do continue, the installer will check to make certain the directory is accessible and will provide a recommendation if the directory is not as secure as it might be.

On the Database Setup screen (see Figure 10-17), you are prompted for access parameters to your database server. At this point, the installer expects that you have already created the database that it will need to write gallery information. If you haven't created the database already, go back and do that now. Then you can enter the login information for the galleryadmin user that you created in the MySQL Administrator.

Figure 10-17. *Enter your database access parameters on the Database Setup screen.*

The Gallery2 installer will check the connection and write the default data into the database tables. That takes care of most of the heavy lifting for the installation. The next screen is the Admin User Setup screen, which lets you configure the username, password, and e-mail address for the administrative user of the Gallery2 application. I would recommend that you make this setting match your Joomla Administrator user for ease of configuration.

Clicking the Continue button on the admin setup screen will execute the procedure to create the Gallery2 configuration file (`config.php` in the `\gallery2` folder). If there is any problem with the creation of the file, you will be notified and given the opportunity to correct it and try again.

Tip The configuration file is critical to the proper functioning of the Gallery2 system. For this reason, I would suggest that you routinely back up the file outside the web server path (for security reasons). If the configuration file becomes corrupted (through manual editing or a system fault), Gallery2 will likely stop functioning. Restoring this file can save you from having to do a reinstall of the system.

Clicking the Continue button will execute the process that installs the gallery core modules. If there are any problems with this stage, once again you will be notified of the problems and given the opportunity to correct them.

The Install Other Modules screen (see Figure 10-18) shows a complete list of the modules available for installation. If you downloaded the full installation, you may see a list that spans several screens and literally dozens of optional modules. Whichever installation package you chose, you can leave all of the modules checked for installation unless you see a module that has functions that you will clearly not need to provide.

The final installation screen provides access to a security guide. Read this guide! It will detail all of the best ways to ensure Gallery2 is as secure as possible. Since the application allows uploads, generates new files on the server, and displays images (a common point of entry for buffer overrun hacks), it is critical that you make your server secure. Even if you're executing the application on a remote server, it is a good idea to read through this security manual.

That should be it! You should be able to access the Gallery2 system through a URL such as this:

```
http://localhost/gallery2
```

Log on to the Gallery2 system as an administrator to begin. Unlike Easy Gallery, Gallery2 uses *albums* to organize images instead of categories, although the difference is only in semantics. Add some albums and photos to make sure the system is working properly. Once you have run through some of the basic functions of the gallery application, you are ready to incorporate it into the Joomla interface.

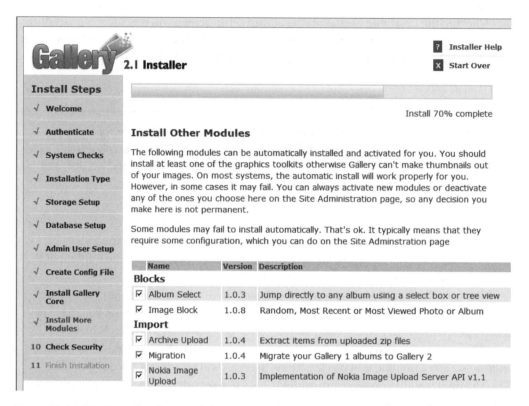

Figure 10-18. *The Install Other Modules screen shows a list of all non-core modules for installation.*

Using Gallery2 from Within Joomla

Gallery2 can be run on a web server as a separate application, as you have it installed now. However, it is much more convenient to integrate it with your existing Joomla site. This way, not only will it run inside the template interface, but Gallery2 can also use the Joomla logins for all users on the system. That way you can use a single registration system. Incorporation of Gallery2 within the overall site interface will also provide a single, consistent user interface for web visitors.

To adapt Gallery2 for use within Joomla, you will need to install a component that wraps the gallery functionality. Known as Gallery2 Bridge, this component provides the services of integrating the interface and coordinating the systems functions.

Installing Gallery2 Bridge

To let Gallery2 interoperate with Joomla, you will need to download the Gallery2 Bridge component and JoomlaLib, which is a library of routines that the component uses. For the most current version of these extensions, check out the main Joomla extension directory (http://extensions.joomla.org). Alternatively, you can find both the component and JoomlaLib at http://trac.4theweb.nl.·

Download both components and install them through the Joomla Extension Manager. You should install JoomlaLib first so that the routines will be available to Gallery2 Bridge. When the Gallery2 Bridge installation is complete, Joomla will notify you (see Figure 10-19).

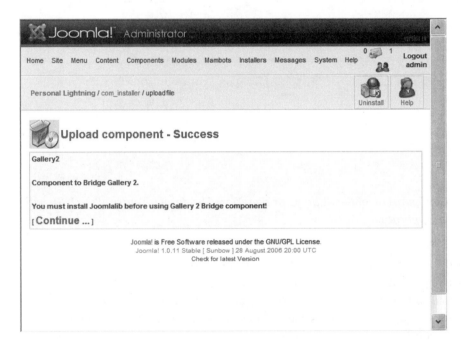

Figure 10-19. *Complete installation of Gallery2 Bridge*

Before you execute Gallery2 within Joomla, you will need to configure the extension so that it will know where to look for the gallery information.

The Gallery2 submenu under the Components menu has three options: Config, User Management, and Album Management. Select the Config option to set up the component to access your existing installation. In the top-right corner of the configuration window, you will see a Wizard button. Click it, and the wizard will take you step by step through the bridge configuration.

When you click the Wizard button, the Gallery2 URL configuration screen will be displayed, as shown in Figure 10-20. This parameter is the most important of the installation, as the bridge uses this path to locate all of the other files it needs for Joomla interoperation.

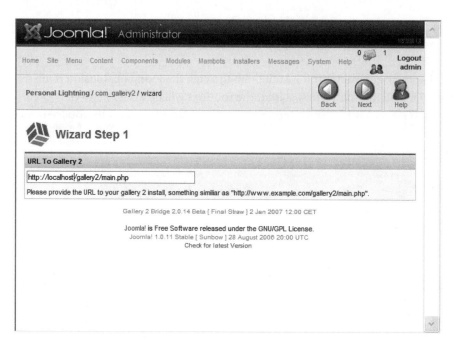

Figure 10-20. *Configuration of the Gallery2 Bridge Wizard begins with entry of the URL path to the Gallery2 application.*

Follow the wizard through the straightforward steps (such as whether you choose to integrate the registered user lists) and the bridge should be operational. Before you can see it displayed within Joomla, however, you will need to add a menu to access it.

The central bridge component is listed simply as Gallery2 in the Components menu. You already know how to add a menu to direct the site to a component. Create a menu item to address the Gallery2 component so that when you click the menu entry, the Gallery2 application will be rendered into the central column of the Joomla template, as shown in Figure 10-21.

In addition to the main component that integrates the core user interface of Gallery2 into Joomla, there are also a number of modules that allow you to display particular items drawn from the gallery interaction. These modules are available through the Gallery2 Bridge web site, where you downloaded the main component.

Figure 10-21. *Gallery2 will appear in the central template column.*

At the time of this writing, there are five available modules:

- *Statistics*: Provides statistics that directly relate to the popularity of a particular gallery. Data includes information on images, albums, comments, and totals of the gallery access.

- *Sidebar*: Displays the sidebar menu that is part of the Gallery2 standalone application. As a module, this menu can be better integrated into the Joomla template interface, and frees up vertical space since the menu doesn't have to be displayed within the component.

- *Image*: Allows selection of a specific image from the gallery to be displayed in the module position. Options include Random Image, Last Added Image, Most Viewed Image, Random Album, Last Added Album, Most Viewed Album, Daily Image, Weekly Image, Monthly Image, Daily Album, Weekly Album, Monthly Album, and Specific Picture.

- *Comments*: Shows the user comments about the various images stored in the Gallery2 system.

- *Album*: Presents a list of current photo albums for more direct access than through the Gallery2 interface.

Each of the modules functions just like a standard Joomla module. Simply install the module, configure it to the parameters that you desire, and add it to a display position.

Other Gallery2 Plug-Ins

If you want to further extend the Joomla/Gallery2 interface, there are a few more plug-ins that offer additional features to bridge these two systems. The following list describes a few of these plug-ins:

- *Search Bot*: This plug-in integrates the photo and gallery descriptions held in Gallery2 into the Joomla search engine. This eliminates dual search requirements and makes the site more consistent.

- *Joomap*: This integrates Gallery2 into the sitemap generated through Joomap (including support for Google Sitemap XML generation). The plug-in supplies the proper URLs of images to the sitemap-generation system.

- *Community Builder*: This plug-in integrates the Gallery2 content with the Community Builder interface. The Community Builder interface can provide much more robust security granularity for images and albums.

Note that all of these extensions are plug-ins and, as such, interface with Joomla at a very low level. Therefore, if you are having slow-downs in performance or untraceable site problems, be sure to check that all your plug-ins are operating correctly.

Conclusion

The photo gallery extensions for Joomla present an incredible opportunity for sharing and/or marketing digital images. The explosion of digital cameras and even cell phone imaging has made the ability to share images an exciting new frontier. With the proper extensions, a Joomla site supplies an excellent foundation for image distribution.

For small or personal sites, the Easy Gallery extension combines simple installation with straightforward administration. It can readily display your images in a user-friendly way that complements Joomla's visual style. Although there is no opportunity for users to upload to the gallery (access to the Administrator interface is required), this gallery is perfect for quickly sharing photographs. The FTP-based interface helps to avoid possible file permission problems.

Larger galleries and commercial image management sites can use Gallery2 to provide everything from multiformat upload to a shopping cart for image purchases. With Gallery2 Bridge, the Gallery2 application can be incorporated into the Joomla deployment for seamless integration. Gallery2 even features its own plug-in architecture for customization and feature augmentation.

While only two gallery extensions were covered in this chapter, there are literally dozens of other gallery options for Joomla. Some of the most impressive gallery applications that have been integrated with Joomla use an Adobe Flash plug-in to offer more vigorous user interaction and display than a traditional web-based gallery.

In Chapter 11, you'll learn about a comprehensive e-commerce extension that will allow you to add catalog and ordering capabilities to your Joomla site for almost any kind of product or service.

■ ■ ■

Joomla! E-commerce

Although Joomla is used for a large number of hobbyist web sites, with the proper extensions it can become a phenomenal commercial platform for e-commerce. On the web, e-commerce has become big business—particularly for B2B (or business-to-business) transactions. To tap into the worldwide customer base that the Internet makes available, you can configure your Joomla site to allow for online purchases or catalog display.

This chapter will focus on a particular open source e-commerce solution called VirtueMart. VirtueMart is a popular web store application with over 600 registered online stores that use its technology to offer online shopping. To show you how Virtue-Mart works, I'll lead you through the steps of creating an online store called Movie Matinee. Your sample store will sell old movies on DVD. By working through a real-world example, you can see exactly how a virtual store can be configured and deployed.

VirtueMart: The Joomla! Store

VirtueMart is an e-commerce solution made specifically for execution within Joomla. It provides complete product catalog, inventory control, and shopping cart capabilities. The entire application can be administered through a web-based interface like Joomla itself. It can also accept the import of an existing product catalog using comma-separated value (CSV) files that contain lists of product prices, descriptions, parameters, cross references, and product details.

One of the most full-featured Joomla e-commerce extensions, VirtueMart provides the following:

- Sales and management of downloadable products (such as software and e-books)

- Presentation as either an online catalog or a catalog with shopping cart capabilities

- Administration interface integrated with the Joomla front-end so that VirtueMart administration is available without full Joomla administrator privileges (so employees can manage the virtual store without having access to the Joomla back-end of the main site)

- Custom attributes for each product, allowing the display of a drop-down list of choices

- Inventory and customer order tracking features

- "Shopper groups" creation and administration for custom tracking and pricing per group

- Shipping rate calculator and interface to shippers such as UPS, USPS, InterShipper, and Canada Post

- Report generation for orders, items sold, and revenue

- Integrated search capabilities

- Interfaces with live payment gateways such as PayPal, eWAY, WorldPay, and Paymate

- Architecture allowing plug-ins for custom authoring of modules, such as for payment and shipping

VirtueMart itself is divided into a number of different extensions, so only the desired parts need to be installed. The minimum VirtueMart deployment requires only a single component and a single module to be installed. The main component that supplies the virtual store interface is very efficient, so the store adds little overhead to the existing Joomla system.

System Requirements

If you are already running Joomla on your server, it is likely that you will be able to use VirtueMart. The minimum configuration is as follows:

- PHP 4.3 or above with the PHP extensions to interface with MySQL, XML, and zlib activated

- MySQL 3.23 or above

- Apache 1.13.19 or above; support for HTTPS (OpenSSL) and cURL recommended

Be sure to check your system configuration before you attempt to install VirtueMart. The application doesn't have a system check for minimum system validation like Joomla does, so the effects on a noncompliant system are unknown.

Download Options

VirtueMart (formerly known as mambo-phpShop) is a free, open source e-commerce solution that is released under the GNU/GPL license (like Joomla). It is available for download from the VirtueMart home page at `www.virtuemart.net`.

VirtueMart is a collection of modules, components, and plug-ins, so there are many ways to download and configure it. Each of the extensions requires separate installation in Joomla. On the home page, there are three packages available for download:

- *Complete installation*: The complete package features the central VirtueMart component, the primary module, ten additional modules (for things such as displaying the latest product or the top ten products), and two plug-ins (for search and content).

- *Joomla installation*: The providers of VirtueMart have created a complete Joomla installation image that includes a configured VirtueMart with the installation. If you already have Joomla installed, you *do not* need this version. This installer makes creating a turnkey VirtueMart site simple and quick.

- *Upgrade installation*: If you have an older version of VirtueMart already installed, upgrade versions are available that can retain your existing data while adding the newer features and bug remedies.

There are ten optional modules (not required for proper VirtueMart execution) included with the complete installation package:

- `mod_product_categories`: Displays the product categories to the visitor

- `mod_productscroller`: Presents a marquee that scrolls information about selected products

- `mod_virtuemart_allinone`: Shows a tabbed display that includes tabs for featured, top ten, random, and latest product lists

- `mod_virtuemart_cart`: Displays a small cart icon link that can take the visitor to the page that shows the current contents of the shopping cart

- `mod_virtuemart_featuredprod`: Shows the products that are selected to be on special sale

- `mod_virtuemart_latestprod`: Presents a list of the latest products added to the catalog

- `mod_virtuemart_manufacturers`: Lists all of the manufacturers or brands of products available and allows listing of products by these categories

- mod_virtuemart_randomprod: Displays a random product from the entire catalog or from a specified category

- mod_virtuemart_search: Shows the search box that allows for catalog searching

- mod_virtuemart_topten: Lists the ten best-selling products on the site

Download the installation file that matches your needs. All archives contain the installer files, which must be extracted before installation is possible. For example, the central VirtueMart cart module, named something like mod_virtuemart_cart_1.0.10.tar.gz, will be contained within the complete archive, possibly named VirtueMart_1.0.10-COMPLETE_PACKAGE.zip.

Begin the installation by extracting the main module. It will have a name similar to mod_virtuemart_1.0.10.tar.gz. Use the Extension Manager to install it. Make sure that you set the position so that it appears somewhere on your site.

After the module is installed, extract the main component, which will have a name similar to com_virtuemart_1.0.10.tar.gz. In the Extension Manager, install this component. Once the installation is complete, the success screen will present a button that can be used to install sample product data (see Figure 11-1). It is a good idea to work from a foundation, so click the button to install the sample data.

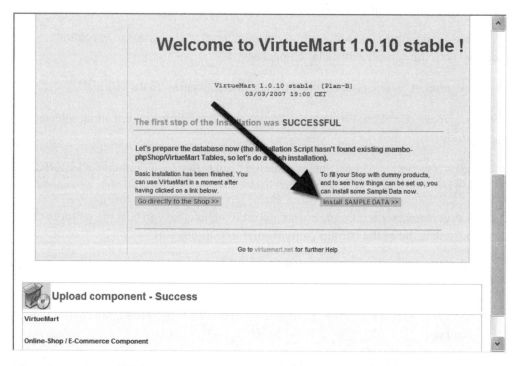

Figure 11-1. *After the installation of the component is complete, you can install sample data.*

Creating a Virtual Store

Once VirtueMart is installed, you can quickly and easily create an online store. One of the best things about this application is the flexibility of configuration. All settings can be changed later, so it is an excellent idea to start now and begin the setup process. There are no mistakes you can't correct later.

As with a Joomla site, however, time invested in planning the structure of the store will benefit the site greatly in the future. By predefining the intended store structure, you can lay out the store from top down—first by creating product categories, and then adding products to each category.

VirtueMart Control Panel

If you selected to install the sample data, after the upload is complete you will be automatically taken to the VirtueMart Control Panel, displayed in the Joomla Administrator interface (although it is accessible through the front-end as well). In the Administrator interface, it is accessible from the VirtueMart menu item on the Components menu. The Control Panel (see Figure 11-2) provides quick access buttons to the most useful screens of the component. The Control Panel also contains virtual store statistics on the right side of the screen for an instantaneous summary of the current store activity.

Figure 11-2. *The Control Panel on the Administrator interface takes you to different parts of the virtual store setup.*

The menu bar displayed on the Control Panel provides access to all of the VirtueMart screens. Most of the setup options, since they do not need to be regularly accessed after initial store creation, are not available as quick access buttons on the Control Panel. Use the menu bar to access them.

Tax Configuration

Due to the serious legal implications of taxation, you should begin your store formulation by creating a tax item that defines a tax rate. The default install includes a single entry for the state of California in the United States. Wherever you're doing business from, make sure that the tax rate is set properly for your region.

To set up a tax rate option that is different from the one installed (or to set up several), select the Add Tax Rate option from the Tax menu. The Add Tax Information screen (see Figure 11-3) will be displayed, on which you can make the appropriate selections.

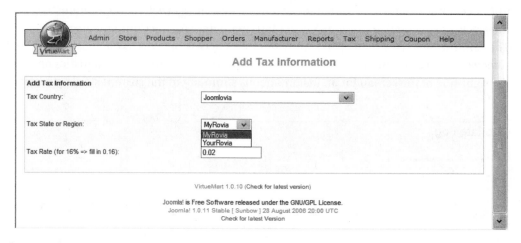

Figure 11-3. *The Add Tax Information screen allows configuration of country, state/region, and tax rate.*

VirtueMart includes an extensive list of countries and regions within those countries. If your country or region isn't included in the list, you can add it through the VirtueMart administrative interface. There is a Country submenu under the Admin menu that holds the Add Country option. This option will add an entry to the jos_vm_country table.

To add a state or region, you have to make the addition manually through MySQL. Open the MySQL Administrator application, right-click the jos_vm_country table, and select the Edit Table Data option. Find the country for which you want to add a region and write down the value in the country_id column for later reference. If you've just added a new country, you will find it in the last row in the list.

Open the jos_vm_state table and create a new record. You can leave the state_id column empty, as the auto-increment setting will automatically assign it an ID. Enter the ID of the associated country you wrote down earlier in the country_id column. Type the name of the state, a three-character abbreviation, and a two-character abbreviation into the appropriate fields, and apply the changes.

Any added entries will now appear in the appropriate drop-down list. Note that these changes will have to be re-created on any other VirtueMart installations. Therefore, be sure to back up your entire Joomla database to allow for full restoration in the event of system failure.

Global Configuration

There are a great many settings available through the Configuration option of the Admin menu. A few options should be configured during the initial setup of your virtual store. When you display the Configuration screen, you are first presented with the Global tab and the associated options (see Figure 11-4).

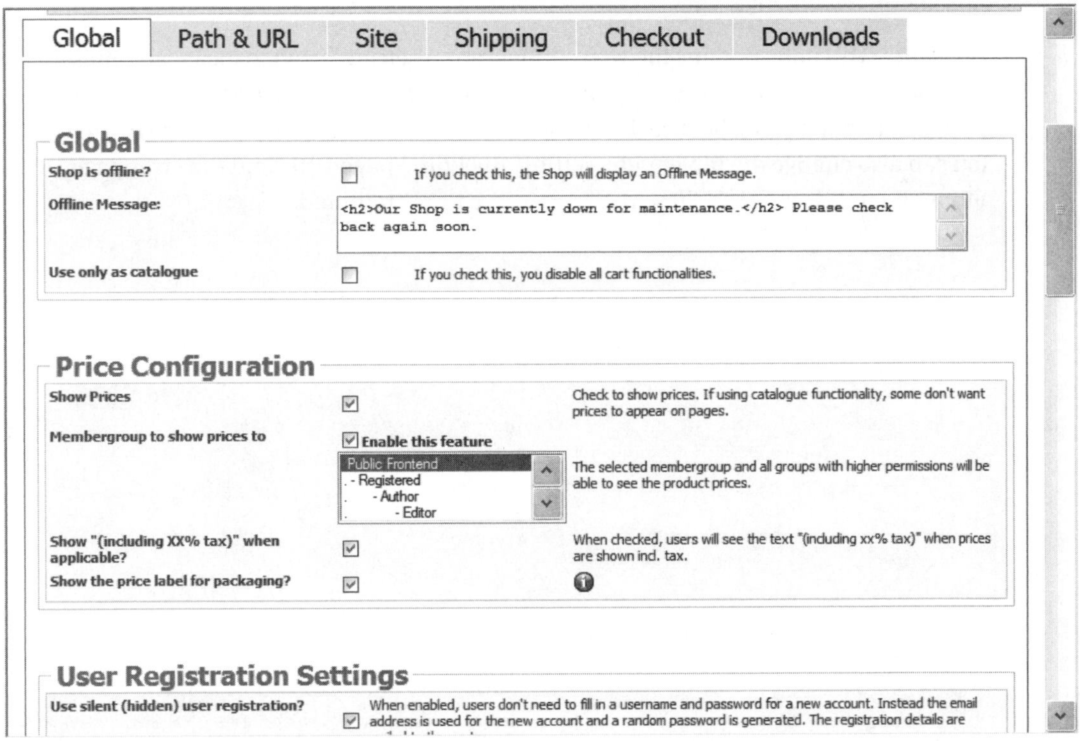

Figure 11-4. *The Configuration screen holds the parameters for all of the global VirtueMart settings.*

Global Tab Settings

To use VirtueMart strictly as an online catalog, you can check the "Use only as catalogue" option. For most users, the default tax options of the Global tab are appropriate, but be sure to check them for your needs.

On the Front-end Features pane, the Enable Customer Review/Rating System setting is active by default. Since this option allows users to not only rate products but also write reviews, consider carefully whether you want to leave it enabled. Unless you are a large company like Wal-Mart, a single bad review can negate a lot of potential sales. However, deleting bad reviews or stuffing the rating ballot box are not the choices most companies should take either. If you choose to keep this enabled, your company will have to take the good with the bad.

You should also review the legal information text displayed in the Legal Information Text field. Since the default text holds such information as the return policy, you are committing your virtual store to the terms found in this copy. Be sure it accurately reflects the policies of your store.

Path & URL Tab Settings

The Path & URL tab contains the web configuration settings used to locate and present information about your store (see Figure 11-5). If you have an SSL certificate (see the "VirtueMart and Secure Sockets Layer" section later), you can configure the URL here. You can also change the table prefix setting, the home page URL, and the error page URL, although modifications to these parameters are rarely required.

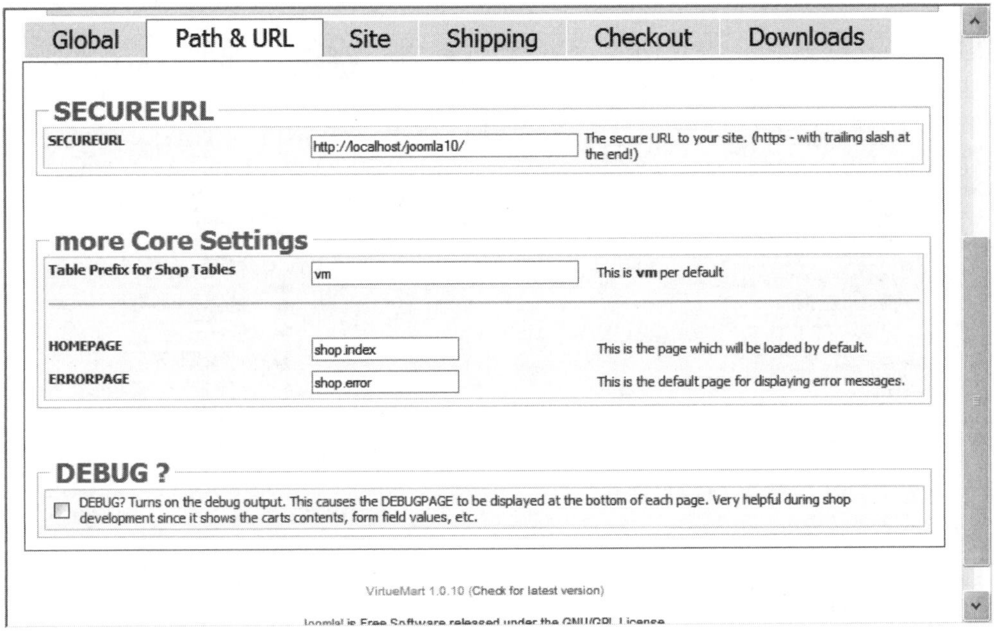

Figure 11-5. *The Path & URL tab contains parameters for the secure path, debugging, the page reference, and the database prefix.*

Other Tab Settings

A majority of the settings available from the other tabs (Site, Shipping, Checkout, and Downloads) can be left as is for the initial site configuration. You may want to make certain the items on the Shipping tab are configured to your desires. Also, if you are selling downloadable items, the Downloads tab will need to be configured with parameters such as the download root directory and the amount of time after purchase that a downloadable item is available to the customer.

If you've completed all of the global configuration settings for your virtual store, click the Save button to store the settings. In VirtueMart, the Save option will return you to the primary tab of the current area that is being used rather than move up one level—unlike the progression of the normal Joomla interface.

Configuring the Store

Before you open your virtual store, you need to configure it to represent your business. Select the Edit Store option under the Store menu. This option will display the Store Information screen (see Figure 11-6), which allows you to edit core business information, such as the store name, URL, address, phone, and site contact information. It allows you to upload a central image for the store. Note that the selected image is not actually uploaded and displayed until the Save button is clicked.

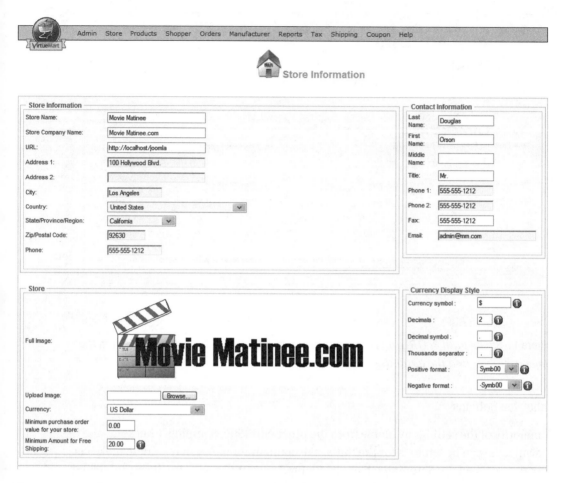

Figure 11-6. *Set the store parameters to match the type of web presence you want to create.*

The Store Information screen also allows you to set the currency type, enter a general description of the store, and include a terms-of-service entry. When the Save button is clicked, VirtueMart presents a basic summary of the information entered.

Creating Categories

In VirtueMart, products are handled just as if a traditional mail catalog were being created. You can begin by adding categories for various products and then placing products in these categories. The categories can be used to sort the product list display for the user as well as for breakdown analysis in the administrative reporting.

Begin by adding a Drama category (see Figure 11-7). Enter the category name and a brief description. The Parent drop-down list makes it possible to define hierarchical categories. The Category Flypage option even lets you create a custom page to be used for the display of products in this category. When you deploy your actual site, it is a good idea to provide a custom page with some category-specific backgrounds and images.

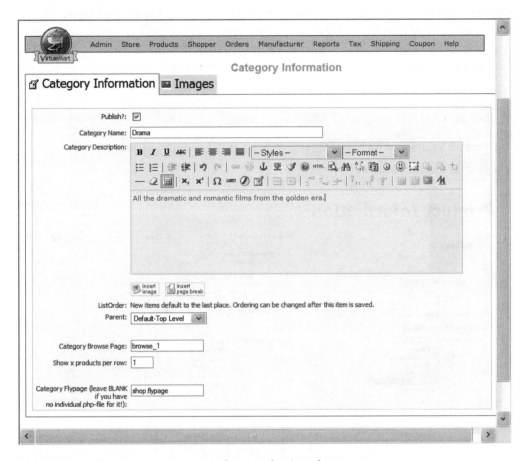

Figure 11-7. *Add a Drama category to the sample virtual store.*

The Category Description field uses the selected Joomla rich text editor (such as TinyMCE). Through this editor you can insert images, make font and style changes, and include other media such as a Flash animation.

Click the Save button to store the category information, and then add a second category to your virtual store. For the Movie Matinee site, I added a Comedy category. You will need at least two categories for proper display on the Frontpage of the site.

Creating Products

To add a product to the catalog, select the Add Product option from the Products menu. Begin the new product definition by setting the title and whatever tracking number you will be using for your products (SKU, bar code, Library of Congress number, or other). Set the category to Drama (see Figure 11-8). For this example, I added the classic movie *Casablanca*. Enter the rest of the information (price, short description, product description, and any other parameters that you will use in your actual site).

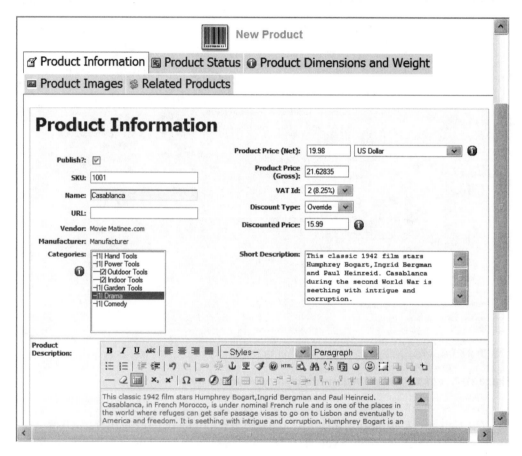

Figure 11-8. *The Product Information tab shows each product and the category in which it is located.*

Click the Product Status tab to enter the inventory information (see Figure 11-9). You can set an *availability date* to allow preordering of announced products. You can also specify availability text and/or a graphic to alert the user of the order fulfillment ship time for this product.

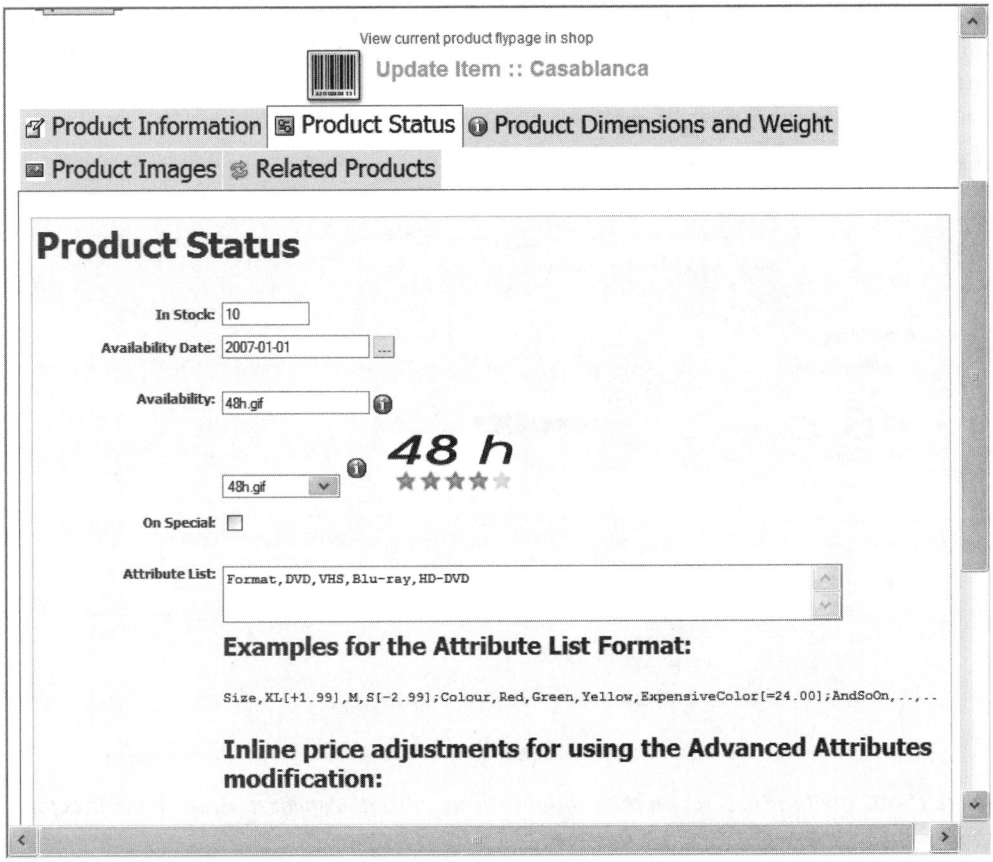

Figure 11-9. *The Product Status parameters determine the number of items in inventory as well as the availability of the product.*

The *attribute list* is one of the many useful features of VirtueMart. A string of parameters can be entered from which the user can select various product options. You can include multiple product option lists by using a semicolon (;) character to separate the lists. A list should begin with the attribute name, followed by the set of options separated by commas.

For example, the Movie Matinee store offers each product in a variety of video formats. These formats can be selected by the customer when they add the product to their shopping cart. The attribute list for the product might look like this:

```
Format,DVD,VHS,Blu-ray,HD-DVD
```

When the user looks at this product through the VirtueMart interface, these options will be presented in a drop-down list, as shown in Figure 11-10. The selection that the user makes is stored with the order. If this were a site specializing in shoe sales, attributes such as stripe pattern, shoe size, shoe width, and color might be included as separate attributes.

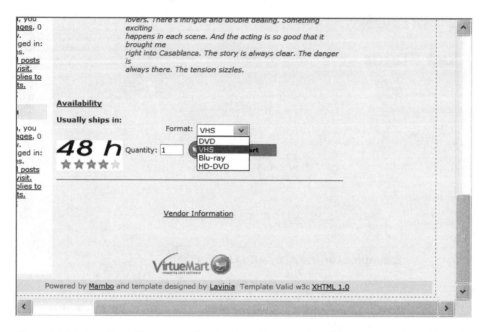

Figure 11-10. *Attribute lists set on the Product Status tab will appear as drop-down lists for the product.*

Click the Product Dimensions and Weight tab to set up the information useful for calculating shipping (see Figure 11-11). These parameters will be used by the various automated shipping applications, which can calculate the actual postage required for an order. If the product is downloadable, you can also specify the filename or browse to select the file for upload. The file isn't actually uploaded into the system until you click the Save button for the product.

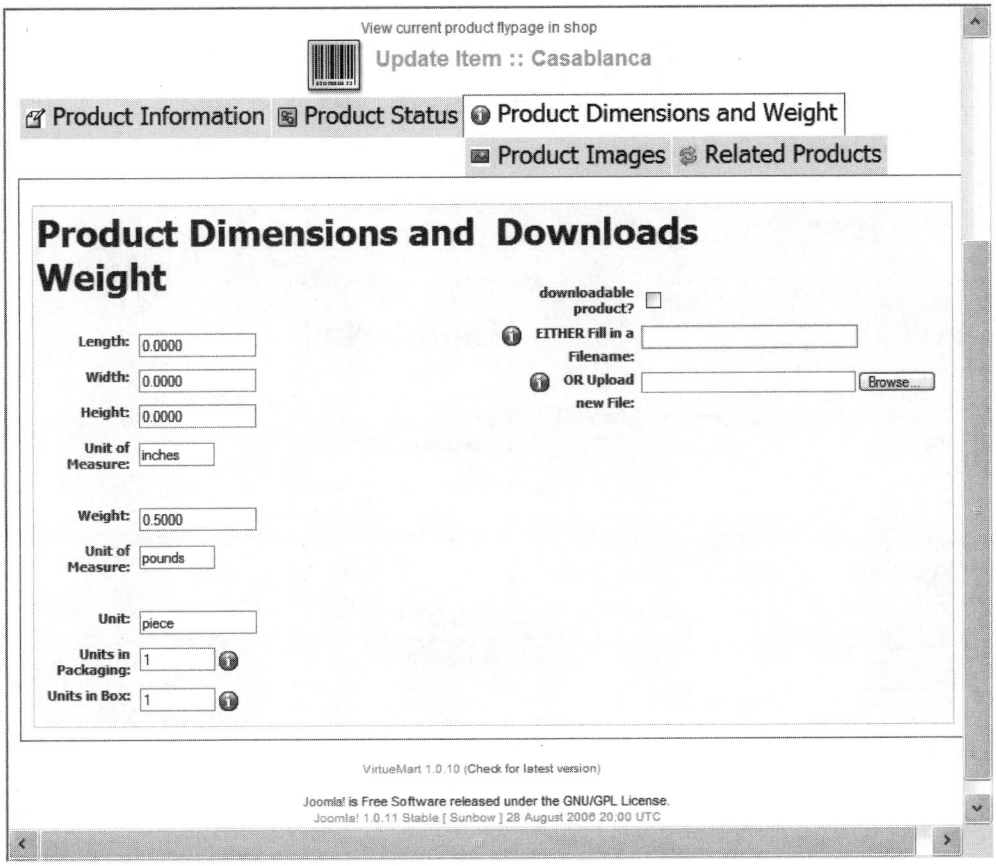

View current product flypage in shop

Update Item :: Casablanca

⌨ Product Information ▦ Product Status | ⓘ Product Dimensions and Weight

▦ Product Images ◈ Related Products

Product Dimensions and Weight — Downloads

downloadable product? ☐

Length: `0.0000`

Width: `0.0000`

Height: `0.0000`

Unit of Measure: `inches`

Weight: `0.5000`

Unit of Measure: `pounds`

Unit: `piece`

Units in Packaging: `1` ⓘ

Units in Box: `1` ⓘ

ⓘ EITHER Fill in a Filename: `_____`

ⓘ OR Upload new File: `_____` [Browse...]

VirtueMart 1.0.10 (Check for latest version)

Joomla! is Free Software released under the GNU/GPL License.
Joomla! 1.0.11 Stable [Sunbow] 28 August 2006 20:00 UTC

Figure 11-11. *The Product Dimensions and Weight tab contains the parameters used for shipping calculation.*

Click the Product Images tab (see Figure 11-12) to upload a product image and thumbnail of the product if desired. VirtueMart will automatically generate a thumbnail from the main image if you haven't created one already. The selected images will not be uploaded into the system until you click the Save button.

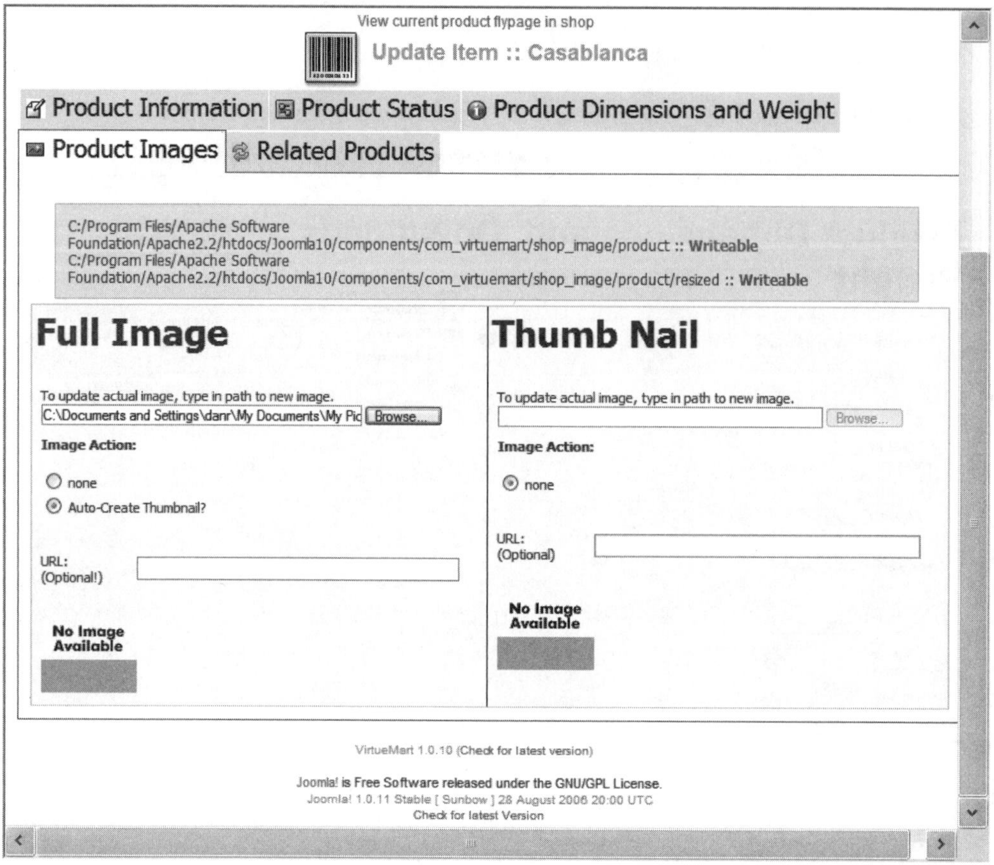

Figure 11-12. *The Product Images tab allows you to upload an image and thumbnail to represent the product.*

Finally, if there are any related products, click the Related Products tab. It will show a list of all the other products held in the system. If there are related products, you can select one or more of them from this list. When the main product is displayed on the site, the bottom of the page will contain a section titled "You may also be interested in this/ these product(s):" and display the thumbnails and titles of any items that you have selected in the list.

Add a few more products so that your catalog provides a rudimentary example of how the site may look. I added an entry for *The Flying Deuces*, starring Laurel and Hardy, and placed it in the Comedy category. I also added another Bogart movie, *To Have and Have Not*.

To view the virtual store, add a menu item that refers to the VirtueMart component in the same way you have with past components. When a browser window is opened to display your Joomla site and the link to the component is selected, the categories available for browsing will be displayed at the top level. Selecting a category will display line items for each one published in the catalog, as shown in Figure 11-13.

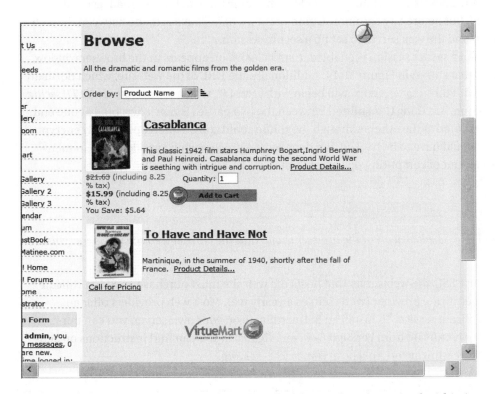

Figure 11-13. *Selecting a category will display all of the products contained within it.*

You've only just begun to configure VirtueMart for true deployment. The extension has many options, but this chapter will only cover the most important ones to get you up and running. Look through the options of the Administrator interface yourself. Most of the items not covered here are actually fairly self-explanatory.

VirtueMart and Secure Sockets Layer

If you are accepting confidential information over the Web (such as credit card numbers or social security data), you need to make sure that transmission and receipt of information is secure. Normally, web information is broadcast in plain text, and the very nature of the foundation technology used by the Internet means that all information is passed through many different computers and routing points. That means that information can possibly be intercepted.

While it is essentially impossible to keep information from being intercepted (by a program known as a packet sniffer), it is possible to encrypt the data. That is the role of the Secure Sockets Layer (SSL). Under SSL, the same information is broadcast and received, but before any communication occurs, a handshake is made between the web browser and the web server to set up a secure session.

When a secure session is enabled, a small lock icon appears in the browser window, such as that shown in Figure 11-14. Additionally, the URL of the web site, which normally begins with the `http://` prefix, will begin with `https://`, which represents an *HTTP secure* connection. Anything transmitted between the two parties is now encrypted at one end and decrypted at the other. Although the traffic could still be intercepted, each encrypted packet would have to be hacked and decoded—a process which would take a tremendous amount of computing power and time.

Figure 11-14. *The lock icon in the browser shows that the current web session is encrypted.*

To use SSL, the web server that hosts the web site must purchase an SSL certificate from a certificate provider (who charges a yearly fee). Most web providers offer an SSL certificate service. To install an SSL certificate on your own server, you can purchase the certificate from VeriSign (`www.verisign.com`). You can find instructions on activating the certificate on Apache at `www.apache-ssl.org`.

■Note At the time of this writing, Apache on Windows (unlike the Linux install) does not support SSL in the downloadable binaries. This means that to use SSL on Apache Windows, you will need to download, configure, and install it yourself. On the Web, search for the Apache SSL module (`mod_ssl`) and installation instructions. Windows IIS natively supports SSL.

Once you have the certificate activated on the server, use the Path & URL tab on the Global Configuration screen of the VirtueMart interface to set the secure HTTP address. VirtueMart can use the security to ensure that all of the transactions relating to the shopping cart are encrypted and secure.

```
Most sites only encrypt the web pages that need the security (such as the credit
card entry pages). Although year after year computers become faster at processing
data, the encryption/decryption cycle is still very computationally intensive even
on a powerful system. Therefore, it is generally a waste of time and processing
power for both the browser and the web server to secure all traffic.
```

Payment Options

Your virtual store can use most of the popular payment services to accept compensation for ordered products. At the time of this writing, VirtueMart features an extensive collection of supported services including 2Checkout, PayPal (IPN), Payflow Pro, Authorize.Net (AIM), eCheck, eProcessingNetwork, eWAY (XML transactions), LinkPoint, Montrada, Nochex, Paymate, Pay-Me-Now, PBS (Danish), Skipjack, and WorldPay. Even better, the system allows you to create your own payment types and define the transaction process for interfacing with new payment systems.

You can set up the transaction methods (to interface with transaction companies such as PayPal, Paymate, eWAY, etc.) by selecting the List Payments option under the Store menu. All payment methods are displayed with their method code, discount, shopper group, payment method type, and enabled status (see Figure 11-15). As the figure shows, you can even limit payment types to particular shopping groups. You can disable payment types not available to your store without removing them from the system, just in case you need to add support for other services in the future.

Figure 11-15. *Existing payment methods can be edited and additional methods can be added.*

If you select an existing payment method or create a new one, the General tab of the payment parameters will be displayed, as shown in Figure 11-16. The General tab displays the summary parameters of the payment. The Code field is the most important field on this screen since it selects the interfaces with the remote system that actually handles the transaction. The code, which is generally given to you by your payment service provider, might include a key or user name.

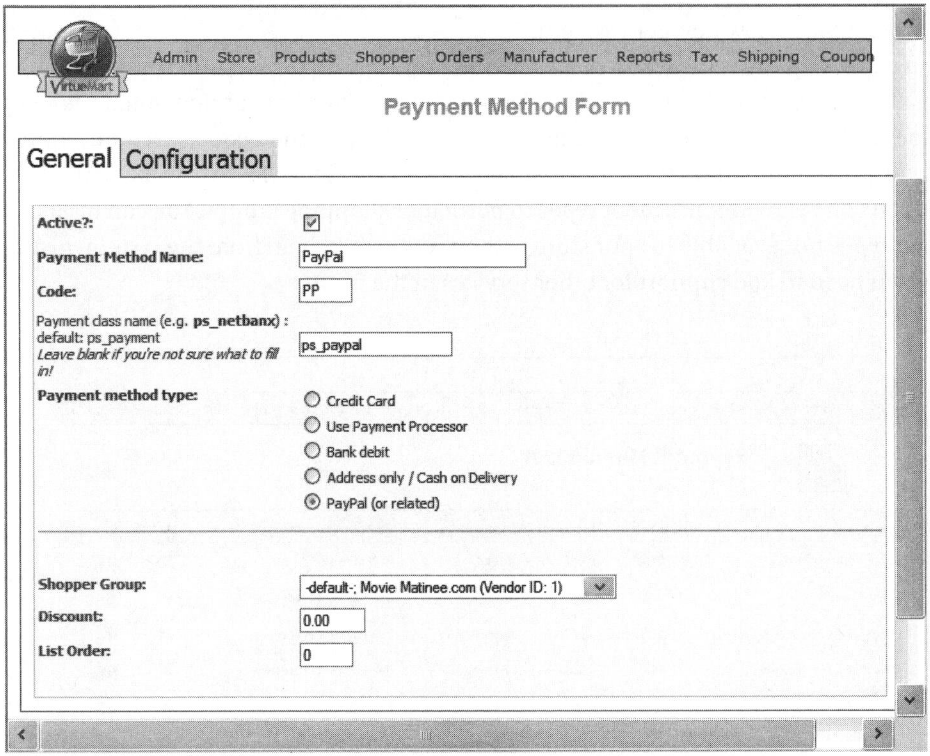

Figure 11-16. *The General tab of the payment editing screen holds the general parameter settings.*

The Configuration tab (see Figure 11-17) of the payment type is used to address the nuts and bolts of the payment interaction. On the Payment Extra info pane, you can insert code given to you by your payment processor that will check the status of the payment. This code will be executed, and the order status in VirtueMart will be automatically updated to reflect the current status. The automatic nature of this payment clearance is most useful in a site that offers downloadable products. The client can enter the payment, and once it clears, will instantly be e-mailed the necessary activation message.

Figure 11-17. *The Configuration tab holds the parameters that define how the service is implemented.*

For stores that accept credit cards, most services handle a variety of card types, from American Express to Diner's Club. When you select the Credit Card List option on the Store menu, the list of supported cards is displayed (see Figure 11-18). Each of these cards can be configured to work with the enabled payment services.

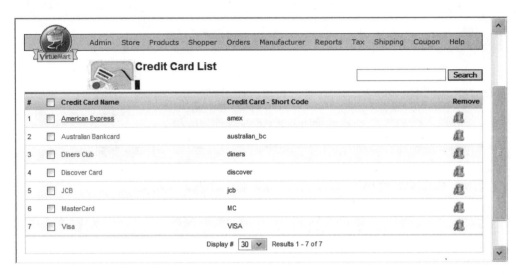

Figure 11-18. *All credit card definitions accepted by VirtueMart are included in the Credit Card List*

Shopper Groups and User Management

One of the most useful features of VirtueMart is the ability to set up *shopper groups*. Shopper groups allow you to create a special category for particular shoppers to see your product catalog. Creating a group may allow you to segregate shoppers (e.g., by geographic area) or cater to them more effectively (e.g., for frequent buyers).

A geographic group might be used when a virtual store is supplementing physical store locations. Often, prices vary depending upon location. A widget sold in a store on Rodeo Drive in Los Angeles is likely to be more expensive than the same product on sale in a small town in Minnesota.

By defining groups based on region, the online prices can match the price differences found in the actual locations. Another common group definition is the *frequent shopper* group. Members receive special discounts and incentives since they are steady repeat customers.

Selecting the List Shopper Groups option from the Shopper menu will display the group list screen. Creating a new group or selecting an existing group will display the Shopper Group Form screen, as shown in Figure 11-19. The parameters of the group are simple and straightforward. The group definition can be used in many places throughout VirtueMart to define special coupon, listing, and shipping options for the members.

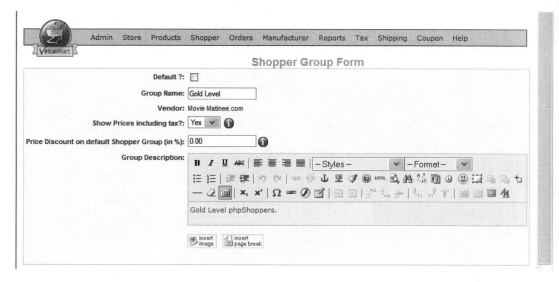

Figure 11-19. *You can define shopper groups to control exactly how group members will see your products.*

Managing Manufacturers/Brands

The Manufacturers menu in the VirtueMart interface is used to manage brands and distributors of the products available through the virtual store. This menu provides options to access, edit, and add to entries of manufacturers and manufacturer categories. Manufacturers can also be configured with contact and web site information if you want your shoppers to be able to directly reference the manufacturers for warranty and product information.

You may have noticed the Manufacturer drop-down list on the Product Information tab when you created a new product. Each product may have one manufacturer designation, and products can be sorted or searched by this parameter.

Setting up manufacturers is an excellent way to allow the web shopper to sort products by brand. For example, a site that sells computer laptops could include manufacturers for Lenovo ThinkPad, Dell, Fujitsu, Sony, and so on. For many types of e-commerce sites, allowing this method of presentation will be exactly what the customer desires.

Shipping Module

VirtueMart has a powerful shipping system implementation. Not only are a large number of shippers preconfigured (see Figure 11-20), but the user interface allows a great deal of specific parameter settings to precisely reflect how the shipping is figured.

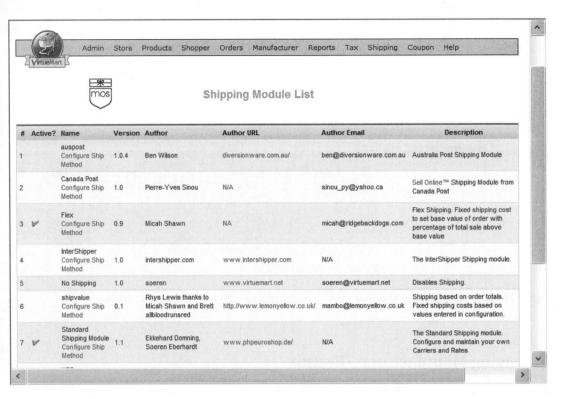

Figure 11-20. *Shippers available on the system*

By default, the Purchase Order and Cash On Delivery payment options are enabled. The rise of credit cards has made these methods of payment far less popular due to the amount of bureaucracy required for a vendor to obtain payment. You should decide whether these payment methods are appropriate for your store before including them on your web site.

Order Management

When VirtueMart receives an order, the new order item will appear in the Order List (see Figure 11-21). You can display the list by selecting the List Orders option on the Orders menu. Clicking the icon in the Print view column will take you to a printable purchase order that you can use to perform product fulfillment.

The Status column shows a drop-down list of status options. You can adjust the status to reflect the current standing of an order by selecting a new option and clicking the Update Status button. If Notify Customer is checked and the user has entered an e-mail during the registration process, a message will be sent to notify the customer of the change in status.

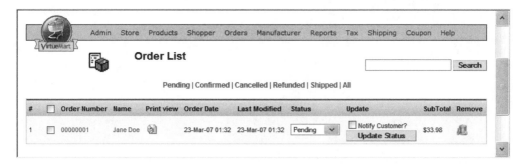

Figure 11-21. *The Order List displays the status of each order and allows display of the order invoice for printing.*

Conclusion

Through VirtueMart, Joomla makes an e-commerce solution not only possible, but attractive and full-featured. VirtueMart has enough capabilities for the small and medium-sized business. With features including a robust shopping cart, automatic payment submission, and inventory management, most businesses will be able to implement the type of virtual store that fits their needs. The ability to offer download-able products expands the range of potential storekeepers even further.

However, if the VirtueMart extension does not provide all of the features that you need, don't give up on Joomla. There are a number of other open source extensions as well as commercial packages (such as EZ-Catalog and osCommerce) that may fit your needs. Joomla has such as large development community; there is a solution available to fit nearly any requirement.

CHAPTER 12

■■■

Search Engine Optimization and Joomla!

No matter how much your site excels in design, implementation, and content, if web users can't locate it, then your efforts are largely wasted. Therefore, ensuring that your site is found by the relevant keywords on Google, MSN, Ask.com, and other popular search engines is worth some effort. A well-placed link on a popular search engine can mean the difference between popularity and anonymity.

There are a number of strategies that will help maximize your search placement. The process of adapting your web site for the best search results is known as search engine optimization (SEO). There are a number of expert companies—such as the Search Agency (www.thesearchagency.com)—that provide skilled consulting services to maximize your web site placement. However, you can do a great deal of work on your own to promote a Joomla site on the search engines.

Search engines use programs called *spiders* that process or "crawl" through each page of a web site and index the content found there for inclusion in the search engine database. A site's ranking in the search database depends a great deal on how effectively and accurately the spider can process the content of your web site.

There are a number of specific configuration settings in Joomla that will optimize it for spider crawling. Further, there are a number of techniques you can adopt to make certain that the content of your site has the best chance of being highly rated. Spending even a couple of hours fine-tuning your Joomla site for SEO can make a world of difference.

SEO on a Joomla! Site

The developers of Joomla recognize the importance of search engine placement for traffic. To assure that Joomla sites have a good chance of being well crawled, they have included a number of features that help increase site visibility and web presence. Various parameters are used to maximize opportunities for web recognition for everything on the site from individual items of content to sitewide configuration.

Since Joomla dynamically creates the web pages sent to a requestor, it has the advantage that changes made to the configuration are immediately effective on a sitewide basis. However, the dynamic nature of a Joomla site also creates a set of disadvantages, since web masters don't have control over the organization and configuration in the way that they do with static web sites. To remedy this problem, Joomla contains parameter settings for all of the major features that affect web spidering. Among the most important of these features is the Search Engine Friendly URLs setting.

Configuring Joomla! to Be Search Engine–Friendly

By default, the page access URLs used by Joomla are not very friendly to a search engine spider. If you've ever looked closely at a URL on a Joomla site with default installation, you may notice that it reads something like this:

```
http://www.example.com/index.php?option=com_content&
    view=category&id=33&Itemid=53
```

That URL may not seem very descriptive to you—and it doesn't seem very descriptive to a spider either. The web address contains parameters that tell the Joomla engine the exact content to retrieve and render. At the time a page is requested, Joomla uses the current template and the requested database content to generate a formatted web page to return to the requestor. While the URL is perfectly understandable to Joomla, a web spider has a hard time with it.

A more straightforward address such as the following is much clearer about the type of content it points toward:

```
http://www.cnn.com/2007/SHOWBIZ/
```

This URL for the CNN web site is formatted like that of a static web site. In contrast to a dynamic site (like Joomla), which renders content on the fly, a static web site stores web page files in various directories (which can be named descriptively) and retrieves them when the proper URL directory path is used.

While search engines can catalog content with a path like the default Joomla URLs, pages with static folder addresses and descriptive links will nearly always outrank the dynamically generated ones. How can this problem be resolved?

Fortunately, the Joomla developers have included two options that allow Joomla to simulate the more descriptive URLs. The options render the URL addresses of the site using a search engine–friendly (SEF) folder-like structure. The native Joomla URLs still won't be as descriptive as ones created by hand (such as the CNN directory path just shown), but they will be good enough that search engines will have no problem finding and cataloging pages properly.

The complication with using the SEF URLs and the reason that this option is turned off by default is that for the feature to work, Joomla needs to be able to dynamically modify the URL on the web server. Some web hosting services will not allow a program to make the URL modifications because a hacker could exploit such capabilities.

Activating the SEF Options

The SEF options are found in the Joomla Administrator on the Global Configuration screen. Notice that the SEO Settings frame (see Figure 12-1) contains two options: Search Engine Friendly URLs and Use mod_rewrite. You will certainly want to set the SEF URLs option to Yes to make links generated by the system appear as the folder-format URLs.

Figure 12-1. *Set the Search Engine Friendly URLs option to Yes.*

When this option is active, the URLs generated by the site will take on the following format:

```
http://www.example.com/index.php/joomla-overview
```

This option uses a routing trick that causes the web server to read the index.php reference in the URL and make that page load and execute. When the index file executes, it processes the folder path that follows it in the URL and supplies the referenced Joomla content. The good news for this technique is that it doesn't require special configuration of the web server to activate the mod_rewrite extension. The bad news is that some web hosts won't work properly using this technique.

If the basic SEF URLs option doesn't work with your host, the server will return an "HTTP 404 - File not found" error when any links are clicked from the Frontpage. In this case, you will want to activate the Use mod_rewrite option. When that is active, the URLs are formatted slightly differently, such that the page referenced earlier will appear as follows:

```
http://www.example.com/home/47-joomla-overview
```

Configuring mod_rewrite on Apache

You will need to check with your web provider to see if mod_rewrite functionality is available. The Apache server needs to have the mod_rewrite module enabled. You can determine if the module is enabled by executing the phpinfo() function (see Chapter 3 for more information). The apache2handler section of the phpinfo() output screen should display mod_rewrite in the module list, as shown in Figure 12-2.

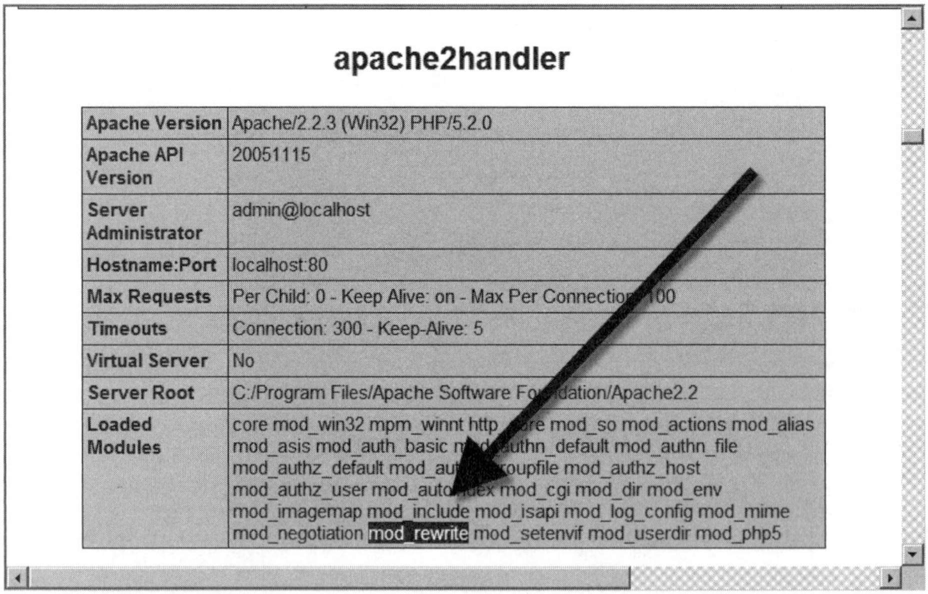

apache2handler

Apache Version	Apache/2.2.3 (Win32) PHP/5.2.0
Apache API Version	20051115
Server Administrator	admin@localhost
Hostname:Port	localhost:80
Max Requests	Per Child: 0 - Keep Alive: on - Max Per Connection: 100
Timeouts	Connection: 300 - Keep-Alive: 5
Virtual Server	No
Server Root	C:/Program Files/Apache Software Foundation/Apache2.2
Loaded Modules	core mod_win32 mpm_winnt http_core mod_so mod_actions mod_alias mod_asis mod_auth_basic mod_authn_default mod_authn_file mod_authz_default mod_authz_groupfile mod_authz_host mod_authz_user mod_autoindex mod_cgi mod_dir mod_env mod_imagemap mod_include mod_isapi mod_log_config mod_mime mod_negotiation mod_rewrite mod_setenvif mod_userdir mod_php5

Figure 12-2. *The Loaded Modules text area of the phpinfo() output screen should include the mod_rewrite listing.*

To activate the module on your Apache server, open the httpd.conf file on the web server. If the module is not being loaded, you should find the following line:

```
#LoadModule rewrite_module modules/mod_rewrite.so
```

To activate it, uncomment the line by removing the pound sign (#). Then you can add the directive that enables the mod_rewrite module:

```
RewriteEngine On
```

To test the mod_rewrite module, you can add a rewrite command. For example, you can add a path to reroute any access to the \myadmin directory to the Joomla \administrator directory. In the httpd.conf file, after the line that enables the RewriteEngine, add the following code:

```
RewriteRule myadmin/(.*) /Administrator/$1 [PT]
```

Restart the Apache server and try to access the \myadmin directory in your browser with a URL like this:

```
http://localhost/myadmin/
```

If the localhost root directory points to your Joomla installation, the \myadmin reference will display the Joomla Administrator login. If you would like to monitor the URL mapping that occurs, you can have Apache write the maps into a log file. Simply add the following two directives to the httpd.conf file:

```
RewriteLog "C:/rewrite.log"
RewriteLogLevel 9
```

With the mod_rewrite module enabled, you're ready to activate the necessary Joomla routing.

Activating the .htaccess File

To allow Apache to properly handle the SEF URLs, you need to set up a custom Joomla .htaccess file in the root directory. For the Apache server, the Joomla installation includes a sample .htaccess file that has the proper configuration settings for the main directory to allow Joomla to handle the URL conversion.

The configuration file, named htaccess.txt, will be located at the root directory of your Joomla site in a default installation file. To allow the Joomla execution of mod_rewrite, you will need to rename the file to .htaccess. To enable the htaccess.txt file included with Joomla, rename it to .htaccess (or ht.acl on Windows; see the following note for more information). Restart the Apache server so that the file will be correctly addressed.

> **Note** On the Windows platform, Windows Explorer won't rename a file to an extension without a main filename (which is how the OS will consider the filename `.htaccess`). You can get around this prohibition by using the command prompt to rename the file, but there is a more elegant solution. You will need to load the `httpd.conf` file for your Apache server into a text editor and add the following line:
>
> `AccessFileName ht.acl .htaccess`
>
> After you've added the line, restart the server. The added directive will allow the `.htaccess` file to have either the traditional filename or the name `ht.acl`.

You can examine the `.htaccess` file to see if any of the special cases listed in the comments section of the file may cause problems on your server. Open the file and you'll see the following setting in the text:

`Options +FollowSymLinks`

This setting may already be set in another part of the Apache configuration (especially on a remote server). If this setting generates an error when you restart Apache, you may need to add a pound sign (#) to the front of the line to make the directive a comment so that it won't execute.

Using Third-Party SEF Plug-Ins

There are a number of SEF plug-ins for Joomla (available on the Joomla extensions site, at `http://extensions.joomla.org`), the most popular being OpenSEF. While the Joomla SEF option is convenient, URLs still have names that may not be as descriptive as you want. The third-party extensions allow you to specify exactly what URL will appear for a given page.

The custom URL mapping supported by the third-party plug-ins is especially useful if you are converting an existing static web site to Joomla. You may already have web pages and directories with good search engine page ranks. By setting up a custom map, you can have Joomla mimic the existent URL and therefore retain the ranking the page has already achieved.

You can download OpenSEF for free from `http://forum.j-prosolution.com/opensef`. After you install it, you will need to use the Administrator interface to configure it to set the SEF output. In the Components menu, you will see the OpenSEF menu, which can be used to display the control panel that allows you to access all the component functions (see Figure 12-3).

Figure 12-3. *The main OpenSEF control panel provides panels for all of the component functions.*

You can craft friendly URLs for any URL that Joomla will use (see Figure 12-4). To set up the custom URL mapping, you need to go to the content where you want to create a friendly address, record that address, and then add it with the SEF address that you want.

Figure 12-4. *You can set friendly URLs for any Joomla URLs.*

■Caution Some of the third-party SEF extensions use a MySQL table to convert between the actual Joomla URL and the SEF version. Therefore, on a page with a great number of URLs (such as a calendar control), the performance on the server can suffer. Therefore, be sure to configure pages with page links to be ignored by the extension.

Using Titles, Meta Descriptions, and Keywords

Joomla has features that aid in proper search engine recognition. Two of the most important are found under the Advanced Parameters tab in the article editor. The *meta description* of an article, which generates the Description tag in the HTML output (see Figure 12-5), is used by most search engines to present a summary of the web page. The description is also examined in conjunction with the title of the page and the headings to ascertain the most relevant information about the page. From this information, the search engine will attempt to file the page under the most relevant keywords.

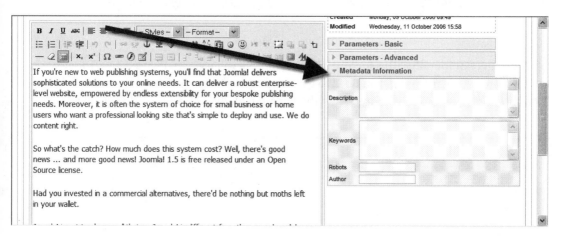

Figure 12-5. *The advanced parameters of an article hold the metadata used by the search engines.*

The keywords for an article used to be very important for classification. Because of the abuse of this information by spammers (who include popular keywords in pages that have no relevance to them), search engines are known to discount or outright ignore these meta keywords. Nonetheless, they can provide just a little extra information and may aid the local search engine in finding articles pertinent to a user query. Therefore, it is prudent to spend a small amount of time entering keywords that are appropriate to each article.

The title of the web page is one of the most overlooked aspects of SEO by new web masters. There are many web sites in which pages have no titles, duplicate titles, or non-descriptive titles. In fact, most search engines put a premium on a web page title for a description of the page—especially if the title matches one of the major page headings. Therefore, try to make your titles as relevant and descriptive as possible.

Sitemaps

Including a sitemap on your page is an excellent way to ensure that the search spider will find and crawl all of the individual pages of the site. Since search engine programs understand sitemaps, their spidering can be guided by the directory provided by the list.

Sitemaps should be limited in length, however. Long sitemaps (those with more than 100 links on a single page) are delayed in mapping. Generally the first 100 links will be spidered promptly with any additional links placed in a queue for spidering later—perhaps even months later. Some of the most popular sitemap generators include Joomap, the Google Sitemap Generator, and SEF Service Map.

Joomap

Joomap is the top sitemap generator for Joomla; it can be downloaded from the Joomap home page, at `http://joomlacode.org/gf/project/joomap/frs`. Joomap not only provides complete mapping for categories and sections, but it can also map items included in the VirtueMart categories (introduced in Chapter 11) if you are using the VirtueMart extension for e-commerce. It can also render the sitemap as a Google Sitemap XML list.

Google Sitemap Generator

If you want to cater to the Google search engine and use technology that is most tuned to Google's specifications, you can use the Google Sitemap Generator. This sitemap generator is written in the Python language and can be downloaded from Google at `www.google.com/webmasters/tools/docs/en/sitemap-generator.html`.

There are many sites that offer to execute the Google Sitemap Generator scripts for you through a web page. XML-Sitemaps (`www.xml-sitemaps.com`), for example, will take you step by step through the rendering of a sitemap for your Joomla site. It will render an XML file that is used by Joomla for the most accurate content rending of your web site. It will also generate a sitemap rendered in the text format used by Yahoo.

SEF Service Map

The SEF Service Map (http://fun.kubera.org) component creates a sitemap dynamically. It also includes a Google Sitemap Generator as well as a Yahoo text format generator for submission to that search engine. This component is compatible with all of the default installation components, as well as Fireboard, Joomlaboard, SMF, DOCMan, Remository, JCal Pro, ExtCalendar 2, RSGallery2, Zoom Gallery, SOBI2, and VirtueMart.

SEF Service Map will even map RSS headlines, links, and contacts. It can also cache its output, so a sitemap doesn't need to be rendered each time it's accessed—saving valuable server resources. The component provides full multilingual support.

One of the most useful features included in SEF Service Map is the ability to exclude menu items or entire menus from being cataloged. This option allows you to prevent private or inconsequential pages from being included in the sitemap.

Breadcrumbs

In web terminology, *breadcrumbs* are the set of links that show the path of the current page as it relates to the greater context of the entire site. For example, if you are on the page for Article A, which is located in Category B within Section C, the breadcrumbs will show a link to the category and section in which the article is held. This user interface convention allows a web visitor to move up the hierarchy, often to look at content of the same general type. The breadcrumbs links on a page will appear something like this:

- Home ➤➤ Section C ➤➤ Category A ➤➤ Article A

More important for SEO, breadcrumbs provide the search engine spider a clearer understanding of the structure of your web site. They also provide internal links that can have a slight but important effect on how the individual pages of your site are rated in the spider's index.

Whatever template you use, try to make sure that breadcrumbs exist on the page. In Joomla, breadcrumbs are displayed as a module (mod_breadcrumbs) and appear at the top of each page in most templates, as shown in Figure 12-6.

By default, the module is configured to appear in the breadcrumbs position of the template. If a template doesn't include such a position, then the breadcrumbs won't be displayed. If your template omits that position, you will need to add it yourself.

To do so, open the index.php file of your template. You can edit the template in your favorite text editor, or you can enter the Template Manager, click the template to which you want to add the breadcrumbs, and click the Edit HTML button, as shown in Figure 12-7. The screen will display the PHP/HTML code of the template main page.

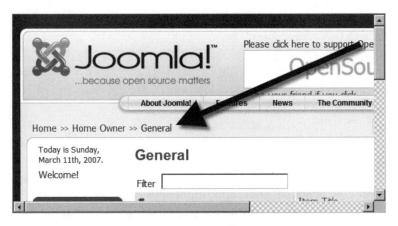

Figure 12-6. *Breadcrumbs appear as a set of links displayed by the Breadcrumbs module.*

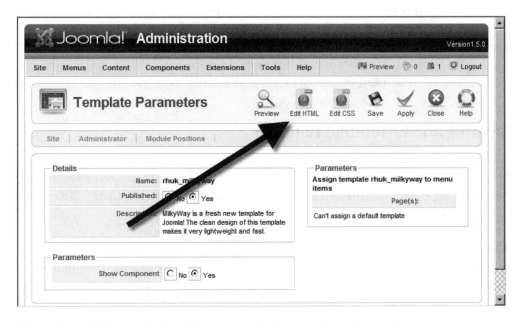

Figure 12-7. *Click the Edit HTML button to edit the template index code.*

It is a good idea to place the breadcrumbs somewhere near the top of the page, although the location will vary from page to page. In the default Joomla template, the module appears to the left of the search engine module (this appears as the user4 position in the code). In the following PHP listing, you can see the reference that displays the Breadcrumbs module:

```
<div id="search">
    <jdoc:include type="modules" name="user4" />
</div>

<div id="pathway">
    <jdoc:include type="module" name="breadcrumbs" />
</div>

<div class="clr"></div>
```

If you duplicate the module reference to the appropriate place in your template code, the breadcrumbs link list will appear. Look at the page and make sure that the list is in the proper position. For correct placement, you can examine the rendering of your Frontpage between edits.

Alternately, you can use the Preview button (on the same screen where the Edit HTML button is located). It will display the current template with dummy content and show where each module position is located. The preview can help you determine whether the template has a location to display the Breadcrumbs module, and also to properly align the module if you are adding it to an existing template.

Creating an SEF Joomla! Template

In Chapter 6, you created a Joomla template that displayed two columns using CSS. By using similar CSS code, you can make the display much more search engine–friendly by rearranging the column display. The new template will increase the visibility of the central content of each page of your site.

When a search engine spider indexes a web site, the text nearest the beginning of the file is indexed first and weighted most heavily in the valuation of content. In a two- or three-column layout, this means that the left navigation panel appears first in the HTML source code, followed by the center column, which holds the meat of the current web page. That's not an ideal situation, since the navigation is not the most important item on the page—the center content that holds the article is far more significant.

The original two-column template has the following code to define the columns:

```
#col1 {
    float:left;width:20%;
    background:#244223;
    padding: 10px;
}
```

```
#col2 {
    float:left;width:75%;
    border:3px solid #244223;
    background:#58a155;
    padding: 10px;
}
```

These style sheets are logical and display properly. However, column 1 must appear first in the source code for this to function properly. If a style sheet could be created in which column 2 appears first in the code, but still displays correctly, everything would work perfectly. Such a CSS design is possible if you use a container element.

If you create a container, the style sheet for column 2 can appear first and simply be assigned to the right side of the container. When column 1 appears in the source code, it specifies a location on the left, and everything is displayed exactly as needed. Change the style sheets for the columns in the CSS file to match the following definitions, and add the container and myclear styles:

```
div#logo {
    width: 110%; height: 100px;
    margin-left: -10px;
    margin-bottom: 10px;
    background: url(../images/LSlogo.jpg) left no-repeat;
    border: 1px solid #244223 ;
    padding: 0px;
}

#col1 {
    float:left;width:20%;
    display:inline;
    background:#244223;
    padding: 10px;
}
#col2 {
    float:right;width:75%;
    display:inline;
    border:3px solid #244223;
    background:#58a155;
    padding: 10px;
}
```

```css
#container {
    float:left;width:85%;
    display:inline;
}

#myclear {
    clear:both;
}
```

With that change, you only need to change the index.php file to position column 1 first. Change the code to match the following (the changes are shown in bold):

```php
<?php echo '<?xml version="1.0" encoding="utf-8"?' .'>'; ?>
<!DOCTYPE html PUBLIC "-//W3C//DTD XHTML 1.0 Transitional//EN"
    "http://www.w3.org/TR/xhtml1/DTD/xhtml1-transitional.dtd">
<html xmlns="http://www.w3.org/1999/xhtml"
lang="<?php echo _LANGUAGE; ?>" xml:lang=
    "<?php echo _LANGUAGE; ?>">
<head>
<jdoc:include type="head" />
<link rel="stylesheet" href="templates/_system/css/general.css"
    type="text/css" />
<link rel="stylesheet" href="templates/
    <?php echo $this->template ?>/css/template.css"
    type="text/css" />
</head>

<body id="page_bg">

<jdoc:include type="message" />
<div id="logo"> </div>
<div id="container">
    <div id="col2">
        <jdoc:include type="component" />
    </div>

    <div id="col1">
        <jdoc:include type="modules" name="left" style="xhtml" />
    </div>
```

```
        <div class="myclear"> </div>
</div>
<jdoc:include type="modules" name="debug" />

</body>
</html>
```

The code shows that both columns are encapsulated within the container structure. Column 2 appears first, which will make the content output by the component appear first in the source code file and therefore be indexed first by the spider.

General Techniques

Joomla includes a number of features that make SEO possible. However, there are other techniques you might consider to make sure your web site is optimized that lie outside of the Joomla configuration. These methods will work on any type of web site—dynamic or static.

Problems of JavaScript, Flash, and Ajax

An increasing number of web sites are adding dynamic interaction either directly through JavaScript (for functions such as drop-down menus) or by using a community of technologies such as Ajax (for dynamic information retrieval). While these new tools provide functionality that can make a web site very flashy and user-friendly, they create special problems for search engine spidering.

For example, a typical Joomla menu is simply an HTML list of links, which makes it easy for the search engine spider to recognize the links and visit the corresponding pages. A JavaScript-enabled menu system, however, is more likely to base link selection upon the current mouse position. Since the search engine spider will not execute the JavaScript code, how can it know which links are available for selection?

Likewise, a Flash-based site may have a great deal of content hidden within an SWF file, which the search spider has no way to effectively address. Search engines cannot read into Flash files or execute Flash code, so all of the content within Flash animations remain invisible to the spider.

Therefore, it is always a good idea to have a non-Flash version of your site for SEO. Each page may have a link to the flashier animated content if desired. However, without a parallel HTML version of the Flash data, search engines will not be able to catalog either the content itself or the links that lead to the content.

HTML-to-Text Ratio

One of the methods search engines use to evaluate and rate content within a page is calculation of the *HTML-to-text ratio*. This ratio indicates whether most of the page's content is HTML code (such as vast tables or substantial JavaScript code) or actual text content. The lower the ratio, the more important the text will seem to the engine.

This is one reason to locate your CSS and JavaScript code in external files. Search spiders do not evaluate these external files as part of the ratio, meaning that the clean content that remains in the main file will be given more priority than if it were lost in a sea of extraneous code.

Spidering Your Own Site

While the exact functions of the search company spiders are closely guarded industrial secrets, you can get an idea about how a spider will view your site by spidering it yourself. There are several free web spiders that you can use to scan and analyze your web site. One popular spider is the Java-based, open source Pavuk Web Spider and Performance Measure, which is available on SourceForge at `http://sourceforge.net/projects/pavuk`.

If you're operating on the Windows platform, you might try Xenu's Link Sleuth, available at `http://home.snafu.de/tilman/xenulink.html`.

Xenu will quickly and completely spider your web site and provide you a variety of information about the site (see Figure 12-8). This utility is very useful because it will show you any problems with your site, including broken links and missing graphics files. The program will generate a report of all the broken links on the pages of the site.

One of the most useful columns in the Xenu report is the Duration column, which reveals how long it took to retrieve the linked file. By looking at the retrieval duration times, you can see which pages (and perhaps which Joomla extensions on specific pages) are slowing down access to site information.

The program will also generate an excellent report of the general content of the web site. At the bottom of the report, a summary will be made that appears something like this:

```
All pages, by result type:
ok 165 URLs 83.76%
not found 10 URLs 5.08%
server error 20 URLs 10.15%
skip type 2 URLs 1.02%
Total 197 URLs 100.00%
```

If the spider report shows a thorough cataloging of your site, search engine spiders will likely have no problem crawling your site and finding all the content.

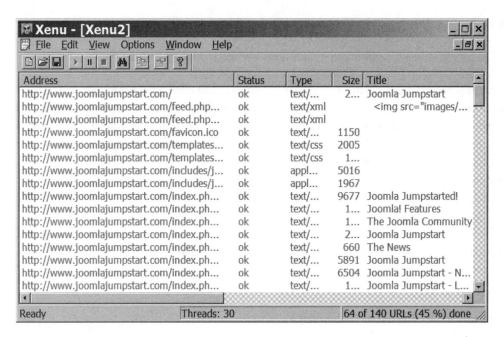

Figure 12-8. *Xenu will spider your web site and identify any broken links or missing files.*

Checking Page Rank

Google originated a value of relative search engine importance, called *page rank*. Each individual web page (pages within a site can vary) is assigned a number from 0 to 10. The 0 value simply means that Google has not yet indexed the page. New pages often have a rank of 2 or 3, while larger, well-established sites are generally in the 6 to 9 range.

To get a very rough approximation of a web site's general search ranking, you can install Google Toolbar (see Figure 12-9). While page ranking is not useful for any precision evaluation of a web site value, it will allow you to get a feel for how important the web site is in the Internet sphere.

Figure 12-9. *Google Toolbar shows a web site's general search ranking.*

When Google first released the page ranking system, optimizers recognized the assigned value as very important. Nowadays, with all the other valuation methods used by search engines, it has become less important. However, it still provides an excellent general assessment of a page's popularity on Google. It can therefore be used in a rough manner to evaluate the popularity of your own site, as well as other associated or competitive sites.

Keyword-Rich Content

Keyword lists should contain all of the important variations of a topic. Whatever the web page is about, the keyword list should contain all the various synonyms of the central terms related to the content in order to encompass each term a person might search for information about. A page on loans, for example, might have a keyword list like this: mortgage, trust deed, grant deed, equity, lending, lender, origination, payee, and note.

Because of the abuse of the technology by spammers, metadata keywords are scarcely given attention by search engine spiders. For search optimization, it is not important to spend much time creating the list of keywords to include in the metadata—except for the advantage of generating the list itself.

The keyword list can be used to ensure that the keywords are located in the content of the article. If all of the important keywords are included in the headlines and body of the article, the search engine indexing system will rate the relevance of the page very highly in terms of loan information because of the association of the common terms.

Preventing Content Listing

Most web sites need to be found by the general public. However, there are some web sites, or even specific pages on a web site, that have reasons to remain invisible. These pages are generally either completely private or needed only by authorized personnel who will be given the URLs individually and won't need to locate the references in a search engine.

A common example of this type of site is a wholesale lending site in the mortgage industry. Since these sites themselves require authorized brokers to have usernames and passwords (and therefore the site address), there is no reason to advertise the site URL to the world. Keeping the site off the search engines prevents unwanted random traffic, confusion by consumers (such as a retail bank customer finding the wholesale loan site of the company and attempting to log in), and targeting by hackers.

You can also be more specific than keeping your entire site off the search engines by explicitly listing individual pages or directories that the spider should ignore. By creating a list of excluded pages, you can hide content that should only be viewed by targeted visitors of the site. For example, you may want to provide a mortgage calculator to potential clients who are geographically local. Having the calculator listed on a search engine will bring worldwide visitors who have no potential to become customers yet still use up your bandwidth.

The excluded files or directories must be listed in a text file that sits at the root directory of the site. The file, named `robots.txt`, contains a case-insensitive list of fields. The pound sign (#) can be used to include comments in the file, which will be ignored by the spider. The `User-agent` field can be used to explicitly specify which spider (such as the Yahoo spider) should use the file. More commonly this parameter is set to the * (which means "all") setting to indicate that all spiders should restrict their spidering based on the file contents.

For example, the `robots.txt` file for restricting the contents of the forum directory and the `clientlist.htm` file would appear like this:

```
# Spidering exclusion file for http://www.example.com/

User-agent: *
Disallow: /forum          # Don't spider anything in the forum directory
Disallow: /clientlist.htm     # Don't spider the client list file.
```

The `Disallow` field for the `\forum` folder excludes all references to items in the directory. You may want to only disallow the index file in a folder, for example, to eliminate spidering of the central listing of all the articles, but allow spidering of articles that are located in the folder but linked from other articles. To exclude only the index file (whether it is `default.htm`, `index.html`, `index.php`, or a different file configured for that web server), you can add an extra forward slash (/) after the directory reference:

```
Disallow: /forum/         # Don't spider anything in the index file
```

Unfortunately, you cannot do exclusion on query string parameters. Therefore, the `robots.txt` file will require you to have the Joomla SEF option turned on for it to work properly. Otherwise, the exclusion file can only be used practically with Joomla to provide exclusion of the entire web site from the search engine spider.

Linking Strategy

It is useful to have a linking strategy in place when you are attempting to increase your placement. Tabulating the number of other important web sites on a particular topic that link to your site is one of the primary methods search engines use to determine if a site has important information on that topic.

For example, ESPN is a very important web site for sports fans. If you run a web site that focuses on football memorabilia, a link from the ESPN site would dramatically elevate your ranking in any searches related to sports. Notice that the link will help you most if it is in your same topic area. A link from a very popular clothing manufacturer would not help the sports memorabilia site nearly as much—even if the clothing site had more popularity than ESPN.

Likewise, a prominent link on a small, rarely visited site is not worth nearly as much as one on a popular site. With this basic understanding of how links from other sites can affect your search engine ranking, you can begin to develop a linking strategy that will help you decide where to focus your efforts in obtaining links from other web sites.

Some ways to obtain links are as follows:

- *Offer reciprocal link placement*: If you can find the administrator e-mail for a popular site, you can offer to exchange reciprocal links. Your web site must have a fair amount of content or a substantial page ranking to make this worth the while of the other site's web master.

- *Write articles for web publication*: There are a number of sites that will publish articles that they will syndicate for republication across the Web (e.g., www.ezinearticles.com and www.onlypunjab.com). An article can contain a link to your web site. Writing a general description article (or more than one) on a topic relevant to your site can be an excellent way to promote yourself as a field expert.

- *Post to relevant message boards with a signature link*: There are forums and message boards on the Web dedicated to almost any topic under the sun. Often these sites have new users posting basic questions that you, as an expert in your field, can answer. It is typically acceptable behavior on these sites to have a small advertisement link for your web site in the signature text that follows your posting. Be sure not to simply spam a forum advertising your wares. Not only will the advertisement likely be removed, but you will also have generated some ill will toward your site. If you can provide value through useful and informative posts, your small link should not raise the ire of any forum members, and could help generate new traffic.

Avoid Keyword Spamming

Most of the advice for adapting your site to make it the most friendly to search engines is also useful advice for simply making your site well designed for your visitors. Likewise, the presentation aspects that can hurt your site rating also generally fall under the category of bad web design.

You should avoid keyword spamming on your page. This form of spamming entails placing a text field at the bottom of your web page that includes hundreds if not thousands of keywords in small or invisible text. Previously, search engines would be fooled by these masses of keywords and increase the site's ranking.

No more. If a search engine recognizes that your site is attempting this sort of rank manipulation, the page may very well be penalized in the search index. In the past, it was generally considered poor form to attempt this strategy—now it can have the opposite of the intended effect.

Conclusion

It requires some effort to ensure that your web site has the highest possible rankings on the search terms relevant to the site. Joomla makes it fairly easy to implement SEO functionality on your web site, and you should take advantage of its features.

Despite having to deal with a little complexity in configuration, one of the first steps you should take in optimizing your site is setting Joomla to use the Search Engine Friendly URLs option for content addressing. The sooner you activate this option, the sooner the search engines will have a proper list of article URLs. This setting alone can significantly increase your web presence. It is worth the trouble of configuring your web server to enable this option.

So far you have used extensions written by other developers for everything from e-commerce to SEF functionality. In the next chapter, you will learn how to create your own modules and components to add any capabilities to a Joomla site that you might need.

Conclusion

CHAPTER 13

■ ■ ■

Creating Extensions

In addition to being very friendly to administrators, the Joomla system is also pleasant to developers. Creating an extension (module, component, or plug-in) can be a pleasure, since the Joomla framework is designed with the developer in mind. In fact, since Joomla takes care of most of the interface presentation and has built-in routines for database access and security, creating a Joomla extension can be quite a bit easier than authoring even a simple standalone PHP application.

In this chapter, you'll learn to create three different types of extensions: a front-end module, an Administrator module, and a component. You'll find that implementation of each of these adds-on is very similar, as Joomla implements both a unified installer that works the same regardless of extension type and common presentation routines that are designed to minimize complexity.

Writing a Front-End Module

As you learned in Chapter 7, modules are primarily used for displaying data. To provide a sample of this capability, I'll walk you through the creation of a module that presents a simple greeting. This module, called mod_hellofrom, has a single parameter, location, that is set in the Module Manager and displayed along with the welcome message. As shown in Figure 13-1, the module will be displayed in the top of the left column.

All front-end modules are stored in the \modules directory by the Extension Manager after installation. The name of each folder matches the name of the module. All the files of the module, including the installation directives file, will be placed in this folder. Later, when you create a component, you'll notice that (unlike a module) the installation directives file is *not* copied into the associated component folder.

Figure 13-1. *The mod_hellofrom module will display the time and date, as well as a greeting.*

■Tip When developing a new extension, the simplest process is usually to begin by roughing out the extension, compressing it into an archive, and then installing it into the Joomla system. The installation process will set up all of the necessary parameters within the Joomla database. Then you can access the actual code files in the \modules folder of the web site to make changes, add features, and perform debugging. When you make changes to the actual file, simply clicking the reload or refresh button of the browser will execute the new code.

Structure of the Module

At the most basic level, every module package contains a minimum of two files: a code file and an XML descriptor file. The code file is a PHP file that holds the execution code of the module display. The XML descriptor file contains all of the installation directives and information about the module. It also holds the module parameters that can be configured through the Module Manager interface.

Begin by creating a folder named mod_hellofrom on your local drive. All of the module files will be placed in this folder, and then an archive file (such as ZIP or TAR file) can be created from it and installed via the Extension Manager.

The mod_hellofrom XML Descriptor File

For the Hello From module, the XML descriptor file will include all of the central elements (installation directives, module name, and file listing) plus some of the optional elements (creation date, version, author, etc.) that are used to document the module. The file also contains a single parameter that can be set to display the current server location.

Create a new file named mod_hellofrom.xml in the \mod_hellofrom folder, and enter the following code:

```
<?xml version="1.0" encoding="utf-8"?>
<install type="module" version="1.5.0">
    <name>Hello From</name>
    <author>Dan Rahmel</author>
    <creationDate>July 2007</creationDate>
    <copyright>(C) 2007 Dan Rahmel.
        All rights reserved.</copyright>
    <authorEmail>admin@joomlajumpstart.org</authorEmail>
    <authorUrl>www.joomlajumpstart.org</authorUrl>
    <version>1.0.0</version>
    <description>Module that displays the date/time of
        the server. <p /> Be sure to set the Location parameter
        in the Module Manager.</description>
    <files>
        <filename module="mod_hellofrom"
        >mod_hellofrom.php</filename>
    </files>
    <params>
        <param name="location" type="text"
            default="Los Angeles, CA"
            label="Server Location"
            description="The location of the server." />
    </params>
</install>
```

The descriptor file begins with a standard XML properties tag. The `<install>` tag that follows tells Joomla about the extension to be installed. The `type` attribute declares the extension type—which in this case is `module`. The `version` attribute specifies that this extension was made to run on Joomla version 1.5 or above.

The `<name>` element specifies the name of the *module instance* that will be created by Joomla when the module is installed. In Chapter 7, you learned that a module type is like a document template, and the module instance is like the document created from it. For this module, the module type is mod_hellofrom and the initial module instance will be named Hello From. The text in the <description> element will be displayed when the module is installed, so it should have any necessary instructions to the administrator regarding the use of the module.

In the <filename> element, note that the module attribute will be stored in the Joomla database and used to reference the module. This name will be the module type that you will select when creating new instances of the module. Once the descriptor file is complete, you can create the PHP file that is the core of the module.

The PHP Code File

The main module file contains all of the PHP code that executes when the module is rendered. This code will strongly resemble standard PHP page code in that it uses the echo statement to send any output text to the user's browser.

You should always begin any extension with a check (under the no direct access section of this module) to ensure that the code is being executed by the Joomla system. This prevents hackers from using a direct URL and executing the extension, possibly using parameters that could compromise security. By ensuring execution through the Joomla framework, the module is shielded by the robust security built into the system.

Create a file named mod_hellofrom.php in the \mod_hellofrom folder and enter the following code:

```php
<?php
/**
 * @version $Id: mod_hellofrom.php 5203 2007-07-17 02:45:14Z Danr $
 * @copyright Copyright (C) 2007 Dan Rahmel. All rights reserved.
 * A module to display a hello from the location of the server.
 */

// no direct access
defined( '_JEXEC' ) or die( 'Restricted access' );

// Get the location parameter that was set in the Module Manager
$myLocation = $params->get('location', 0);
// Set a formatted date string
$myDateTime =  date("l, F dS, Y");

// Output the greeting
echo "<small>" . JText::_('Hello from ') . '<b>' .
    $myLocation . "</b>.";
echo JText::_(" Right now, it is ") . $myDateTime .
    JText::_(" here.") . "</small><br />";?>
```

If you understand PHP coding, the process of this module should be straightforward. After the check to make sure the code is executing under Joomla, the $myLocation variable is created. You can see that it uses the get() method of the $params object to obtain the current value of the module parameter called location, which was defined earlier in the XML descriptor file.

A second variable, named $myDateTime, is set to a formatted string holding the current system time and date. If you want to actually use this module, you may have to make some adjustments to the time if the web server that hosts your site resides in a different time zone than the location parameter indicates. The lines of code that follow these definitions use the echo() function to output the text to the browser page.

You might notice that all of the text is sent to the JText::_() method. This Joomla method sends any text passed to it to the Language Manager. If a language other than the default is selected for display, and the Language Manager (or Joom!Fish) has a translation of the current text in the selected language, the translation will be substituted and returned by the method. If not, the same text that was sent will simply be returned. Using this method allows your extension to expose itself to the Joomla internationalization features where, if translation text exists in the system, it can output text that can be read in one of the dozens of languages Joomla supports.

Archive the folder with both files into a file named after the module (e.g., mod_hellofrom.zip). To install this module, go to the Extension Manager, browse to the archive file, and install it. Once installed, you can publish the module, set the location parameter (see Figure 13-2), and select where the module will be displayed in the Module Manager. Click the Save button to store these parameters to the Joomla system.

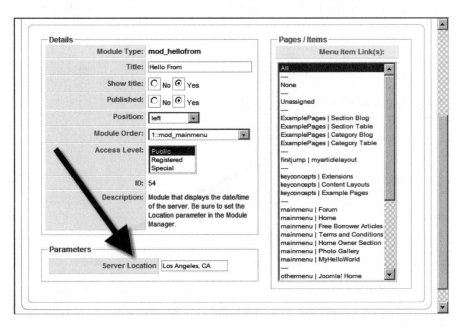

Figure 13-2. *Set the location parameter to match the geographic location of your web server.*

If you set the module to display in the left column location, open a browser window and you should see the greeting displayed. If you didn't change the order of the module in the Module Manager to appear first in the left column, you may have to scroll to the bottom of the column to see the display.

Congratulations! You've just implemented your first extension. However, this primitive module is probably not anything you would want to use in a real Joomla deployment. Most modules have more complex functions and often need to perform database access. The next module will add to the complexity of the current one and also throw in another twist—it will be an Administrator module.

Writing a Missing Metadata Administrator Module

Administrator modules function in the same way as front-end modules, but they are used within the Administrator interface. An Administrator module is never seen by a front-end user because it generally exposes private system information and may help with maintenance and administration of the site—neither of which you want shown to the visiting public. In this example, the module will list content articles that are missing key information—the article metadata.

For proper SEO, each web page should contain two pieces of unique metadata information: the metadescription and metakeywords fields. These fields are used by the search engine spider to determine how to index and display the content. In fact, Google uses the metadescription field of an article to display the brief summary of the page, as shown in Figure 13-3.

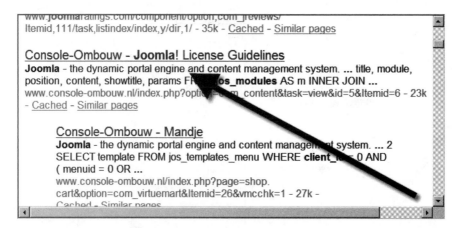

Figure 13-3. *The metadescription field of a web page is displayed as the summary in search engines such as Google.*

Despite the importance of this information, many Joomla sites have numerous articles where this information is left blank. Blank metadata fields can hurt the search engine ranking of the site and also make it more difficult for search engine users to know which pages they might want to examine. It is preferable for every article to have these two fields completed.

To solve this problem, you'll create an Administrator module that lists all articles that have empty metadata fields. Each article title will be an edit link, so an administrator can simply click the title and the article will be displayed in Edit mode. The missing information can then be immediately added to the content. Only articles that are published will be displayed in the list presented by the module (unpublished and archived articles will not be displayed).

Begin by creating a folder named \mod_missingmeta on your local drive. Inside you will put the XML descriptor file and the module code file.

Creating the XML Descriptor

The XML descriptor file is much the same as the file for the previous Hello From module. This module also consists of a single code file (mod_missingmeta.php) that contains all of the querying code. In the \mod_missingmeta folder, create a file named mod_missingmeta.xml and enter the following code:

```
<?xml version="1.0" encoding="utf-8"?>
<install type="module" version="1.5.0" client="administrator">
    <name>Missing Metadata Items</name>
    <author>Dan Rahmel</author>
    <creationDate>July 2007</creationDate>
    <copyright>(C) 2007 Dan Rahmel. All rights reserved.</copyright>
    <authorEmail>admin@joomlajumpstart.org</authorEmail>
    <authorUrl>www.joomlajumpstart.org</authorUrl>
    <version>1.0.0</version>
    <description>Module to display any articles that have missing
    metadescription or metakeywords fields.</description>
    <files>
        <filename module="mod_missingmeta"
            >mod_missingmeta.php</filename>
    </files>
</install>
```

Notice that the <install> tag has an additional attribute named client that wasn't used in the previous module. If the client attribute is not included, the module is assumed to be a front-end module and is assigned the site client type. Since you want this module to only be available through the Administrator interface, set the client type as administrator, which will make the module an Administrator module and place it in the \administrator\modules directory.

Creating the Module File

The actual code for the Missing Metadata Items module requires both presentation code and logic. In a more sophisticated application, it would be wise to break up these two pieces like you did earlier in the book when you created a template. By putting the presentation aspects in a separate file such as a CSS file or a template file, they can be developed and modified independently. This module, however, is fairly simple, and in the interest of maintaining simplicity, all of the code will be contained in a single file.

Create a new file named mod_missingdata.php in the \mod_missingdata folder, and enter the following code:

```php
<?php
/**
 * @version $Id: mod_missingmeta.php 2007-07-12 21:49:30Z Danr $
 */

// no direct access
defined( '_JEXEC' ) or die( 'Restricted access' );

$db =& JFactory::getDBO();
// Find all empty strings in metakey and metadesc and
// make sure the article is published (state=1).
$where = "(metakey = '' or metadesc = '') and state = 1 ";
$query = "SELECT id, title, metakey, metadesc"
    . " FROM #__content WHERE "
    . $where . " ORDER BY title ASC";
$db->setQuery( $query, 0);
?>

<table class="adminlist">
<tr>
    <td class="title">
        <strong><?php echo JText::_( 'Article' ); ?></strong>
    </td>
    <td class="title">
        <strong><?php echo JText::_( 'Empty Description' ); ?></strong>
    </td>
```

```php
    <td class="title">
        <strong><?php echo JText::_( 'Empty Keys' ); ?></strong>
    </td>
</tr>

<?php
    // Make sure some rows match query
    if ($rows = $db->loadObjectList()) {
        foreach ($rows as $row) {
            // Create url to allow user to click & jump to edit article
            $url = "index.php?option=com_content&task=edit&" .
                "&id=" . $row->id;
            // Check meta fields for record and set Yes/No value
            if ($row->metadesc =="") $metad = JText::_("Yes");
                else $metad = JText::_("No");
            if ($row->metakey =="") $metak = JText::_("Yes");
                else $metak = JText::_("No");

            echo "<tr>";
            // Place article title inside link
            echo "<td><a href='" . $url . "'>" .
                $row->title . "</a></td>";
            // Display status of empty meta column
            echo "<td>" . $metad . "</td>";
            echo "<td>" . $metak . "</td>";
            echo "</tr>";
        }
    } else {
            // No articles with missing metadata found
            echo '<tr><td>None</td>';
            echo '<td>n/a</td>';
            echo '<td>n/a</td></tr>';
    }
?>
</table>
```

This module has code that is quite a bit more sophisticated than the earlier greeting module. The first section of PHP code requests a reference to the database object and stores it in the $db variable. Then a WHERE statement is created for the MySQL query, which will only select records that have either a metakey or metadesc field that is empty. The query also requires that the state of the article be set to a value of 1, which indicates that the article is published.

The $query variable is created to contain the entire search query and select the id, title, metakey, and metadesc columns to be returned in the data set. The query uses the #__content statement to specify that the Joomla content table should be searched. The #__ directive tells Joomla to add the current table prefix set by the user—usually the jos_ default prefix is used. The setQuery() method of the database object is called to store the query string.

The section that follows the PHP code is HTML display code to create a table to display the article list. The table is set to use class attributes (such as adminlist and title) so that the style complies with the current template settings. Three columns are created to display the article title link, the indicator for whether the metadesc field is empty, and the indicator for whether the metakey field for page keywords is empty.

The second batch of PHP code actually outputs the article list. An if statement tests to make sure there are in fact articles with missing meta information. If the data set is empty, then the code execution jumps down and displays a single row with the values None, n/a, and n/a.

When there are articles that comply with the query parameters, a foreach loop cycles through each row or record. First, a URL is created for the links that will be added on the titles. Note that the URL includes the task parameter set to edit. This parameter will cause the link to bring up the article in Edit mode when it is clicked.

The two following if statements check to see if the fields are empty and set variables to display the word *Yes* or *No* in the appropriate column. Once again, the JText::_() method is used to convert the words *Yes* and *No* to the configured language if necessary. The remaining code outputs a three-column row for each record including the title link and indicators of which field is empty.

Place this file along with the XML descriptor file inside an archive file (such as mod_missingmeta.zip) and use the Extension Manager to install it to the system. Bring up the Module Manager—notice that the file isn't present in the initial list. By default, the Module Manager displays all of the site or front-end modules, but not the Administrator modules. Click the Administrator link, as shown in Figure 13-4. The list that appears will show the Missing Metadata Items module.

Click the module name to bring up the editing screen. By default, a module is placed in the left position—even if the Administrator template doesn't have a left position. Set the Position drop-down list to cpanel to display the module in the main Administrator Control Panel (see Figure 13-5). Click the Save button to store your changes in the database.

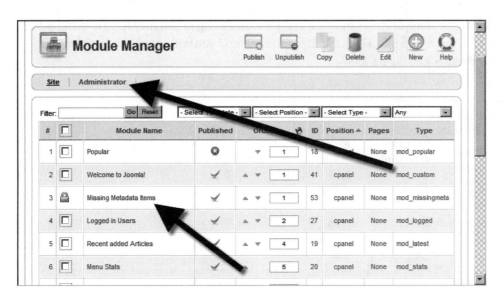

Figure 13-4. *Click the Administrator link to display the Administrator modules.*

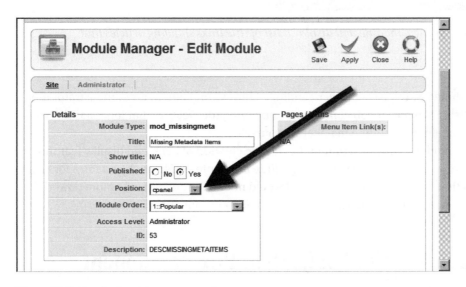

Figure 13-5. *Set the position to cpanel.*

Go to the Control Panel and look in the list on the right. You may have to scroll down to see the module listing. Click the Expand arrow and you will see a list of articles that lack metadata (see Figure 13-6).

Article	Empty Description	Empty Keys
Cocktails for Two	No	Yes
My First Article	Yes	Yes

Figure 13-6. *The new module will display a list of title links showing articles that lack metadata.*

You should now have an understanding of how to implement an Administrator module in Joomla. Whenever you come across a maintenance feature that Joomla lacks, you have the capability of adding that feature yourself.

These modules provide a foundation for the creation of back-end display features to Joomla. But what if you need something a little more interactive, such as a form for user entry? In that case, the preferred method would not be the creation of a more powerful module; instead, you would want to develop a new component.

Structure of the Suggestion Box Component

A component has a structure very similar to a module. The primary difference comes from the user interface portions of the extension. A component can have a complete Administrator interface, whereas a module is limited to simple parameter settings. The interface for a component is accessible through the Components menu of the Administrator interface.

Additionally, since components are included in the central column of most templates, they have a great deal more control over the presentation of screen output than modules do. Components can also have direct menu links that take the user to the component display. Components can accept parameters, which you'll see in this section as you implement the Suggestion Box component.

One great way to improve your site is to encourage visitor feedback. An effective method of doing this is to include a suggestion box. A user can enter a suggestion that is stored to a database table for later examination by the administrator.

To create a Suggestion Box component, begin by creating a folder titled \com_suggestionbox on your local drive. You'll place all of the component files within this folder.

The XML Descriptor File

The descriptor file for the component is virtually identical to that of a module. One difference is that the `<installer>` element has the type attribute set to component, instead of indicating a module. There is also an additional section encapsulated by `<administration>` tags. The information held within this element defines the Administrator interface for the component.

In the case of the Suggestion Box component, there is no Administrator interface, yet in the following code, I have set the standard component interface to be displayed when the component is selected from the Components menu in the Administrator interface. Why bother to do this?

When Joomla installs a component, if it doesn't have an Administrator interface, it will not be listed in the Components menu. Most components should be listed in this menu whether they have a specialized interface or not so that an administrator can quickly and easily verify if the component is installed.

More importantly, a component must have an Administrator interface to be registered in the database for linking via a Joomla menu. Since you want the Suggestion Box component to be listed in the Main Menu on the Joomla Frontpage, it must have an `<administration>` section in the XML descriptor file.

In the \com_suggestionbox folder, create a file named suggestionbox.xml and enter the following code:

```
<?xml version="1.0" encoding="utf-8"?>
<install version="1.5.0" type="component">
    <name>SuggestionBox</name>
    <author>Dan Rahmel</author>
    <version>1.0.0</version>
    <description>Displays a suggestions form and records
      suggestions in the jos_suggestion table.</description>
    <files>
        <filename component="com_suggestionbox"
            >suggestionbox.php</filename>
    </files>
```

```
    <administration>
        <menu>Suggestion Box</menu>
        <files>
            <filename component="com_suggestionbox"
                >suggestionbox.php</filename>
        </files>
    </administration>
</install>
```

The descriptor file should be ready to go. Now you will need to create the code file that contains the execution logic of the component.

The PHP Code File

The component code will perform a number of different operations. First of all, it will check to see if any parameters were posted by a form. For the component, the same URL will be used for the first stage of the suggestion box (presenting a form for user entry of the suggestion) as the second stage (writing the suggestion into the database). The first stage will post the form information, and the code, if it detects the form data, will write it into the table.

In the \com_suggestionbox folder, create a file named suggestionbox.php and enter the following code:

```php
<?php
/**
* @version $Id: suggestion.php 5203 2007-07-27 02:45:14Z DanR $
* @copyright Copyright (C) 2007 Dan Rahmel. All rights reserved.
* This component accepts suggestions and stores them in a database.
*/

// no direct access
defined( '_JEXEC' ) or die( 'Restricted access' );

if(JRequest::getVar( 'suggestion' )) {

    $db =& JFactory::getDBO();

    // Automatically try to create the table. If it already exists, this creation
    // Will be ignored.
    $createTable = "CREATE TABLE IF NOT EXISTS `#__suggestions`" .
```

```
            "(`id` INTEGER UNSIGNED NOT NULL AUTO_INCREMENT, ".
            "`suggestion` text NOT NULL, `email` VARCHAR(45)," .
            "`location` VARCHAR(45), `created` TIMESTAMP NOT NULL, " .
            "`userip` VARCHAR(16), PRIMARY KEY(`id`))";
        $db->setQuery( $createTable, 0);
        // Execute table creation
        $db->query();

        // Grab and format all of the variable entries from the form.
        $fldSuggest = "'" . $db->getEscaped(JRequest::getVar('suggestion')) . "'";
        $fldEmail = "'" . $db->getEscaped(JRequest::getVar( 'email')) . "'";
        $fldLocation = "'" . $db->getEscaped(JRequest::getVar( 'location' )) . "'";
        // Store the IP of the user submitting the suggestion
        $userIp = "'" . $_SERVER['REMOTE_ADDR'] . "'";

        // Insert all variables into the jos_suggestions table
        $insertFields = "INSERT INTO #__suggestions " .
            "(suggestion, email, location, userip) " .
            "VALUES (" . $fldSuggest . "," . $fldEmail . "," . $fldLocation .
            "," . $userIp . ");";
        $db->setQuery( $insertFields, 0);
        $db->query();
?>

<h1 class="contentheading">Thanks for the suggestion!</h1>
    <?php } else {
?>

<h1 class="contentheading">Suggestion form</h1>

<form id="form1" name="form1" method="post"
    action="index.php?option=com_suggestionbox">
  <p>Enter suggestion here:<br />
    <textarea name="suggestion" cols="40" rows="4" id="suggestion"></textarea>
  </p>
  <p>Email (optional) :
    <input name="email" type="text" id="email" />
</p>
```

```
<p>
  <label>Location (optional) : </label>
  <input name="location" type="text" id="location" />
</p>
<p>
  <input type="submit" name="Submit" value="Send Suggestion" />
</p>
</form>

<?php    } ?>
```

The first part of the code checks if any form variables have been posted—specifically the suggestion field. If there is a suggestion variable passed to the component, the component begins processing the information. The code loads a reference to the database object.

It then performs a CREATE TABLE operation. In this case, it uses the IF NOT EXISTS qualifier so that if the table already exists, the operation is ignored. If not, it creates a table using the current table prefix (most likely creating a table named jos_suggestions) to hold the user data.

In the table definition, there are two fields generated by the MySQL system: id and created. The id field has a number that is automatically incremented by the database server so that every record has a unique key. The created field has the timestamp type, so when the suggestion is submitted, each record will automatically be logged with a time and date stamp to show when it was created.

After the table is created, the three fields of the suggestion form (suggestion, email, and location) are parsed and stored into variables. The getEscaped() method is used on each user entry to add any necessary escape characters to ensure that the text writes into the database properly. For example, if the user typed quotation marks within the suggestion, these would foul up the insertion routine if they were not modified by the getEscaped() method.

A fourth variable is created to store the IP address of the suggestion submitter. Although IP addresses that are sent with form data can be faked, or "spoofed," many abusers won't take the time or energy to counterfeit this information. Storing this value gives the administrator a chance to track down someone who abuses the system or, in extreme cases, to ban their IP address from accessing the system.

With all four variables properly set, an Insert Into command is used to write the new record into the table. After the storage is completed, the user is thanked for their submission.

The remainder of the component is only displayed if there are no form variables detected. In this case, the suggestion entry form is presented for user entry. There are only two items in the form code that are worthy of note. First, the <H1> headline is set to a specific style via the `class="contentheading"` statement. By using the `contentheading` style, the component ensures that it will match the heading style of the currently selected template.

The second item of note is the `action` attribute of the form. It is set to the value of `index.php?option=com_suggestionbox` so that once the web visitor clicks the Submit button, the form will simply call the component again. When the component is called, it will detect the submitted form fields and the suggestion will be written into the database.

Installing the Component

From the `\com_suggestionbox` folder, create an archive by the name of `com_suggestionbox.zip` for upload into the Joomla system via the Extension Manager. Once the component is installed, you will have to click the Components tab of the Extension Manager and publish the component (by default components are unpublished).

The Components menu should now display a menu for the new component. You don't need to select it—just make sure it's there. Under the Menus menu, select the Main Menu option. Click the New button to create a new menu reference; in the Select Menu Item Type list, you should select the Suggestion Box component listed (see Figure 13-7).

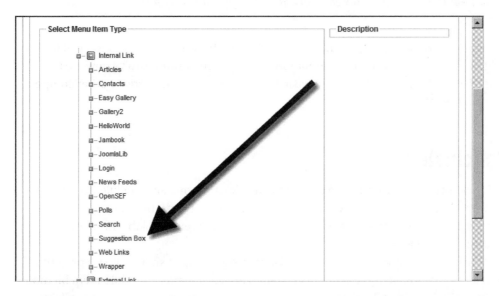

Figure 13-7. *Select the Suggestion Box component to create a menu linking to it.*

Name the component **My Suggestion Box** and open a browser window to the site Frontpage. In the Main Menu on the left, you should see the menu item listing. Click the link and you will be presented with the suggestion entry form, as shown in Figure 13-8.

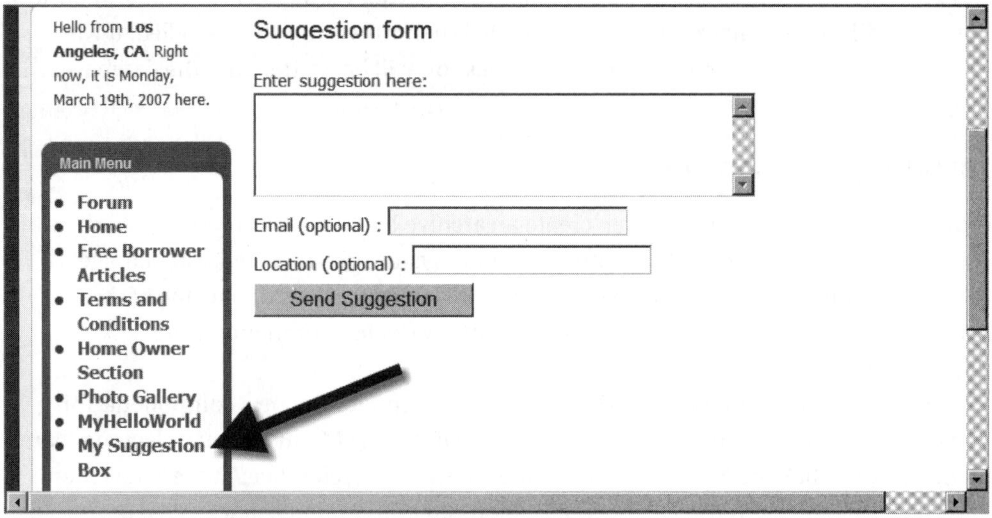

Figure 13-8. *The Suggestion Box component will display an entry form.*

Enter a sample suggestion and click the Submit button. The suggestion will be written into the database for examination by the Administrator. You've now created your first component and have the basic framework you need to create other components in the future.

Conclusion

In this chapter, you created three different extensions: a front-end module, an Administrator module, and a component. For most development needs, modules and components will allow you to add missing features that aren't available from existing third-party extensions.

While the first module only displayed a simple greeting, it showed how a presentation can be integrated into the Joomla system. The Administrator module was a bit more complex since it added database access and set the proper parameters to be available only from the Administrator interface. Finally, the component was the most complex of all, as it consisted of two parts: the data entry form and the database storage logic. The extension demonstrated how a component can modify its behavior based on parameters passed to it.

I hope you've enjoyed this book on Joomla and have learned quite a bit about what is perhaps the most promising CMS available. Joomla can be used to create web sites for everything from hobbyist information to complete e-commerce solutions. I hope that you'll join the Joomla community and make a contribution of information, money to the development team via the nonprofit Open Source Matters (see `www.joomla.org` and `www.opensourcematters.org` for more information), new templates, new extensions, or simply goodwill.

The Joomla community is made up of tens of thousands of enthusiast users. I hope you will join us and become another proud Joomla supporter. See you online!

Index

You Need the Companion eBook

Your purchase of this book entitles you to buy the companion PDF-version eBook for only $10. Take the weightless companion with you anywhere.

We believe this Apress title will prove so indispensable that you'll want to carry it with you everywhere, which is why we are offering the companion eBook (in PDF format) for $10 to customers who purchase this book now. Convenient and fully searchable, the PDF version of any content-rich, page-heavy Apress book makes a valuable addition to your programming library. You can easily find and copy code—or perform examples by quickly toggling between instructions and the application. Even simultaneously tackling a donut, diet soda, and complex code becomes simplified with hands-free eBooks!

Once you purchase your book, getting the $10 companion eBook is simple:

❶ Visit **www.apress.com/promo/tendollars/**.

❷ Complete a basic registration form to receive a randomly generated question about this title.

❸ Answer the question correctly in 60 seconds, and you will receive a promotional code to redeem for the $10.00 eBook.

2560 Ninth Street • Suite 219 • Berkeley, CA 94710

eBookshop

THE EXPERT'S VOICE™

Offer valid through 1/23/08.

LP110